T0154357

Rebel Alliances

The means and ends of contemporary British anarchisms

Benjamin Franks

AK Press and **Dark Star**
2006

Rebel Alliances
The means and ends of contemporary British anarchisms

ISBN: 1904859402

ISBN13: 9781904859406

First published 2006 by:

AK Press	AK Press
PO Box 12766	674-A 23rd Street
Edinburgh	Oakland
Scotland	CA 94612-1163
EH8 9YE	USA
www.akuk.com	www.akpress.org
ak@akedin.demon.co.uk	akpress@akpress.org

Catalogue records for this book are available from the British
Library and from the Library of Congress

Design and layout by Euan Sutherland

Printed in Great Britain by Bell & Bain Ltd., Glasgow

Rebel Alliances

The means and ends of contemporary British anarchisms

Benjamin Franks

To my parents, Susan and David Franks, with much love.

Contents

Acknowledgements

This manuscript was originally begun in September 1991. It has taken over fourteen years from the start of the research to its publication. Nonetheless, it is this, the last page to be consigned to paper, which has proven the most difficult to write. There are so many people to whom I am deeply indebted, for their love, friendship and patience, that it is difficult to know where to start. As a result, this brief section already runs the risk of appearing like the Oscar night acceptance speech of a particularly neurotic actor. There are also the concerns of overlooking those who have made significant sacrifices – and of naming those who would prefer to remain anonymous. In listing people there is the additional hazard of those at the top being considered of greater importance than those in the middle or end, so except for the first few names, everyone else is listed in reverse alphabetical order. I have to start, however, by thanking my partner Lesley for her love, good humour, patient proofreading and encouragement, and my parents Susan and David Franks for their constant support, love and hot food. It would be quite amiss not to acknowledge the carefully considered, academic guidance provided by Jon Simons of the University of Nottingham, supported by the kindly words of Prof. Richard King.

My thanks are also due to Paul M. of London Class War, Mike & Clare of the Anarchist Federation, Trevor B. of Movement Against the Monarchy, Millie W. of the Advisory Service for Squatters and Bill Godwin formerly of the Anarchist Trade Union Network for their comments. Their relevant and good-humoured advice was pertinent, if not always welcome. The advice and support offered by Malcolm of Dark Star and Michael Harris of AK Press was also invaluable. I would also like to thank Euan Sutherland and Alexis McKay of AK Press for their invaluable assistance.

My gratitude to the following is also quite beyond words: Rowan Wilson, Kathy Williams, Millie Wild, Bill Whitehead, Colin West, Mark Tindley, Claire Taylor, Robert Smith, Simon Sadler, Helen Rodriguez-Grunfeld, Sarah Merrick, David McLellan, Angie McClanahan, Brian and Suzanne Leveson (Cumper), David Lamb, Richard King, Sarah Kerr, Rita Kay (z"l), Sean Johnston, Adenike Johnson, Benedict Jenkins, Natalie Ireland, Steven Gillespie, Rebecca Howard, Stephen Harper, Stephen Hanshaw, Jim Hanshaw, Stuart Hanscomb, John and Gina Garner, Tim Franks, Esme Choonara, Mike Craven, Larry Chase, Russell Challenor, Carolyn Budow, David Borthwick, Ian Bone, Julie Bernstein, Mark Ben-David (z"l), Trevor Bark, Clare Bark and thanks also to the domestics at Dudley Road Hospital (1991-2), participants at the Goldsmiths' College, extra-mural philosophy classes (1992-4), WEA current affairs courses Derby (1997-2000) and Nottingham (2000), University of Nottingham politics classes (1997-2000), fellow staff members at Blackwells University Bookshop, Nottingham University (1997-9), students and staff at the University of Glasgow, Crichton Campus (2001-), and my friends in numerous anarchist and Leninist groups.

This book, like many other recent texts dealing with radical politics, was going to start with a detailed account of one of the numerous anti-globalisation protests.[1] There are attractions with starting with vivid accounts of these demonstrations; dramatic narratives can capture the colour and carnival of the fancy-dressed dandies, protesting stilt walkers and semi-clad demonstrators, the chaotic rhythms of electronic dance music, samba-bands and police sirens. Mixed into this vibrant concoction is exhilaration at assaults on the property of sweatshop profiteers, humbling politicians by restricting them to house arrest inside their luxury hotels, and the mass collegiality of shared dissent. Then there is the hi-tech shock and awe of the heavily armoured state forces, ending sometimes, as in the case of Carlo Giuliani, a 23-year-old Italian anarchist, in brutal tragedy.[2] In comparison, few writing on politics, even the vivacious discourse of contemporary anarchisms, can match the emotional descriptions of exuberant mass action. It is unsurprising, therefore, that these eye-catching, high-profile gatherings have become a central theme in contemporary assessments of radical politics.

The first draft of this book began with an extended narrative that described the 'Carnival Against Capitalism' of Friday June 18th 1999 (otherwise known as J18). It covered the London-end of the global protest against the G8, where leaders of the eight top industrialised countries met to discuss and agree further steps towards freer trade. There was an account of the assaults on the facades of billion dollar corporations, the occupation of Congress House, the head quarters of the Trade Union Congress (TUC), by those angry at the official labour movement's involvement in supporting the dictates of the government. That version included the selective torching of luxury cars and other creative acts of destruction aimed at the beneficiaries of global capitalism, and the invasion of the LIFFE building (a trading exchange), where City traders, furious that their turf had been occupied by joyous assortments of anti-market pranksters and class struggle mobs, hurled abuse at the invaders of the free trade area. It was a rare day, for seldom had stock-market dealers, Tom Wolffe's 'masters of the universe', been so threatened. The extended account covered the tactics at avoiding detection, the CCTV camera covered up by plastic bags, the banners proclaiming poetic rebellion strung up through the square mile, preventing the easy movement of the mounted police. The account also covered the identities of those taking part in J18, which included many explicitly class struggle libertarians, plus those with a distinct influence from this direction.[3] Noticeably absent on the day were participants from the once powerful Leninist organisations. Although some of the groups taking part in J18 were not explicitly class struggle, the modes of organisation, the targets and the methods were consistent with contemporary anarchism.

But the original description of J18 and the anti-capitalist events has been curtailed Whilst the anti-globalisation and anti-capitalist movements do contain a substantial element of anarchists and anarchist inspired groupings, there has been too great an emphasis on the recent anti-globalisation movements that has risked both ignoring the other manifestations of anarchist activity and also subsuming the other currents in the anti-capitalist movement that are antipathetic to anarchism into the libertarian fold. In the context of the United Kingdom, these would include anti-Third World debt campaigners initiated by Christian churches, social democrats like the trade unions and Green Party, state-socialists like the Socialist Workers Party (SWP) and Scottish Socialist Party (SSP) and more philosophically conservative political groupings. The anti-capitalist movement has also undergone significant transformation, most notably since late 2001.[4] It is also relatively new, and even since the late 1990s, when it developed as a significant phenomenon, it has been only mobilised sporadically. Concentrating too much on this form of protest overlooks the other more long-standing, and often more pressing areas of libertarian concern than those of the 'anarchists' travelling circus', as Prime Minister Tony Blair referred to the anti-capitalist protestors.[5] The often anarchic anti-globalisation protests did not occur in a vacuum, but are part of a process of radical challenge to particular forms of oppression. One of the themes of this book is tracing and classifying the myriad methods employed by class struggle anarchist groups and assessing them according to how far they reflect and embody their complex, multiple objectives.

Terminology: 'Class struggle anarchism'

In order to carry out this examination and evaluation, some clarification of the terminology employed throughout the text is required. The organisations identified under the heading of 'class struggle anarchism' include those that identify themselves as such, as well as those from autonomist marxist[6] and situationist-inspired traditions. The organisations and propaganda groups examined include the Anarchist Black Cross (ABC), Anarchist Federation (AF) (formerly the Anarchist Communist Federation (ACF)), Anarchist Youth Network (AYN), Anarchist Workers Group (AWG), Aufheben, Black Flag, Class War Federation (CWF), Earth First! (EF!), Here and Now, Industrial Workers of the World (IWW), Reclaim the Streets (RTS), Solidarity, Solidarity Federation (SolFed) (formerly the Direct Action Movement (DAM)), Subversion, White Overall Movement Building Libertarian Effective Struggles (WOMBLES), Wildcat and Workers Solidarity Movement (WSM), many local and regional federations such as Haringey Solidarity Group, Herefordshire Anarchists and Surrey Anarchist Group as well as the precursors to all these associations.

These organisations and their tactics can be said to form a semi-coherent subject for this book as they meet four hesitantly proposed criteria. The first is a complete rejection of capitalism and the market economy, which demarcates anarchism from reformist politics and extreme liberal variants (often referred to as 'anarcho-capitalism' or in America as 'libertarianism'). The second criteria is an egalitarian concern for the interests and freedoms of others as part of creating non-hierarchical social relations; the third is a complete rejection of state power and other quasi-state mediating forces, which distinguishes libertarianism from Leninism. The final criterion, alongside the other three, is the basis for the framework used here for assessing anarchist methods: a recognition that means have to prefigure ends. The first three criteria contain elements of 'anti-representation', dismissing oppressive practices that construct identities through market principles of class or wealth, party or nation, leader or citizen. The last criterion, prefiguration, is indicative of the reflexivity of anarchist methods which not only react against existing conditions but are also 'self-creative'. These four criteria create the 'ideal type' used to assess the actions of contemporary groups.

These four identifiable standards contrast with the view of the political philosopher David Miller, who considered that the confusing multiplicity associated with anarchism meant that, unlike marxism, it had no identifying core assumptions and consequently could barely be called a political ideology.[7] The multitude of often incompatible interpretations of 'anarchism' would give Miller good grounds for this assertion. The label has been applied to Stirnerite individualism, Tolstoyan Christian pacifism, the hyper-capitalism of the Libertarian Alliance, as well as the class struggle traditions of anarchist communism, anarcho-syndicalism, situationism and autonomist marxism.[8] By limiting the scope to the revolutionary socialist variants of libertarianism, however, a distinctive group of ideas and practices can be identified through the aforementioned four criteria.

It was necessary to provide criteria to limit the scope of the subjects for analysis. Choosing appropriate standards for classifying political movements is always a precarious business. It is especially difficult to select appropriate measures for classifying class struggle anarchism as it constantly responds to changing circumstances and approves multiple forms of revolt. Yet there is a strong case for classifying class struggle anarchism using the four criteria. Historically, anarchist groups can be traced using these standards. John Quail, in his account of the growth of British anarchism, characterises anarchism using the first three criteria: 'Anarchism is a political philosophy which states that it is both possible and desirable to live in a society based on co-operation, not coercion, organised without hierarchy [....]. More specifically it marks a rejection of the political structure which the bourgeoisie sought to establish – parliamentary democracy'.[9] And the commitment to these principles can be found in libertarian groups themselves, for instance in the definition of anarchism provided in 1967 by the Solidarity group[10] and in the shorter explanation in the *Anarchist 1993 Yearbook*. There are other statements proclaiming the same norms in the 'Aims and Principles' sections of most anarchist publications, [11] such as those of AF, Class War and SolFed .[12]

Even with this clarification of the four criteria, the label 'anarchism' and other vital parts of the revolutionary lexicon have been subject to criticism by proponents and opponents of socialist libertarian traditions. Andy and Mark Anderson claim that the terminology of the revolutionary socialist groups under consideration is too vague and the objectives consequently obscure, thereby making debate confusing and alienating.[13] Such a problem concerning definition is not new; the first edition of Seymour's *The Anarchist* discusses confusion surrounding the term as indeed do early copies of Kropotkin's *Freedom*.[14] The Andersons' objections are not without foundation, but a recognisable set of groups, movements and events can be categorised as part of the class struggle variant of anarchism. The differentiation is not precise or absolute. Groups such as Earth First! (EF!) initially saw themselves as unconcerned with issues of class and capitalism but, in Britain especially, many EF! sections have come to regard environmental activism as interwoven with more general class struggles.[15]

It should be noted that occasionally one trend or other would fall outside the criteria. However, to use more inclusive criteria, as David Morland recognises, would mean drawing up principles so vague as to be meaningless.[16] Anarchism's constant evolution, its suspicion of universal tenets and its localist philosophy risk making any gauge for one epoch or region seem wholly inappropriate to another. Yet these criteria do hold remarkably well, within the relatively short time-span of the post-1984 period, of a fairly limited geographical region (predominantly the UK context).

Anarchism is a historically located set of movements. The opening chapter illustrates this by placing current groups and tactics in a wider context and introducing some of the main debates. The second chapter develops a framework for assessing anarchist actions, and ties this method of evaluation to the distinctive category of libertarian tactics known as 'direct action'. The third chapter elucidates the importance of the appropriate agent, and examines what sort of revolutionary subject anarchism should embrace if it is to remain consistent to its principles. The fourth and fifth chapters categorise and assess anarchist organisational forms and tactics according to the types of group involved and their suitability according to the framework.

In the past, the class struggle trend was attractive to a broad swathe of the industrial working class, especially the Jewish immigrant communities of the late nineteenth century. Chapter One demonstrates that the socialist variants of anarchism were the most important ones within the more general libertarian milieu, where they competed with individualist, liberal and anarcho-capitalist anarchist alternatives and also, often detrimentally, with state-socialism. The latter became increasingly important from 1917, when Vladimir Lenin's triumphant Bolshevik forces were thought by many radicals to have provided the successful blueprint for the revolutionary movement. Anarchism has often been in debate with Leninism, and as a result, discussion of anarchist tactics goes hand-in-hand with critiques of orthodox marxist strategies.

The powerful, hegemonic influence of Leninism began to fade most significantly after Kruschev's speech denouncing Stalin. This was followed by the Soviet invasion of Hungary in 1956, and orthodox Communism continued to decline culminating in the fall of the Soviet Empire in 1989. However, its influence has not entirely disappeared

– it still lingers within revolutionary socialist movements, including aspects of anarchist organisational and tactical activities. The significance of the conflict between Leninism and anarchism is one of the major themes of this book, as anarchist methods are partly the result of a rejection of authoritarian socialism. The decline of Leninist movements has also coincided with the weakening in influence of individualist anarchist currents.

Terminology: 'Liberal Anarchism'

The liberal versions of anarchism had a position of dominance within the relatively restrictive anarchist milieu between the post-Second World War period and the Miners' Strike of 1984-5; however, since then liberal anarchism has gone into decline, as class struggle groupings have become predominant. The contrast and often *conflict* between class struggle and liberal traditions is mirrored in America in the clash between social and lifestyle libertarians.[17] The latter, 'self-centred' or liberal anarchists, consider the individual to be an ahistoric 'free-booting, self-seeking, egoistic monad [....] immensely *de*-individuated for want of any aim beyond the satisfaction of their own needs and pleasures'.[18] Liberal, or lifestyle, anarchists have a view of the individual which is fixed and conforms to the criteria of rational egoism associated with capitalism. The social or class struggle anarchist, by contrast, whilst recognising that individuals are self-motivated and capable of autonomous decision-making, also maintains that agents are historically and socially located.[19] The way individuals act and see themselves is partly a result of their social context, and this formative environment is constantly changing.

By concentrating on class struggle libertarianism, this book stands in contrast to much speculative writing on the subject coming out of universities in the 1970s, '80s and '90s. Academics such as Robert Wolff and Robert Nozick have associated the term with individualism and economic liberalism.[20]

Postanarchism

The four principles of class struggle anarchism are consistent with contemporary poststructuralist anarchism (sometimes referred to as 'post-anarchism' or 'postanarchism').[21] Todd May's *The Political Philosophy of Poststructuralist Anarchism*[22] has been influential in the development of postanarchisms. May develops a libertarian philosophy that rejects a universal vanguard and asserts the importance of a prefigurative ethic, in which the means are consistent with the ends. This *postanarchism* is in agreement with the non-essentialist theories of the more politically-engaged contemporary theorists such as Michel Foucault, Gilles Deleuze and Felix Guattari.

The moral framework that comes out of the four principles is developed in Chapter Two. This ideal framework, of an anarchism consistent with the key axioms, is evaluated against competing moral theories, in particular those of ends-based moral theories, especially utilitarianism and Leninism, which argue that the justness of an act is based on the outcome. In the technical language of moral philosophy these types of assessment are termed 'consequentialist'. The anarchist ethic is also contrasted with rights-based moral theories, which considered ends to be unimportant, and held that only the duties and freedoms of individuals matter. These means-based approaches, associated with Immanuel Kant (and referred to as 'deontology'), inform contemporary liberalisms. Ideal type anarchism differs significantly from these orthodox ethical models, as it holds that the ends must be reflected in the means. This way of thinking is captured in the notion of 'direct action', which is of critical importance to current anarchist practice.

Anarchism approves of direct action because, as a liberation movement, it asserts that the oppressed must take the primary role in overthrowing their oppression. Chapter Three identifies the moral agent of change approved by the anarchist ideal. In analysing this concept of the revolutionary agent, the starting point is with the marxist notion of the 'working class' based on the economic subjugation of those without control of the means of production. However, this concept is widened beyond a single group with a fixed identity determined wholly by the economy; instead, consistent anarchism recognises that agents of change are multiple and in flux. Oppressive practices combine differently in specific contexts. Whether it is economic subjugation, patriarchy or racism, these forces appear, overlap in different ways depending on context, with no one form having total sway in all contexts.

Such an account stands in contrast to Leninist versions of the revolutionary subject, the influence of which can still be identified in some parts of the libertarian movement. In Leninism the term 'working class' refers to solely economic determined identities as opposed to the plethora of radical subjectivities which are denoted in contemporary anarchisms' uses of the term. This is not to deny the importance of economic conflict. In most, if not all, circumstances, the economic conditions of capitalism play a dominant (but not exclusive) oppressive role, hence the continuation of terminology based in marxist analysis.

Chapters Four and Five identify and classify a wide variety of contemporary anarchist organisational methods and their (anti-)political tactics.[23] The division between non-workplace (referred to for convenience as 'community') and workplace organisation and the corresponding division in tactics is explored. The ideal type constructed in Chapters Two and Three is used to assess anarchist formal structures and their favoured methods. Many tactics and organisational structures condemned by some critics as inconsistent with anarchism are latterly shown to be reconcilable, in particular contexts, with the prefigurative archetype. However, other stratagems, although normally associated with anarchist practice, are shown to be fundamentally flawed as they create a vanguard acting *on behalf of* the oppressed.

Scope

The main, but not the only, region under analysis for this study is the area known up until 1922 as the 'British Isles'. The reason for the inclusion of the 26 County WSM[24] is not due to any imperialist bias but a recognition that English, Scottish, Welsh and the Six Counties' anarchist histories are intimately linked, partly through anti-imperialism, with that of the 26 counties.[25] The WSM are also important as they represent one version of a particular type of class struggle grouping. These groups use the controversial centralising organisational principles outlined in the *Organisational Platform of the Libertarian Communists*.[26]

The definition of 'Britishness' is geographical rather than cultural, to take into account the contribution of immigrants. One of the first anarchist newspapers printed in this country was written in German, not English. Amongst the earliest major groups of anarchists in Britain was *Der Arbeiter Fraint* (The Workers' Friend), comprised of Jewish refugees fleeing from Tsarist persecution, who carried out their activities in Yiddish.[27] In the 1930s, the arrival of Italian and Spanish activists inspired and influenced anarchism in Britain.

The concentration on the British Isles should not overlook the fact that anarchism is an internationalist movement, and organisations often reflect this. In the past, *Der Arbeiter Fraint* was a member of the cross-channel Federation of Jewish Anarchist Groups in Britain and Paris, while the SolFed is part of the International Workers' Association of anarcho-syndicalists, which has the Spanish CNT-AIT (*Confederacion Nacional del Trabajo – Asociacion Internacional Trabajadores*) as its most famous and influential constituent. The AF are part of a wide libertarian communist network including groups on three continents.

Oppression is understood to be contextual and based on opposing dominating forces as they affect that locality, rather than a single universal form of domination that determines all hierarchies. As a result, it is not possible to represent the whole anarchist movement through one or two key groups, regions or individuals, or through particular canonical texts. The anarchist movement, to quote the activist George Cores, 'was due to the activities of working men and women most of whom did not appear as orators or as writers in printed papers'.[28] The types of material considered, and the approach taken here, reflect anarchism's concern for localised micropolitical, as well as more extensive, global narratives.

An accurate account of anarchism requires a combination of the actors' own perceptions and an appreciation of the wider context.[29] Accounts based only on the actors' own perceptions would omit the broader contextualising relationship which helps shape these beliefs.[30] To use an example drawn from the socialist theorist, Andre Gorz, individual soldiers may not be in a position to fully understand their role in the wider military conflict.[31] A comprehensive account of warfare, nonetheless, must still take into account the experiences of service personnel.

The views of anarchist participants are derived from the propaganda sources created by the groups identified above and the analysis of their activities through self-reports, participant-observation and supporting interviews with members of class struggle libertarian groupings. Materials collected and analysed are by no means complete or exhaustive and no such holding exists. A number of the articles, especially of pre-First World War materials, were found at the British Library and the Colindale newspaper depository. The specialist Kate Sharpley Library (KSL) holds many anarchist periodicals, although it too has absences, and access for UK scholars has become more difficult since the archive moved to the United States. Accounts of the main groups have tried to be as complete as possible but the localised nature of many anarchist publications has meant that the concentration has been on those that attempt to be nationally available (but may fall well short). Additionally it must be admitted that an element of chance and arbitrariness is unavoidable in the selection of material.

Texts and Actions

The concentration on both written texts as well as action may seem to contradict the dubious distinction, problematised in the following paragraphs, between writings and events. Anarchists tend to consider the latter to be more important than the former (in certain academic circles they reverse this order by placing greater emphasis on classical texts). George McKay comments that the environmentalists he champions give pre-eminence to deeds over words.[32] This distinction occurs in much anarchist self-analysis. One of the founders of Class War, Ian Bone, for instance, prioritises action as most desirable and criticises former comrades for spending too long on theorising rather than acting. Bone himself is criticised in similar terms by his libertarian opponents.[33] Yet the distinction between deeds and words does not stand up to rigorous scrutiny.

The philosopher J. L. Austin fundamentally collapsed the opposition between speaking and acting in *How to do Things with Words*. Speaking is an act in itself and not only an abstract expression of meaningful (or meaningless) propositions. Speaking/writing is not just a dispassionate exercise in academic communication but is also an action. Anarchists, including Bone, have also acknowledged this.[34] They reject the rights of organised fascists to speak publicly, for example, as such activities are also recognised as provocative acts and expressions of power. Nationalist newspaper sales, leaflets and public oratory are not merely ways of broadcasting ideas and means for encouraging debate. As speech-acts they also serve to marginalise and exclude sections of society and mark geographical regions as restricted to privileged groups.[35] Speech-acts, then, are performative. So too events have a communicative purpose that can be read textually. An example of direct action, such as tearing up genetically modified crops, can be read as a symbol of wider ecological concern or as a provocative inquiry that questions rights to land ownership. The apparent distinction between theorising and action is really about who is involved in their performance and those whom the act intends to influence.

If speech-acts are activities just like any other, then on what grounds can this study justify concentrating on contemporary events and propaganda, and downplaying classical theoretical texts? The answer involves acknowledging the importance of the identities of the agents involved in the actions and the types of agent appealed to. It is on the grounds of the involvement and identity of active and affected agents that distinctions are drawn between propaganda and theorising. Theorising is interpreted by Bone as discourse created by and towards elite groups (especially those not involved in the events to which the speech acts refer). The greater the distance from those involved or intended to be involved in the acts, the greater designation its designation as mere 'theory'. This explains Bone's disapproval of pure theorising, such as discussions in and between revolutionary groups and the organisation of conferences aimed at a select group, over and above the participation of the wider revolutionary agent. Action, then, for Bone, aims at and aspires to include, as autonomous participants, wider groups of individuals – in particular the revolutionary agent of change. Thus certain speech-acts, such as leafleting and speaking tours in response to the activities of organised racists in working class communities, are forms of political action.[36] The same activities in a different context, with a different range of influence, might be dismissed as theorising. Publication and distribution of tracts by the classical anarchist thinkers was originally part of popular agitation. However, in the principal period addressed by this study (1984 - 2002), the publication of these same writers is more often associated with distribution to a specialised, academically-privileged audience and therefore designated pejoratively as theorising.[37] To re-cap, the identity of the agents involved in rebellion is fundamental to the demarcation between anarchist and non-anarchist variants of direct action. In anarchist direct action the agents are those immediately affected by the problem under consideration, whereas other forms of direct action promote benevolent (and sometimes malevolent) paternalism.

Drawbacks and Dangers

By undertaking a critique that is sensitive to, and draws heavily upon, the accounts of the activists themselves, the objective is to avoid some of the pitfalls identified by Simon Sadler in the introduction to his book *The Situationist City*. Sadler notes that university-based researchers engaging in analysis of revolutionary movements (in his case the Situationist International) provoke numerous criticisms from revolutionary activists. These reproaches suggest that the researcher is misrepresenting the subject by using the tools and debates that are the concerns of an intellectual elite rather than the participants themselves, or that the author is domesticating the revolutionary potential of their subject by integrating it into academic discourse. My response differs from Sadler's reply, although acknowledging the veracity of his rejoinder that the university can provide a means to transmit such ideas, and that the small magazines of the purist revolutionary groups rarely avoid the elitism of which they accuse others. It would be disingenuous to deny that universities (especially the ones which assisted this project) were not elite institutions and that any research, even that which is self-consciously radical, is not only going to be damned by association but risks only being of interest or available to those who seek to police autonomous, egalitarian activity. Nonetheless, efforts have been made to resist the reduction of anarchism into a subject of study for the dominant class, and to this end a particular methodology is employed.

The procedure developed has at its core the recognition that anarchism is primarily a mode of revolutionary action rather than a set of theoretical texts. As a result this book concentrates on the materials of the revolutionary groups, their magazines, newspapers, journals, books, pamphlets, posters, stickers, graffiti and websites as well as describing their actions. This stands in contrast to the approach of many critics of anarchism, such as James Joll, George Woodcock and Peter Marshall, who have examined the movement largely through the supposed canon of the classical anarchist thinkers; but few contemporary anarchists are directly inspired by these writers.

It would be surprising if the thousands participating in libertarian events had read the standard texts by Michael Bakunin, Pierre-Joseph Proudhon or Emma Goldman. Consequently the works of the classical writers are referred to, but only in order to elucidate the explanations of more recent activists.

This book attempts to describe contemporary anarchist movements and to show they are significant and important forms of (anti-)political thought. The form of assessment I have developed aims to be sympathetic to, and consistent with, the evaluative techniques of anarchism itself (see above). Yet it does not avoid all the problems associated with 'academic' research, despite the fact that for a significant period this text was written external to the university. This was not a matter of principle but due to the unpopularity of the subject, matched maybe by a similar suspicion of the author, amongst grant awarding bodies.

As mentioned above, there is serious concern in avoiding the misrepresentation of past and existing groups, and more importantly in ensuring that no-one's security is jeopardised by inadvertently making known sources that desire anonymity. Consequently, I am grateful to the many friends in working class and/or anarchist groups who have assisted me and read parts or all of this text to check for such unwarranted disclosures and factual inaccuracies. Nonetheless there are still many weaknesses within the text that I am unable to resolve. Reductionism and omission has unavoidably occurred – even in a document of this size. My apparent tone of confidence in providing a linear narrative is similarly inappropriate for a movement that is contingent, fluid and diffuse. As a result, there are many groups, journals and individuals who have been unjustly excluded (or included to their chagrin) or whose original, thoughtful and inspiring ideas and actions have been diminished or overlooked. In such instances I offer my regrets and hope that these aberrations do not discourage any 'senseless acts of beauty' and that my deficiencies cause others to create superior accounts.

Chapter One

Histories of British Anarchism

Foreword

Looking at the histories of anarchism, primarily in the British context, not only helps characterise some of the debates inherited by contemporary libertarians but also illustrates that it is not an isolated national phenomenon, but developed out of worldwide movements. The different guises that class struggle anarchisms have adopted are indicative of their varied tactical and theoretical formulations as well as the diverse contexts in which they have developed.

There is, at present, no single text that covers the history of British anarchism, so this account draws upon a large number of competing, partial accounts. For the pre-First World War period, William Fishman's and John Quail's chronologies of Jewish immigrant and indigenous radicalism were used alongside the general histories of anarchism provided by George Woodcock, Peter Marshall and James Joll. Also of significant relevance were the first hand accounts of activists of the period such as Rudolph Rocker and Errico Malatesta and the pamphlets reissued by the Kate Sharpley Library (KSL), an archive that not only preserves anarchist texts but reprints and distributes previously overlooked accounts. These include publishing the autobiographical offerings of militants Tom Brown, Wilf McCartney and George Cores. KSL concentrates on the lived experiences of the ordinary activist rather than the deeds of the leading personalities.

However, many more scholarly works have been useful and inspiring such as Fishman's (1975) *East End Jewish Radicals*, Quail's (1978) *Slow Burning Fuse* and Daniel Guérin's (1970) *Anarchism*. The first stops at the First World War, the second ends in the 1920s with the rise of the hegemonic influence of the Communist Party, and the last ends with the failure of the Spanish Civil War. 1939 is the terminal date of Woodcock's first edition of *Anarchism*.[1] Later works, such as

Marshall (1992), do include a few brief mentions of more contemporary groups, but these are often side issues to larger historic themes, so they are brief and occasionally inaccurate.[2] Texts by contemporary and near-contemporary activists and organisations provide more comprehensive information. Class struggle newspapers, magazines, pamphlets and websites provide reports of their own events and those of other liberatory movements. The founders of the ABC and *Black Flag*, Stuart Christie and Albert Meltzer, in their respective autobiographies,[3] as well as in Meltzer's own histories of British anarchism,[4] include evaluative descriptions of the development of the libertarian milieu. Critical accounts of anarchist activities also appear in orthodox marxist publications such as *Socialist Review* and *Red Action*. Reference is also made to reports found in general histories of Britain in which anarchists have played a small part, for instance George Dangerfield's *The Strange Death of Liberal England* and, post-war, Nigel Fountain's *Underground* and Robert Hewison's *Too Much*.[5]

1. Problems in Writing Anarchist Histories

There are enormous difficulties with writing a history of British anarchism and the histogram (fig 1.1.) has unavoidably reproduced some of them. The confusion of groups, with different organisations having the same title, groups affiliating and disaffiliating, appearing, disappearing and reappearing in quick succession, are by no means unique to anarchism but are, nevertheless, significant features of this political movement. These are the consequences of the particular anarchist approaches to organisation; the revolutionary role of the association differs significantly from that of their orthodox socialist and communist counterparts.

Leninists believe that their party is essential to the success of the revolutionary project: 'The Communist Party is the decisive Party of the working class and necessary to lead it to victory.'[6] More recently, the SWP argues 'there are those in the West – like members of the Socialist Workers Party – who continue to adhere to revolutionary

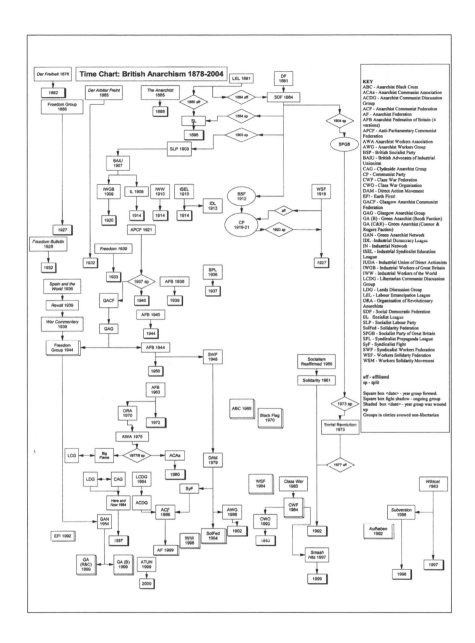

Figure 1.1. Time Chart of Main British Anarchist Groups 1878-2004.

Leninist organisation and who see it as the only answer to fighting the capitalist system... it is an essential part of working class struggle.'[7] The importance of the party means that organisational integrity is vital; it also has the consequence that Leninist groups tend to keep accurate records that provide a good source of evidence. This is not the case with most anarchist groups.

The types of group proposed by anarchists stress that. as far as possible, formal structures should develop the autonomy of participants, so groups are often federal in structure and maintain a large amount of local initiative. Thus, small groups that nevertheless may have been hugely influential in their locale, have unfortunately been excluded from the histogram. Tracking the multitude of such smaller groups, influential though they may be on particular events, is an almost impossible task. McKay, in his history of post-1960s counterculture, comments on the difficult task of developing a master narrative out of the autonomous events and networks which criss-cross the country, but which nevertheless represent an identifiable 'bricolage or patchwork' of oppositional activity and culture.[8]

To add to the confusion, prior to the Bolshevik Revolution the divisions within the socialist camps were not hard and fast. Many groups, such as the SDF, contained both statist marxists and anarchists amongst their ranks, and numerous individuals alternated between the two movements. Some did not recognise a distinction or straddled both camps.[9] Even in the 1970s the Libertarian Communist Group (LCG) worked with the non-anarchist Big Flame group and ended up entering the Labour Party.[10]

Given the problems of mapping groups coherently, some commentators have presented anarchism spatially, through the interconnectedness of ideas, rather than historically through the interaction of organisation (fig. 1.2.). The diagram from the 1980s libertarian magazine *Fatuous Times* illustrates the many different theorists and movements that create the terrain of libertarianism. A more contemporary version might extend the area 'under deconstruction', given the recent increase in interest between forms of poststructuralism and anarchism from the likes of David Morland, Tadzio Mueller and postanarchists like May and Saul Newman.[11]

2. Origins

The origins of British anarchism are not clear-cut. Many different movements have been posited as precursors, from the Peasant's Revolt led by Wat Tyler[12], to Winstanley's Diggers[13] and the Chartists.[14] For European anarchism, Greil Marcus, following Norman Cohn, saw significant anarchistic elements in the religious radicals of the Medieval period.[15] There has been a desire to create a respectable historical tradition for anarchism. This aspiration often leads to the creation of inappropriate forebears and an inaccurate account of the movement. In his history of anarchism, Marshall cites figures as diverse as the conservative theorist Edmund Burke, the nationalist Tom Paine and even the Christian messiah as 'forerunners of anarchism' – a revolutionary, anti-state, egalitarian movement.[16] Certainly many of these can be regarded as *influences on* anarchism as they have inspired many contemporary activists (for instance, Tyler featured in the anti-Poll Tax publicity), rather than being classed as libertarian themselves. Anarchism is, in part,

Figure 1.2. from *Fatuous Times*, No. 4.

a product of industrialism and post-industrialism, modernity and post-modernity. Actions from preceding eras can be emancipatory and conform to the basic criteria of anarchism, as outlined in the introduction, but the types of subjects or participants are not those associated with anarchism.

3. The Heroic Period: A history of British anarchism up to 1914

Anarchism in Britain had foreign origins but would not have taken root unless there was a native born population receptive to its message and prepared by its own historical experiences. It grew from small and exotic beginnings to become a major cause of concern for the British State and an influence in breaking down divisions of race and ethnicity.

The first person in the modern epoch to use the phrase 'anarchist' in a non-pejorative sense was Pierre-Joseph Proudhon who, in his book, *What is Property?*, declared in 1846, 'I am an Anarchist.' In this text he positioned anarchism as a coherent political movement:

> "[Y]ou are a republican." – Republican, yes, but this word defines nothing. *Res publica*; this is the public thing. Now, whoever is concerned with public affairs, under whatever form of government may call himself a republican. Even kings are republicans. "Well, then you are a democrat?" – No. – "What! You are a monarchist?" – No. "A constitutionalist?" – God forbid – "You are then an aristocrat?" – Not at all. – "You want mixed government?" – Still less. – "So then what are you?" I am an anarchist.[17]

And

> Although a friend of order, I am, in every sense of the term, an anarchist.[18]

Proudhon gained much support and notoriety in France for his views, yet his ideas remained, for the most part, confined to his native country. Outside of France, interest in Proudhon is mainly due to the interest shown in him by Marx and his reclamation of the name 'anarchist'. It was Michael Bakunin who spread the ideas of anarchism.[19] It was Bakunin's, not Proudhon's, name that appeared in the earliest editions of the anarchist newspapers in Britain.[20]

If the first criterion, self-identification as anarchists, is used to assess the start of the British anarchist movement, then it starts as late as the 1880s and is based on immigrant personalities and influences.[21] The Jewish immigrants who settled in Britain having fled Tsarist persecution were the foundation of a strong anarchist movement, as indeed were similar communities in France and America. Furthermore, Britain received an influx of anarchists from the Continent, fleeing oppression from their countries of origin, amongst them Peter Kropotkin, Errico Malatesta, Johann Most and Rudolph Rocker. The models of anarchism had many international sources but found advocates and sympathisers amongst the native-born as well as recent immigrant communities. Initial hostility between the recent immigrants and the longer established communities was replaced by mutual support between the ethnic groups.

One of the native radical traditions was the Chartist movement, the precursor to the British socialist movement from which the anarchist movement developed. Although the heyday of the Chartists was between 1838-1848, it continued to have an identifiable influence later into the nineteenth century. Joe Lane and Frank Kitz, later to become active in the early anarchist movement, were supporters of the Chartists, the latter having taken part in the Hyde Park rally and disorders.[22] Other broad-based socialist groups and movements grew out of the Chartist clubs, amongst them the Democratic Federation (DF) and the Social Democratic Federation (SDF). These are relevant to the history of British anarchism because there were no clear-cut distinctions between anarchists and other versions of radicalism.

This remained the case until the Bolshevik revolution. Despite the infamous split between Michael Bakunin and Karl Marx in the First International in 1871, many working class activists admired both anarchist and orthodox socialist personalities.[23]

It was out of the DF and SDF that Lane and Kitz launched the Labour Emancipation League (LEL), which according to the ACF (whose account of this period draws upon Quail): 'was in many ways an organisation that represented the transition of radical ideas from Chartism to revolutionary socialism.'[24] The LEL created the Socialist League (SL), which distributed Kropotkin's *Freedom*, although there was mutual suspicion between the anarchists in the League and those of the Freedom Group.[25] Groups such as the DF, SDF and then the SL contained more orthodox (parliamentary) socialists and anarchists, as well as those who flitted between the two positions, as the radicals Cores and McCartney explain.[26] This fluidity between marxist and anarchist movements also indicates a culture of solidarity in pursuit of socialist causes.

The first of the influential foreign revolutionaries to come to Britain was Johann Most. He epitomised one of the ways in which anarchism emerged from the socialist movement. He was originally a radical member of the Social Democratic Party, an elected member of the Reichstag from 1874 to 1878, but moved to a more explicitly anarchist position as he grew older, and he is widely regarded as a leading proponent of 'propaganda by deed', violent direct action. Following a contretemps with Bismarck, Most was forced to flee Berlin and arrived in London in 1878. Here he published his newspaper *Freiheit* in 1879, originally subtitled 'The Organ of Social Democracy', but throughout 1880 articles which were more seditious and anarchic in tone were published – by 1882 it was subtitled 'an Organ of Revolutionary Socialists'. *Freiheit* thereby stakes a strong claim to being the first anarchist newspaper printed in Britain, although it was intended for export back to Germany.[27]

3.1. Age of Terror

On March 15, 1881, Most held a rally to celebrate the assassination of the Tsar Alexander II that had taken place earlier that year. Four days later, he also wrote an editorial in praise of the killing. In Most's direct and lurid style, which finds its echo in early editions of *Class War* and *Lancaster Bomber* of more recent times, he wrote:

> One of the vilest tyrants corroded through and through by corruption is no more [.... the bomb] fell at the despot's feet, shattered his legs, ripped open his belly and inflicted many wounds [....] Conveyed to his palace, and for an hour and a half in the greatest of suffering, the autocrat meditated on his guilt. Then he died as he deserved to die – like a dog.[28]

For this, Most was arrested for incitement to murder, and was indicted at Bow Street Magistrates Court. The subsequent trial at the Central Criminal Court, the later appeal and the sentence of sixteen months caused much press and public interest, especially as the conviction was considered a restriction on the freedom of the press. The newspaper reports of the trial brought anarchism to a wider public. A week after he was released from prison Most emigrated to New York, taking his periodical with him. However, he did leave behind a group of committed radicals that sought to promote socialism through direct action.

Most's dramatic support for violent direct action was more fully explained in his book *The Science of Revolutionary Warfare*, which also gave a detailed account of how to pursue well-prepared guerrilla attacks. In this way it is similar to, although more scientifically accurate than, the more infamous *Anarchist Cookbook*.[29] Propaganda by deed was frequent on the continent of Europe. The highlights were:

> - 1881, the assassination of Russian Tsar Alexander II by the People's Will.

- 1881, attempt on the life Gambetta, a Republican leader, by Emile Florain.
- 1883-84, bombings, in France, of churches and employers' houses.
- 1884, a more accurate attempt on the Mother Superior of the convent at Marseilles by Louis Chaves.
- 1891-92, bombing campaign against judiciary and police by Ravachol (né Koenigstein).
- January 1894, nail bomb attack on the Chamber of Deputies in Paris, by August Vaillant.
- 1900, King Umberto of Italy shot by Gaetano Bresci.

America also faced similar incidents, following state repression of industrial militants. These included Alexander Berkman's attempt to take the life of Henry Clay Frick in 1892 and the 1901 assassination of President McKinley by Leon Czolgosz. These events promoted the association of anarchism with terrorism throughout Europe and America. There was a general perception that a worldwide conspiracy of assassins existed.[30] Although individual anarchist assassins were aware of the deeds of others from the libertarian press, there was no formal conspiracy.

Because in Britain political repression was less severe than elsewhere in Europe, propaganda by mouth was possible, meaning that propaganda by deed was less frequent. However, this is not to say that the tactic of terror promulgated by Most was utterly neglected here. The Walsall anarchists, Charles, Cailes and Battola, were accused of conspiracy to conduct a terror campaign and held on explosives charges. How far there was any real conspiracy for a French style bombing campaign, or whether it was a pre-emptive strike by the nascent British political police fearing such a campaign, remains a matter of some dispute.[31] More famously there was the 1894 bomb in Greenwich Park, which killed the anarchist who was planting it. The incident at Greenwich was immortalised in Joseph Conrad's 1907 novel *The Secret Agent*. Other popular, fictive accounts of anarchists as terrorists were Henry James' (1886) *The Princess Casamassima*, H. G. Wells' (1894) *The Stolen Bacillus* and G. K. Chesterton's (1908) *The Man Who Was Thursday*.[32] Journalistic accounts treated anarchism and terrorism synonymously, such that terrorist acts were attributed to anarchists, no matter who carried them out.

The terroristic strand of anarchist activity was also evident in the incidents surrounding *Leesma* (Flame) cell number 5, a group of anti-tsarist revolutionaries originally from the Letts province of Russia involved in the December 1910 Sidney Street siege. The robbery at a jewellery shop to provide funds for comrades back home went awry. In making their escape the thieves shot dead three policemen and injured two more. The revolutionaries were tracked down to a house at 100 Sidney Street in Stepney in the East End (now a multi-storey residential block of flats called 'Siege House'). The events ended with Winston Churchill, the then Home Secretary, overseeing the deployment of Scots Guards to support the police, creating a 1000-strong combined force to capture two cornered men, Fritz Svaars and William Sokolow. Peter Piaktow (Peter-the-Painter), who is most frequently associated with the events, had already fled. Svaars and Sokolow died in the house.[33] The incidents entered East End mythology: parents would threaten their recalcitrant offspring that if they failed to behave 'Peter-the-Painter would get them'. Unsuccessful efforts were made to further incriminate the general anarchist movement. The Italian militant, engineer and electrician, Malatesta, was charged with involvement in the crime, as he had innocently provided the gang with the equipment to make a cutting torch, but he was released.[34]

Propaganda by deed was just one form of anarchist activity, although it was the one with which anarchists were most strongly associated. This was not because anarchists placed greater emphasis on this rather than other tactics, but that they were unusual in accepting it as a legitimate tactic, under appropriate circumstances. Propagandists of all types, including Kropotkin, supported it. So although anarchists, like other socialist groupings at the time, were also active in industrial organisation, it was the uniqueness of their occasional advocacy of propaganda by deed that was their most distinctive characteristic. Even some of the French illegalists, who mainly used propaganda by deed, regarded it as just one method amongst many others.[35]

3.2. Workers Arise: Anarchism and industrial organisation

Anarchist industrial organisation had a great influence upon the Jewish immigrants in Britain who had fled from Tsarist Russia. The arrival of these refugees had been met with a marked increase in popular xenophobia. Even the anarchists had been promoters of racism and anti-semitism. The French utopian socialist Charles Fourier, and allegedly Proudhon, had argued that Jews were habitually middlemen and exploiters, incapable of common feeling with their fellow man.[36] The incoming immigrants, desperate for work, were blamed by socialists for strikebreaking and under-cutting pay rates.

Socialists and trade unionists such as Ben Tillett were anti-refugee.[37] By 1888, 43 trade unions had 'condemned unrestricted immigration'.[38] Many of the native British workers' groups repeated the stereotypes of Jewry as the parasitical enemies of the gentile population, found in the remarks of Proudhon and Fourier. In the East End, where many of the immigrants settled, the anti-semitism of established left-wing groups assisted in the formation of the ultra-patriotic British Brother's League. A petition demanding the exclusion of immigrants from Britain attracted 45,000 signatures in Tower Hamlets alone.[39]

Against this background of anti-alien prejudice, Aron Lieberman, a Lithuanian socialist, tried to organise the immigrant poor, first to help them in their plight and second to show the established workers' movement that the refugees were capable of socialism. The principles of his Hebrew Socialist Union had much in common with anarchism.[40] An alliance of state authorities and the ruling class within the Jewish community (*Jewish Chronicle*, Board of Guardians and Chief Rabbi's Office) thwarted Lieberman's plans. The *Jewish Chronicle* libelled the movement, claiming that it was a front for Christian missionaries. This constituted a particularly effective piece of propaganda, as it questioned the integrity of the movement and united with the dominant culture's anti-semitic views that Jewry and socialism were incompatible. The Chief Rabbi's agents also deliberately disturbed the meetings, so that the police were called and the gathering broken up. Partly as a result of this harassment, Lieberman later left for America.

One of Lieberman's fellow socialists, Morris Winchevsky, set up the first Yiddish socialist journal in Britain, *Poilishe Yidl* (*The Polish Jew*). Winchevsky left the paper when it supported the parliamentary candidature of the anti-socialist Sam Montagu, and set up in its place *Der Arbeiter Fraint*. It quickly gained a distinctive anarchist outlook, promoting equality, liberty, atheism and anti-capitalism (from 1892 it called itself 'The organ of anarchist communism'). During the period from 1885 to 1896, the group around the paper gained the support of the English-speaking anarchist movement, as well as a sizeable section of the Jewish immigrant community; however it was with the assistance of Rudolf Rocker that its progress was most significant.

Although not Jewish, Rocker had worked with Jewish anarchists in France.[41] In 1895 he had arrived to stay in London and came into contact with the Jewish anarchists there. He was sympathetic to the plight of the refugees and learnt Yiddish in order to help them. In 1898, he went up to Liverpool to edit *Der Freie Vort* (*The Free Word*). Its success prompted a request from *Der Arbeiter Fraint* for Rocker to come back and relaunch their paper. The editorial and presentational skills of Rocker, along with his organisational and agitational abilities, transformed the Jewish movement into one of the most effective anarchist groupings in British history.

Rocker was a syndicalist, and he encouraged the tactic of organising unions. The early *Der Arbeiter Fraint* had been unenthusiastic, regarding unions as a reformist distraction from building the immediate revolution. They had concentrated instead on communal agitation, particularly against rabbinical authorities. Under Rocker's lead this workplace strategy was adopted. It proved to be successful. Workplace agitation was attractive to Jewish refugees, as the ruling elite within this ethnic community championed social peace by claiming that Jewish interests were the same, whether worker or owner, whereas unionism recognised the vital differences in circumstances between employee and employer.

Syndicalism was a multi-faceted organisational tactic. It demonstrated the primacy of class division over ethnic division. It was a structure that could bring about a general transformation of society by being part of a General Strike and it could provide the basic administrative framework for the running of the new society.[42] In the short term it also brought about recognisable results. The unions organised effective strikes within the workshops where immigrant workers were found. The growth of radicalism meant that by 7 January 1906 the *Jewish Chronicle* was reporting that, 'hardly a day passes without a fresh strike breaking out.'[43] However, the continuing streams of immigrants, desperate and disorientated, provided an ample source of potential strikebreakers.

The period from 1910 to 1914 saw an increase in general industrial militancy with dockers, shipwrights, railwaymen and miners taking major strike action.[44] In 1912 when a strike of largely gentile West End tailors was called, it was feared that East End garment workers would continue working. *Der Arbeiter Fraint* set to work by calling a general strike. Rocker reports that: 'Over 8,000 Jewish workers packed the Assembly Hall... More than 3,000 stood outside.'[45] Within two days 13,000 tailors were out on a strike. Throughout the two weeks of the strike (approximately May 10 - 24) *Der Arbeiter Fraint* appeared daily in order to inform workers of the strike's progress. It was almost certainly the first and last (to date) daily anarchist paper in Britain. The strike was successful; immigrant and native workers struggled together to improve their lot, winning shorter hours, the abolition of piece work, and an improvement in the sanitation of their working conditions.

The SDF had been unenthusiastic about the role of trade unions, seeing them as restricted to skilled workers and being little more than friendly societies. In their place, they favoured parliamentary tactics.[46] Yet industrial organisation was becoming more frequent after the mid 1880s. Most unions took a more reformist line like the Trades Union Congress (TUC), but after the turn of the century the more radical Socialist Labour Party (SLP) and an offshoot, the Advocates of Industrial Unionism (AIU), were formed. These bodies increasingly prioritised revolutionary syndicalism over party building, just as the Industrial Workers of the World (IWW) was doing in the USA.[47] The main anarchist section, Kropotkin's Freedom Group, noticing this move towards industrial organisation, started to produce a syndicalist journal, *The Voice of Labour*.[48]

Syndicalists did not cause the increased industrial unrest that flared during the early part of the twentieth century but the wave of strikes confirmed that such tactics were a relevant form of action.[49] Although propagandists for syndicalism had little influence on events there was small need for them to do so: agitation in industry was already high and taking a syndicalist direction.[50] Noah Ablett, alongside other members of the unofficial rank-and-file reform committee of the Miners' Federation of Britain (a forerunner of the National Union of Miners), produced *The Miners' Next Step*. It was a lucid statement of revolutionary syndicalism, promoting democratic workers' bodies to run industry. A pocket of syndicalism continued in Welsh mining communities for decades, even at the height of Communist influence.[51] Fear that the revolutionary industrial message was winning support was such that by 1912 the labour organiser Tom Mann was arrested for publishing a reprint of a leaflet in his paper *The Syndicalist* asking troops not to shoot at strikers. *The Syndicalist* was the newspaper of the Industrial Syndicalist Education League and claimed a circulation of 20,000.[52] The authorities clearly felt that his message might find a receptive audience. The political motivation behind Mann's arrest is even more stark when one considers that a year later the Conservative Party leader, Andrew Bonar Law, called on the army to mutiny over the issue of Home Rule for Ireland, without facing any similar prosecution.[53]

3.3. Propaganda and Anarchist Organisation

In the last two decades of the nineteenth century there were a number of anarchist newspapers available that began to reflect the diversity of anarchist methods and beliefs. The aforementioned *Freiheit*, with its links to revolutionary socialism and propaganda by deed, spawned an English language version in 1882, published to rally support for Johann Most during his trial. Extending the tradition back into British working class struggle was the former Chartist Dan Chatterton's *Commune – the Atheist Scorcher* of 1884.[54] Also published in this era was Henry Seymour's *The Anarchist* and a fellow individualist-anarchist paper from the USA, Benjamin Tucker's *Liberty*.[55] Anarchist newspapers of all kinds provided both a means of propaganda as well as a tangible product around which an organisation could be based. The papers acted as a means of communicating with other socialist militants and with the workers (the potential agents of social change). Newssheets enabled the co-ordination of tactics such as public meetings, rallies and strikes. Their distribution at rallies and meetings helped to put individuals in touch with groups and clubs. Successful periodicals also provided a source of finance: the importance of the newspaper to the revolutionary movement is discussed in more detail in the last chapter.

The activists behind *Der Arbeiter Fraint* created anarchist meeting places in Whitechapel in London which acted like more recent radical social centres such as Emmaz in London, 1 in 12 Centre in Bradford and The Chalkboard in Glasgow. Like the contemporary versions, the Jubilee Street club organised educational as well as social events. Entertainments such as dances attracted wider sections of working class communities into the anarchist milieu. Even if the participants did not become full anarchist militants, they were, at least, more likely to be sympathetic. Through lectures and anarchist papers, the clubs provided a source of radical ideas and debate – an arena in which to clarify and exchange political theories.

Newspapers, too, provided a role for such interchange. Seymour's *The Anarchist*, for example, printed articles discussing the differences between individualism, anarchist socialism and 'collectivist socialism'.[56] Seymour invited Kropotkin to contribute, but the association did not last long – the collaboration lasted just one issue.[57] Kropotkin and his followers set up their own anarchist paper, *Freedom,* in 1886, which became Britain's most important English-language anarchist paper for the next 35 years.[58]

From the beginning, *Freedom* developed alliances with socialist and anarchist groups and periodicals throughout Britain and beyond.[59] By building up a wide coalition of sympathisers they could mobilise support far exceeding the formal membership of anarchist organisations. The willingness of socialists and anarchists, immigrants and locals to work together was evident in the large demonstrations against Tsarist oppression.[60] This co-operation helped Malatesta when in 1912 he faced deportation after being found guilty of criminal libel, for suggesting that an Italian called Belleli was 'a police spy'. A campaign was started calling for his release that united labour, socialist and anarchist movements. Support came from trade unionists such as the London Trades' Council, *Der Arbeiter Fraint* group, the Independent Labour Party (ILP) and MPs such as George Lansbury and J. C. Wedgewood.[61]

Debate and solidarity does not mean that there were not also significant theoretical differences between the groups . One of the principal ones has been between the industrial organisation of anarcho-syndicalism and the wider communal structures of anarchist communism. Another has been on theories of distribution and exchange based on mutualism, collectivism or communism: each suggested different forms of organisation, different tactics and appealed to distinct types of agency.

3.4. Ideological Differences in Class-Struggle Anarchism

With Kropotkin's growing influence within British anarchism, the movement was becoming increasingly anarchist communist. This move from mutualism and collectivism to communism was not merely a change of name but a shift in specific ideals. Collectivism, promoted by Bakunin, was a system of distribution whereby commodities were given a value based on the number of labour hours necessary to produce them. These were then to be exchanged with goods that had an equal labour value. A day's work by a surgeon was worth exactly the same as that done by a plumber. If barter was not possible, then labour vouchers recording the labour-value of the product would be provided and exchanged for goods. Labour was the key to value – it could be centrally determined by a collective council of labourers. Consequently collectivism was often associated with syndicalism, although some syndicalists have been anarchist communists, especially since the end of the Second World War.

Mutualism, a system preferred by Proudhon, was an intermediary stage towards a fully collectivist economy. At the centre of the operation was the Peoples' Bank, a non-profit, non-interest charging organisation. Mutualists would join the bank as co-operative groups of workers. Labour cheques would be converted into the currency of the period until the economy was fully mutualist. The bank would sell the members' products on the open market, with the market, rather than a committee, deciding the value of the goods.[62] As more groups entered the People's Bank, the power of the state and capital would diminish, allowing people to enter into free contracts with each other based on the principle that, '*A day's work equals a day's work.*'[63]

Anarchist communism was a break with collectivism and mutualism. For Kropotkin these systems were a recreation of the wage economy, with labour vouchers replacing traditional capitalist currencies.[64] In his introduction to anarchist communism, Berkman explains some of the areas of disagreement between the mutualist and the communist anarchists. First, mutualists believed that an anarchist society could come about without a social revolution, through the progress of the People's Bank, while anarchist communists argued that the ruling class would use force to protect their privileged position. Second, mutualists believed in the immutability of private property rights, while anarchist communists held that use determined ownership – the means of production should be free and equally accessible to all. Third, for mutualists the ideal was for a society without government, where voluntary commercial transactions would become the norm and such free market activity would prevent the build up of monopolies. Anarchist communists on the other hand desired the abolition of the market economy.[65]

Anarchist communists also dismissed the labour vouchers system that had been the basis for collectivism. How could equivalent labour time create equivalent value? 'Suppose the carpenter worked three hours to make a kitchen chair, while the surgeon took only half an hour to perform an operation that saved your life. If the amount of labour used determines value, then the chair is worth more than your life. Obvious nonsense.'[66] The surgeon's training might, also, be no longer than an artisan's apprenticeship. Furthermore, it is hard to determine where and when labour starts for certain professions, such as for acting, writing or child-minding.

Freedom under Kropotkin's editorship pursued a clear anarchist communist line. It considered mutualism and Bakuninist collectivism to be little better than capitalism. Mutualists aim:

[T]o secure every individual neither more nor less than the exact amount of wealth resulting from the exercise of his own capacities. Are not the scandalous inequalities in the distribution of wealth today merely the culminative effect of the principle that every man is justified in securing to himself everything that his chances and capacities enable him to lay his hands on.[67]

Individualist-anarchism, which has similarities with, but is not identical to, anarcho-capitalism, was condemned on the same grounds. Anarchist communism became throughout the end of the nineteenth century the dominant current in British libertarianism.

Even in the period prior to the First World War, the separation between workplace and community organisation, which was regarded as the distinction between anarcho-syndicalism and anarchist communism, was often more tactical than universal. Anarchist communists were active in industrial organisation as well as supporting propaganda by deed. Kropotkin himself defended certain of these spectacular acts and also wrote of the need for revolutionary syndicates.[68] Propaganda was carried out on two fronts: industrial activism and community organisation. As a result of working on these different fronts, links were built across anarchist groups and into the wider socialist and labour movements.

Propaganda by word, through meetings, rallies, papers and pamphlets, was not a pacifist alternative to other forms of action. Liberal commentators are often embarrassed by Kropotkin's advocacy of both industrial methods and propaganda by deed, as well as respectable propaganda by word.[69] These were not, however, mutually exclusive currents, but complementary measures. Each was used independently or in combination, depending on circumstances, to develop and encourage emancipation for the oppressed classes from repressive situations. By 1914 the anarchist movement was still marginal in terms of its numbers, but anarchist ideas on tactics and objectives had grown into a minority current in many industries and had permeated into various large communities. However, at this point the movement went into rapid decline. The reasons for this are not hard to discern.

4. Anarchism During the First World War, 1914 - 1918

With the outbreak of war, anarchism's advocacy of anti-militarism and internationalism was out of keeping with the new jingoistic mood throughout Europe. The excitement of innovative forms of battle seemed far more enticing than the outmoded idea of universal fellowship. The start of international conflict also meant that prominent refugee organisers were interned as enemy aliens. For Rocker, this included being held on a prison ship moored off the south coast.[70] He was not released until 1918 and then only into The Netherlands. He remained an active anarchist setting up the anarcho-syndicalist International Workers' Association in 1922, but he never returned to Britain.

The war not only lost potential recruits to the anarchist cause through conscription but, as Meltzer suggests, it also provided a cover for the British State to use political foul play against its opponents. Evidence to support this allegation includes the significant number of disappearances of radicals during the period of the First World War.[71] As a result, the talk held on the 5th of February, 1915 by *Der Arbeiter Fraint*, entitled 'The Present Crisis', could be seen as a commentary on the precarious state of the anarchist movement as much as the European wartime situation.

Those socialists who had remained loyal to their internationalist ideals during the feverish jingoism of the early war years had forged a strong bond of unity. 'Everywhere the Socialists were aggressive and everywhere they moved in solidarity. No attention was paid to party barriers'.[72] As the conflict continued and the casualties mounted in horrifying numbers, nationalistic fervour began to diminish. As a result, the revolutionary anti-war movement, of which anarchism had been a part (Kropotkin's support for the allies being a rare exception), began to regain public support. They received a further short term fillip with the successful Russian Revolutions of 1917 (February and October), although the latter was shortly to have a devastating effect on the global anarchist movement.

A consequence of working closely with the marxists was that a mutual appreciation of each other's theories developed. Anarchists adopted Marx's analysis of class society, while socialists began to oppose social democratic tactics.[73] The Bolshevik Revolution was initially greeted favourably by the anarchists. Only a few immigrant-community anarchist groups in America condemned the Leninist insurrection from the beginning. Nearly all the others, including the normally sceptical, and by then veteran anarchist, Emma Goldman, greeted it with delight. *Freedom*, although suspicious of the Bolsheviks, sang the praises of the revolution in 1918 as it was 'compelled by events to adopt many ideas put forward by anarchists', a view endorsed in Guy Aldred's anti-parliamentary communist paper *The Spur*.[74] Slowly, however, the Bolshevik Revolution began to sap the anarchist movement of its strength, through the domination of the revolutionary movements by the Leninists.[75]

The events of October 1917 were regarded as the decisive theoretical and tactical breakthrough and many left, or were dissuaded from anarchist groups, in favour of Communist Parties. Other sympathisers were lost when Jewish male Russian immigrants (who had provided the core support to the anarchist movement, especially to *Der Arbeiter Fraint*), returned to the motherland after the revolution, seizing the opportunity to go home and build a socialist utopia.[76] Other sections of the original immigrant community, as it became anglicised, found that the Yiddish speaking anarchist movement no longer held as great an attraction. By the end of the war the influence of the anarchist movement had sharply declined.

5. The Decline of Anarchism and the Rise of the Leninist Model, 1918 - 1936

Disputes on aims and tactics between anarchists and marxists precede the battle between Bakunin and Marx in the First International. However, by and large, anarchists and marxists of the turn of the century had the same vision of a utopian society. It was of free labour, in which people had the opportunity to undertake the types of activity they wished to carry out, the type of society described by Marx in *The German Ideology*:

> [I]n a communist society, where nobody has one exclusive sphere of activity but each can become accomplished in any breach he wishes, society regulates the general production and thus makes it possible for me to do one thing today and another tomorrow, to hunt in the morning, fish in the afternoon, rear cattle in the evening, criticise after dinner, just as I have a mind, without ever becoming hunter, fisherman, cowherd or critic.[77]

The difference at first was seen as tactical, as Lenin in *The State and Revolution* suggests. Both anarchists and Leninists claimed that they wanted the abolition of the state, but anarchists desired its immediate eradication. They claimed that it was impossible to use the state in a libertarian manner, whereas Lenin, following Friedrich Engels, wanted to make temporary use of it (which he idiosyncratically defined as the exercise of 'organised violence') for communist ends.[78] The victory of the Bolshevik forces gave Lenin incredible power within revolutionary circles. He used his success as validation of his methods, and his biting invective and Russia's financial reserves (the infamous 'Moscow Gold') to encourage other revolutionaries to follow suit.[79] Revolutionary socialist groups were amassed into a Third International with Lenin's strategic plan providing the political blueprint. Those groupings that remained outside were harshly criticised by Lenin, as his political formula required only one Communist Party for each country. In Quail's words, since this single grouping approved by Lenin 'represented the only path to revolution, [so] all other groups were not just wrong but *counter-revolutionary*.'[80] On January 1921, under the direction of Lenin, the Communist Party of Great Britain (CPGB) was formed out of three formerly separate communist parties.[81] The aim was to dominate and control the British revolutionary movement.

As we have seen, in its early years anarchism had developed as part of a broad socialist movement and, as such, suffered equally with the revival of patriotism at the outbreak of the First World War. In the immediate post-war period, anarchism received a boost as opposition to the war had enabled associations to be built which cut across party divisions. The Bolshevik Revolution did little to increase solidarity, however. Under Lenin's direction, organisational diversity was deplored and the differences exacerbated between anarchists and orthodox marxists.

The Russian Revolution encouraged large numbers of radicals to follow the Bolshevik path, but while many anarchists were won over to Bolshevism, a few socialists rejected Lenin's centralism. Groups such as the Communist League, formed in 1919 and dying in the same year, brought together anarchists from *Freedom*, Guy Aldred's *The Spur* and anti-parliamentarians from the Socialist Labour Party (SLP) (a group which had links to the American IWW). In Europe the KAPD (Communist Workers Party of Germany) formed in opposition to the Leninist German Communist Party (KPD). The KAPD argued for tactics more in keeping with the demands of workers' autonomy associated with anarchism.[82] In Holland a parallel group of left communists also formed. The leading theoreticians of this movement, Anton Pannekoek, Herman Gorter and Otto Rühle (later to be referred to as council communists), were placed alongside the anarchists in Lenin's polemical critique, *Left-Wing Communism: An infantile disorder.*

Non-Leninist communists aimed to compete with their statist counterparts. Reports of growing authoritarianism within the Leninist regime became an increasingly common feature in anarchist papers from 1922 onwards.[83] The Kronstadt rebellion, carried out by workers and sailors wanting a return to the principles of the revolution, and supported by anarchists and left-wing revolutionaries, was crushed by the armed forces under the control of Leon Trotsky and Grigorii Zinoviev[84]. 'March 17. [1921] – Kronstadt has fallen today. Thousands of sailors and workers lie dead in its streets. Summary executions of prisoners and hostages continues.'[85] There was additional suppression of anarchists with the imprisoning of activists in Moscow.[86] From the early 1920s onwards, the Soviet Union was recognised in anarchist circles as being just another form of dictatorship, and they identified Leninism with counterrevolution.

The Communist Party of Great Britain (CPGB and sometimes CP),[87] formed in 1921, not only competed with independent, libertarian movements, it also actively intervened to prevent working class activity that was not under its control. The early 1920s movement of the jobless was sabotaged by the CPGB who wanted the National Unemployed Workers Movement to be run by their appointees.[88] The apparent success of centralised party organisation and the subsequent closure of opportunity for autonomous activities caused anarchist self-confidence to collapse and by 1924 the movement was 'in deep depression and disarray'.[89] By the time of the General Strike of 1926 anarchists had next to no influence, except in an individual capacity.

In a survey carried out in 1933 by Espero White for a mooted Federation of Groups, there were about 500 anarchist militants, people who were members of groups or regular subscribers to anarchist papers, in the whole country. Even at this low ebb, however, there were still a far larger number who sympathised with anarchism.[90] Nevertheless, the reduction in anarchist ranks was such that by the time that the iconic anarchist firebrand Goldman came over to visit old comrades in London in 1935, most had moved into the CPGB or the Labour Party.[91] Others, like Tom Keell, *Freedom*'s editor after the departure of Kropotkin, had retired to the Whiteway Colony, an anarchist commune in the Cotswolds.[92]

6. Decay of Working Class Organisations: The Spanish Civil War to the Hungarian Revolution, 1936 - 1956

In the early 1930s the occasional anarchist paper was still being produced, but it seemed to be more of a monument than a movement.

Papers like *Freedom Bulletin*, produced by Keell from the Whiteway Colony, were filled with obituaries and reminiscences rather than practical calls to action. It was the Spanish Civil War that gave anarchism a boost, not simply through providing a cause to rally around, but through the arrival of foreign anarchists to Britain, providing a core of activists to revitalise a largely moribund British scene.

The anti-fascist movement in Britain was dominated by the CPGB. The left-intellectual milieu was dominated by pro-Soviet Union sentiment, to the extent that all active opposition to Franco was credited to the Communists. The Communists accused the CNT-FAI (*Confederacion Nacional Del Trabajo – Federacion Anarquista Iberica*) and the non-aligned marxist POUM (*Partido Obrero de Unificacion Marxista*) of being 'fascist agents'.[93] The anarchists, already sensitised to the perils of state-communism by the experience of Russia, saw that the situation in Spain represented a dangerous opportunity for further extension of Stalinist domination of working class movements. Spain provided an occasion for anarchism to break away from the shadow of other forms of socialism.

Following the outbreak of the Spanish Civil War, British anarchists took an increasingly syndicalist stance influenced by the CNT-FAI who opened a London Bureau.[94] An Anarcho-Syndicalist Union (ASU) was formed, as well as the already existing Syndicalist Propaganda League. The ASU's work was mostly dedicated to rallying support for the anarchists in Spain, although it was involved in one minor industrial dispute on the home-front.[95] Vernon Richards (Vero Recchioni) and Marie-Louise Berneri, both children of Italian anarchists, produced the paper *Spain and the World*, around which support for the Spanish anarchists was co-ordinated. The Freedom Group closed their newspaper in order to put their energy into the new *Spain and the World* as did the Anarchist Communist Federation, run by Aldred in Scotland, with its paper *Solidarity*.[96] The remnants of Freedom reorganised themselves as distributors of anarchist literature.[97]

With the fate of British anarchist groups tied to those of their comrades in Spain, the fracturing of loyalist forces resulted in a reorganisation in Britain. The split in Spanish anarchist ranks concerning the rightness of supporting a government, was repeated in Britain. Most took the view of Buenaventura Durruti, who opposed the compromise and participation in the Popular Front, as did Marie-Louise Berneri's father, Camillo, who was killed by Stalinists in the 'tragic week of May' when Communist forces turned on the left-wing opposition.[98] 1939 saw the end of the Spanish campaign. This decline in activity led in the same year to an attempt to create an Anarchist Federation of Britain (AFB) (a similar enterprise earlier in the thirties had come to nothing).[99] The AFB admitted a wide selection of support, from those interested in civil liberty, anarcho-syndicalists (ASU), councilists (Committee for Workers' Control), anti-parliamentary communists (Anarchist Federation of Glasgow), anti-fascists and trade-union anarchists and various small parties from the various Freedom Groups.[100] Before long the Federation felt the strain of internal feuding. It broke back into its various individual constituents, the Freedom Press Group of Richards, Marie-Louise Berneri and Philip Samson being one section.

The growing hysteria surrounding the international military situation with Germany also further demoralised the anarchist movement, as it had done in the First World War, although there were far fewer cases of internment of anarchists this time around.[101] With the outbreak of hostilities, *Spain and the World* was replaced by *War Commentary*, again edited by Richards and Berneri, but with the addition of Meltzer and Tom Brown. *War Commentary* and the Anti-Parliamentary Communist Federation's (APCF) *Solidarity* opposed the war, not on pacifist grounds, but because the conflict served the interests of the ruling class. They both somewhat unrealistically argued for global working class action to overthrow the bodies that had brought about the conflict.[102]

Those producing *War Commentary* became increasingly involved in the circulation of anti-militarist material. With victory over Nazi Germany growing increasingly assured, the paper was growing in popularity amongst those in the armed forces (including Colin Ward and later the Jazz performer George Melly). As a result, the authorities instituted raids on the press, and four of the editors of *War Commentary* were charged with 'conspiracy to seduce His Majesty's Forces'.[103] Three of them, Richards, Philip Samson and John Hewetson, were imprisoned just as the war in Europe concluded. The case solidified the support of a number of intellectuals who were linked to the movement. These included Alex Comfort,[104] the painter Augustus John and art critic Herbert Read. After the final cessation of the conflict in August 1945 *War Commentary* changed its name to *Freedom*.

The War, as before, polarised opinion. Communism and Liberal Democracy were on one side and Fascism and the axis dictatorships on the other, with little room for alternatives. This division led to examples of unfortunate, contradictory and downright unprincipled coalitions. Aldred, having left the APCF prior to the conflict, aligned his anti-war paper *The Word* with the pro-Nazi Duke of Bedford. Elsewhere, due to the anarchists' opposition to fighting the war, libertarianism began to develop a pacifist following such as in the North East London Anarchist Group.[105] Similarly the Spanish anarchists, in the isolation of exile and the despondency of defeat, made dishonourable alliances. The CNT in exile supported the allies during the Second World War, and hoped that after defeating Hitler they would go on to liberate Spain from the nominally neutral Franco.[106] As a result of these compromises on fundamental principles, the British libertarian movement had, by the end of 1945, two different groups calling themselves anarchists: '[T]he dead wood of social-democratic pseudo-libertarianism still parading the theory of the 'just' war (as exemplified by the National committee of the CNT in Toulouse) [...] and on the other hand [...] the liberal-pacifist cult.'[107] Anarchism took on, in most areas, either a pacifist or social-democratic demeanour.

This was incompatible with the revolutionary character of the original British movement and with the necessarily violent Spanish groups of the civil war period.

The changing character of British anarchism from a working class based revolutionary movement to a more liberal-pacifist, intellectual and artistic centred avant-garde was exemplified when the Anarchist Federation split in 1944. According to Marshall, the break came because the syndicalists had gained prominent positions in the AFB.[108] Meltzer, however, felt that an ideological explanation was superimposed after the event, as the split was more of a personality difference.[109] The remaining syndicalist rump of the AFB re-titled themselves the Syndicalist Workers Federation (SWF) in 1954, later becoming the Direct Action Movement (DAM) and latterly the Solidarity Federation (SolFed).

The anarchist movement's drift away from revolution to peaceful, liberal co-existence fitted into the post-war mood of the times. The elation following the victory over fascism, and the Labour landslide of 1945, with the implementation of the *Beveridge Report* by Clement Attlee's Government, won over a huge swathe of the British public to parliamentary reform. This model of political activism became the paradigm just as the Bolshevik revolution had been the standard for socialism nearly three decades earlier.

After the war, the League for Workers' Control and the 1953 Anarcho-Syndicalist Committee continued with a syndicalist strategy but they made little impact. The consensual approach to politics in Britain and the post-war economic boom had curtailed radical revolt. The disaffected gravitated towards the CPGB, which, after the war, was still looked upon benignly by large sections of the British public. This political and social restraint was broken by three important events of the mid 1950s: the Suez Crisis, the birth of the anti-bomb movement and the Hungarian Uprising.[110]

7. Spring and Fall of the New Left, 1956 - 1976

On February 25th 1956, Nikita Kruschev, in a speech at the XXth Conference of the Communist Party of the Soviet Union, admitted to the abuses and tyranny of Stalin's rule. If it was meant to be a sign of a thaw in the Cold War then the invasion of Hungary by Soviet forces in November the same year indicated that Russian rule was far from softening. Those within the CPGB had been able to dismiss reports of Soviet oppression as being merely the propaganda of the bourgeois press, until their admission by the highest official within the USSR. Kruschev's confession and the subsequent suppression of the Hungarian working class by Russian tanks in Budapest resulted in the disillusionment of many socialists with Stalinism.[111] In the two years between 1956 and 1958 the CPGB lost 10,000 members – a 30 per cent reduction in its membership.[112]

Many of these former Communists remained Leninist in principle and supported pre-existing Trotskyist and marxist groupings such as the Revolutionary Socialist League (RSL) and the Socialist Labour League (SLL).[113] However, the libertarian socialist Solidarity[114] group was formed out of disillusioned CPGB members thrown out of the SLL. Solidarity had a small part to play in the British anarchist revival of the 1960s and '70s, and members of this group continued to participate in British anarchism in the 1990s.

7.1. Changing Constituency

The decline in Britain's world standing was made apparent with the Suez Crisis, also in 1956. Britain's ruling elite attempted to maintain their nation's status as an imperial power by resorting to military action, which, under pressure from America, was quickly aborted. The decision to use force, and the availability of weapons capable of killing on a global scale, led to the rise of the Campaign for Nuclear Disarmament (CND), which was given added impetus by the Cuban missile crisis in 1962. This pressure group provided a further source of potential recruits for the developing political New Left as well as for the counterculture. In a postal survey of CND members and Young

CND members carried out in 1965-1966, 7% of the former and 10% of the latter described themselves as anarchists. The overwhelming majority became anarchists after joining CND.[115] However, the types of people who were attracted to CND came predominantly from the middle classes.[116] They were not from the sections of society to which anarchism had traditionally sought to appeal. Nevertheless, this new interest group did afford 'a pool in which to swim [.... Anarchist] ideas were able to be heard for the first time by a larger audience'.[117] CND, and their direct action spin off, Committee of 100, provided a meeting point for young people interested in wider political and social questions.[118]

These new converts encouraged the reformation of the Anarchist Federation of Britain (AFB) in 1963. Its anarchist principles were, however, unclear and confused, as the ACF explain:

> [T]he revolutionary core of Anarchism, already deeply affected by the erroneous ideas of the Synthesis as devised by Voline and [Sebastien] Faure (which sought a fusion between individualism, syndicalism and libertarian communism within the same organisation) was further diluted in Britain.[119]

The plural approach attracted pacifists, extreme-liberals and individualists as well as more traditional anarchist communists and anarcho-syndicalists. The aims of the different sections were not just diverse, they were often contradictory. As a result, the reformed AFB had no clear tactical or organisational strategy. Annoyed with the appearance of liberals within anarchism, Stuart Christie (Scottish anarcho-syndicalist and co-founder of the ABC) sought out contacts with the more militant European libertarian movement. Arrested in Spain, with Ferrado Carballo, for carrying explosives, he was charged by the Francoist authorities with attempting to assassinate the fascist dictator.[120] Christie was given a twenty-year sentence although he served only three.[121]

Throughout the 1960s and 1970s, the post-war political consensus began to unravel. There were a number of causes. The increased birth rates in the years after the Second World War meant that by the time this cohort reached maturity they were a demographic challenge to the depleted ranks of the older generation. The general improvement in prosperity made their parents' mores, based on rationing and fear of shortage, seem anachronistic in the new, affluent 'pop' society. Furthermore, despite the general increase in prosperity, longstanding social problems, such as housing shortages, had not been resolved.

Discontent grew against the paternalistic state. Left-wing intellectuals complained that bureaucracy at local and national levels, in the form of punitive planning, censorship and public order legislation, was restricting individual freedoms and artistic imagination.[122] The welfare state, for all its advantages, was regarded as acting on, or for, individuals, but was not actually under their control. Additionally, the growing economy required an expansion in higher education to train new sections of the community for the managerial positions that had been created. Increased strain on university resources, alongside the problems caused by an obstructive state, led to the phenomenon of student radicalism. This had its origins in the American civil rights campaigns in the South, and grew into the organisation Students for a Democratic Society (SDS). The rebellion of the predominantly educated, White, young, was given further impetus by the bloody conflict in Southeast Asia.

The New Left, as historian Wini Breines describes in her analysis, proved attractive to this post-Second World War generation, partly because it rejected the division between organisational means and political ends that had marked the older revolutionary left.[123] Instead they prioritised a prefigurative politics, one in which the means were an embodiment of the ends. This involved political actors, through their everyday interactions with each other and those beyond the activist sub-group, creating 'the beloved community' that makes possible the realisation of revolutionary or non-hierachical values,[124] such as co-operation, human dignity and justice.

This rise of a politicised, white collar, youthful demographic, was tapped into, in Britain, by the Freedom Press Group. From 1961 onwards, it had targeted a new, younger, more academic readership with a new magazine, *Anarchy*, with some success. *Anarchy*'s circulation grew to 4,500, while its readership was many times that amount,[125] in part due to Colin Ward who edited its first 100 issues. During Ward's editorship, *Anarchy* took anarchist ideas and applied them to aspects of society not covered by previous libertarian publications. It was judged by some of the class struggle anarchists to represent 'Revisionist Anarchism little different from Liberalism'[126] because it prioritised protest rather than revolution.

Even in this form Ward's magazine did introduce various features of anarchism to a wider, previously uninformed readership. British libertarianism prospered with this influx of new blood, but not all were happy. Christie, amongst others, felt that the movement was being 'side-tracked by the new left, anti-bomb, militant-liberal-conscience element away from being a revolutionary working class movement. This was not anarchism as I understood it'.[127] However, some of the new anarchists disparaged by more traditional members later adopted revolutionary positions.[128]

The British anarchist movement strayed further away from its traditional working class roots – a trend apparent in the 1940s but more evident in the 1960s. A 1962 survey of *Freedom* readers found that:

> [O]nly 15 per cent of them [...] belonged to the traditional groupings of workers and peasants; of the 85 per cent of 'white-collar' workers the largest group consisted of teachers and students, and there were also many architects and doctors, as well as people employed in the arts, sciences and journalism. Even more significant was the class shift among the young. 45 per cent of the readers over 60 were manual workers, as against 23 per cent of those in their thirties and 10 per cent of those in their twenties.[129]

The fall in proletarian composition within anarchism partly reflected the changing class composition of the wider society from manual work to clerical and administrative employment. The trend throughout the 1960s within most popular libertarian movements was to move further away from their traditional sources of support in the conventional working class, towards the new social movements. The change in the nature of support in anarchist groups had a reciprocal effect on the categories of people and tactic deemed suitable to bring about emancipatory change.

7.2. Alternative Revolutionary Subjects

The civil rights and anti-war movements in America and the growing student protests in Europe throughout the 1960s saw a combination of liberal causes being reassessed using collectivist analytical tools. Interest was renewed in libertarianism and the other minor revolutionary traditions.[130] The non-Bolshevik revolutionary socialist trends that Leninism had first ridiculed and marginalised, and which Stalinism then liquidated from the socialist canon, were being rediscovered. Student activists in France, such as Daniel Cohn-Bendit ('Danny the Red') with his brother Gabriel in their book *Obsolete Communism the Left-Wing Alternative*,[131] cited the anti-Bolshevik revolutionaries of Nestor Makhno,[132] the Kronstadt rebels,[133] anarcho-syndicalism especially the Durruti Column,[134] and the council-communists.[135] These examples of autonomous workers' struggles were also discussed and promoted by the Situationists, most famously Michele Bernstein, Guy Debord, Mustapha Khayati and Raoul Vaneigem.[136]

There was what Alfred Willener calls a 'double juncture' between '[m]arxism/anarchism, politics/culture'.[137] With the rejection of Stalinism, the ideological restraints had been broken, so that marxism was released from being a specific set of dogmas and rediscovered as an interpretative device and tactical tool. The combination of anarchism and marxism was not new, as Christie and Meltzer explain. Class struggle anarchists such as anarcho-syndicalists had disagreed with the prescriptions of marxism, not its economic analysis of social problems.[138] It was the extension of this analysis into aspects of modern life, which Marx could barely have imagined, which provided one of the original stimuli for the 1960s rebellion.[139]

Debates and indeed arguments still existed between the various heterodox groups but there was also a spirit of co-operation between many of the participants that was reminiscent of the collaborative endeavours that characterised the previous growth period for libertarianism (the classical age up to 1914). Politics in France was being extended into the wider culture – art, theatre and poetry.[140] So too in Britain, radical politics expanded beyond the small, special interest groups or quadrennial visits to a polling booth into forming a separate 'underground' counterculture. The new politics entered into cultural life because the oppressive power it sought to negate was not merely generated by, nor did it only operate in, the economic and political arenas. A host of other institutions and practices beyond the spheres of production and political representation intruded and disciplined oppressed groups. Even the trade unions and the orthodox left, originally set up to protect the interests of the oppressed, were acknowledged to be part of the repressive institutional framework, which integrated revolt into the existing system. Capitalist methods of production and exchange modified, glamorised, and yet rendered all social interchange banal, causing atomisation of the public realm. Individuals became capable only of interacting through the hierarchical power structures of consumption. They sought compensation through commodities, yet such a solution only worsened the sense of dislocation.[141]

In this respect the 1960s radicals were returning to some of the concerns that anarchism had stressed in its classical period. Libertarianism had always regarded oppression in much wider terms than merely the economic and political. Goldman, for instance, had railed against sexism,[142] whilst Kropotkin wrote on the effects of prisons on the prisoner, on the wider community and as a representation of a particular ideology in operation.[143] The range of oppressive practices was wider than just factory and wage conditions and consequently the areas of resistance and potential radical subjects were broader than the category of industrial proletariat at the point of production.

British anarchists were influenced by the activities taking place throughout the rest of the world. 1968 was a touchstone for revolutionaries. The potential for students and workers to combine in autonomous struggle for a total re-shaping of reality under egalitarian, participatory organisation had an intense influence on the left, both libertarian and authoritarian. Nostalgia for the lost possibilities of this time can be traced even in writers barely old enough to have been born in 1968.[144] The Paris uprising was regarded as a model for libertarian possibilities. At the time many British groups were inspired by the events across the Channel, amongst them was Solidarity, which already had links to France's *Socialisme ou Barbarie*. Solidarity sent a couple of members to Paris in May 1968 and they returned highly impressed by the autonomous student-worker activities. The Solidarity members were particularly encouraged by the efforts of both groups to resist the machinations of the French Communist Party and its trade unions, reinterpreting the rebellion against the state into the traditional framework of wage-demands.[145] Similarly the prefigurative politics of the SDS made a great impact, as did the highly publicised pranks of the American hippie-radicals, the Yippies.

With the strength of the student movement, and the stress in the popular press reports of May '68 on the acts of the young rather than trade unionists, a new revolutionary agent was thought to be developing.[146] Some forms of anarchism did appear to go along with this and reject the working class as the revolutionary agent. The events in Vietnam and Central America produced interest in the peasantry in countries under colonial rule. Previously repressed issues and concerns became prominent: the women's movements, Gay (and later – Lesbian) liberation, environmental crises, Irish Catholics, Black and

Asian immigrant communities, and the mentally ill. While some have maintained that these forms of oppression could be assimilated into more orthodox economic analyses, others regarded the oppositions of Black versus White or equality versus patriarchy as a replacement of class antagonisms.[147] The women's movement, in particular, with its questioning of hierarchy and experiments in egalitarian organisation, was a particularly potent influence on British anarchism.

The women's movements introduced new critiques of organisational practices that had dominated the revolutionary movements. Feminists challenged assumptions concerning the agent and location of revolt. The presumption had been that the central agent of change was the male, industrial worker located at the point of production in heavy manufacturing. Women's groups re-conceptualised social problems. Feminists focused on exploitation and hierarchy in other aspects of social life such as education, the home and culture, rather than solely in the traditional workplace. In doing so they introduced a lexicon that differed from solely class-based critiques.

Feminists re-appraised the organisational structures of self-proclaimed radical groupings and found that they often imitated the sexual divisions of labour and hierarchical structures of the detested hegemonic organisations. In 'alternative' newspapers women's views were denigrated and patronised, while their female members were allocated specifically secretarial tasks rather than more highly esteemed journalistic ones.[148] As Peggy Kornegger laments: 'Anarchist men have been little better than males elsewhere in their subjection of women'.[149]

New practices and women-centred groups developed to counter the sexism of the revolutionary movements. The democratic structures of radical organisation were examined and modified.[150] Tactics included supporting and building women's only groups, Rape Crisis Centres and refuges and also projects that questioned women's traditional roles in the workplace and the home.[151] These not only became features of distinctive anarcha-feminist movements, but also began to filter through into the general anarchist milieu.[152] Sexist behaviours still exist within more general anarchist movements[153] and are consequently the subject of continued censure and mockery from anarcha-feminists.[154]

Feminism extended the economic category of the working class beyond the European, White, male stereotype and (re-)introduced other perspectives. With the growth in interest of ecological concerns, new repressive conditions and sites of conflict were identified. Murray Bookchin is credited with having re-integrated the question of humanity's relationship to the natural environment, which had been a feature of Kropotkin's anarchist communism, back into libertarianism and the wider protest movement. Environmentalism rose in prominence, with the publication of Rachel Carson's *Silent Spring* on the effect of pesticides, and Bookchin's *Our Synthetic Environment*. These texts reflected growing public concern with the ecological damage wrought by the industrial post-war boom. Many of those in the environmental movement questioned the revolutionary agency of the working class, and many were indeed rejecting revolution as both aim and means. As the green anarchist author PNR indicates, it was Schumacher's Buddhist principles that informed his *Small is Beautiful* thesis. This, claims the writer from the Green Anarchist movement, inspired people to 'drop-out' and form communes attempting a self-sufficient existence.[155]

7.3. Tactical Responses

The end of 1968 saw a growing counterculture, which was attractive to the young who had different values from the older generations. One method of meeting their desires was the creation of communes in which young people experimented with new types of domestic arrangements. These experiments in collective living can be divided into two groups: those which saw the communes as a basis for more radical activities which confronted heteronomous power, and those which ignored existing power structures but attempted to create liberated zones within them.[156] Some communes used the cheap space and supportive atmosphere to create new products as well as providing markets for goods on the fringes of the economy: drugs, music and media which reflected their lifestyles. There was a huge growth in radical newspapers and magazines, *Black Dwarf*, *Frendz*, *Ink*, *International Times*, *Red Mole*, *Oz*, and the opening of radical bookshops in which they could be bought and sold. Thus, radical left-wing causes were mixed with liberalising values and developing popular tastes.

Creating and satisfying fringe markets was seen as a method of fashioning more egalitarian social relations. The original draft of the founding document of the SDS – the Port Huron Statement – included a remark about how free market relations could be potentially emancipatory. '[P]rivate enterprise is not inherently immoral or undemocratic indeed it may at times contribute to offset elitist tendencies.'[157] In this period in the late 1960s and into the 1970s, the distinctions between the New Left and the New Right had yet to be formed.

In the 1960s, the New Right as a particular set of institutions, ideas and theorists had yet to coalesce into an identifiable camp. Prior to the New Right's consolidation of power, assisted by the election of Margaret Thatcher to the leadership of the Conservative Party in 1975, the underground contained many concepts and some of the people which were to become associated with the Thatcher era. There was correspondence between New Right and New Left in their enemies: trade unions and their leaders, the state and the bureaucrats. The language of the New Left and soon to be New Right were also similar; both rejected 'paternalism' and 'welfarism', both wanted 'choice' and 'freedom', even if these terms were interpreted in diametrically opposed ways. Because the lines of demarcation between different ideologies and groups were unclear, orthodox Marxists, radical liberals, free market libertarians and anti-market communists found themselves acting in the same loose milieu: the

Non-Plan, published in the left-liberal *New Society*, written by such protest culture luminaries as Cedric Price[158] and Reynor Banham, was accepted as part of the left although its aim was for the creation of free market solutions to architecture and planning problems.

Some left-libertarian countercultural activities were a challenge to market relations and embodied the participatory, prefigurative features of egalitarian anarchism. The communes formed by the squatting movement, which began in Redbridge on the London/Essex border in the winter of 1968-69, were a reaction to the continuing housing shortage. The accommodation crisis was brought again into the public mind by the repeated showing of the television drama *Cathy Come Home*. Squatting sought to create a remedy for the situation, by assisting hostel residents into vacant council houses and luxury apartments. It directly confronted the principle of private property and brought squatters into conflict with the state, at both local and national levels. As Chris Broad, one of the 1969 Redbridge squatters, pointed out nearly a decade later, squatting was part of a wider revolutionary programme.[159]

On the other side of London, in Notting Hill, the Situationist-inspired King Mob, which included Malcolm McLaren amongst its ranks,[160] celebrated anti-social criminality and carried out pranks showing up the oppression behind the spectacle of capitalism. This involved employing the SI tactic *détournement*: altering the symbols of the dominant order to illustrate how they influenced and controlled desire. It was, according to the Situationists, more than just inverting an image. It involved the twisting around of the everyday image or event, such that the oppressive ends and the mechanisms by which it operated were illuminated.[161]

One of the situations created by the Mob involved one of their number dressing up as Father Christmas and entering Selfridges where he started to hand out free presents from the shop's stock to children. The security staff were called, who had to grab the presents back off the disappointed infants who then witnessed the arrest of Santa.[162] King Mob did not survive long, and many, 'once their youthful hijinks were played out,... [were] becoming part of the post '68 new middle classes'.[163]

The changing class composition of anarchist movements, with a concomitant change in the identification of the revolutionary agent, led some former anarchists into Leninist groups such as the International Socialists (IS), later to become the Socialist Workers Party (SWP). Christie, dissatisfied with British anarchism's slump into liberalism, had sought out contacts with European anarchist movements, who remained linked to working class activism. On his return to Britain, after his prison sentence in Spain, Christie along with Meltzer ran a class struggle anarchist magazine, *Black Flag* – originally the magazine of the Anarchist Black Cross (ABC).[164] It supported the smaller anarcho-syndicalist sections in Britain and also formed links with terrorist groups such as the Red Army Faction (RAF), which grew out of the European New Left after the decline of the student unrest. These groups were supported because they still promoted the working class as the revolutionary agent. *Black Flag* also sympathetically reported the activities of the Angry Brigade. Because of Christie's involvement in *Black Flag,* its coverage of incendiary activities, and the background to his previous arrest in Spain, Christie became one of the 'Stoke Newington Eight', prosecuted on conspiracy and explosive charges related to Angry Brigade events. He was acquitted.

Despite liberal accounts attempting to disassociate the AB from anarchism,[165] the milieu they moved around in was one imbued with anarchist ideas. The origins of some of the personnel accused of AB activities came from within a self-consciously anarchist background[166] and some alleged members accused of AB conspiracies are still part of the current British anarchist scene. The targets and *modus operandi* of the AB were informed by the ideals of the libertarian tradition, with a particularly strong tinge of situationist theory. The situationist tone of the Angry Brigade is captured in their communiqués with their attack on 'Spectacles'[167] and direct quotations from Vaneigem.[168] The anarchist prerequisite of egalitarian, unmediated action is also at the fore:

> Our revolution is autonomous rank and file action – we create it *OURSELVES*. [...] Our strategy is clear: How can we smash the system? How can the people take Power?

> We must ATTACK, we cannot delegate our desire to take the offensive, Sabotage is a reality [...] We are against any external structure, whether it's called [Robert] Carr [Conservative minister], [Tom] Jackson [trade union official], IS [International Socialists], CP or SLL [Socialist Labour League] is irrelevant – they're all one and the same.[169]

Unlike others labelled 'terrorists', the AB sought only the destruction of property.[170] It portrayed itself as having no formal membership and hence was not an elitist organisation. 'Without any Central Committee and no hierarchy to classify our members, we can only know strange faces as friends through their actions.'[171] The idea was to encourage direct action by anonymous groups of individuals *alongside* other working class activity, rather than as a replacement for it.

Against the earlier propagandists by deed whose interventions were supposed to lead or replace working class actions, AB activities were to be just another tactical method alongside more established industrial tactics. 'Organised militant struggle and organised terrorism go side by side.'[172] Convicted AB-member John Barker was involved in claimants unions and industrial-based radical publications such as *Strike* and the *Daily Grind*, a supplement of *International Times*.[173]

The AB attacks on the property of the Ford Chairman William Batty and contractor for Birmingham's Bryant Homes Chris Bryant and the trade ministers' residences (Carr) were directly influenced by the industrial struggles of the day. But, like the Situationists, the AB also regarded oppression as existing beyond the confines of industrial production. The offices of the state (police computer centre at Tintangel House, Post Office Tower) and the entertainment and consumer spectacle (Miss World, Biba's Boutique) were also targeted.

The attacks were embarrassing for both the officials of the state and the security forces. To the conservative factions of the ruling class, the Angry Brigade were another symptom of the disease of permissiveness infecting Britain. The authorities reacted by placing large sections of the politicised counterculture under surveillance, and subjecting them to raid and arrest.

7.4. Fall of the New Left

The increased interest by the security forces was just one of the many changes in circumstance that led to the fragmentation and decline of the New Left. From January 1971 until early spring, the homes of known political activists and members of the 'hippie' counterculture were raided and activists arrested. In July, the editors of *Oz* were on trial for obscenity over the schoolkids' edition that pictured a sexually active Rupert the Bear. The *Oz* defendants were originally sentenced to between 9 and 15 months although these prison terms were reduced on appeal.[174]

The Angry Brigade trial was due to start in the autumn of 1971.[175] After a long trial of the eight defendants – John Barker, Chris Bott, Stuart Christie, Hilary Creek, Jim Greenfield, Kate McLean, Anna Mendleson and Angela Weir [176] – four were acquitted: the jury also asked for clemency for the other four.[177] Although '[n]ot a single person was ever convicted for actually committing any of the twenty-seven bombings and shootings attributed to the three-year-long conspiracy',[178] the four convicted were each sentenced to 10 years. Unlike the Lady Chatterley and *Oz* trials, the AB accused was defended neither by the great and the good from the liberal establishment, nor by the orthodox left.[179] With the harsh sentences for those convicted and the general crackdown by the authorities on countercultural activities, the libertarian milieu began to suffer. The combination of politics and culture, marxism and anarchism, which had seen the radical movement grow, was fragmenting.

Other wider, social influences also had an effect. The economic conditions altered when the sixties boom, along with its optimism and willingness to take risks, was replaced by the economic downturn of the 1970s. Advertising in the radical press diminished, causing the closure of magazines that had supported militant action. Those that tried to continue faced competition from established media, who had recognised the new market and were keen to supply goods to meet its new demands. With the rise of the women's movement, the sexual titillation that had provided a readership for magazines such as *IT* was no longer tolerated. This market, and others that the radical press had served, was taken over by the mainstream popular press. Revolutionary deeds became subjected to market forces and were commodified. As the SI had recognised, 'ideology tries to integrate even the most radical acts'.[180]

Apart from greater antagonism towards anarchist activities from the state and the press, the 1960s also failed to garner any significant working class support. The AB had tried to avoid becoming a vanguard movement yet its 'militarisation of struggle' (to use Barker's phrase) nevertheless created a covert and secretive elite acting on behalf of the working classes. The AB were consequently associated with other terrorist groups operating at the time – the IRA and the Red Army Faction, which were not anarchist. The creation of a vanguard was not only antipathetic to anarchism's egalitarian and prefigurative ethic, but was a tacit admission that the potentially revolutionary agent for change (the working class/es) was not moving in an anarchic direction. Incendiary tactics met only with stronger sanction from the judiciary and wider public distaste.[181]

Accusations of terrorism against anarchists and the counterculture continued with the unsuccessful 'Person's Unknown' prosecution of 1978-9. Six anarchists, Ronan Bennett, Trevor Dawton, Taff Ladd, Mills, Vince Stevenson and the separately-tried Stewart Carr, were arrested in 1978 and accused of planning a bombing campaign in the manner of the Red Army Faction and the Red Brigades. Despite an exhaustive police investigation and the imprisonment of the six, the prosecution failed because no trace of explosive was ever discovered, although it did allow the mainstream press to run stories connecting anarchism with terrorism.[182]

Terrorist strategies either ignored or patronisingly caricatured large sections of the working class, leaving the oppressed little role in the revolutionary 'armed struggle'. Similarly, few industrial workers had actively participated in the '60s political or cultural alternatives. *Oz* journalist David Widgery, a member of the IS, commented: 'Occasionally you'd meet shop stewards at conferences who were interested in the underground press [...] or got stoned, or were interested in radical music. That was always very fruitful. Otherwise there wasn't much apparent link between the workers' struggles and – this psychedelic flowering.'[183] This view was confirmed by reports that working class skinheads watching the anti-Vietnam War demonstration, held in Grosvenor Square in March 1968 derided the protestors as the police violrntly confronted them: 'Students, students, ha, ha ha'.[184]

Workers did engage in apparently autonomous action, but not of the sort advocated by radicals. In April 1968, after Ted Heath sacked Enoch Powell from the shadow cabinet for the inflammatory 'rivers of blood' speech, 1,000 London dockers staged a seemingly spontaneous march in support of Powell. Reactionary groupings led by the evangelical Christian Festival of Light gained mass support and the National Front forced its way into public prominence. '[W]orkers [.... were] no longer ashamed to shout Keep Britain White.'[185] These events sapped the confidence of the radicals: while they had 'toyed with revolution, and while the underground had played with toys, workers were on the move, and in the wrong direction'.[186]

In 1970, Heath replaced Harold Wilson and the 'inch of difference', that pivotal space in which the counterculture had prospered, diminished. Yet the Heath government reactivated traditional working class opposition. Trade unions became the centre for popular agitation against the Conservative government. Most of the radical left, including the anarchists, had despised the unions for a number of reasons. For the hippies, unions were organisations of the straight workforce, whereas for the radicals they represented the old 'Stalinist' left. Unions mediated between employer and employee in resolving industrial problems. Union leaders had a significant role in the corporatist state and hence were considered to have had closer interests with the officers of the state than with their own rank-and-file. Yet the unions, rather than integrating the working class into capitalism, were now leading the assault on the Conservatives through opposition to the Industrial Relations Act (1971). The radicals' confidence in their own analysis was severely dented, as was their credibility.

The result was that large sections of the libertarian milieu returned to more traditional forms of anarchist activity. The Organisation of Revolutionary Anarchists (ORA), a grouping within the AFB, while critical of union bureaucrats, did not dismiss trade union activity.[187] In 1975, ORA changed its name to the Anarchist Workers Association (AWA), reflecting its reaffirmation of the revolutionary role ascribed to the working class. The AWA paper reported the industrial struggles, yet its audience, although larger than most anarchist periodicals, was still small, selling 1500-2000 copies an issue.[188]

It was the successes as well as the failures that lead to the dissolution of the radical environment. The most significant victory for the radical left was the American withdrawal from Vietnam in 1975. Yet this removed the main political cause, opposition to a war against a civilian peasant population, which had unified the radical movements. The hippie counterculture that had included the burst of libertarian experimentation was replaced with a more aggressive current.

8. Punk and DiY Culture, 1976 - 1984

The skinheads who had derided the predominantly academically-privileged anti-war protestors at Grosvenor Square (described above) were a source of inspiration for the King Mob. King Mob 'aspire[d] to be a "street gang with analysis"'[189], an ambition seemingly adopted by later anarchist groups such as Class War. King Mob member McLaren, a clothing entrepreneur, wanted to appeal to the street hooligans. McLaren, along with his then partner Vivienne Westwood, turned clothing into provocation and helped to enliven the moribund anarchist movements. McLaren also knew Jamie Reid, a radical graphic designer, who, like other libertarians, had been involved in creating a militant, local periodical, *Suburban Press*. *Suburban Press* combined a prankish situationist approach with a specific local interest in the new London satellite towns. It was successful enough in its catchment area and claimed to sell 5,000 copies. It was active in promoting squatters' and claimants' groups. However, it was never sufficiently large to threaten the authorities – not even the local council who Reid maintained were corrupt.[190] McLaren invited Reid to London to assist him on his latest project, that of creating and promoting the Sex Pistols.

Reid was already becoming disenchanted with revolutionary politics as it was being practised, believing it to have become staid, formulaic and insular. Reid accepted McLaren's proposal as it 'seemed very much a perfect vehicle to communicate the ideas that had been formulated during that period [....] to people who weren't getting the message out of the left-wing politics at the time'.[191] The Sex Pistols not only jolted one of Britain's largest economic sectors – the music industry – but also drew a whole new section of the public into anarchism.

The Pistols and many other punk bands set out deliberately to manipulate the mass media in order to provide free publicity for the band and provoke the established order. A few swear words during the Bill Grundy interview on television created a scandal in the mainstream newspapers and hence promotion for the group.[192]

Playing up to and shocking the media into reporting activities was a trick which others, in particular Ian Bone of Class War, attempted to emulate, and in Bone's case with some success.[193]

Stewart Home, a frequent critic of British anarchism, interprets punk as having a reactionary focus because Home concentrates on McLaren's aim of using the new musical form for commercial gain.[194] Certainly punk's aesthetic was used to promote a variety of ideologies including commercialism and the far-right (for instance nationalist punk like Chelsea and Screwdriver), but for many it represented working class identity and a rejection of consumerism. The passive role of the audience as spectator was denigrated as punk crowds revelled in participation and creative disorder.[195] The gender balance of the key actors in the movement, and the roles they were assigned, was altered by the active involvement of women such as Siouxsie Sioux, Poly Styrene and The Slits,[196] a tradition that stretched into the 1990s with the Riot Grrrls.

There was a disdain for the commercialisation of protest. Contempt was aimed at the '60s counterculture that had become integrated into the existing systems of oppression. 'The hippies now wear Black. The system wears hippie.'[197] In response to the institutionalisation of rebellion, punk's dynamism led to the endorsement of do-it-yourself (DiY) principles. The participatory nature of punk was evident in the alternative press that grew up around it. *Sniffing Glue* was London's most famous punk fanzine, but such media spread back into the suburbs where Reid's *Suburban Press* had first started: *Zero* in Welwyn Gardens, *Harsh Reality* from Kent. Some, like *No Class*, explicitly picked up on and covered anarchist politics.

The types of autonomous politics associated with punk could involve finding personal solutions to larger socio-political problems. Penny Rimbaud of the band Crass, active from 1978 to 1984, was prominent in promoting individual self-help responses to larger crises. This was later derided by class struggle anarchists such as Nigel Fox of the AWG as 'lifestylist romanticism' (or 'lifestylism'). Crass's DiY aesthetic often seemed to substitute pleasant, individualistic activities, such as growing medicinal herbs and forming co-ops, for 'developing and testing out a coherent strategy that could win people over to the struggle against capitalism'.[198] In other words, this form of punk autonomy accepted the possibility of personal liberation while the vast majority was still oppressed.

Crass's politics were diverse; its vision was often closer to that of pacifist individualism than to radical anti-capitalism. For this reason it was derided as merely 'prosaic laissez-faire individualism'.[199] On other occasions it promoted an anarcha-feminist sensibility alongside a forceful anti-militarism.[200] The sizeable following around Crass became interested in environmental direct action, animal rights, vegetarianism and veganism.[201]

The anarcho-punk agent of change was unclear. On the few occasions it was explicitly elucidated it seemed to reject class, and appealed to the same great hope of the '60s hippie culture – 'youth'. As a result of such shared characteristics, it is no surprise that punk met a similar fate to that of the 1960s (counter)cultures it originally despised. It became a youth orientated marketing niche, subsumed into the mainstream of corporate business. Punk clothing and records could be found in the companies owned by multinationals.

Punk, nevertheless, directed a whole new section of people, predominantly the White, male young into anarchist groups. The new entrants' aggressive attitude helped to revitalise libertarian movements. Despite Crass's own pacifist origins, its politics was often only a starting point for its youthful audience's more aggressive and collective activity. Crass's popularity also assisted anarchist and related causes more directly through their benefit gigs. Their success helped to promote a chic anarchist message, much in the way that the group Chumbawamba advanced a similar moral aesthetic throughout the late 1980s and '90s.

This increase of interest caught several of the anarchist groups unaware. In many instances these movements were in disarray. In 1977 the AWA split in two, with one group becoming the Anarchist Communist Association (ACA), which died out in 1980, and the remains of the AWA changing its name to the Libertarian Communist Group (LCG) and attempting to refine its organisation.[202] The LCG's opposition to Trotskyism did not prevent them from co-operating with avowedly marxist groupings such as Big Flame.[203] As a result, some activists became influenced by Trotskyist tactics at the time and joined the Labour Party.[204] Other groups also changed their structures as a result of the influx of new *punkier* anarchists. The Direct Action Movement (DAM) managed to preserve some organisational coherence when it was formed in 1979 out of the last surviving remnants of the 1950s SWF and it grew throughout the early years of the 1980s.[205] Elsewhere the renewal of interest in anarchism resulted in the formation of smaller, regional groups, organising around local issues.

The election in 1979 selected a radical right-wing Prime Minister, one of whose principle aims was the control of the trade unions. Industrial unrest had brought down the last Labour and Conservative administrations. The effects of Margaret Thatcher's policies were to break the power of organised labour by a strategy of mass unemployment and the criminalising of previously legitimate industrial methods. The destruction of jobs and wealth in the working class centres of major conurbations saw the escalation of inner-city riots. To some anarchists, the massive urban unrest of 1981 was a symbol of utopian promise, 'like a summer with a thousand Julys' to borrow a phrase.[206] They welcomed the actions of large numbers of inner-city residents, uniting from all races, ethnicities and sub-cultures (Rastafarians, Asians, Jews, skinheads, punks), attacking centres of oppression (police stations), redistributing goods and challenging the control of the state.[207] Such acts were collective but autonomous. The uprisings were completely outside the orbit of the Labour Party or the trade unions and beyond the comprehension of any of the many revolutionary vanguards.[208] These spontaneous insurrections terrified the ruling class.

The Conservative government appeared to actively exacerbate social, economic and ethnic divisions. Supported by members of what were, at the time, considered the far right, the government helped to intensify the Cold War.[209] This stimulated public interest in CND, and drew in a substantial number of Women's Groups such as Women Oppose Nuclear Threat (WONT) and the Feminist & Nonviolence Study Group (F&NSG). The Peace movement provided opportunities for greater participation by women. One such example was the creation of women-controlled protest camps such as Greenham Common. This in turn promoted feminist analyses of social conflict and created new methods of protest. Women's groups developed organisational structures that had many parallels with anarchism, favouring localised activities and inclusive, flexible, democratic structures. Feminism opened up questions concerning not only the limits of class struggle anarchism's traditional analysis of capitalism, but also of formal structures of radical organisations. This revived the old prejudice that feminism was weakening the class struggle.[210] Feminism also raised the question of whether all forms of hierarchy were reducible to the economic or whether patriarchy and other oppressive forces such as racism and militarism predated capitalism.

It was within the context of renewed interest in unilateralist mobilisation that Class War first appeared. A local group produced the newspaper *Class War* in Swansea in early 1983 – the same group had produced the influential *Alarm* newssheet that had repeatedly embarrassed the corrupt local council.[211] The original creators of *Class War* were: 'Long-time anarchists who, being well-versed in the movement's history, were able to apply this knowledge to the production of.'[212] While the liberal anarchist movement drew support from CND, Class War gloried in ridiculing their pacifism and its middle-class paternalism.[213]

The first Thatcher government's economic and industrial policies provoked the Labour Party to become more left-wing, albeit in a statist and paternalistic form, with Tony Benn gaining greater influence. This period also saw the ascendance of small Trotskyist groups who had entered the Labour Party, the most prominent being Militant Tendency, which promoted a strategy of confrontation through local municipal councils. The dominant organisational tactic to oppose the free market reconstruction of society was through entry into the Labour Party. The LCG, already compromised by close co-operation with Trotskyist groupings, ended up supporting Labour Party radicals.

9. The Revival of Class struggle Anarchism:
The Miners' Strike to anti-capitalism, 1984 - 2004

The main enemy of the Conservative administration on entering government was the National Union of Miners (NUM), whose industrial activities in 1972-4 had led to the fall from power of Heath, Thatcher's Conservative predecessor. In opposition, leading Conservatives had plotted how to destroy the power of organised labour and in particular the powerful Miners' union (the Ridley Plan). In 1984, the Conservatives were still popular following the successful

Figure 1.3. Policing the Miners' Strike from *Do or Die*, No. 8.

defence of the Falkland Islands. The police were given substantial pay rises as 'a precaution against any police force doubting whose side they were on in the civic struggles to come'.[214] After a false start in 1981, when coal stocks were too low and miners' unity too steadfast, by 1984 circumstances were opportune to crush the miners.[215]

The Miners' Strike looms large in all recent histories of British anarchism, for it indicated a firm return to its class struggle origins. As Ian MacGregor, the chairman of the NCB, proclaims: 'It *was* civil war'.[216] It was a class conflict between a vengeful government supported by a rabid media and para-military police force[217], against a militant industrial workforce supported by their local communities (fig. 1.3.) and co-ordinated by a trade union with a history of radicalism piloted by an autocratic, and increasingly unpopular, leader.

The strike events in 1984-5 were a direct class-based confrontation of the government's energy, industrial and finance policies. Dave Douglass, a NUM delegate for Hatfield who was sympathetic to syndicalism and Class War, argues that if the miners had won '[it] is doubtful whether Thatcher could have survived and all the misery, war and deprivation caused by her government, need never have happened.'[218] For Class War and the other main anarchist groups, the working class was recognised as the revolutionary force that could obstruct the programmes of the almost impregnable Conservative government. However, the defeat of the miners led the buoyant Thatcher government, in support of the media-owners who had supported the para-military tactics so enthusiastically, in breaking another sector of well-organised industrial labour, the print-workers' union. The Wapping dispute (as it was known) confirmed the judgement that it was unfeasible to doubt the importance and relevance of class in confronting state power. The government used a large range of state apparatuses to destroy collective power in the workplace and to restructure potentially disruptive local communities (fig. 1.4). Strike support, however, raised new questions about the appropriate reaction to trade unions. The ACF continued to reject, in theory in any case, any involvement while Class War had members, such as Douglass, who held union positions.

Class War's darkly humorous propaganda had originally been aimed at the post-punk milieu of hippie-punk squatters and prostitutes who lived in the same area. The social conflict in the coalfields enabled Class War to link up with groups and individuals outside of the anarcho-punk ghetto.[219] Close links were created between Class War and a group of Doncaster miners, in which the anarchists provided propaganda and financial support. Class War gained significant support from strikers because of its populist publicity in favour of miners' autonomous activities. The 'Hit Squads' (groups of miners who carried out direct action on scabs and NCB property) were despised by the NCB and their governmental supporters, and disowned by the NUM and their fellow travellers. Yet the strikers supported their actions. Although Class War never had more than 150 formal members it had significantly more supporters.[220] At its height *Class War* claims to have sold 15,000 to 20,000 copies per issue: 'miners

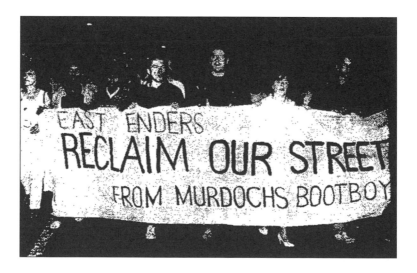

Figure 1.4. Locals support Wapping strikers against Murdoch and the police, from McNaughton, *Wapping: The story of a struggle*, 1988e.

queued 20 or more for the paper at the big Mansfield demonstration in 1984', success of a size which 'to be honest we could hardly believe ourselves.'[221]

Class War built up its reputation in the popular imagination by playing on the worst fears and prejudices of the 1980s ruling class, using the ignorance and naivety of mainstream journalists to full effect.[222] Class War glorified everything that Thatcherism condemned: working class solidarity, anti-market-communism, and violent hatred of the rich. In the two years between the appearance of the first *Class War* newspaper in 1983 and the 'hot autumn' of '85, the British media began to write of an 'anarchist menace' which was the equal of any 'red scare'. For the first time since the Angry Brigade bombings of the early seventies, anarchism was perceived as a threat to the British establishment.[223]

Class War took part in the Stop the City (STC) demonstrations that took place from September 1983 to September 1985. STC involved disrupting the functioning of the financial districts of major cities through low level sabotage, such as blocking up the locks of major institutions and gluing up bank machines. It organised stunts that would build up the solidarity of its supporters, scare the ruling class and gain media publicity for their brand of free-communism. In 1985 Class War restructured itself into a formal organisation, the Class War Federation (CWF) blending a loose amalgam of like-minded groups and individuals into a more formal membership organisation. At first this changing structure increased their ambition. In 1987-88 CWF organised a Rock Against the Rich tour with Joe Strummer, formerly from the punk band The Clash.[224] CWF organised a Bash the Rich demonstration held in the affluent Kensington area of London in May 1985, upsetting, to participants' delight, local residents. This was repeated in Hampstead (in September 1985) with less success as the police had learnt how to control the mob.[225]

Class War cherished the urban rioters. As opposed to anarcho-syndicalists, Class War believed that, in terms of practical tactics, communities rather than workplaces were the centre of resistance to middle class forces.

> Battles in the community – over control of territory, space and time – have become the pivotal point of today's struggle.

> The only paper that reflected this new battleground was *Class War*. The ungovernability of our class was celebrated in its pages whenever and wherever it broke out.[226]

Workplace battles were still important, but the changes in the economy had restricted their effectiveness, albeit temporarily. As a result of this emphasis on community revolt, Class War was widely associated with the promotion of, and involvement in, urban rioting. Journalists for the mainstream press blamed CWF for starting the riots. Along with other class struggle anarchist groups, Class War were also held responsible for the disturbances after the London Poll Tax demonstration of 1990 and the commotion after the march against the British National Party (BNP) at Welling in 1993.[227] The coverage CWF received was viewed with some jealousy by the orthodox left, yet even its critics admitted that CWF's populist approach attracted a new constituency into revolutionary politics.[228]

CWF thrived during the build-up of opposition to the Poll Tax, but soon afterwards went into decline. In 1992 the Conservative government under John Major announced the massive pit closure policy, that Scargill had earlier predicted and which had been denounced as 'lies' by MacGregor. The coal policy brought about the destruction of the British industry.[229] A quarter of million people took part in a protest march, but the miners, defeated in 1985, were in no position to undergo another long strike. The protests fizzled out. In the CWF, arguments over the response to this renewed attack on the miners exacerbated existing tensions. The large demonstrations, which provided a market for Class War's paper, had receded, and Bone and many others, who had been responsible for their most imaginative stunts, had left.

Tim Scargill led a short-lived, tiny breakaway faction in 1993, the Class War Organisation (CWO).[230] By 1997 the remainder of CWF split again. One side announced the closure of the organisation and produced an edition of the newspaper that was supposed to be the last: 'Class War is dead... Long live the class war!'[231] The other side continued to produce a version of the paper in an unavailing attempt to reproduce its earlier vivacity. The section of the CWF that wished to disband hoped to work more closely with other anarchist groups.[232] These included the A(C)F and the environmental, but non-class struggle, grouping Reclaim The Streets (RTS).[233] Despite lingering acrimony, both sides of the CWF split co-operated with each other and continued to work with the AF and other anarchists in campaigns such as the Anti-Elections Alliance (AEA) and Movement Against the Monarchy (MA'M) as well as in the June 18th 1999 Carnival Against Capitalism (also known as J18) and in creating blocs for later anti-war demonstrations.

The most enduring class struggle anarchist group in Britain is the Solidarity Federation (SolFed). This was previously known as the Direct Action Movement (DAM) and traces continuous links back to the SWF, the syndicalist section of the AFB of the 1950s. Whereas the CWF and AF prioritise community struggles, anarcho-syndicalists have traditionally identified the workplace as the most suitable site for class conflict. The favoured structures were the revolutionary syndicates made up of workers in particular industries, rather than split into trades.

Prior to 1987, DAM had sought support for anarcho-syndicalist unions elsewhere in the world, but due to organisational weakness and the strength of trade unionism here, it merely supported general industrial militancy in Britain. Between 1987 and 1988 it grew more ambitious and attempted unsuccessfully to set up separate anarcho-syndicalist unions to rival reformist trade unions. The only independent union they formed was the Dispatch Industry Workers Union (DIWU), to assist the non-unionised bicycle, motorcycle and van-driver couriers in 1989.[234] Despite some minor successes the DIWU lasted less than five years.

In 1994 DAM changed its name to the Solidarity Federation (SolFed) and altered its industrial strategy. It no longer attempts to build separate anarcho-syndicalist unions but instead aims to create networks of militants within sectors of industry: transport, education, communication and public services. These have their own publications in addition to the general *Direct Action* magazine. It also organises 'locals': community-based organisations made up of SolFed members.[235] SolFed remains a member of the International Workers Association in which the Spanish CNT is still the major section. A Six Counties' group, Organise, was also a signatory until it folded in 1999. Also working on a syndicalist strategy are British branches of the remnants of the American IWW. Occasionally networks such as the Trade Union Network of Anarchists (TUNA, also referred to as @TU) have tried to combine syndicalists, trade union activists and dual strategists, but these efforts have had little success.[236]

DAM's change in policy in 1987 to form separate unions led to a split from a group called the Anarchist Workers Group (AWG). They considered the DAM project to be an inappropriate use of their efforts, as all unions, including anarcho-syndicalist ones, were reformist. This was because the function of unions was to negotiate with employers. Separate anarcho-syndicalist unions merely split radicals from their constituents.[237] In their place, the AWG strategy proposed setting up rank-and-file movements in existing unions.[238] These rank-and-file groups would consist of trade unionist (excluding union officials) revolutionaries who would propagandise and build up militancy.

The AWG adopted *The Platform of Libertarian Communism* (*The Platform*) and a cadre form of organisation. *The Platform* was written by Russian anarchists who had fled from the Bolshevik counterrevolution. These had included Nestor Makhno, Piotr Arshinov and Ida Mett. It argued for a tighter organisational framework. Many regarded *The Platform* at the time as an attempt to Bolshevise anarchism; consequently other British libertarians accused the AWG of Leninism. The AWG's membership never rose above 20 and its influence was further reduced, partly as a result of taking sides with the Iraqi dictatorship during the 1991 Gulf War.[239] As if to confirm its critics' accusations of incipient Bolshevism, several of its members joined the Revolutionary Communist Party (RCP).[240] The only remaining openly platformist grouping in the British Isles is the 26 Counties-based Workers Solidarity Movement (WSM). Unusually for an anarchist group, it actively participates in constitutional procedures, supporting referenda options for abortion and divorce.

Amongst the other major anarchist groups were the ACF, which developed from individuals who had left the wreckage of the LCG. These individuals formed the Libertarian Communist Discussion Group (LCDG) in 1984 distributing former LCG materials, including *The Platform*. While originally interested in *The Platform*, the ACF later turned to Georges Fontenis' less centralist *Manifesto of Libertarian Communism* as their guide.

The LCDG became friendly with an individual who had produced his own anarcho-socialist magazine, *Virus*, which became their journal.[241] The group then changed its name to the Anarchist Communist Discussion Group (ACDG) and through *Virus* promoted anarchist communism and distributed *Solidarity* materials.[242] In 1986 the ACDG was joined by Syndicalist Fight (SyF), a splinter group from DAM. The combined group became the ACF.[243] In 1991 the Economic League considered the ACF to be '[i]n its militancy and commitment to violence [...] second only to Class War.'[244] In 1999 the ACF changed its name again to the Anarchist Federation (AF) but this does not indicate a change in its (anti-)political orientation.

Despite its relatively low numbers (counted in their dozens rather than the hundreds), the AF has significant influence because of its cordial relationships with other groups.[245] As well as working with both sides of the CWF it also held joint meetings with other groupings such as the autonomous marxist Subversion group, based in the North West of England. Subversion and the A(C)F had much in common, both being consistent in their opposition to national liberation movements and trade unionism.

Subversion was a split from the council communist Wildcat group. Subversion not only co-operated with the ACF but also with libertarian marxist groupings such as Red Menace.[246] Although Subversion was tiny in terms of its formal membership, it produced a regular free magazine (*Subversion*) and it was vigorous throughout the period of the Poll Tax, especially in the North West of England. It was also involved in claimants' campaigns before petering out in 1998. A loose federation of autonomous marxist sections still operates which centres on the Brighton-based Aufheben collective.

Wildcat was the most libertarian of the council-communist groupings in Britain (others still existing include the International Communist Current (ICC) and Communist Workers Organisation). Wildcat, however, became more sympathetic to a primitivist orientation.[247] Primitivism, with its roots in Sorel's *The Illusions of Progress*, rejects aspects of Marx's theory of history, in particular the view that communism can only come about once capitalism has progressed to a particularly advanced technological stage. Primitivism celebrates societies that are independent of complex technologies; it rejects industrially complex civilisation as ahuman and alienating.

The main primitivist current today is Green Anarchist (GA). It was formed after the 1984 STC demonstration called by London Greenpeace[248] – a radical environmental group with no direct link to Greenpeace. London Greenpeace was famous in the 1990s for the heroic activities of two of its members, Dave Morris and Helen Steel, who were the stoical defendants named by McDonalds in Britain's longest libel trial. The so-called McLibel Two were spied upon and prosecuted by the billion-dollar fast-food business for distributing leaflets criticising the working conditions, nutritional composition and environmental damage associated with the company's product.

The magazine *Green Anarchist* (which later became a newspaper) was produced by activists inspired by the environmental movements of the 1960s and '70s, and who had been on the fringes of the Ecology Party (now the Green Party). Albon, one of the earliest members of the editorial team was a pacifist writer for *Freedom* and as a result, early editions of *Green Anarchist* followed similar non-violent and liberal lines.[249] *Green Anarchist* did not recognise the class implications of the Wapping dispute; Albon's editorial for the magazine condemned the striking print-workers for their sexism and racism and previous lack of solidarity. Although the News International printers had been an unsympathetic lot,[250] Albon's editorial 'created a sectarian gulf between GA and the Class Struggle Anarchists [sic.], which lingers on to this day.'[251]

The commitment to pacifism promoted by Albon was out of keeping with the spirit of the time and further alienated the network of environmental anarchists from the rest of the libertarian movement who were becoming increasingly involved in practical class struggle on the picket lines. The violence of the industrial disputes and the police riot against the modern nomads, the travellers, in the Battle of the Beanfield in 1985 demonstrated the lengths to which the state was prepared to go to attack those who rejected the values of the free market.[252]

The long-standing radical environmentalist Richard Hunt joined the editorial board of *Green Anarchist* in the mid-1980s. The result was that under Hunt's influence the magazine pursued a version of class politics at the expense of the Christian, pacifist supporters.[253] The potential revolutionary agents were those who lived on the economic periphery, that is, the peasantry in the Third World. The affluence of the industrial workers in the western hemisphere made them a revolutionary irrelevance.[254] This further divided GA from the wider class struggle anarchist movement and indeed fron other members of the editorial board. Hunt left to set up his own magazine, *Alternative Green*, when he was unable to impose his will on the editorial board of *Green Anarchist* – especially on the issue of the 1991-2 Gulf War (in which Hunt supported western intervention).

Hunt's new journal promoted a range of theories antipathetic with anarchist ideals, including support for structures based on a 'pecking order' and the sexual division of labour in which males had the patriarchal role of protecting females.[255] *Alternative Green* was subsequently denounced by GA, which developed a more overtly Primitivist project. The latter argued that technology, and the scientific rationale that underpins it, was imposing a specific form of domination on nature. Amongst the writers endorsed by *Green Anarchist* was Theodore (Ted) Kaczynski, the convicted Unabomber, who targeted, with explosive packages, technologically dominant institutions, such as Boeing and American university research departments.[256] As Sheehan notes, the Primitivist analysis adopted by Green Anarchist often ignored the economic dynamic that encourages the enclosure and imposition of technological control over the wilderness.[257]

Despite these setbacks, GA's continued commitment to direct action in pursuit of animal rights, environmental issues and in particular, anti-road campaigns, has maintained the popularity of their newspaper. They sell around 4,000 copies an issue. The connection between the Animal Liberation Front (ALF) and Green Anarchist has been the main feature of state interest in GA. Police raided bookshops selling *Green Anarchist* in 1995 and instituted the GANDALF (GA-aND-ALF) trial. In a throwback to the Person's Unknown trial, six editors of *Green Anarchist* and *ALF Supporters Group Newsletter* faced prosecution for reporting ALF activities. The authorities believed that these accounts were inciting similar actions.[258] The defendants in November 1997 received custodial sentences of up to three years, without the prosecution ever having to show that the publications had inspired one criminal act. They were eventually released after an appeal. In 2001, the editors of *Green Anarchist*, John Connor, Stephen Booth and Paul Rogers, fell out over the decision by Rogers to sell an interview with Kaczynski to the soft-porn magazine *Penthouse* for $3,750.[259] As a result of this rift, two separate journals of the same name are published with varying regularity.

Also active in the environmental anarchist arena are Earth First! (EF!), a group which has its origins in an American ecological campaigning movement of the same name.[260] Although EF! formed because they considered Greenpeace to be too tactically restrained, Green Anarchists such as Booth have in turn criticised EF! for their bureaucratic tendencies and a preference for symbolic rather than direct action.[261] Class War have, in the past, similarly criticised environmentalists for their liberalism. Groupings like the Green Party (GP) and Friends of the Earth (FoE) are accused of attempting to create a cross-class alliance against environmental threats that should be understood as the result of exploitation.[262]

The division between class struggle anarchist and environmental radicals has substantially lessened. Their histories and tactics have encouraged avenues of co-operation between class struggle groupings and those originally hostile such as Reclaim the Streets (RTS) and British EF!. Class struggle groupings have increasingly involved themselves in environmental actions, such as joining in anti-roads protests, and recognised the class-based issues arising from ecological actions.[263] So too radical environmental groupings have developed a corresponding interest in class-related perspectives. RTS, which started out organising rave-style street protests against the domination of urban space by the motor car and had its origins in the 'alternative community ghetto', by 1996/97 started making links with the locked out Liverpool dock workers and striking London Underground employees. This co-operation between RTS, the other radical environmental groups and workers in conflict, culminated in the March for Social Justice in April 1997 in which 20,000 people participated (See figure 1.5).[264]

The creation of new alliances and links of solidarity between differently situated oppressed groups was partly inspired by the Zapatista revolt in Mexico. The rural revolt against neo-liberal economic policies and government land seizures created alliances between indigenous peoples and radicals. They also attempted to organise in a manner that evaded hierarchical forms, and as part of their struggle encouraged participation in an international *encuentro* (Encounter). Here people from across the globe gathered to discuss issues of common interest and develop forms of mutually beneficial action. This tendency to take on more global perspective became apparent in the 1998 protests against the G8 in Birmingham.[265]

The mass action in Birmingham primarily against global debt united class struggle and environmentalist activists. The thousands of

Figure 1.5. Anarchists march past Parliament as part of the March for Social Justice, 1997 (photo by Bill W.)

anarchists who helped block the streets of Britain's Second City[266] were, nonetheless, a tiny faction of the protestors present that day, made up largely of socially-concerned Church groups. However, by the following year's 'Carnival Against Capitalism' on June 18th 1999 (J18) the initiative was predominantly from libertarian radicals; there was not even a noticeable Leninist presence. Since then there have been a plethora of highly publicised anti-capitalist and anti-globalisation protests against the institutions that promote, regulate and enforce global trade: G8, International Monetary Fund (IMF) and World Trade Organisation (WTO). None has had the success of the Seattle protests of November 1999, in which the mass protests managed to prevent the delegates from meeting. Since then state intervention, in more lethal form, has more successfully restrained the protestors, making popular incursions less effective.

The distinction between 'anti-globalisation' and 'anti-capitalism' is not clear-cut, and the terms have been used interchangeably. The term 'globalisation' in particular has been subject to numerous interpretations by both proponents and the discontented. 'Globalisation' originally came from telecommunications, in which information in real-time could be transmitted and received anywhere on the planet, a dislocation of time and space that was to have a huge impact on culture and the economy.[267] The economic interpretation was developed in Japan where it meant marketing goods on a world wide scale rather than for the local market.[268] It latterly has developed into a more monolithic vision where free market trade, and the corresponding systems of law and culture that are associated with this method of organising production and exchange, is imposed on every region of the globe, strengthening the powers of mighty corporations and increasing socio-economic inequalities.[269] As a result, anti-capitalism and anti-globalisation have considerable overlap, although many anti-globalisers simply want a central state to manipulate prices in order to protect local production.

Anti-capitalist movements, especially those supported by anarchists, reject reform (but not abolition) of the price mechanism as this would require a centralised social structure.[270] However, protestors, in keeping with an anti-hierarchical perspective, support globalisation from below, where activists build networks of solidarity across national boundaries that are separate from (and hostile to) capitalist hegemony.[271] The networks of co-operation across national boundaries are indicative of a renewal of anarchism's rejection of national chauvinism.

The co-operative ventures of J18 and later Mayday anti-capitalist events demonstrated a greater degree of confidence amongst the libertarian milieu. Prior to the Poll Tax, most anarchist activity was centred upon following Leninist campaigns and offering critiques rather than initiating distinct campaigns. The significance of Leninist groups, however, diminished even faster after the fall of the Berlin Wall, although they had already gone into decline. The disintegration of much of the Revolutionary Left meant that is no longer possible, nor relevant, to tail-end the events organised by them.

The high media profile of anarchism, partly as a result of Class War's stunts, and the crumbling of the dominance of Leninism, resulted in considerable interest in anarchism from constituencies who might previously have been attracted by orthodox marxism. The victorious campaign against the Poll Tax also provided experience in organising events and arranging publicity, and raised the level of aspiration. Anarchists became more willing to organise their own events and develop the co-operative networks instigated by the Anti-Poll Tax campaign.

The Gulf Wars of 1990-91 and 2003, prompted the setting up of the No War But The Class War (NWBTCW) grouping made up of all the main anarchist groups, but for (in the 1990-91 conflict) the AWG. The AWG, exceptionally, supported the Iraqi state against western imperialism.[272] Like Kropotkin in 1914, who by taking sides in the

First World War was shunned by the wider anarchist movement, the AWG's support for the Saddam imperial ambition left them with few friends in the movement. NWBTCW tried to create an understanding of imperialism and global capitalism which was independent of Leninism, yet, according to Aufheben NWBTCW in 1991 was still concerned with defining itself against state-socialism rather than undertaking autonomous activity.[273] The NWBTCW network has been reactivated many times in recent years to respond to conflicts in the Balkans (1999), Afghanistan (2002-) and Iraq (2003-) once more.

Anarchist networks throughout the 1990s became increasingly ambitious. In April 1992 1,500 people took part in an anarchist organised Anti-Elections demonstration,[274] even though permission for the march had been withdrawn by the state, making it then the largest anarchist organised demonstration for decades (subsequently exceeded by J18). For the first time in a century tiny factions of the Left were tail-ending anarchic initiatives rather than the other way around. These networks have become more sophisticated and adventurous. In local areas class struggle groups and environmental campaigns have come together to swap information and find areas for solidarity. Brighton's Rebel Alliance was the first, followed by Norwich Solidarity, Manchester Direct Action, Nottingham Association of Subversive Activists, and London Underground, amongst others. Many dissolve, but the internet is providing other forums for groups to share information and plan mutually-supportive actions.

British anarchism remains continually in flux with groups appearing, dissolving, reappearing and combining. It is made up of organisations with distinct structures, who appeal to different constituencies and promote different tactics. At the end of the nineteenth century, it was immigrant workers and radical industrial organisation that characterised anarchism. In the 1930s it was refugees from fascism and the support for CNT that united the British anarchist movement. In the late 1950s and into the 1960s the New Left and the corresponding counterculture provided opportunities for new forms of expression and experimentation in communal arrangements, although these rarely challenged economic relations. With the recession of the 1970s and Conservative retrenchment of the 1980s anarchism began to rediscover the importance of economic as well as other forms of oppression. In the most recent period under review, 1984-2004, anarchists have been involved in a host of organisations and used a multitude of tactics. They have set up social centres, some legal, others by reclaiming empty properties, that have helped house the homeless, offered an organisational space for anti-militarist groupings and been venues for myriad social and cultural activities from educational circles to raves and cafes. Anarchists have been involved in distributing technical welfare advice to squatters and provided fund-raising for strikers and prisoners. Most spectacularly, they have been at the forefront of anti-capitalist and anti-government riots, such as the protests against the 1994 Criminal Justice Act and the anti-capitalist festivities of J18 and recent Mayday contestations in Britain's urban centres.

These disturbances, such the 1994 riot in the West End of London, once again saw the Hyde Park railings become weapons in the hands of anarchists, just as they had for Kitz and Lane over a century earlier. For behind the apparent diversity of actions, a result of the historical context in which they occur, there is amongst the main anarchist strands a consistent framework which sees means, ends and agency as inseparable.

Chapter Two

The Anarchist Ethic

This chapter is divided into two sections. The first, 'The 'Anarchist Ethical Framework' (Part One), devises a procedure for evaluating anarchism that is consistent with libertarianism. The second section (Part Two) examines the category of behaviour associated with anarchism, 'direct action', and shows how it accords with the anarchist ethic. This latter section, which demarcates direct action from other more conventional types of politics, also explores the vexed question of violence, in particular whether a consistent anarchist ethic rules out behaviours normally classified as 'violent'.

The system of evaluation is constructed from writings from theorists and activists that broadly accept the categorising principles of class struggle anarchism discussed in the introduction. The model of appraisal involves the means being consistent with the desired ends, that is to say the outcomes are *prefigured* by the methods. Another important feature, which is covered in Chapter Three, is that particular types of agent must be in charge of the action. An ideal, consistent, type of anarchism is developed, and this is used to assess various examples of contemporary British libertarian behaviour. In their ideal form, anarchist tactics have immediate practical consequences as well as pursuing wider social goals. The longer-term objectives are achieved through the extension of, and interaction with, other prefigurative behaviours. This anarchist ethic of *prefiguration* is assessed against competing moral theories in order to demonstrate its distinctiveness and strengths in terms of methods and organisation.[1]

Prefiguration is the feature that is specific to 'direct action' – a category of (anti-)political behaviour favoured by anarchists. (The term '(anti-)political' is applied to those non-statist tactics that challenge the disproportionate power to influence other people's realities). The importance of this class of tactics is the subject of Part Two. Tactics of this type embody the aim. In the ideal anarchist form of direct action, the oppressed themselves are directly involved in resisting oppressive power, rather than relying on more powerful others. It is in relation to direct action that the most frequently debated questions arising from prefiguration appear. In particular, it considers the hotly disputed conundrum of whether the commitment to direct action requires a commitment to pacifism. It will illustrate that a consistent anarchism does not require an obligation to solely pacifist methods. Close scrutiny shows that many behaviours that are conventionally labelled 'violent' can be compatible with anarchism.

PART I

The Anarchist Ethical Framework

Introduction

Part One discusses the morality of anarchist methods, yet applying ethics to revolutionary activity faces three objections. The first category of criticism concerns the problems of identifying 'anarchism'. The second set deals with the unwillingness by some class struggle libertarians to accept that ethics has any part to play in evaluating their methods. The third concern is the problem of finding a suitable method for such an assessment. This chapter does not cover the first category, as the difficulties in defining 'anarchism' are covered in the introduction and developed through the description of the main groups and movements in the opening chapter. The primary focus of this chapter concerns raising and resolving the second and third of these criticisms. This first part concentrates on sketching out a consistent (or ideal) anarchist ethic, and demonstrates its advantages over the traditional approaches of ends-based moral theories, referred to in the technical literature as 'consquentialist', and means-based approaches favoured by Immanuel Kant, which prioritise the rights of the individual and are known in the specialist literature as 'deontological'. However, it is pertinent to start by explaining the relevance of ethical evaluation to anarchist behaviours.

1. Against Ethics

Some anarchists reject, out of hand, the relevance of moral evaluation. One such argument advanced takes as its basis economic determinism, a theory that concludes that change is dependent on the workings of the economy, a view associated with more mechanistic interpretations of marxism. As the productive forces are the motor for change the subjective intentions of actors are immaterial (superstructural) and therefore any form of moral evaluation is irrelevant.[2] Other critics consider ethics to be a middle class preoccupation where those in elite positions, who cannot comprehend the situations on which they pontificate, place an unsuitable evaluative framework on anarchist tactics. Notwithstanding these criticisms, some critics have attempted ethical evaluations of class struggle methods, some with a degree of sophistication, others by simply applying an inappropriate moral template derived from Immanuel Kant's liberal ethics.[3] The latter have thereby inadvertently confirmed the naïve anarchist criticism of moral evaluation. Liberal, Kantian categories not only have general meta-ethical shortcomings, but are also particularly ineffectual in assessing class struggle methods.

A widespread anti-ethical stance can be traced to the wider socialist political movements. It is exemplified by a phrase ascribed to Brecht: 'Bread first, then ethics'. The political philosopher Alan Carling describes the view that, as human action is economically determined, the struggle of the oppressed is not amenable to ethics. Consequently, relevant behaviour is either heteronomously fixed or morality is a 'luxury item, and the poor cannot afford luxuries.'[4] Such divisions between the subjectivities of individuals and the economic base have long been criticised, by autonomist marxists such as Harry Cleaver, for inappropriately restricting the identification of the realm of economic oppression.[5] Purely determinist accounts, such as Brecht's, rob oppressed groups of any agency. They are therefore incompatible with anarchism, as it is a liberation movement for the oppressed in which the oppressed themselves create non-hierarchical practices that challenge or elude forms of domination.

The second of the criticisms raised by Carling – that the resolution of unbearable social conditions allows for no discrimination in methods – appears occasionally in anarchist propaganda but does not stand up to scrutiny.[6] There is justifiable hostility from the oppressed towards those, like tabloid columnists and politicians, who are distanced from privation, but cast critical judgement on the actions of the oppressed. Ethical questions still arise when considering the circumstances that lead to the division between the dominant and subservient, and which methods are most appropriate for resolving this disparity.

Moral evaluation of (anti-)political behaviour is not alien to anarchism. On the contrary, the WSM illustrate that the recognition of the importance of ethical considerations marks libertarianism off from many traditional marxist groups. In a critique of Leninist policies, Andrew Flood of the WSM describes how:

> [M]any can admit the Russian revolution was in part destroyed by the politics of Bolshevism, but they can only do so after first making clear that their critique is not related to the 'moralism' of the anarchists. This is the hallmark of an organisation which never sees itself as addressing 'ordinary people'. Who in their right mind would approach such a discussion with 'I've nothing against shooting leftists to achieve revolution, but it does not work.' The anarchists were full of moral indignation and quite right too! But they also argue that terror was crushing the revolution by destroying initiative and debate.[7]

Morality is neither separate from, nor identical to, practical results, but the one informs the other. Flood states that not only must the ends be humane, emancipatory and diverse, but the methods also have to be morally acceptable, *independently* of the ends. The question is not whether to use a moral framework to assess anarchist methods, but which should be used?

Inappropriate ethical assessments derived from other ideological positions are likely to disfigure and dismiss anarchism. Academic approaches to political writings often omit the most important features of revolutionary writings. As Cleaver suggests, works such as Marx's *Capital* are wrongly viewed as being primarily exercises in political economy or ontological theorising rather than as practical advice to oppressed subject groups.[8] An analysis of anarchism should use a method which recognises that libertarianism comes from and addresses particular audiences. The prefigurative framework that forms the ideal type anarchist model is derived from anarchism's own professed evaluative approaches. Ideal type anarchism is used to assess the tactics (including organisational structures) of contemporary libertarians. The latter part of the chapter elucidates this method in connection with 'direct action' – the category of (anti-) political methods identified with anarchism.

2. The Prefigurative Method.
An interest in, and development of, a method of ethical evaluation is not new to anarchism. Kropotkin's last (and incomplete) work was a treatise on ethics.[9] Consciously or not, anarchist activists frequently evaluate their actions and those of their opponents in ethical terms. It is the consideration of whether libertarian methods are 1) consistent with the type of agency they wish to appeal to and 2) the aims they wish to achieve – that provides the framework of evaluation for this review. It is a form of assessment that can be discerned in the earliest predecessors of many forms of anarchism. It also provides a useful method for indicating areas that lack clarity and reveals contradictions or omissions in various anarchist programmes.

The dialogues between anarchism and other forms of political action, primarily Leninism and liberal democracy, have often focused on the question of tactics. These debates have frequently been about determining the relationship of means reflecting ends. The anarchist position has been characterised by the oft-quoted comment of James Guillaume, a colleague of Bakunin: 'How could one want an equalitarian and free society to issue from authoritarian organisation? It is impossible.'[10] Similarly, the difference between Kropotkin and Sergei Nechaev, as the anarchist historian Paul Avrich remarks, is one in which the first maintained that the ends and means were inseparable while the latter prioritised objectives exclusively.[11]

The persistent claim that there is a dynamic relationship between the methods and ends also appears in contemporary groups. The ACF states: 'Anarchists believe that there is a strong correlation between means and ends and this means freedom is not something that can be granted to us by politicians.'[12] This tactical question of methods embodying the aims and also involving the subjugated agents themselves marks libertarianism out from its socialist competitors. The abandonment of any predisposition for either means or ends is also a repudiation of both traditional ethical approaches. It contests the priority given to ends found in Leninist and social democratic approaches, and is a rejection of the approach to sovereign rights that marks the Kantian, deontological influence on free market liberalism.

The ideal type anarchism constructed here rejects consequentialism because it recognises that it is impossible to impose a specific universal end which is applicable to all in every circumstance and known in advance. To use the terminology of the poststructural anarchist Todd May, anarchism is tactical rather than strategic. Tactical philosophies acknowledge a multitude of oppressive irreducible powers with no objective position that can identify how they would operate acontextually. Leninism, by contrast, is strategic; it proposes that there is one central struggle which can be understood scientifically.[13]

Anarchism acknowledges that there are consequences to actions. The satisfaction of desires, or the frustration of goals, has to be taken into account. Yet these ends are pragmatic and temporary and the legitimacy of an act does not rest on end-states alone. The four anarchist criteria described in the introduction (which exemplify anti-representation and anti-hierarchy), in an ideal form, do not impose a singular strategy of resistance, as such a positive methodology would only impose a regulative set of social relations. As will be seen, applying a utopian blueprint would involve enforcing others to live under a social model designed by just a few individuals, thereby restricting autonomy and hence (re-)creating patterns of domination. Anarchist principles cannot be applied externally onto the subjugated agents. For a tactic to be regarded as liberatory, it must come from the resistance of the dominated group themselves, rather than be governed by the judgement of a group of revolutionaries, anarchists or otherwise (or any other mediating vanguard), a point returned to in the next chapter.

Anarchist principles are reflexive and self-creative, as they do not assess social practices against a universally prescribed end-point, as some utopian theorists have done, but through a process of immanent critique. The precepts behind an ideology are examined to show whether they are internally consistent or whether they contradict with that ideology in practice. In carrying out this sort of appraisal of existing social forms, new practices and social relations are formed. The process of critical assessment creates a medium of communication that is consistent with anarchist ambitions.[14]

Through criticising and opposing the existing order, anarchists develop emancipatory alternatives. For ideal type anarchism, means and ends are irreducible parts of the same process – and as a result one cannot be considered more important than the other. By contrast, Leninism asserts for itself an objective position from which it assesses situations and prescribes solutions. It regards ultimate aims as being scientifically determined and promotes specific ends over means. Lenin claims that a revolutionary project must concentrate on ends, such that even the methods associated with repression are acceptable:

'[W]e must temporarily make use of the instruments, resources, and methods of the state power *against* the exploiters.'[15] Leninism is instrumental; anarchism, in its ideal form, is prefigurative.

2.1. The Means-Ends Distinction

Aristotle was the first philosopher of note to make a distinction between means and ends. He developed a taxonomy in his *Ethics* through which acts could be understood and assessed. Aristotle's scientific approach was one in which choices of behaviour were identified through the application of categories such as means, ends and actors. This method remains influential in moral philosophy. The scientific approach was taken to extremes with Jeremy Bentham's 'hedonic calculus', a complex mathematical schema by which the skilled utilitarian could objectively measure happiness with industrial precision.

Aristotle ranks acts into a hierarchy according to their proximity to the ultimate aim – namely achieving a state of *eudaemonia* or societal prosperity.[16] Aristotle was not a strict consequentialist. He conceded that results were not the sole moral ground for assessing different acts as even unsuccessful endeavours can be virtuous, a view endorsed by anarchists.[17] Anarchists also share Aristotle's link between virtuous behaviour and the moral agent, in which acts help form the identity of the subject that will perform the moral act. However, there are important differences between the Ancient Greeks' and contemporary anarchism's approach to identifying this moral agent.

For Aristotle, slaves and women were too irrational to be significant moral subjects. Instead, Aristotle sought to influence the powerful oligarchs and tyrants – to turn them into heroic individuals.[18] Anarchists, on the other hand, consider that ethical change comes about when those affected by oppression overcome it through their actions. The agent of change in this scenario is democratic, fluctuating and wide ranging, as opposed to the Aristotelian champion, who is fixed into a hierarchy. While anarchists and Aristotle differ over the types of agency and the relationship between means and ends, it is through these moral categories developed in Aristotle's *Ethics* that anarchist tactics are analysed in this book.

3. Ends-based Approaches

Foremost in the ethical theories that assess the efficacy of an action according to its success at attaining a particular end, is utilitarianism. Consequentialism, of which utilitarianism is a prime example, is also apparent in Leninism and certain forms of utopianism, in which predetermined end-points are prioritised as the ultimate goal. However, it should be noted that contemporary utopian writings play a different role, no longer based on encouraging the acceptance of a social blueprint of predestined ends.

Neither the motives nor the intentions of the moral agent are significant for an ends-based ethical theory: only the consequences of an act are relevant to its moral evaluation. Utilitarianism, for instance, involves the application of a simple formula (devised by Bentham and later described by John Stuart Mill), which outlines an ends-based schema for assessment: 'actions are right in proportion as they tend to promote happiness, wrong as they tend to produce the reverse of happiness. By happiness is intended pleasure and the absence of pain; by unhappiness, pain, and the privation of pleasure.'[19] It is the end point, a more restrictive notion of *eudaemonia* considered solely in terms of happiness, that provides the method for weighing the correctness or otherwise of an act. Even ignoring the potential difficulties of measuring the potential and actual happiness or misery of others (a task made no easier by Bentham's utility calculus), there are still major drawbacks in determining the appropriateness of an act depending on its efficiency in delivering a predetermined end.

Instrumental rationality, as categorised by Max Weber, ensues when methods are solely guided by consideration of the ends. The success of a plan is determined by its efficiency in meeting the objectives. 'A person acts rationally in the "means-ends" sense when his action is guided by consideration of ends, means and secondary consequence.'[20]

This is considered problematic for anarchists as it presumes having advanced knowledge of the desired aim. This is rejected by the tactical nature of anarchism (again covered in more detail in Chapter Three). Secondly, instrumentalism allows for oppressed subject groups to be used as mere implements, further reducing their autonomy.

3.1. Prefiguration Versus Consequentialism

Examples of instrumentalism appear in a variety of political propaganda. It appears not only in Leninism but also in the writings of fascists, in which any action, including using other autonomous agents as mere instruments, is justified in pursuit of the ultimate goal of preserving the dominance of the 'White race'.[21] There are also examples of instrumentalism within the anarchist canon. However, consistent anarchism, unlike the revolutionary alternative with which libertarianism has often unsuccessfully competed, rejects such instances as incompatible with its prefigurative ethic.

Foremost as an alternative to anarchism within working class movements was Leninism. Lenin constructed a model of political behaviour based on a consequentialist account. In *"Left-Wing" Communism, An Infantile Disorder*, Lenin proposes a wholly ends-determined framework for assessing and justifying political behaviours. Boycotts or participation in parliamentary elections, for example, are appraised on their ability to bring about revolutionary situations.[22] The direction of the masses through the model of the centralised party is similarly warranted on the basis of eventual ends.[23]

David Lamb, formerly of Solidarity, writing for the anarchist magazine *Animal*, explains the anarchist rejection of the Leninist approach thus:

> [T]he distinction between *ends* and means has been drawn between humans and the natural world, masters and slaves, men and women, employers and employees, rulers and ruled.

> To be reduced to a means or an instrument is to be robbed
> of autonomy and responsibility and consequently to be of no
> direct moral significance.[24]

Lamb's criticism of Leninism captures part of the twofold problem of consequentialism: that it undermines the autonomy of the subjugated group. Paternalistic socialism predetermines the objectives and imposes these ends onto the already subjugated classes. The client class – the proletariat – becomes the instrument used to reach this end.[25] To quickly reach the desired end they can, therefore, be treated in an authoritarian manner.[26] This turning of the autonomous subject into an object, a tool, for others is also the basis of alienation in capitalism, as self-conscious beings are used as mere human resources in the production process. This is in contrast to consistent, ideal type anarchism, in which the process of overthrowing existing alienating conditions involves creating countervailing, non-hierarchical, social relations that avoid creating a group who act *on behalf of* the subjugated.

The second part of the problem of consequentialism is also criticised by Lamb – that in creating a hierarchy of means and ends, the former becomes a substitute for the latter. Explaining the Hegelian origins of this criticism of Leninism, Lamb recounts the 'Dialectic of Master and Slave', in which the slave mediates between the master's desires (end) and the natural world in order to fulfil the master's wishes. In doing so the slave learns the skills, while the master becomes dependent on the servant. As a result, the slave (the means) becomes dominant over the lord (the ends). This dialectical process of means dominating ends is illustrated for libertarians by the domination of the bureaucracy in the post-1917 Soviet Union. The Party, which was supposed to be the means, becomes the ends.[27] By rejecting the necessity of a mediating group, anarchism avoids the creation of a new hierarchy. Prefiguration avoids this Hegelian dilemma as means and ends are identical. The dialectical process of methods replacing objectives no longer applies.

3.2. Anarchist Consequentialism

Not everyone within the libertarian tradition rejects a consequentialist approach. Even those who repudiate utilitarianism recognise positive features of branches of ends-based moral theory in that they propose integrating social welfare with, in Mill's case, individual freedom.[28] Some follow Benthamite utilitarianism and place pre-eminence on eventual happiness. Others – Johann Most and Sergei Nechaev, a confidant of Bakunin – urged a results-based approach:

> Ethics? The end of revolution is freedom; the end justifies the means. The struggle for freedom is a war; wars are to be won and therefore to be waged with all energy, ruthlessly [...] using all there is to be used, including the latest in technology and the first of chemistry, to kill oppressors forthwith....[29]

and

> The revolutionary despises all doctrinairism and has rejected the mundane sciences leaving them to future generations. He knows only one science, the science of destruction. To this end, and this end alone, he will study mechanics, physics, chemistry and perhaps medicine [....] His sole and constant object is the immediate destruction of this vile order.[30]

Most and Nechaev's ends-based entreaties have apparent parallels with some contemporary anarchists[31] although they are inconsistent with prefiguration of ideal type anarchism. For Nechaev, the autonomy of the oppressed was unimportant – anyone could be used as an instrument to achieve the predetermined end.[32] The instrumentalism of this approach led the historian Michael Prawdin to consider Nechaev a precursor to Leninism, rather than anarchism.[33]

Consequentialism can also be identified in the utopianism associated with anarchism. Socialist blueprints that envisioned imaginative, heterodox forms of communal living and ingenious forms of manufacture and agriculture were drawn up by, for instance, Charles Fourier with his model communities (Phalanxes). Older utopian visions can be seen in Tommaso Campanella's City of the Sun and Thomas More's *Utopia*, as well as later proposals in the form of Nechaev's dictatorial, almost borstal-style, post-revolutionary existence and Ivan Chtcheglov's Situationist, experimental city.[34] More recently, GA's Stephen Booth portrays a 'utopian' society in *City Death*.[35] Booth's plan can act as the basis for measuring contemporary society's shortcomings by comparison with the suggested utopia. It also provides a gauge for assessing the success of current methods by considering if current strategies are helping to reach the millennial community.

Recent utopian studies have suggested re-evaluating imaginative idealised societies by considering them as performing more sophisticated functions than just blueprints.[36] Utopias can illustrate anarchist principles, with a presentation of how they might work in practice, a fictionalised version of the New Left's 'beloved community'. They can also act as a source of inspiration and an alternative discourse for political ideas, or as an impetus for action. Their function could be akin to Sorel's myths; for example, Richard Humphrey argues that there are distinctions between myths and utopias as the former are irrational and unaffected by the failure to be realised.[37] Contemporary anarchist utopias work, however, precisely because of their mythic qualities. Neither the xenophobia of Booth's utopian community, nor the unrealistic ease in which divisions of gender, race and sexuality are overcome in *Breaking Free*, detract from the role these utopias play in symbolically portraying anarchist principles and dealing in fictional forms with problems which affect anarchism.[38] Anarchist utopias are not just used to identify a universal end point; instead, anarchist visionary literature plays other roles. It demonstrates and plays with tactical methods, encourages and inspires readers, provides a literary form for presenting critiques of current and proposed practices as well as supplying a form of pleasurable escape.

Utopianism as a blueprint is rejected not just because so many proposed perfect societies are distasteful, such as Booth's and Nechaev's, but also because it involves a general imposition on the whole of humanity of the creation of just a few minds. This runs counter to the ideal of anarchism whereby the oppressed themselves must take priority in formulating and producing their own patterns of living. Totalising philosophies of the modernist era (such as Leninism), in which eventual ends are scientifically determined and implemented, have been superseded by poststructuralist theories that replace these large-scale meta-narratives with the liberating possibilities of diversity and change. Ideal type anarchisms reject a singular totalising end point and the concomitant manipulation of individuals to fit this predetermined plan; they therefore engage more productively than Leninism with postmodernism.[39]

The traditional alternative to the consequentialist approach has been deontological ethics. Some anarchists, especially those in the liberal anarchist tradition, have explicitly used this form of moral evaluation. However, this too is incompatible with class struggle anarchism's prefigurative ethic.

4. Means-Centred Approaches

The attractions of Kantian ethics (deontology) for anarchists are not hard to detect. Kant sought a rational basis for ethics that would eradicate dependence on a metaphysical ground and thereby free morality from religious control. Reason is the essential faculty for Kant as through its use individuals can overcome their instincts and choose for themselves. This notion of the autonomous agent is shared by liberal anarchists.[40] It represents the ability of the individual to make choices. This individual 'will', the autonomous agency, is 'the highest good and the condition of all others.'[41]

For Kant, autonomy is of central importance; what makes an act susceptible to moral consideration is that it is voluntary. If an act is impelled by instinctive responses or by the imposition of particular ends, then the moral agent has no sovereignty. For Kant, ends cannot be imposed; choices of action must be free. The guarantor for autonomy in choosing between possible alternatives is the use of reason.[42] Kant calls 'imperatives' those ethical principles that instruct particular behaviours.[43] These imperatives are of two types. Hypothetical imperatives are driven by particular ends, for instance, 'for a healthy life one ought to exercise regularly'. This is goal driven. The second type of imperative – categorical – is 'without having any other end.'[44] An example of a non-consequential duty would be 'never break a promise'. The categorical imperative provides the basis of Kantian morality.

Categorical imperatives are the most important because they are not end dependent; they are unchanging and universal. Categorical imperatives are derived by the use of reason and are valid for all rational people. It transpires that all categorical imperatives can be reduced to a single one, namely: 'Act only according to that maxim by which you can at the same time will that it should become a universal law.'[45] For the deed to be justified, the general principle, of which the particular act is an example, must be universally applicable (the universalisability criterion).

The aspect of the categorical imperative picked up on by many anarchists is the notion of *autonomy*. The anarchist ideal criticises Kantian notions of autonomy (the self-governing agent) but does not advocate, in its place, heteronomy (the imposition of external rules or constraints). Autonomy is an important feature of the anarchist prefigurative ethic, but unlike Kant, consistent class struggle anarchists formulate it in an anti-essentialist, rather than an individualised, sense (see below). Kant formulates sovereignty in terms of treating people as ends in themselves, rather than using others solely as means to reach heteronomous objectives. Limits are placed upon each individual, restraining them from infringing on the autonomy of others, guided by the categorical imperative. Through the application of absolutely binding moral duties, one is obliged to carry out an act regardless of its consequences. The most famous example is where a Kantian moral actor is ethically impelled to return a borrowed axe to a homicidal neighbour in order to keep a promise to return property. Not to do so would be to break a pledge. There is a categorical imperative, according to Kant, to maintain one's word because if everyone broke a promise then promises would become meaningless. For Kant, prioritising duties, even at the cost of actual appalling consequences, is fundamental.

There are a number of apparent attractions of deontology for anarchists from both class struggle and individualist traditions. The features that seem most advantageous are those that avoid the excesses of consequentialism, namely, respect for each subject's ability to make rational choices and the obligation to avoid treating people as means to an end. The provision of a rational framework with guarantees for sovereignty without recourse to metaphysical authorities, makes Kantianism appealing to many under the anarchist banner, especially (but not exclusively) those from liberal, egoistic and anarcho-capitalist strands.[46]

4.1. Deontology and Contractual Relationships
Despite the many apparent hierarchical characteristics and repercussions of deontology, many described as 'anarchists' have embraced Kantianism, at least in part. Liberal humanist anarchists, such as Baldelli, have embraced one interpretation of the categorical imperative, while anarcho-capitalists have endorsed the notion of sovereignty within a liberal economic framework. Both these positions are incompatible with the prefigurative anarchist ideal.

4.1.1. Anarcho-Capitalism and Liberal Anarchism
Anarcho-capitalists and extreme free marketeers, such as the social scientist Friedrich von Hayek, maintain that advocacy of ends is necessarily authoritarian. Hayek's condemnation is overtly Kantian: to reach the selected goal involves restricting the autonomy of the individual to freely choose.[47] Consequentialism therefore imposes the

pre-determined will of others onto sovereign individuals. According to Hayek, determining ends is impossible as the individual's ambitions alter in response to other people's autonomous behaviour. Anarcho-capitalists, by contrast, prioritise means: the ideal of rational sovereign agents making free contracts to achieve their ambitions.

Anarcho-capitalists endorse 'voluntary' contractual agreements as the basis for social relationships. Free marketeers share with Kant the belief that autonomous individuals have the right to determine their own ends and to do so through free contract. In the words of anarcho-capitalist Chris Cooper: 'freedom means nothing if it does not mean the freedom to make mutually beneficial exchanges with others.'[48] Fellow individualists, like Ludwig von Mises (one of Hayek's key influences), consider that sovereignty of the individual is assured through market relationships: 'There is in the operation of the market no compulsion and coercion.'[49] Individual contracts enforced by privatised legal practices are considered the ideal model for social interaction. Proudhon, too, advocated a society run entirely on the basis of free contract.[50] This position is endorsed by the liberal anarchist tradition, represented by the Canadian writer Robert Graham. He claims that contractual obligations are only wrong in capitalist society because they are not made between equals. They would, however, be admissible as the basis of exchange in a liberal anarchist society.[51]

Class struggle anarchists advance a number of criticisms of this free market application of deontology. Contractual duties are based on the intention to maintain a promise, regardless of how the resultant situation may differ from the intention behind the duty. In the example used earlier, in which a person is obliged to return the axe to his/her homicidal neighbour, the Kantian ethic is dependent on the distinction between foreseeability and intentionality. The moral agent had no desire to assist in the murder of his/her neighbour's family, yet this was the foreseeable result of returning the borrowed axe. The distinction between the possible likely results and the desired consequences is important, but an unequivocal moral separation between the two, as Kantianism requires, is difficult to preserve without offering a view of the individual as abstracted from all social networks. Extreme individualists may offer such a defence, but even some liberals recognise the moral concept of negligence. The person returning the axe to his neighbour is guilty of just such nonchalant disregard for others. Class struggle anarchists, by contrast, accept that individuals are constitutive parts of wider social networks. To deny the significance to the likely results of one's actions in order to perform a duty appears at odds with a benevolent moral philosophy, and would be a principle incapable of being universalised.

4.1.2. Free Contracts
Class struggle anarchists dispute the efficacy of contracts, as they still imply heteronomous obligation. If the activities are mutually beneficial the question arises as to why agreements have to be enforced, or why formalised agreements are needed at all. Contracts in a free market are rarely between equal partners and exacerbate inequalities. In order to meet their basic needs, the least powerful are often compelled into agreements that further restrict their liberty. More socially-minded anarchists, such as Most, have promoted a different view of a 'free contract' in which people can withdraw from contracts at any point without financial penalty. Such free contracts certainly avoid the problems of freezing social relations by having as their basis predetermined agreements, regardless of changing circumstance. But there are shortcomings with Most's suggestion. He still includes a mild sanction through loss of reputation for those who do not keep the contract.[52]

Contracts indicate that one act has a value with respect to another. As anarchist commentator Alain Pengam explained, even the liberal view of contract necessitates someone being in credit or debit (the latter being open to light sanction).[53] Communism, the autonomous composition of new types of living, rejects any recreation of the law of value. As Berkman explains, non-hierarchical social relations require only 'concord and co-operation' whereas contracts require an apparatus of enforcement. Such heteronomous interventions are only necessary when social structures are already repressive and are not a solution to such forms of domination.[54]

By contrast, extreme liberals claim that being bound by contractual obligations protects individual sovereignty. If a person has agreed to labour for a given wage, then industrial action, which breaks this agreement, is unacceptable. This is because the obligation to maintain the contract is binding on all rational parties. This is regardless of the fact that most individuals have to sell their labour in order to survive, and thus their choices are economically constrained.[55] No consistent anarchist would accept this neo-liberal hypothesis, as they accept that, in part, wider social forces constitute individuals. Class struggle anarchists' support for strikes and occupations rests upon recognising that different power structures are at work that affect the social power of particular groups and individuals. Enforcing Kantian contracts can reinforce these social inequalities rather than counter them.

4.2. Liberal Anarchist Deontology
Anarchists of all denominations are aware that Kant's universalisability criterion provides a useful device for choosing between acts, as Kropotkin recognised:

> Besides this principle of treating others as one wishes to be treated, what is it but the very same principle as equality, the fundamental principle of anarchism? And how can anyone manage to believe himself an anarchist unless he practices it?[56]

As Kropotkin indicates, it is not just the anarcho-capitalists who were influenced by Kantian philosophy, although Kropotkin felt there were significant weaknesses with the theory.[57] The shortcomings we will concentrate upon are its universal and abstract individualised moral agent.

In liberal anarchism, exemplified by Baldelli, the agent of change is that predicated on Kantian ethics: the dispassionate, objective citizen, abstract 'Man'.[58] For Kant, abstract individuals agree to give up freedoms for the rights of living under civil law. A prerequisite for this social contract is an equal opportunity to influence legislation.[59] What is at question for individualists is that no such contract has been made.[60] The criticisms by class struggle anarchists are twofold. Firstly, the model of the equal citizen with equivalence of opportunity to change the law does not exist when hierarchies of power are in place, such as in capitalist society.[61] Secondly, and of more importance, is the atomised individualist identity of Kantian liberal and anarcho-capitalist moral agents.

Todd May, amongst others, recognises an essentialism within classical anarchism in which there is a fixed, benign human nature which forms the core of the individual actor.[62] Dependence on this benevolent metaphysical (and therefore fundamentally unknowable) construct hampers rather than encourages moral evaluation. It suggests a universal actor independent of context or circumstance; the same duties are imposed on the very poor as on the obscenely wealthy. Arguments predicated on a humanist essentialism restrict action to opposing power in order to allow the expression of 'natural goodness'. Essentialism stands opposed to theories (often regarded as poststructuralist) that propose that other forms of power can construct non-hierarchical social relations and identities. Ideal type anarchism is, in this sense, poststructural, as it recognises the fluidity of subject identities and rejects a singular essential human nature.

Alberto Melucci, a researcher on collective action, discusses the paucity of individualist methodologies for ethical analysis. To be comprehensible, collective action must involve the use of general categories such as 'solidarity', in which collective identities are assumed and mutually recognised amongst the participants.[63] These explanatory classifications are irreducible to statements concerning individuals. Class struggle anarchists maintain the importance of autonomy but accept that this will often take a collective as well as individual form. Group decision-making in deciding upon suitable means and ends for carrying out such action is a rejection of the imposition of ultimate objectives and predetermined instrumental methods onto subject groups. It resists the reduction of agents to mere tools.[64] Chapter Four examines collective decision-making methods within anarchist groupings.

4.3. Anarchism Against Liberal Rights
In ideal anarchism, the liberatory act is defined by the ability of oppressed agents to create new social structures that avoid hierarchy and representation. In creating their own social relations in contrast to those of oppressive power (a process called self-valorisation by autonomist marxists), the subjugated class creates new types of practices and seeks out new forms of solidarity.[65] The agents of change contest the inequalities in social power and seek their equalisation. 'Social power', a term discussed in greater detail in the next chapter, refers to the amount of autonomy agents have in formulating and acting upon their goals and how much influence they have in creating the realities of others. Low social power, in a given context, refers to a predominant order-taker role, high social power to an order-giver.[66] Countervailing methods aim to create alternative non-hierarchical social relations and these tactics are particular to specific domineering disciplines.

The importance of the appropriate agent in anarchist prefiguration cannot be over-stressed. Other groups, such as racist organisations, argue that their actions are guided by prefigurative considerations. Attacking individual members of minority groups, they might suggest, is indicative of their wider (anti-)social ambitions.[67] In this way racist means prefigure the wider repressive political programme. But their methods are antithetical to the egalitarian principles of anarchism, as power relations remain fundamentally imbalanced, and appeal to a different agent or set of agents than that promoted by class struggle anarchism. The appropriate agent which anarchism aspires to influence is discussed in the next chapter. However, in short, the appropriate agents for change are those who are subjected to power, individuals placed in unprivileged positions within a given social context, that is to say with low social power. The prefigurative act, as used by anarchists, aims to resist this oppression.

Prefigurative ethics collapse the problematic distinction between means and ends. This moral framework requires appropriate agents of change who act autonomously to end their own oppression. Such methods are pragmatic and local, as no ultimate or universal ground for 'the good' exists. Anarchist methods are associated with seeking immediate results. Anarchist actions are aimed at achieving useful results (ones that allow for greater autonomy, albeit only temporarily). This practicality reduces the gap between means and ends; however, immediate goals are not the sole grounds for assessment. The local agent determines the pertinence of the event. This is the model of direct action found in a great deal of contemporary libertarian propaganda.

Anarchism's prefigurative, pragmatic approach is in contrast to instrumentalist strategies that appeal to the ultimate millennial events such as 'the revolution'. Either the revolution never occurs, thereby providing no possible basis for distinguishing between methods, or the successful uprising turns into a dictatorship, negating the very methods that had early been central to the emancipatory strategy. For the contemporary anarchist ideal, tactics embody the forms of social relation that the actors wish to see develop. They are contextual and require the oppressed themselves having a primary role in eradicating subjugating conditions. As methods mirror the ends, radical behaviour evokes the playful and the carnivalesque, attempting to dissolve divisions particular to specific forms of oppressive power, such as those between production, pleasure and play. These prefigurative approaches are commonly referred to as 'direct action'.

PART II

Direct Action

Introduction

Direct action has long been identified with anarchism, an association that stretches back to the nineteenth century syndicalists.[68] The term, despite many misinterpretations, is widely applied to anarchist behaviours because 'direct action' refers to practical prefigurative activity carried out by subjugated groups in order to lessen or vanquish their oppression. Further complications occur because some within the wider anarchist tradition (predominantly liberal anarchists) suggest that only non-violent direct action is consistent with anarchist prefiguration. Examining the differences between direct action and other (anti-)political approaches illustrates both the appropriateness of this form of activity for anarchism and the unsuitability of alternative methods such as symbolic or constitutional action. It also reveals the importance of the appropriate agent. As a result, unlike civil disobedience, which by definition claims to be non-violent,[69] direct action may take forms which opponents could justifiably consider to be physically coercive.

Anarchists take great pride in their association with direct action. During the First World War *Freedom* declared that the best tactics for revolutionary activity were 'appeals to reason and direct action'.[70] The strength of the association for anarchism was such that the anarcho-syndicalist SolFed called itself the Direct Action Movement (DAM) from 1979 to 1994, and continues to call its magazine *Direct Action* (fig. 2.1.).[71]

Although different anarchist groups use the same terminology, it does not mean that they are organisationally linked, have similar ideals or interpret key phrases in identical ways. SolFed, for instance, concentrates on the industrial front as the main arena for revolutionary activity and when talking of 'direct action' refers to strike action, workplace occupation and sabotage on the industrial front. The Animal Liberation Front (ALF), by contrast, regards the exploitation of animals to be the primary site of struggle. Thet use the term 'direct action' to signify, for example, attacks on laboratories where vivisection takes place and vandalism of shops engaging in unethical enterprise.

All the above groups recognise 'direct action' as involving a threat to oppression, yet the forms of oppression, and the types of behaviour aimed at its overthrow, leave the term open to multifarious interpretations. Such diversity is reflected in the differing accounts of the subject from academics. April Carter, for instance, defines direct action in a number of competing ways. In an overtly propagandist piece for CND, *Direct Action*, she contrasted it primarily with constitutional and symbolic action,[72] which reflects the manner in which anarchists have sought to justify their approval for prefigurative (anti-)political behaviour.[73] In a later analysis, *Direct Action and Liberal Democracy*, Carter describes direct action as a form of behaviour which can be consistent with the previously oppositional categories of constitutional and symbolic action.

5. Direct Action: Means and Ends
As Carter recognises, the phrase 'direct action' is highly ambiguous.[74] It has been indiscriminately applied to behaviour more properly identified as civil disobedience. The two differ in numerous ways

Figure 2.1. Heading of Direct Action Movement (since 1994 Solidarity Federation) newspaper, *Direct Action*, 1985.

not least in the differing commitments to non-violence, law breaking and prefiguration.[75] As a result of journalistic misappropriation, the expression 'direct action' has become almost meaningless.[76]

Carter's attempt at clarification in order to resurrect this term as a meaningful category of political behaviour is, however, unsatisfactory. Her method is to reject definition 'in terms of method, goal or of the persons using it' as being 'sterile and misleading'.[77] In its place she suggests that the best way of 'understanding [...] what is entailed in the idea of direct action is to consider which movements have consciously used direct action, and what theoretical connotations surround their use of the phrase'.[78] While not denying the importance of looking at its use and the ideological orientation of those exponents who use it, Carter's methodology is question-begging. It requires a prior conception of direct action in order to determine the scope of the search and to identify which groups of people are using it. Without an initial understanding of the term Carter would neither be able to identify relevant examples nor deal with contradictory claims.

The best way to understand direct action is through using the criteria that Carter develops in her earlier essay, where she distinguishes between different types of action precisely on the grounds of the means employed, ends desired and the agents involved. These categories can be used to illustrate the tripartite division between constitutional, symbolic and direct action, under which most political behaviour falls. Direct action competes with symbolic and especially constitutional methods, and the specific features of the first can be assessed through contrast with the latter two. These categories of analysis also help elucidate the debates surrounding direct action, those concerning the role of theory, and the importance of agency. They also clarify the debate surrounding prefiguration and violence, which has long been regarded as one of the most contentious within anarchism.

Direct action is prefigurative in that the means adopted to achieve objectives are characteristic of the ends, with the oppressed acting against their subjugation. Direct action resists mediation. For example, two different proposals have been advanced to deal with the problems of homelessness and inadequate housing. The first would be to encourage the homeless to squat in empty buildings. This, as Carter and contemporary anarchists agree, is direct action.[79] The alternative is to lobby parliament to raise the matter of inadequate housing in the legislature. This is not direct action as the campaign itself does not practically resolve the social problem, nor are the primary agents of change – parliamentarians – the ones directly affected by the housing shortage. Constitutional acts are separate forms of behaviour.[80] Direct action is prefigurative: what is desired must also be involved in reaching this aim.[81] The former editor of *Anarchy*, Colin Ward, seems to concur: he borrows American anarchist theorist David Wieck's distinction between 'direct' and 'indirect action' in which the first is prefigurative while the latter is justified only consequentially.[82]

Direct action is *synecdochic* – where a small part of an entity represents the whole thing. It stands both as a practical response in its own right to a given situation, but also as a symbol of the larger vision of societal change. For anarchists, direct action involves equalising power relations and altering relations of production and exchange, as this is part of their envisioned aim. As such, direct action is part of a wider (anti-) political strategy. It involves a 'conscious will to resist or to affect policy'.[83] It is both particular and general. Anarchist direct action alleviates specific hardships consistent with the general principles of libertarianism.

The identities of the agents involved in direct action is one of the necessary – but not sole – characteristics of anarchist direct action that demarcates it from its non-anarchist variants, and distinguishes direct action from paternalistic behaviour. In anarchist direct action the agents are those directly affected by the problem under consideration. Other forms of direct action promote benevolent (and sometimes malevolent) paternalism. In 1976-7 senior politicians, including Shirley Williams, joined the picket lines of strikers at

Grunwick, yet this is not an example of ideal type direct action as these parliamentarians were not directly affected. Anarchists claim that the involvement of politicians is an instrument to their gaining electoral power and political privilege, so their activities are not prefigurative of libertarianism. Yet these same acts constitute direct action – and are consistent with anarchism – when they are carried out by the Grunwick employees or others affected by the result of the dispute.

Consistent anarchists do not consider their role as pivotal. It does not require a class of 'community politicians' or self-identified activists to carry out these acts. Anarchism does not require anarchists; indeed, as the Situationists argued, the creation of 'specialists in freedom' creates new hierarchies and divisions.[84] The core of anarchism is that the oppressed themselves carry out their own liberation. There are, however, examples of anarchist groups who have considered themselves to be a separate vanguard, but in doing so these groups are in conflict with their own prefigurative ethic.[85]

5.1. Direct Action and Agency

Carter provides plenty of examples of anarchist direct action: prisoners leading strikes against their conditions, workers occupying factories to save them from closure or as part of pay negotiations, black citizens boycotting buses which promote racial segregation.[86] There are, however, occasions when some have used the phrase 'direct action' in an improper fashion. For instance, animal rights activists are not behaving in a liberatory manner if their aim is animal liberation:

> The actions of ALF and others are on the contrary not the actions of one group struggling for its own interests. Unfortunately, animals are unable to do this. As such they have no 'rights'. What animals have are the actions of altruistically minded humans who object to the way animals are treated.[87]

Subversion, like many other class struggle libertarian groups, regard ALF-style activity as non-anarchist direct action, as it is not carried out by the oppressed person (or group). If the same ALF-style actions were carried out against oligarchical agribusinesses by dissatisfied employees, consumers angry at the paucity and expense (both monetarily and environmentally) of the food offered or by those whose livelihoods are placed under threat by the expansion of technology and capital-intensive modes of production, then this would constitute direct action of an anarchistic variety.

The aim of engaging those directly affected by oppression may lead to a concentration on campaigns surrounding local issues, as Trevor Smith, a commentator on radical action from the early 1970s, reports:

> [T]he need [is] to encourage individual participation... [T]o do this, issues must be selected which are close at hand. The world has become too complex for any individual to cultivate his own macro-cosmic view of it which might guide his actions and possibly those of others; the only solution is to avoid such lofty considerations and concentrate one's energies instead at a level of society and within a range of issues which one can fully comprehend.[88]

The notion of agency is clarified later on to include an international subject (that of a multi-identitied working class), allowing the types of issue to stretch beyond the merely parochial. Yet Smith is right to identify decentralisation and stress on the micro-level as characteristics of anarchist methods. 'Think global – Act local' has long been a motto for anarchist environmentalists, syndicalists and communists alike, and the slogan has almost become a cliché.[89] When local actions or micropolitics are undertaken, conceptions of the agents of change, their motivations and the forms of organisation are shown to be different to those posited by the grander Leninist traditions. Orthodox marxists propose a unified working class homogenised into a single organisational structure, while the anarchist ideal acknowledges multiple structures as being both desirable and necessary to a shifting and diverse anarchist revolutionary agent of change.

5.2. Practicality and Direct Action

Anarchists propose direct action as a pragmatic response to the social problems they identify. There have been a significant number of do-it-yourself protest movements around environmental and civil liberties issues throughout the 1990s and into the new millennium. The participatory approach, evident in punk subcultures, was overtly championed by the ecological activists in events such as the land occupations in Wandsworth (Pure Genius site), Wanstead, Pollok and Newbury. These unmediated experiments involved significant numbers of libertarians and have been represented as anarchic moments.[90]

Given the association of anarchism with utopianism and impossiblism, the importance of practical responses may seem surprising. Yet notwithstanding the small minority of anarchists who reject all reform as inadequate and a restraint on the revolutionary potential of the oppressed, most anarchists welcome changes that enhance the power of the revolutionary agency at the expense of the countervailing power (however defined).[91] Anarchist objectives sometimes appear to be distant and unrealisable even in the lifetimes of current activists, and this can be disempowering.[92] Demonstrably useful ventures encourage activists and promote support, as the celebrations surrounding the abolition of the Poll Tax illustrate.[93] Some anarchists do occasionally promote a strict consequentialism, regarding success to be only the achievement of a defining moment of liberation, often couched in terms of social revolution.[94] This might be termed 'a millennial event', the occasion from which everything is transformed. It is the achievement of this singular instant which determines the value of an act: anything short of the millennial event is judged to be inadequate. It is therefore consequentialist: anything is justified to achieve this millennial event and thus used to legitimate oppressive practices in reaching this goal. As a result, such millennialism is out of keeping with the prefigurative approach of consistent anarchism.

The practical consequences of direct action are not limited to immediate small improvements in conditions. A reform may not occur as a result of a single direct act, but as part of an on-going campaign. The road protestors did not expect that the invasion of a single by-pass construction camp would alter governmental policy immediately, but that change would come through a continuous crusade, and that the experience itself would be an example of libertarian enrichment.[95] The distinction between short-term and long-term for prefigurative acts is insignificant except in terms of size. Short-term aims are more localised; longer-term objectives are the progressive culmination of the more immediate acts. Even when localised direct acts do not meet their immediate ends, their prefigurative features mean that the participants have benefited from the involvement. Contributors not only gain, as Burns notes in relation to the anti-Poll Tax movements, an insight into the type of promised future society, but also develop practical competencies, such as craft-skills and organisational and communicative faculties.[96] Micropolitical acts are unmediated, being controlled by those affected. As suggested above, this stands in contrast to other political methods, symbolic and constitutional action.

6. Constitutional Proceedings Versus Direct Action
'Macro-politics' takes place on the grand scale, it involves gaining control/influence of the state.[97] Constitutional action is macro-political, it aims to sway the legislature or judiciary through legal means such as organising and signing petitions, lobbies of parliament, local councils or other legislative bodies. As Herbert Marcuse points out, such action confirms the legitimacy of the state as it accepts that the institutions and individuals in charge are amenable to change and that the existing constitutional systems are adequate and representative.[98] Anarchists reject constitutional methods because they utilise hierarchical structures.

Although many anarchists, like Bakunin, grudgingly admit that liberal democracy is less pernicious than overt tyranny, they reject participation in constitutional processes.[99] Historically, anarchists have been opposed to parliamentary government because of its oppressive elitism. Anarchists today continue to be equally antagonistic; one of the activities that unites anarchists in Britain is participation in Anti-Election activities (fig. 2.2.).[100] Indeed, as Lenin points out, the rejection of parliamentarianism has been so strongly associated with anarchism that it is often mistaken for anarchism.[101] The rejection of parliamentarianism was the foundation of a profound split in the communist movement in the aftermath of the October Revolution. Lenin's *Left-Wing Communism: An Infantile Disorder* was a response to critics in Germany (Herman Gorter), Netherlands (Anton Pannekoek), Italy (Amadeo Bordiga) and Britain (Sylvia Pankhurst) of the Bolsheviks' parliamentary tactics. This led to the formation of a small communist current opposed to Leninism, and thus with significant similarities to class struggle anarchism.[102]

Anarchists' reasons for rejecting legalistic methods differ amongst the various tendencies. For the extreme individualists such as Stirner, government by will of the majority is no less an infringement on the individual than that of monarchical tyranny.[103] For class struggle anarchists, representative democracy is rejected on three grounds. These criticisms are based on a pragmatic assessment of electoral methods with respect to anarchist

Figure 2.2. Anti-Elections Alliance sticker, 1997.

principles (including prefiguration). These counter-constitutional positions have become so accepted that they have gained, within parts of class struggle anarchism, the status of *a priori* truths (statements that are true by definition, and thus unquestionably accepted). The desire for practical but still principled responses, however, has led to some questioning of these positions, an area which will be discussed in the final chapter.[104] The positions that reject constitutional activity are as follows:

1. Representative democracy involves voters relinquishing their own powers and giving them to others to exercise on their behalf.

2. Liberal democracy creates a political class whose interests are not the same as their electors.

3. Under capitalism, the executive and legislature is not where power is really found and so constitutional activity is misdirected.

These arguments refute constitutional methods as incompatible with class struggle libertarianism. For contemporary British anarchism, the agents involved have to be the oppressed, the power relations that the method employs must conform to egalitarian and libertarian principles, and the sites of conflict identified have to be immediate. Constitutional methods fail on all three grounds.

6.1. Abdication of Power

The first of the above criticisms by anarchists is that representative democracy, by definition, creates a group of people with more power than those who elected them. As Robert Chaase, an American situationist, explained: 'Bourgeois [representative] democracy is the appropriation of the political power of individuals, renamed constituencies, by representatives'.[105] Voters give up their political power to others who exercise it on their behalf. This behaviour is out of keeping with the egalitarian aims of anarchism. As the ACF points out, by 'ceding political power to someone or some party' those they yield to will inevitably have different interests.[106] Consequently, the constitutional response, of abdicating responsibility to another, has to be rejected. Direct action, by contrast, increases the power of the revolutionary class, even if the act is not immediately successful.

The presupposition from the anarchists is that representative democracy, *pace* Jean-Jacques Rousseau, is a form of feudalism for it assumes that citizens cannot represent themselves and require others to do so.[107] By passing on authority to others, Rousseau explains, citizens enslave themselves to a new set of masters. 'The moment a people allows itself to be represented, it is no longer free....'[108] For Rousseau, the subjugation of individuals is an unavoidable consequence of representative democracy not found in more direct forms. Many anarchists show a deep attachment to Rousseau. The Primitivists, in particular, share his preference for *amour de soi* (pre-rational, instinctive equality) over *amour-propre* (values which support self-interest and inequality which are generated by civilisation) and agree with his critique of the restrictions inherent within a developed society, without accepting Rousseau's rejection of returning to a pre-social state. Yet, for other anarchists, this criticism of representative democracy is more contingent than necessary, built upon countless examples of representative democracy replacing direct democracy which then developed into a further lowering of the status of the electorate.[109]

Advocates of representative government reject these criticisms. Thomas Paine maintains that representative democracy provides for all relevant interests to have an influence without the inconvenience of direct democracy. Representative democracy is far more efficient for large populations.[110] For other liberal theorists such as John Locke, democratic government, whether as a Greek popular legislative assembly, elective oligarchy or constitutional monarchy, provides a bulwark against the development of a more powerful class. Governments serve by the approval of the citizens and hence are the servants of the people, charged with protecting their rights.

For Locke, these rights involve the protection of the individual's 'life, liberty and property' (a slogan taken up by the anarcho-capitalist Libertarian Alliance). In the final instance power remains with the electorate, such that if the administration loses the trust of the people then the people have the right to alter it. Abuses of power lead the people to scrutinise the role of government and provoke appropriate responses including open revolt.[111]

Anarchists in reply make three related observations. Firstly, even in idealistic, egalitarian movements, representatives can assume hierarchical powers, since through their exclusive experience of decision-making they gain unequalled knowledge. As a result, these representatives coalesce into a new class who gain acceptance because the electorate have no opportunity to assess the suitability of their decisions.[112] While class struggle anarchists accept that governments exist to protect individual private property rights, they consider this to be neither desirable nor legitimate. In protecting these rights governments become weighted towards the interests of the mightiest.[113]

Secondly, a government that abuses power to become master of the destiny of others does not, in most western democratic nations, advertise the fact through the open use of coercion predicted by Locke. Instead, governments ensure compliance through, to quote the American libertarian Noam Chomsky, the 'manufacture of consent'.[114] The effect is to hide rather than display abuse and to manipulate acceptance. The task of overthrowing inegalitarian constitutional government is hindered by its guise of equality and democracy.

Thirdly, anarchists recognise that representative forms of government are sometimes required for certain limited forms of organisation where factors, such as the geographical size of the enterprise, make direct participation impractical. In examples such as these, anarchists propose a number of modifications to representative organisations to prevent the creation of a governing class. These will be discussed in

Chapter Four. To touch on them briefly, they include a restriction on the number and duration of full-time posts, prohibition on the right to stand for consecutive elective positions and the right to immediately recall delegates.[115] Stress too is placed on autonomous activity for groups and individuals within an organisation, direct democracy and federal structures, in which decisions are taken as locally as possible rather than centralised into a single powerful executive. Many associated with the periodical *Green Anarchist* regard these additions as inadequate. They maintain, like Rousseau, that all representative methods necessarily reduce the electorate to serfs. They argue that only small scale, localised movements are acceptable and regard all forms of mass organisation as totalitarian.[116]

6.2. Creating New Masters

Tom Paine defined many of the advantages of democratic government over monarchy. These compensations include the idea that the commoner would have relevant knowledge of the needs and abilities of the general public, whereas a hereditary leader would not.[117] Yet the dynamics of representative democracy create a new dominant class. The functionaries gain their authority from the voters. These officials act in a mediating role between the voters and the fulfilment of the voters' desires. The elected, however, become a privileged class, according to class struggle anarchists, who implicitly, and explicitly, develop the Hegelian notion of the mediator becoming dominant.[118] As Bakunin explains, the representatives have more social power, different social experiences of work and higher levels of respect than their electorate and consequently have different interests. 'On the one side there is the feeling of superiority necessarily inspired by a superior position; on the other there is the feeling of inferiority induced by the attitude of superiority on the part of the teacher exercising executive or legislative power.'[119] As the Irish anarchist J R White put it: 'Don't ask them [the workers] to saddle themselves with political masters, who the day after they conquer state power will want, like all conquerors, to remain the masters.'[120]

This social distinction occurs even if the elected representative comes from the same social class as its constituency. Bakunin asks what would occur if working class deputies, for all their financial disadvantages, succeed in being elected? He concludes that the class origins would make no difference:

> [D]o you know what will be the result? The inevitable result will be that workers' deputies, transferred to a purely bourgeois environment and into an atmosphere of purely bourgeois ideas, ceasing in fact to be workers and becoming statesmen instead, will become middle class in their outlook, perhaps even more so than the bourgeois themselves.[121]

This is a point repeated by the ACF: namely, that the class interests and concerns of representatives alter once they gain elective power such that working class MPs inevitably lose touch with their communities.[122]

The division between governor and governed in representative democracy, heightened by the desire for those in charge not to have an inquisitive electorate overseeing them, means that the populace are kept ignorant. The masses are therefore less capable of controlling their political masters and, consequently, their own destinies.[123] Participating in representative democracy does not fundamentally alter the unequal relations of social power and in some circumstances actually exacerbates them. By contrast, direct action breaks down the distinctions between leaders and followers in order to equalise power relations.

6.3. Misdirected Sites of Power

The most trenchant criticism of encouraging change through constitutional elective activity is that power does not really reside in the hands of governments. This claim is often summed up in the phrase: 'if voting changed anything... it would be illegal'.[124] The reasoning behind such a blanket condemnation of the franchise is explained by Britain's Class War:

The British State is supposed to be controlled by the politicians and the politicians elected by us. This, we are told, allows us through the ballot box to change things. So why does the State act in the interests of the ruling class regardless of whoever is in power – Labour, Tory or Liberal? It is because to function and succeed politicians and their parties are ultimately controlled by the capitalists and the State's own permanent unelected officials.[125]

The owners and controllers of a country's wealth, the senior officials in the civil service, the judiciary and the armed forces, are considered by anarchists to be the real organisers of social life. Changing the personnel in Augustus Pugin and Charles Barry's Palace of Westminster cannot dismantle the structural power imbalances of western countries.

This recognition that the elected offices of the state do not have determining control of social relations is shared with Leninists. Anarchists distinguish themselves from the Leninist perspective by rejecting a strictly instrumentalist view of national bureaucratic structures. Orthodox marxists have argued that the state is a commission of the dominant class:

> The bourgeoisie has at last, since the establishment of Modern Industry and of the world market, conquered for itself, in the modern representative State, exclusive political sway. The executive of the modern state is but a committee for managing the common affairs of the whole bourgeoisie.[126]

The moral philosopher Alan Carter explains how the anarchist analysis of the state, developed from Bakunin, differs from orthodox marxism. The executive as an instrument of the bourgeoisie is shown to subsequently gain relative autonomy. The interests of the state are no longer identical with the class it serves, its primary interest being to protect itself. The interests of these two groups can (and do) frequently correspond, but they can also conflict. Where taxes are levied to pay for the operation of a state, for example, these interests may cause opposition amongst the entrepreneurial middle classes.[127] Attacking the bourgeois class alone, or concentrating on just the state, will not bring about an egalitarian social order, as Carter explains:

> In other words, the state might transform the mode of production because it is in its interests to do so. But new relations of production which promised a greater surplus to the state would not be egalitarian ones, nor would they allow a libertarian social order. The state is not, therefore, an appropriate tool for bringing about a classless post-capitalist society.[128]

Some anarchists maintain the stronger hypothesis that social structures remain the same regardless of the change in personnel in the political class: hence the anarchist slogan, 'whoever you vote for the government always gets in'.[129] Yet underneath the rhetoric there is the recognition that changing government does have wider social effects. The electoral victories of the Conservative Party, for example, had specific consequences for manufacturing sectors and state enterprise.[130] Anarchists are aware that a fascist or ecological government might make drastic changes to social and economic relations and alter forms of oppression.[131] But even a radical socialist seizure of the state will not produce an egalitarian social order.

Increasingly, the choice between different electoral parties has come to be seen as progressively less significant. Richard Morris of the AWG predicted what would have been the result if the Labour Party had been victorious in 1992. 'Behind the waffle and a few token initiatives, their economic policies are identical to the Tories.'[132] The extension of capitalism into all aspects of social life has meant that all the main political parties have accepted economic liberalism not just pragmatically but as an ideal. So close are the main political parties on their social and economic policies that the tendency in British anarchism is increasingly towards the stronger hypothesis that the elections between the main parties offer no choice at all.[133]

If an oppositional government does stand in the way of the groups with real power, and does not have the means to defend itself, then it will be overthrown either by a military coup, such as Salvador Allende's in Chile in 1973, by intrigue, such as Harold Wilson's Labour government of 1974-76,[134] or through funding and publicising the merits of the favoured opposition. The anarchists' point is not that parliament is unimportant: it is, after all, where the legitimacy of the British legislative system is mythically supposed to lie. Their point is that it is part of the apparatus of class domination and consequently cannot be used to forward egalitarian aims.[135]

In contrast to representative politics, direct action operates in the multiple locations (geographical and functional) where oppression lies. As such, it is associated with localised campaigns. Constitutional politics, on the other hand, is committed to remedying social problems through institutions that are not directly involved with the issue. Such constitutional activity transfers the geography of rebellion from the home ground of the activist to the protected walls of the Palace of Westminster. Legislative politics, therefore, mediates change, whilst for direct action it is those who are immediately affected who are in charge.

While Lenin agreed that the sites of power lay outside of parliamentary institutions, he maintained that parliamentarianism is necessary for propaganda purposes: it demonstrates the dissolute and repressive nature of liberal institutions.[136] Parliamentarianism also helps to develop revolutionary leaders and encourages party unity.[137] But this means, as Marcuse points out, that even those parties which historically were revolutionary are '"condemned" to be non-radical' once they accept the constitutional rules and serve to further integrate opposition into support for the existing system.[138] The revolutionary party apes the repressive characteristics of the constitutional parties in order to play the parliamentary game.

British anarchists take great delight in highlighting how professedly revolutionary groups demonstrate their repressive character by using parliamentary tactics. Class War, AF, Black Flag and in particular Trotwatch, for example, illustrate how some orthodox marxist groups actually conform to the very social structuress they purport to confront. 'Tommy Sheridan (recent Parliamentary candidate for Scottish Militant Labour) and Steve Nally (both Militant men) have never for one minute let the interests of effective working class resistance to the Poll Tax, come before the interests of their party, or the Metropolitan Police for that matter.'[139] Constitutional processes involve rewriting political demands in terms that are acceptable to those who hold constitutional power. Jane Jacobs, a theorist on city planning, relates how a community campaign in New York required the involvement of representatives of the local power elite to ensure success. Without this support, fighting local government through constitutional means would be futile.[140] Playing by constitutional rules involves accepting the existing hierarchies of power.

In theory, the appeal to electors does not contradict anarchism, as the oppressed are in the majority.[141] However, electoral success requires involvement with the media – multi-national, capitalist corporations who are at odds with anarchistic methods/aims. In Britain this takes the form of wooing of the major media magnates. Rupert Murdoch's support for Tony Blair, for example, was widely seen as a key feature in the defeat of John Major and the long serving Conservative administration.[142] The owners and controllers of the main media outlets are hugely powerful people whose interests will not be those of the vast majority.[143] Meaningful participation in constitutional elections involves appealing to agencies whose interests are inimical to working class anarchism.

Political groupings aiming to gain power through electoral means place less emphasis on action to solve current social problems in the hope that they will be resolved once they gain office. The Labour Party's refusal to support anti-Poll Tax activity, for example, was justified on the grounds that they would abolish this form of local taxation once they gained office, that state power was a more effective and legitimate response than that of the Poll Tax resistors. The Labour Party sought to undermine immediate local popular resistance as they regarded the legitimate arena for political activity to be in one singular geographically distinct area (the Palace of Westminster). If the political party is unsuccessful in being elected then activity is directed towards 'party work, bar-room debate and buying the correct newspaper'.[144] Internal democracy also has to take second place, as the presentation of the party to the electorate takes precedence.[145]

For anarchists there is a practical implication of direct action which cannot be evaluated in terms of achievement of goals: even when direct action fails in winning its long-term or immediate ends, by taking part the agents of change have enhanced their autonomy as a result of their involvement. By contrast, when constitutional activity fails, its activists, claim Class War, have only gained skills for advancement into managerial activities within the system they claimed to oppose.[146]

The rejection of representation by anarchists does not apply just to the constitutional political process. Political representation is merely the most obvious form in which one group seeks to speak for another. Anarchists attempt, as May points out, to wrest control back into all other planes, 'the ethical, the social and the psychological, for instance'.[147] Liberation refuses mediation, as only the oppressed can emancipate themselves: no group, however benevolent, can liberate another. Autonomy and liberation involves oppressed groups determining their own values rather than embracing those of the hegemonic authority.

7. Symbolic Action and Direct Action
Symbolic actions are those acts that aim to raise awareness of an issue or injustice, but by themselves they do not resolve the problem. They are acts that signify other acts. There are many forms of overtly

political symbolic action: parades, marches, vigils, fasts, slogans, songs, festivals, badges, flags and salutes.[148] It can be argued that all direct action is symbolic in that its means are a partial example of the wider set of anti-hierarchical interactions. What marks out consistent anarchist versions of direct action is that they are synecdochic, that is to say the sign is a small part of what it is representing. Anarchist action embodies a glimpse at the types of social arrangement of a more liberated society.

Direct action, therefore, may act as a totem of wider protest. The squats, such as the ones in Wanstead in the early 1990s, created barricades sculpted out of abandoned cars, huge webs of rooftop webbing and towering monuments (figure 2.3.). These were designed to slow down the development of controversial and ecologically destructive new roads. They also acted as a dramatic emblem of wider environmental protest. Direct action is prefigurative. Such tactics immediately empower the oppressed class. Symbolic action, on the other hand, is often mediated and the objectives are not embodied in the methods. The efficacy of symbolic action is dependant on mediating power for translation.

Figure 2.3. Anti-Road protestors' network of squats,
Claremont Road, from *Do or Die*, No. 7., 1997.

In her discussion of direct action in her book-long treatment of the issue, April Carter does not explicitly refer to symbolic action, although others have connected and contrasted the two, such as the anarchist academic Lindsay Hart. He places certain forms of symbolic behaviour in the category of direct action, for instance 'bearing witness', where groups observe and publicise wrongdoing. However, Hart recognises that unless symbolic action is tied to an 'effective part of a broader whole' it has no practical consequence. Hart suggests that only when symbolic action has practical characteristics can it be also included in the category of direct action.[149]

The category 'symbolic action' is restricted here to those events which are not in themselves an attempt to resolve the problem at hand *directly* but are *metonymical* (an attribute of a phenonema used to signify the whole), for instance, making the hand-in-fist salute to stand for resistance to heteronomous power[150] or displaying a poster of parliament in flames as an image of more general revolt.[151] Symbolic action can also be *metaphorical*. Examples include vigils outside prisons and detention centres.[152] Symbolic acts and direct action are not necessarily distinct. Yelling slogans (apparently symbolic acts) is used to raise courage and frighten the enemy prior to breaking through a police line (direct action). However, purely symbolic action is rejected by egalitarian anarchists because of its limitations. There appears to be little point, from a consistent anarchist perspective, in screaming at the growing forces of state power and then leaving the police lines intact.

Symbolic acts, which appear to refer solely to the representative realm, can, nonetheless, alter the very relationships of knowledge-power that underpin the order of signification and inspire practical prefigurative action. The political scientist David Apter identifies the way that symbolic actions affect the self-identification of those contesting and *détourning* the symbol.[153] The *détournement* of advertising hoardings and the manipulation of everyday language, such as the juxtaposition of previously unconnected words ('demand the impossible', 'senseless acts of beauty') demonstrates the ideological hold of the dominant culture and can also be classed as direct action.[154] The process of resistance creates different perceptions that break the hold of the status quo. Anarchists are rightly critical of tactics whose aim is to limit the extension of action, such as symbolic acts that have a prescribed reference applied to them, or allow only an elite group to determine their signification.

Attack International criticise purely symbolic actions such as marches and rallies, as they encourage passivity and hierarchical divisions between the 'leaders' and 'followers'. Symbolic acts can have their meanings prescribed by those with greater social power. In an ironic swipe at such symbolic actions, Attack International recreate a mock leaflet for a dignified 'March Against Anything'[155] which covers the main reasons for opposing such actions. Particular targets are the organisers who control the signification of the act:

> Let us march as one to show our governments how cross we are about the state of the world.
>
> But for this demonstration to be effective, we must march with dignity and unity. Comrades, a disciplined march is essential, if we are to avoid losing the support of the media, the international press and the police. So please remember to follow the rules of the demonstration [....] And please obey all commands given by the stewards and police, who will be working together throughout the afternoon to ensure peace.
>
> At the end of the march, there will be a long rally, with speeches by several very important people. After the rally, please disperse as quickly as possible and make your way home peacefully....
>
> With your co-operation, we can make today a massive success, and start building for a repeat performance next year.[156]

Not only are symbolic meanings fixed by those in dominant hierarchical positions, but in securing them the signs reflect this restraint. For instance, the highly structured and passive marches through indifferent streets less symbolise resistance to oppressive power than the passivity of the crowd. The demonstration does not resolve the problem it sought to highlight, but accents the political power of those who manage the march, and the liberality of the state which allows opposition (albeit toothless) onto the streets. The organisers do not facilitate the desired social change, as this would end their role of leaders of the campaign. The end result is that the organisers control the opposition and profit from it – an attitude characterised by the phrase 'Join the struggle buy the t-shirts'.[157]

Symbolic actions are an opportunity for those with a grievance to let off steam. The ACF report of the demonstrations held on October 25 and 30, 1992, to save the coal mines (due to close by order of the Conservative government) stresses that despite the massive size of the demonstration the pit closure plan went ahead unchanged:

> The demonstrations and related activity were designed to divert and demoralise. People were meant to feel that they had done their bit, that after all, nothing could be changed, and after a dreary walk through driving rain, they must go home and accept 'Things as they are'.[158]

Although demonstrations appear to engage those who are oppressed in some way by the current state of affairs, they encourage submission. Anarchists promote instead active confrontation of oppression by those directly affected. Class War handed out their leaflets at the marches against the 1994 Criminal Justice Act encouraging marchers to act directly themselves, to break out from the pre-set symbolic representation into practical action.[159]

Marches need to gain media coverage to be symbolically effective, so the real agents are not those participating but the recorders of the event. As Nicholas Garnham, in his critical analysis of democratic participation, points out:

> People who stage demonstrations in order to obtain media coverage have been persuaded by the media to forget what direct action is all about. For surely one of the basic motives behind direct action is just to escape from the image and substitute for it a concrete reality, an action. Direct action is a revolt against the use of language in political communication. Instead of talking or writing about democratic participation, it acts it out, and by doing so it cuts down the manipulative possibilities inherent in any language.[160]

Symbolic action is twice mediated. The agents who bring about change are not those that are in a subjugated position, as such methods rely upon the media. Institutions of effective mass communication are not subject to democratic participation.[161] Moreover, such symbolic action brings about change not in the current situation but in the future. Direct action, on the other hand, aims to have, at least some, immediate consequences. Such propinquity (nearness at hand) discourages mediating forces. It therefore allows participants to ascribe their own interpretations onto events. It also ensures that, while the interests of those in the future are considered, the subjects of oppression also benefit more immediately.

Signifiers (such as terms, symbols, images) are given particular meanings by the dominant structures in society, interpretations which consequently reinforce these structures' governing positions. Radical action attempts to disrupt these established meanings and thus undermine their dominance. Such subversion of established methods of signification also leads to alterations in the sense of identity of those involved. Radical teachers, such as Ivan Illich and Paulo Friere, questioned the whole hierarchy of traditional teaching methods (one of the forms in which prevailing interpretations are legitimised) and also came to question their own role as specialist 'educators'.[162] Behaviour, apparently taking place solely in the realm of the symbolic, that dislocates established meanings and identities based on these interpretations, risks severe punishment, the acts being labelled pejoratively as 'blasphemy', 'terrorism' or 'violence'.[163] Thus, certain forms of symbolic action are indistinguishable from the model of direct action, in that they assault mediating powers' ability to impose their hierarchic interpretations.

8. Direct Action and Violence

The question of violence and whether it is compatible with prefiguration has caused much debate within anarchist circles. Critical accounts of anarchism have frequently concentrated upon the tactical approaches to violence within libertarian traditions. No other political or anti-political philosophies have had to contend with such consistent (and de-contextualised) interrogation on this point. Despite the bloodier histories of free market individualism, conservativism and state socialism, the caricature of these movements rarely embraces hooliganism, and few commentators interrogate these movements on whether they advocate violence. The traditional stereotype of the anarchist as a bearded, black-cloaked bomb-thrower, or, more recently, the chaotic, masked hooligan, has led some activists and theorists to disassociate themselves from such unpalatable connotations. Thus, they create the title anarchist-pacifist or anarcho-pacifist – where there are no corresponding pacifist-conservatives or nationalist-pacifists. The existence of this influential minority within anarchism suggests that those libertarians who do not distinguish themselves in these overt peace-loving terms are, by contrast, hopelessly wedded to violence. The further problem is that through this discussion of anarchism with respect to violence, one once again re-associates these terms, although the objective of this section is to disentangle and demystify this connection.

The adherence of anarchism to prefiguration would seem to imply that anarchists must rule out using violent means to reach a peaceful end. The argument is often put in the following form: the aim of anarchists is a liberated, non-violent society. As the means of bringing this about must match the objectives then anarchists must commit themselves to the use of solely pacifist tactics as violent means would contravene the prefigurative imperative: 'Only by adopting non-violent means [...] can we ever hope to achieve a non-violent society'.[164]

Baldelli restates the Kantian rejection of instrumentalism (discussed in the first part of the chapter), and then affirms the claim that a prefigurative ethic prescribes a commitment to pacifism:

> The renunciation of violence and deception, however motivated, is the first and fundamental condition to the achievement of freedom and peaceful existence as well as to their preservation once achieved. This renunciation is thus a means-cum-end, a truly moral value.[165]

In 1995 Chan summarises the pacifist-anarchist position:

> If an act of violence was wrong, then it was wrong no matter who perpetrated it. If anarchists wanted a society based on mutual respect and rational persuasion then they should prove their commitment to this by practising what they preached.[166]

The preference for non-violence based on prefigurative grounds has been a consistent issue in anarchist debate, from the anti-nuclear campaigners of the early 1980s – such as the Feminist and Non-Violent Study Group (F&NSG)[167] – to the road and anti-Criminal Justice Act protestors of more recent periods.[168] Not all anarchists accept this disposition. On the contrary, the influence of pacifists within contemporary British anarchism is probably overstated.[169]

The anarchist movement in Britain is divided between the pacifists and the non-pacifists. The first includes mostly liberal groupings such as, for most of this period, the Freedom Press Group,[170] Advance Party and Freedom Network, and an informal coalition derisively referred to as the 'Fluffies'.[171] The other side includes class struggle groups such as AF, Black Flag, Class War and Solfed. Green Anarchist originally had pacifist origins but has long since abandoned this principle. Class struggle anarchists are not, however, contravening their prefigurative criteria by accepting violent tactics, as will be discussed below. The pacifist argument rests on a confused and contradictory conception of violence.

8.1. Identifying Violence

Class struggle anarchists reject holding pacifism as a universal principle. They consider that violence is often necessary to protect and advance the revolutionary subject. As a result, it is occasionally desirable and does not conflict with prefiguration. The general social context, in which the injustices of the everyday are so ingrained that they are hardly questioned, means that many forms of violence are ignored. Beneficiaries of 'institutional' or 'structural' violence are so assured of the legitimacy of their coercive behaviour that it passes without comment. Class struggle anarchists reject the passive acceptance of institutional force.

Depending on characterisations of violence, one could argue – in opposition to the pacifist position – that anarchism does not presume that all violence would be absent from non-hierarchical social relations. Martial arts sparring or consensual sado-masochistic role-playing would still be classed as violent but are not precluded from a liberated social order. One can, therefore, distinguish between morally neutral *violent acts*, such as sparring, and more morally questionable *acts of violence*, such as assault and intimidation (a taxonomy developed by John Harris).[172]

The argument for non-violence could then be re-written in terms of non-coercive behaviour.[173] Indeed, many of the advocates of pacifism in the West have leant on Kantian notions of rights in defence of their position.[174] However, class struggle anarchists maintain that they are still being consistent with the prefigurative criteria by not refusing all coercive activity, as it may be justified according to the social context in which it is used and the actor who uses it.

The category of 'violence' is certainly confused. During the Gulf War of 1991-2, CND opposed the use of military weaponry against Iraq. They argued instead for economic sanctions, a form of coercion, against the country. These sanctions have caused the deaths of hundreds of thousands of Iraqi citizens. So, too, Miller has posited Gandhi's economic boycotts as 'non-violent forms of resistance to the state',[175] but others, including Reinhold Niebuhr, have explained that these embargoes caused considerable hardship to Lancashire textile workers who had little influence on policy decisions in India.[176] Class struggle anarchists are shown not to be more favourably disposed to violence than others, but merely less hesitant in admitting that they use it.[177]

The absolutist position on non-violence requires non-action in circumstances in which violence is the only possible reaction, and it therefore leads to quietism and passivity.[178] As a result of this acquiescence, greater avoidable acts of violence occur. The F&NSG argued along these lines in their recognition of abortion as an act of violence which was permissible as the alternative of state restraints on the autonomy of women would be a greater wrong. Thus, it becomes not a matter of rejecting violence as a whole, but particular acts of violence.

The problem of identifying 'violence' is exacerbated because the term is not an analytical category, but is constructed as an expression of class prejudice.[179] The institutional violence of everyday living, whether in the alienation of the workplace or the discipline of state apparatuses, is excluded from the calculations of liberal-pacifist traditions. The mainstream commercial media that castigated the events of Mayday 2000 for their hostility and carnage, in particular the graffiti on the cenotaph war memorial, were similarly celebratory in support of the conflicts in Serbia the previous year and latterly in Afghanistan and Iraq, where tens of thousands of civilians were killed or maimed by allied action. Yet the acts of violence perpetuated with the support of the ruling class are rarely described in terms of violence – the term is used solely as a pejorative label for actions that are disapproved of by those in a position to apply the taxonomy.[180] Niebuhr endorses this view. He noted that the middle classes claim to abhor violence but often use it for their own end, while also failing to recognise that violence might be a response to their physical force.[181]

Various diagnostic tools for the identification of violence have been posited in order to maintain the pacifist position, none of which are successful. One such method relies on the acts and omissions doctrine. In a situation where there is a choice between an act or inaction, both of which have equal probability of leading to a violent or coercive conclusion, the doctrine suggests inaction is morally preferable. The doctrine states that: '[I]n certain contexts, failure to perform an act, with certain foreseen bad consequences of that failure, is morally less bad than to perform a different act which has the identical foreseen bad consequences.'[182] There are a number of objections to this doctrine. Jonathan Glover presents many examples where inaction is worse than action. Refraining to give food and allowing people to starve to death, for example, indicates that there is nothing inherent in inaction that assures its moral supremacy. In some instances inaction or omission can be reinterpreted as purposive acts. Not feeding a prisoner, for instance, is not merely an omission but the act of starving an inmate.

Niebuhr tries to give a workable definition of violence based on the 'intent to destroy either life or property'.[183] This definition proves inadequate on a number of grounds, however, as it fails to take into account injuries that are not life threatening. Even if these were included, a consistent pacifist position on the definition of violence would still prove to be problematic. Failure to carry out a minor destructive act may be to permit far greater excesses. Tolstoy, for instance, considered it a breach of pacifist principles to kill a murderer who was about to slaughter a child, even if this was the only way of saving the victim. Blanket prohibition on the use of violence can permit far greater harm.

Pacifists may counter that the violence resulting from the non-interference with Tolstoy's murderer is not the intended result of the pacifist's principled passivity, but rather just the foreseeable consequence of the failure to act – in the same way as a cigarette smoker might foresee but not intend foreshortening his/her life. This argument has previously been discussed with respect to Kant's axe-returning neighbour (covered in the first part of this chapter). This depends on a clear distinction between the foreseeable and the intentional. As Aufheben discusses, the anarchist-pacifist argument regards personal commitment to avoiding violence as more important than saving life. It cannot be considered prefigurative of the desired set of social relations. Aufheben argues that this form of absolutist pacifism is indicative of liberal thinking. Like lifestyle anarchism, it stresses individuals, their actions and intentions, as the ultimate basis for evaluation, in isolation from the wider social context in which the act takes place.[184]

Pacifists, such as Baldelli, Morland and *Peace News*, and certain sections of *Freedom* and *Green Anarchist*,[185] see all individuals as the same, condemning both the aggressor and also the victim if the latter uses coercion to overcome their oppression. Class struggle anarchists, on the other hand, point to the differences in social power and recognise that the prevention of further oppression may require resistance that is sometimes physically coercive. Creating non-hierarchical associations may involve breaking authoritarian relations. Those who benefited from oppressive power-structures would consider such transgression to be violent.

By contrast, consistent egalitarian anarchists do not prioritise deliberate inaction over similarly intended actions. Black Flag, in a response to the pacifist-anarchist Anark, give examples of not only excusable, but also morally desirable and possibly mandatory, coercive violence such as resistance to the Nazis and Communist secret police.[186] By refusing to act in a coercive manner one would be conniving with existing totalitarian governance. Assaults that sought to create non-hierarchical social relations may well be violent, but would be more in keeping with the ends than peaceful inaction or martyrdom.

Non-coercive techniques advocated by pacifists are often covertly tyrannical, as in the reduction of education to propaganda.[187] Other radicals, such as the assassinated Black revolutionary George Jackson, argue that Gandhian non-violence – 'soul-force' – which seeks to change the minds of the oppressors through reason and positive example, confers onto the adversary qualities which they do not have or which would not be in their interests to exercise.[188] The proponents of 'soul-force' make the oppressors the agents of change, as it is from them that transformation is desired.

8.2. Violence and the Working Class

Chapter Three examines the taxonomy and identity of the 'working class', understood by anarchists to be the appropriate agent of social change. Yet some attempt must be made at this point to explain the association of violence with class struggle anarchism. While there were pacifists in the 1950s Syndicalist Workers Federation,[189] and those who approve of violence who are members/supporters of contemporary non-class struggle groups such as GA and those behind Lancaster Bomber, there is a strong correlation between class struggle groups and the rejection of pacifism, an association which requires an explanation. For some writers, like George McKay, the acceptance of violence is equivalent to leftism and class struggle.[190] Class struggle anarchists not only permit but also encourage those facing oppression to overthrow it, even if this involves the use of physical coercion. Socialist libertarians recognise that existing structures of domination maintain their authority through violence and that in resisting further subjugation, and in creating non-hierarchical social relations, conflict with these oppressive institutions is inevitable.

Martin Wright, a co-founder of Class War, discussed the different patterns of rejection of pacifism amongst working class and middle class anarchists.[191] In the late 1960s to the early 1980s, Wright, and the then few working class members of anarchist groups, saw violent means as a natural expression for confronting heteronomous power, and therefore to be welcomed. Middle class anarchists considered such responses to be barely distinct from fascism. Wright argued that the reason for this difference between the middle and working class activists was down to their respective life experiences. Working class people, he argued, grew up amongst greater violence, at schools, in family relationships and in the generality of working class culture, as part of the preparation for – and result of – more physically demanding labour. As a result, violence becomes just another aspect of the communication between and within the working class, which is absent from the middle classes who regard it as alien.

Criticisms can be levelled at Wright's analysis. There have been significant changes in employment patterns since his youth.[192] Manual labour no longer employs the majority of working class people. Furthermore, it is by no means true that working class families are any more violent or have a greater propensity to use physical coercion than middle class ones. Domestic violence, for instance, exists throughout the entire class system. Indeed, it is argued, that the barbarities of elite boarding schools would compare unfavourably with contemporary comprehensive education where corporal punishment has been banned since 1986. It might be argued that if Wright's analysis had any verisimilitude (correspondence with reality) in earlier decades, then it would hold less true in the late 1990s and early 2000s, with the decline of unskilled manual labour and the growth of the tedious and demeaning, but less physically arduous, service sector.

A number of replies can be made. Firstly, there is strong anecdotal evidence, as well as the reports of sociologists such as Robins and Cohen, which indicates that because of their position in society, working class people face greater harassment and violence than the middle classes, whether this be the casual assaults of street-crime, structural physical coercion, or from state bodies such as the police.[193] As welfare provision has diminished, the state has become less a benign enabler and more a controller, whose mechanisms of restraint impose themselves on many areas of social life. As their social position is maintained by institutional violence, even if it is not overtly defined as such, members of the working class may be more conscious that meaningful change might require a physical response. As a result, they might regard political violence in a more positive light.

Class War, like Sorel, regards violence much more positively. Both identify pacifism with consent to the rules and conventions of the dominant class, and celebrate examples of working class violence:

> Violence is the key to *working class confidence*. Where the class is confident it fights back....

> When it comes to violence remember – THEY STARTED IT!

> Remember – the police have murdered loads of black and white people over the years. We have killed no-one, yet it is us who are labelled 'violent yobs'!! This is real capitalist/media double speak.[194]

They both regard violence as essential to historical progress and the revolutionary project. Acquiescence encourages peaceful, continuous repression. Conversely, for Sorel, violence is synonymous with virility and dynamism. Destructiveness helps to strengthen class resolve amongst the workers and releases their repressed desires.[195] Class War restates that violence represented the vitality of class struggle, turning it (once again) into a festival for the oppressed to gain materially and rediscover their strength.[196] Violence is celebrated, then, because it is necessary for the development of the revolutionary class.

In contrast, the advocates of 'bearing witness' felt that the spur to action could be found in representations of brutal oppression against 'innocent victims'. Class War pointed out that such representations of working class people as passive or innocent victims of state violence, found in left-wing newspapers, demoralised rather than encouraged agents of change.[197] In their place they published the crumpled figures of bleeding police officers.[198] The photographs helped to illustrate the vulnerability of dominating forces and the possibility that oppressed groups could overcome their persecutors. Class struggle anarchists' justification for violence is based on an acceptance that methods which forge egalitarian social relations will conflict with existing hierarchical social practices.

The context in which pacifists find it hard to maintain their absolute rejection of violence is self-defence. The question of the legitimacy of self-defence involves defining what one means by self. Many pacifists conform to the liberal tag placed upon them by class struggle libertarians and see violence in terms of immediate harm to the abstract individual. Some of those interviewed by Chan do indeed differ from Gandhi and accept the legitimacy of self-defence as either moral or value-neutral. They cite cases of women protecting themselves (and their children) from spousal (parental) abuse as legitimate activities.[199] The inconsistencies of the pacifist approach become apparent when pacifists accept activities such as strike action or ecotage (sabotage carried out for environmental aims) in defence of individual well-being. Such action causes considerable destruction to property, and physical inconvenience. In contrast, social anarchists consider actions provoked by risk of harm to the community to be self-defence.[200] Those who are the subject of oppression are not only permitted but also encouraged by anarchists to overthrow the forces oppressing them, even if this involves the use of violent coercion.

In many examples those who call themselves pacifists reject an absolutist position, seeking merely to limit violence to its minimum. This position is similar to that of class struggle anarchists, except the latter include in their assessment the everyday intimidation of dominant practices which often go unnoticed.[201] Thus, certain 'pacifists' do not reject all acts of violence but, like non-pacifists, make distinctions between justifiable and unjustifiable forms. April Carter, for instance, identifies acceptable forceful tactics as those that aim to resist heteronomous power, which are performed by those affected and have a good chance of success. For Carter, this latter stipulation also implies popular support for the act.[202] Her formulation is close, but not identical, to the class struggle anarchist position. The difference is that anarchists would accept (on the whole) violent acts in certain contexts where the ends are unlikely to be fulfilled. Brave but doomed efforts at self-defence, for example, are seen as prefigurative in that the forms of resistance provide opportunities to create anti-hierarchical, creative social relations. In addition, an oppressed minority might still legitimately use force against an aggressive, powerful majority. Yet, this does not justify all acts of individual violence. Whilst anarchists advance specific types of resistance because they provide opportunities to engage in solidarity with other similarly oppressed individuals, they also consider that certain methods of contestation, like particular types of terrorism, restrict avenues for solidarity and reify subject identities, as will be discussed in Chapters Four and Five.

8.3. Tactical Violence

There are positive side effects to non-violence that provide a good tactical, rather than principled, basis for its contingent adoption. The methods covered by NVDA make it harder for the state to use extreme oppressive countervailing power, whereas the ostentatious promotion of violence, such as the carrying of weaponry by the Black Panthers, provides cover for extreme state intervention.[203] Similarly, it is argued that in cases of brutal intercession by the state, whether in Sharpville or Bloody Sunday, public opinion can turn sharply against the state.

Thus, non-violence is seen to have pragmatic virtues in winning popular support and avoiding extreme consequences for activists.

Aufheben criticise this argument, claiming that it is not violence which promotes physical attack, but the success of a campaign. 'Of course, cops don't always need "excuses"; so long as they're physically capable, they trash you if they think you're *effective*, not just when you are "violent"'.[204] But the fact that oppressive forces have to go to the trouble of either covering up their actions (such as the Battle of the Beanfield 1985) or using *agent provocateurs* (such as the Littlejohn brothers in the war in Ireland) suggests that the state recognise that improper action is a more risky strategy against less obviously violent movements.[205] This positive side effect (which is not true in all situations), does not, however, justify a blanket rejection of violent activities. Support for non-violence on the grounds of effectiveness is contingent and tactical, not the basis for an absolute principle.

Another benefit associated with non-violence is increased popular support and ease of organisation.[206] However, there is no convincing evidence that the broad mass of people support pacifism. Unwillingness to use more effective, violent measures may be indicative of bad faith. The Poll Tax riots led to no noticeable decrease in support for the wider campaign against the Community Charge. In contrast to the difficulties in violent, (anti-)political organisation, non-violent groups are less subject to state interference. Yet, not all violent tactics require organisation as they can be undertaken spontaneously. A later chapter will discuss forms of organisation, but the standard conception of anarchist organisations, admired by Miller, as open, consensual groupings, need not be the only form consistent with prefigurative politics.

The defence of violence put forward by class struggle anarchists does not mean that they advocate it as the only response. Certainly, violence can help break the consensus that has kept certain groups in an inferior position, and can act as a symbol of their discontent, which had previously been easier to ignore. Likewise class struggle anarchists, even Class War, do not consider all acts of violence to be uniformly advisable, nor do they consider non-violence necessarily as a sign of weakness. Aufheben and the London anarchists behind the one-off free-sheet *Hungry Brigade* (1997) accept that non-violence, in certain circumstances, is a better tactic than those more commonly used by revolutionaries.

British anarchists advanced violent methods because the pacifist tactics that dominated the early 1980s protest had been successfully neutralised by the strategies of the state. Tactics such as lying in the middle of the road to block traffic and provoke arrest (sit downs) had become little more than empty rituals for the participants. NVDA had become elite symbolic activities. However, by 1997, many of the non-pacifist tactics used by the anarchists over a decade earlier had also been successfully contained by the state. The ruck with the police which had startled the assembled officers at Molesworth in 1984, was by the time of the 1997 March for Social Justice (also known as Reclaim the Future) in central London, just as much a ritual as CND's sit downs.[207] Dominating powers learn to control and integrate tactical developments, and their meanings are constrained by state intervention. The failure to adopt fresh methods results in ossification and reification.

While class struggle activists may question certain violent tactics, and regard others categorised as 'non-violent' as more appropriate, they refuse to advocate non-violence as a principle. Class struggle activists increasingly see NVDA to be tactically appropriate in specific contexts. If other means are more effectively prefigurative, then they should be used even if they involve violence.[208]

Evaluation of anarchist positions according to the prefigurative ethics they espouse, implicitly or explicitly, provides a diagnostic for highlighting the inconsistencies in their own accounts of social change, and contradictions within their methods. Central to the prefigurative approach, exemplified in direct action, is the role of agency. Egalitarian anarchists prioritise the working class as the agent of change. They do so at a time when most other theorists have renounced class analysis. Anarchism's conception of the revolutionary class differs from that of traditional marxist conceptions from the Second International. It is against this alternative socialist approach to agency and the additional weaknesses of class analysis provided by feminist and poststructuralist accounts, that an ideal type anarchist notion of agency is developed, one that is consistent with the prefigurative ethic. This paradigm also shares key characteristics with politically engaged poststructuralisms.

Chapter Three

Agents of Change

Introduction

In assessing anarchist tactics, the question arises: who can transform society in a libertarian manner? To put it another way: who is it that anarchism needs to appeal to in order to be consistent and effective? Libertarian action requires not only that the methods prefigure the ends but also that appropriate agents must instigate the means. Those subjected to oppression must be the primary actors in overcoming it, and must do so in a manner in keeping with anarchist principles. The task here, therefore, is to illustrate what forms of subjugated agents would be consistent with the anti-hierarchical, prefigurative *ideal*. A second, inter-related task of this chapter is to assess whether the actual revolutionary subjects addressed by contemporary anarchist groups are compatible with this ideal.

The identification of the appropriate agent that will assume the role of the revolutionary subject is fundamental to the success of liberatory tactics, and as such is also essential for an evaluation of current methods. This section looks at how modes of oppression help create the identities of the agents of change and how the category of moral agent differs significantly from Leninist classifications and those of other strategic theorists and extends beyond the category of the proletariat. The theory of the anarchist ideal subject involves engaging with autonomist marxist and poststructural conceptions of power.

The aim of this chapter is to trace some of the sources from which the archetypal anarchist agency appears. Starting by tracking some of the histories of class in anarchism, it continues to show the way in which the notion was progressively extended to include other groups and subject positions. Marxism, and its Leninist interpretation, is still an important influence on revolutionary politics in Britain.

Although anarchists differentiate themselves from orthodox marxism, many still retain a commitment to the economic determinism and strategic politics characteristic of Leninism. The revisions by neo-marxist and marxian radicals, such as Gorz, the autonomists and Situationists, are significant alterations in recognising the scope of capitalist oppression and consequently extend the range of potential revolutionary subjects. Yet these revisions still ascribe priority to the economic base as a determinant of social relations. The anarchist ideal extends the notion further by not tying oppression to an objectively knowable singular power, but realises that different forces operate in different contexts. As such, it shares important characteristics with the politically-engaged poststructuralisms of the likes of Jacques Derrida, Michel Foucault, Jean-François Lyotard, Gilles Deleuze and Felix Guattari.[1]

The consistent anarchist agents of change are those groups of people that through self-created, anti-hierarchical relationships can successfully challenge oppressive practices. The revolutionary subject is described in class terms, yet is distinct from that of orthodox marxism. Class relations extend beyond the immediate economic sphere of production. Although economic forces are acknowledged as dominant in many contexts, other repressive practices operate that are not reducible to capitalism alone. The notion of the working class is not a pre-designated identity, economic or otherwise, but the identification of oppressed subject positions, which are increasingly products of economic forces. A feature of these subject positions is that they have particular tactical advantages within these contexts, such as more flexible and fluid responses to repression.

1. The Anarchist Ideal: A concept of class agents
Anarchism holds that it is the oppressed subjects who are the agents for making liberatory social change (they are the 'moral agents'), but the identities of these agents alter according to context. An individual or group in one social position may be subject to forces that place them in a subordinate position, yet in another context

they may wield oppressive authority. Oppression does not have one ultimate source, so consequently there is no vanguard or universal agent whose liberation ends all oppression. Nevertheless, the concept of 'class' is still important to anarchism because in most contexts (if not all) capitalism is one of the main oppressive powers, albeit in a much wider sense than the Leninist model dictates (see below). In the contexts where anarchists self-identify, capitalism may be the main form of domination. As a result, the anarchist agent of change, even in the ideal form, is still described in terms of the 'working class'.

The libertarian groups that have been the focus of this text have regarded economic exploitation as a major form of oppression and consequently have tended to see liberation in terms of class struggle. Many of these groups recognise that there are other forms of oppression which are not reducible to capitalism alone and that in certain locations other oppressed subjects are formed. The dominance of class-based terminology led to many groups still referring to other oppressed subjects under the singular (economic) category of the 'working class'. The continued application of the vocabulary of economics can give the impression that they are subsuming all subject identities under a single designation. Their intention in using this term is often, however, to signal plurality, as they regard oppression to be multiform.

The revolutionary subject of the anarchist ideal, even when misleadingly termed the 'working class', is, however, diverse and evolving. The multiplicity of oppressed subject positions reflects the variety of forms that capitalist domination takes in pursuing surplus labour in areas beyond the mere point of production. By inhabiting many different locations, oppressed agents can see similarities in apparently distinct forms of hierarchy. Feminist writers, for instance, recognised similarities in the operation of power in the workplace, leisure facilities and private sphere, which developed into a general concept of patriarchy, whose operation subtly alters depending on context.[2] For the anarchist ideal, oppression, such as homophobia, sexism, anti-semitism and racism, is not restricted just to the extraction of profit.

At the heart of anarchism is the rejection of hierarchical relations. Repressive practices can come about through mediation, so consistent anarchism avoids representing others. Ideal type anarchism is motivated by the quest for liberation: the oppressed must have primacy in overthrowing their oppression. In the words of Marx, reaffirmed by the Situationist International, 'the emancipation of the proletariat will be the work of the proletariat itself.'[3] The oppressed are the only ones capable of being the class in itself. The distinction between the class in (or by) itself and the class for itself is one found in Marx's writings and is endorsed by many contemporary libertarians.[4]

This division has also been subject to further critical development by the marxian theorist Marcuse. He explains that the group that can overthrow the existing system of production and exchange is in itself the revolutionary subject. The revolutionary subject 'for itself' is the group (or groups) that has an immediate vital desire for revolution, being self-consciously aware of its oppression and seeking to overthrow it. The section of the community that is in decisive need, or is otherwise willing to risk what they have for an entirely different social system, is the revolutionary subject for itself. Marcuse suggested that the western, industrial working class of the 1960s was still the revolutionary subject in itself but not for itself.[5]

Other class struggle groups have used slightly different terminology but made a similar demarcation between the revolutionary agent and the section(s) of the populace from which it emerges. The autonomists talk of 'class composition' and 'decomposition', composition being the process by which the working class unifies and grows in technical, cultural and organisational effectiveness. Decomposition comes about when the opponents of the working class succeed in breaking down their power. In the 1980s this occurred with the dismantling of the welfare state and the de-centring of industry, which restrained the powers of the organisations of the mass workers such as trade unions.[6] The stronger the composition of the working class the more significant it is as a revolutionary force and the more potent the threat to capital.[7]

Criticisms have been raised by a host of theorists concerning the formulation of the class for itself coming from the class in itself. Writers in *Green Anarchist* and the social critic Richard Sennet, amongst others, reject the view that the working class(es) is (are) a revolutionary subject. These critics argue that those sections of the community that have little or nothing to lose have not been prominently involved in revolutionary activity in the western post-war context. Indeed, the comparatively large number of middle class radicals, in contrast to the apparent apathy of those suffering from impoverished conditions, seems to support these commentators' case.[8]

The existence of an assembly of elite 'revolutionaries' is not fundamental to the success or otherwise of libertarian uprisings, as liberation cannot come from a mediating power. The anarchist ideal rejects the notion of an objectively identifiable set of universal 'revolutionaries'.[9] It is through self-creative action that the revolutionary class in itself transforms into the class for itself. Dominant practices and values are rejected and replaced by autonomous activity based on anti-hierarchical and egalitarian anarchic principles.[10] The movement for the creation of anarchism is itself anarchist. The process of change involves those who do not identify themselves through the 'anarchist' label but nevertheless are oppressed and use tactics that are in accord with libertarian precepts. No group, including those who announce themselves as 'anarchists', can take the prior role in emancipating others, although they can, and do, take part in action that opposes their own oppressions.[11]

The anarchist ideal recognises that the revolutionary class for itself is not identical to the class in itself. Those who mistake the first for the latter reject areas of potential solidarity. An example would be *Green Anarchist*'s refusal to support the sacked News International strikers as they had printed reactionary, racist and sexist publications.[12] The Irrationalists, a group close to Green Anarchist, have contempt for the dispossessed and disadvantaged because they do not measure up to a predetermined revolutionary model. Irrationalists describe subjugated groupings as the 'passive herd' and portray them, in their cartoons, in a scatalogical fashion.[13] The flipside is to consider the sociological class as being innately for itself. According to the romantic vision of 'workerism', the working class in its current state is equivalent to an already revolutionary grouping.[14] The archetypal anarchist response is not that the oppressed are already revolutionary, but that it is only through their self-activity that these groups can achieve liberation.

As May explains, anarchism's principle of direct participation of the oppressed in their own emancipation makes it responsive to the poststructuralism of Lyotard, Foucault and Deleuze. According to the anti-representative feature of libertarianism, one group may not decide upon the fate of, or claim the ability to speak for, another. There are two closely related reasons. First, as discussed in the previous section, representation (and this extends beyond political representation) leads to the abuse of power and the (re)creation of hierarchical divisions between the powerful and powerless. The second reason, shared by poststructuralists and consistent, contemporary anarchists, is that as there are a multiplicity of irreducible forces that form the intersecting networks of power which constitute society, there is no privileged universal class. At each location different forces interact. Social space is constituted by these forces – it is not something ahistoric and separate that contains them.[15]

May uses Deleuze and Guattari's rhizome metaphor to explain the non-hierarchical relationship between forces.[16] Unlike trees, whose branches stem from a simply traced origin, rhizomes spread out roots, which connect up to other roots, such that no single tuber constitutes the source. Consequently, as the multiple forms of power do not operate uniformly, or to the same degree at different points, different political identities develop.[17] There is no central political struggle, nor a universal group, that represents all struggles.

A vanguard would paternalistically impose one set of interests onto another. Instead, poststructural (or ideal type) anarchism recognises that different oppressed subjects appear in various contexts, with no singular entity having universal priority. When anarchists talk of working class resistance, they refer not to a single identity, but to a diverse changing multiplicity of resisting agents. The anarchist agent of change is context-dependent such that although an individual or grouping in one geographical or historical context is subjected to heteronomous power, in another it can be regarded as an oppressive agency. Examples would include unemployed people who intimidate their gay neighbours, or businesspeople that face domestic violence or racial prejudice in other aspects of their life.

There are a number of different interpretations of the agent of change within contemporary anarchism. Some libertarians, still under the influence of Leninism, have a strategic analysis regarding all forms of oppression as emanating from a single objectively identifiable source. Other contemporary anarchists are closer to the ideal in which the identities are multiple and fluid and dependent on the diversity of forces operating locally, an approach that is consistent with poststructuralism. The extension from the single subject of Leninism (the industrial proletariat) to the anarchist ideal can be traced through the influential theories of libertarian thinkers from the New Left, and autonomist marxist currents (including council communism and situationist theory).

1.1. Agents in Anarchist Propaganda
The ideal model of the anarchist conceptions of class and class struggle is often neither explicit nor fully formed. It can, however, be identified in and reconstructed from contemporary groupings such as the A(C)F, Black Flag, Class War and SolFed. The definitions and

explanations of the archetypal libertarian agent of change borrow heavily from the interrelated autonomist and situationist traditions which helped form contemporary British anarchism and take on board their criticisms of traditional marxism.[18] The anarchist ideal maintains that only the oppressed themselves are the revolutionary agents, and the oppressed, in almost all contexts, is the working class. Alternatives to the tactical ideal are also present within British anarchist texts. Leninist conceptions of the revolutionary agent of change are also an important influence on anarchism as historically some libertarian groups have attempted to recreate the apparent success of the Bolsheviks by replicating their analysis, whilst other anarchists reacted to the authoritarianism of the Soviet experiment by developing antagonistic recommendations. The complex and multi-identitied ideal type anarchism agent becomes more comprehensible by examining its strengths against the limitations of Leninist and other models that have helped create the ideal.

There is no single position on the identity of the revolutionary agent in contemporary British anarchist writings. Indeed, a single edition of *Green Anarchist* contained articles which proposed three distinct views on class, two of which dismiss class analysis as meaningless or tantamount to promoting a repressive theology, while the other sought to revise marxist models in line with changes in the global economy.[19] Similarly, Class War, Subversion and Working Class Times have engaged in epistolary debates over identifying and categorising the working class.[20] Leninist influences on anarchism are also evident. In some of the propaganda emanating from within these class struggle groups the revolutionary class is restricted to preconceived categories based on western industrial, predominantly male workers.[21] Liberal anarchists, such as Donald Rooum, also have a distinct view on the appropriate agent of change, regarding it in terms of the abstract rational individual.[22]

The paradigmatic characterisation of the revolutionary subject and other libertarian conceptions of class are best understood through comparisons with other competing theories from within the socialist camp. As Marx's work has been so widely interpreted, to justify one version as authentically his against competing exegeses would be a task too great for the limited space of any single text not specifically dedicated to the task. Instead, marxist ideas in this chapter are discussed through his various interpreters, predominantly those within the tradition of the Leninist Second International.[23]

1.2. The Decline and Rise of Class Within British Radicalism

In the major libertarian movements, even before the end of the First World War, anarchists surmised that the agent of change was the working class. Libertarians, such as Rocker and Berkman, acknowledged that they were part of the working class who were in a conflict with another class, in a struggle based on competing economic interests. Their writings were based on encouraging class conflict. Ignoring this feature would make their propaganda incomprehensible. As the American syndicalist Elizabeth Gurly Flynn explained in her defence of sabotage to promote economic emancipation: 'If you believe that a point can be reached whereby the worker can get enough, a point of amicable adjustment of industrial warfare and economic distribution, then there is no justification and no explanation of sabotage intelligible to you.'[24] The division in capitalism between capital and labour is absolute and cannot be reconciled, as incarnated in Harry Cleaver's remark: '*there are always two perspectives, capital's versus the working class's!.*'[25] Any consequent attempt at an objective social science is dismissed as 'futile'. Claims of universal validity are rejected. The archetypal anarchist position, derived in part from the autonomist tradition to which Cleaver belongs, accepts that capitalism divides subject positions (i.e. it creates distinctive classes which are born into distinctive contexts and consequently have different sets of experiences, forms of knowledge and loyalties), but does not consider this the only separation.

The contemporary British anarchist groups that are the focus of this study regard themselves as emanating from, and referring to, the 'working class'. This term has many differing interpretations and in the ideal form cannot be specified apart from the context of oppression, although some groups like the 1990s anarchic Splat collective profess to have very clear universal demarcations for class.[26] The identifying features of the libertarian ideal (prefiguration, rejection of both capitalism and other forms of hierarchy) can be reinterpreted in terms of the identification and reaffirmation of the working class as revolutionary subject, albeit a 'class' which is more diverse and irreducible than the Leninist formulation. The agent of change in itself transforms into the (revolutionary) class for itself through the reflexive application of anarchist principles. Examining the constituency that forms the anarchist revolutionary subject also uncovers the libertarian notion of power and assists in understanding the relevance of multiple forms of organisation and tactic that characterises contemporary British anarchism (as covered in the final two chapters).

The main anarchist currents operating in Britain identify themselves primarily as anarcho-syndicalists, anarchist communists, councilists and autonomous marxists, as such they maintain that the working class is the revolutionary agent of change.[27] This view challenges the dominant interpretation of anarchism that, since the 1950s, has often been associated with a position which repudiated this agent. Indeed, in some cases, as Fox reports, the ascription of the revolutionary subject has been transferred to groups such as students or dropouts.[28] Similarly, in America, as Cleaver describes, the New Left identified only particular parts of the working class as the agent for change, namely the lumpenproletariat and third world peasantry.[29]

Others went further by explicitly or implicitly rejecting class analysis altogether.[30] This rejection is deemed by class-based opponents such as Christie and Meltzer to be little more than 'militant liberalism'.[31] Revolutionary anarchist groups felt that their movement had been contaminated with 'liberal and leftist ideas' which had come about through a 'lack of theory and class based analysis'.[32] While Ward and the Freedom group have often been accused of helping to create British reformist anarchism, others have been much more charitable.[33]

The perceived downturn in the utopian promise of 1960s class struggle in the following decade (which reached its nadir when the Iranian Revolution ended in theocracy) led to an exodus of radicals into the then more cosseted world of academia, a migration that resulted in a revival in class analysis amongst critical and cultural theorists. The reinvigoration of class analysis had its heyday with the promulgation of Gramscian and Althusserian marxist revisions of communism by, amongst others, Birmingham University's Centre for Contemporary Cultural Studies (which became the enfeebled Department of Cultural Studies before closing in 2003).[34] Even at the height of interest in class analysis the form used was one consistent with elitist forms of socialism. It made few connections to the supposed agent of change, and concentrated on a staid vision of the working class as predominantly Occidental and male, which dealt only superficially and often patronisingly with other concerns. There has been a rise in popularity, over the same period, of poststructuralist critics who, recognising the weakness with this version of class analysis, stress the divisions and inconsistencies within unifying identities. These theorists have questioned the viability of discourses which exclude gender or race, such as those programmes that operate solely in terms of class (and a restrictive interpretation of 'class' at that).

With the decline of monolothic marxist theory, there has been a corresponding decrease in the status of revolutionary groups on the orthodox left. Militant (now the (Scottish) Socialist Party), the Workers Revolutionary Party and the Communist Party, who used to count their members in thousands and their supporters in the tens of thousands, have either folded or been reduced to groupings with memberships counted in dozens.[35] In the anarchist movement in Britain, the opposite trend has occurred. Since 1984, the main egalitarian libertarian groupings have grown in size, while the pacifist-liberal tradition prominent in the 1960s has gone into decline.

Even the environmental movement, which has been portrayed as the meeting point for many activists who reject class struggle,[36] actually includes substantial groupings, such as the militant British sections of Earth First!, who recognise the importance of class.[37]

It would be simplistic to see British anarchism's return to revolutionary socialist preoccupations with class as a result solely of the aggressive policies of the Thatcher governments (1979-90). Some commentators have cited the main industrial landmarks of these administrations, the Miners' Strike (1984-5) and the Wapping Dispute (1986) as the impetus for this change in direction.[38] Although this account of the extension of class analysis within British anarchism captures some important features of the dynamics of anarchist discourse, it is not wholly satisfactory.

Viewing the Miners' Strike as the central cause for the restoration of class in British anarchism risks overlooking the significant class struggle groups (Syndicalist Workers Federation, Anarchist Workers Association and Black Flag) which existed even in the more consensual political epochs. These, too, faced moments of expansion and decline prior to the appearance of the New Right. Class War itself had chosen its descriptive, combative name prior to the Miners' Strike. Even amongst those that did not employ classic marxist terminology, and even claimed to have superseded it, there was still a similar view of agency to that promulgated by contemporary class struggle groups.[39] Many egalitarian anarchists in the 1980s were hesitant to employ overtly class terms because such language had strong associations with the totalitarian Soviet States and their advocates in Britain. State socialists had defined themselves as marxist and claimed a pre-eminent status as representatives of the global proletariat using the discourse of class struggle. The discourse of class struggle was identified with hierarchical state socialism, as an article in Class War's *Heavy Stuff* journal explains: 'The more talk of class struggle the more Stalinist.'[40]

Soviet-style states were defined by the anarchist movement from 1921-onward (and by some before that) as having an authoritarian and elitist social order, little different to that of the capitalist states.[41] In order to distance themselves from these movements many anarchists sought to avoid the terminology associated with the Soviet tyrannies, and consciously or not, they resisted employing a vocabulary associated with class analysis. With the decline of the Stalinist parties, and the relative upsurge of interest in anarchism, there was greater confidence in reclaiming this discourse for libertarian revolutionary purposes. Starker expressions of class enmity were also found to be useful in shaking off the (militant) liberal influences on British radical politics.[42]

2. Leninist Model of Class

While the archetypal anarchist notion of class developed here differs from that of the traditional marxist notion of class, this simple binary opposition still has its adherents within British libertarianism. Marx defines the class position as depending on the relationship to the means of production,[43] a view that is shared by libertarians such as Subversion.[44] In orthodox marxism the workers engage in daily struggle with capital, pursuing higher wages and better conditions while capitalism aims to maximise profits by lowering pay and benefits. It is this contradiction which is central to traditional marxism. Anarchists accept that although this economic conflict is an important aspect of class it is not the only one.[45]

For traditional (Leninist) marxists such as Chris Harman,[46] priority is given to the industrial working class. For Harman, the social agent capable of achieving communism is only found in the modern conditions of western industrialised states. It is only here that the working class can be gathered together in sufficient numbers to form cohesive organisations and develop its collective strength:

> [L]ife under capitalism prepares workers in many ways to take control of society. For example, capitalism needs workers who

are skilled and educated. Also capitalism forces thousands of people into huge workplaces in huge conurbations where they are in close contact with one another, and where they can be a powerful force for changing society.[47]

As Marx explained, each historical era is marked by particular modes of production, such as feudalism or capitalism, which have specific relations of production. These relations and modes of production create the 'mode of production of material life' or superstructure which is the 'general process of social, political and intellectual life.'[48] Social conflict and revolution takes place when the productive forces come into conflict with existing social relations, for instance when emerging capitalism came into conflict with the laws and political processes of the preceding period of aristocracy. What is particular about the era of industrial capitalism is that it is only in this epoch that there is sufficient affluence for restrictive modes of production to be redundant and for an agent to be formed that can create communism.[49] (The historically specific feature of Marx's materialism is examined below. What is concentrated upon in this sub-section is the role of the industrial worker as being uniquely qualified for the task of liberation.)

There are two unique characteristics that distinguish the proletariat as the revolutionary subject. The first is that the modes of production specific to the industrial period require a geographical concentration of the workforce in a disciplined fashion. The second is that technical means have been formed to cross national frontiers so that the working class can combine. Modern capitalism, for Harman, provides the potential international revolutionary force. Additionally, as will be discussed below, capitalism not only reduces labourers from selling the products of their labour to selling just their labour power, but further immiserates them, as the imperative to maximise surplus value from their labour reduces wages. This classical model of marxism has a strategic implication. There is one central problem: the resolution of economic class contradictions.

The forces of production create new social relations through conflict with current social relations. In other epochs, the tension between the two has led to the transformation of serfdom to liberal citizenship, and it is only in the modern epoch that the transition to socialism is possible. Technical progress has to be supported to promote the development of capitalism so that the material conditions for communism can come into being.[50] Consequently, Harman considers the industrial worker created by capitalism to be *the* revolutionary subject. In this he follows Lenin: '[T]he proletariat is the only class that is consistently revolutionary, the only class able to unite all the working and exploited people in the struggle against the bourgeoisie, in completely replacing it.'[51] Only the proletariat have this historic mission.

Indeed, it is specifically the industrial working class that is capable of the transformation into communism. Colleagues of Harman, such as Tony Cliff, explain that the authoritarian turn of Lenin's Bolsheviks was as a result of an insufficiently large working class in Russia. A large proletariat was required to gain power over other classes, including the peasantry. Without it the Communist Party had to substitute its rule for that of the numerically weak proletariat.[52] Cliff maintains that agricultural workers are not revolutionary subjects.

Harman's version of historical materialism, ascribed to Marx by Andre Gorz[53] and libertarians such as Wildcat, restricts the communist agent of change to a particular epoch, that of industrial capitalism.[54] The anarchist archetype agent has similarities with the founding axiom of primitivism, according to which there has always been sufficient abundance for a libertarian form of society. Leninists, such as Harman, prioritise the current epoch because, they argue, it is only now that the capitalist relations of production have generated sufficient economic surplus to create socialism. The proletariat for Harman are in a unique epoch in which they are no longer constrained by scarcity and have no material interest in the continuation of this pattern of production.[55]

According to Thomas, it is Marx's prioritising of the proletariat over other sections of the working class which distinguished his views from Bakunin.[56] As the ACF comment, Bakunin saw the revolution emanating from: 'The overthrow of one oppressing class by another oppressed class [....]. The oppressed class [...] he variously described as commoners, the people, the masses or the workers....'[57] Because anarchists hold to a broader view of the working class, which includes the lumpenproletariat, they have been accused of promoting this section above others. This standard marxist interpretation of anarchism is inaccurate; anarchists simply include the lumpenproletariat as part of the working class, rather than exclude or exalt it.

The emphasis upon the industrial workforce, which is not unique to Leninists, is so great that the term 'working class' appears to be synonymous with 'industrial labour'. For instance, the health and size of the working class has often been reduced to questions concerning the size and influence of industrial and trade labour unions.[58] Other socialist theorists, amongst them Gorz and post-marxists Ernesto Laclau and Chantal Mouffe, have questioned this privileging of the industrial proletariat. Anarchists as diverse as the primitivists and class based libertarians such as the ACF and Sam Dolgoff also dismiss this emphasis on the industrial worker for, amongst other reasons, providing succour to capitalism and presenting a Eurocentric geography of struggle.

Libertarians such as Dolgoff consider the orthodox marxist view of historical progress to be inaccurate. They ascribe to Marx the proposition that when material productive forces (technology and industrial organisation) are constrained by the social relations of production, a revolutionary situation comes about. Traditional marxism therefore requires the development of these material productive forces (such as new types of technology, new forms of energy) to provide the material conditions without which the conclusive conflict between capital and the proletariat will not come about. As a consequence, libertarian forms of peasant and artisan struggle in underdeveloped countries and in non-industrial epochs are rejected by Leninists in favour of supporting capitalist domination so that an industrial working class is formed.[59] Economic determinist versions of history have Eurocentric repercussions, as the arena of revolutionary struggle is deemed to be in those areas that are most industrialised, namely western Europe and North America. Such determinism also leads to British Leninists supporting the developing bourgeois movements in the colonial and post-colonial nations not only against the colonial and post-colonial powers but also against the local peasantry.[60]

In contrast to the above view, libertarians (especially, but not exclusively, the primitivists) hold that any historic epoch has had sufficient abundance for communism to develop. Drawing on the research of Marshall Sahlins, Kropotkin and the writings of John Zerzan and Fredy Perlman,[61] they propose that 'resistance to civilisation has always had the potential to lead to the global community'.[62] What is unique about the current situation is that local libertarian enclaves are more quickly overrun by the expansion of oppressive forces.[63] Moreover, the globalisation of the industrial economy means that in any case most modes of production increasingly fall within the framework of capitalism.[64]

The prioritisation, by Leninists, of the proletariat over other sections of the working class was not only fundamentally mistaken but also effectively repressive as it assisted in the development of the capitalist mode of domination. Conflicts before the industrial era involving artisans, peasants and dissenters could have been taken to free communist conclusions. According to the anarchist conception, revolutionary subjects are confined neither to a particular historic epoch, nor to the arena of production alone. As capitalism extends globally, the social conditions needed to increase surplus value also extend beyond the site of manufacture, a view endorsed by autonomists and situationists.

There are a few anarchists who share the simple binary model of orthodox marxism, yet there are others, on the edges of the movement, who overtly reject any form of historical materialism[65] preferring an Idealist (mind-based), mystical explanation of events which escapes the hold of the rational.[66] Differences arise between traditional marxists and the archetypal anarchists. The latter accept that changes in society have a materialist basis but they also regard certain features that are considered by their orthodox socialist opponents to be merely products of the forces of production as sufficiently influential to affect these forces and to develop an autonomous dynamic. Orthodox marxists hold that only industrial workers can be agents of liberation in a particular historical era and that the primary site of conflict is economic in all cases, whereas anarchists have a wider interpretation of oppression and consequently a broader, more complex concept of the agent of change.

The Leninist account restricts the class in itself to a historically-specific, economically-determined group tied to specific social locations. Lenin's account of the transformation of the class in itself into the class for itself has other strategic features. Lenin's immiserated and active working class is incapable of recognising the roots of its own oppression. 'The history of all countries shows that the working class, solely by its own force, is able to work out merely trade-union consciousness.' What is needed is 'consciousness [...] brought to them from outside'.[67] Lenin's proposition has three important features. First, there is a predetermined state to be reached (an ideal type of consciousness, knowledge of a precise type of economic analysis). Second, it is a section of the 'bourgeois intelligentsia' who can know this state independently of those who reach it.[68] Thirdly, those who need to reach revolutionary consciousness cannot attain it without another external group to guide them (a vanguard). The revolutionary party, as described in the next chapter is, for Leninism, the quintessential catalyst for the change from the class in itself to the class for itself. This organisational structure, and the paternalistic ideology which promotes it, is widely seen as leading to the re-establishing of a ruling class in socialist regimes.[69]

Some anarchists have also considered that there is a considerable distance between the revolutionary class for itself and the subjugated class in itself and, like the Leninists, have proposed that a revolutionary elite is required to guide, albeit temporarily, the backward sections. The groups organised around *The Organisational Platform of Libertarian Communism* (*The Platform*), such as the WSM and particularly the AWG, place considerable importance on the role of the revolutionary cadre and organisation in transforming the class in itself into the class for itself. Yet they are criticised by other major anarchist currents for this paternalistic strategy.

The anarchist ideal, by contrast, rejects mediation by others, including even those professing to be revolutionaries. It is the different approaches for the transformative 'class becoming for itself' which distinguishes anarchism in its ideal form from other socialist traditions such as Leninism.[70] An example comes from Class War's Jon Barr who identifies the Bolshevik Revolution, the pivotal event of contemporary Leninism, as an example of paternalistic rebellion. Barr argues that such bourgeois insurrection is not liberation, as the oppressed themselves were not in control of the process of change but had it done for them, so the revolution could only lead to the re-creation of class society.[71] So what can anarchists do if they want to avoid paternalism?

Anarchists are not condemned to inactivity. Class struggle libertarians who come from oppressed subject groups can consequently act for their own liberation by operating in an anti-hierarchical manner in confronting disciplining practices. Anarchists from outside these subjugated identities cannot directly intervene in these struggles in a liberatory manner.[72] In addition, co-operative networks of support between subjugated groups can form where mutual areas of struggle are recognised. For instance, trade unionists, workplace activists, ravers and travellers came together to create libertarian networks of common support to confront the 1994 Criminal Justice Bill, as it affected all these different groups. Inside and alongside these groups were sections of the community who had already withstood harm inflicted by the administration that was proposing the new legislation. So too the intertwined anti-capitalist and anti-globalisation movements involve new and ever-changing, non-paternalistic coalitions.[73]

The act of the oppressed co-operating under the specific context of their subjugation provides the motivation for widespread solidarity between subject groups. The class in itself becomes for itself by acknowledging a prefigurative application of libertarian principles. Self-valorisation manifests itself in tactics which avoid hierarchical relations (such as, but not uniquely, capitalism) as well as representation which tends towards the recreation of oppressive structures and creates new grounds for solidarity with other oppressed groups. It is through the process of confrontation that forms of oppression become recognised and solutions sought. The process of struggle generates new forms of resistance and new identities for the agents of change that cannot be predicted in advance. The events of May 1968 brought out into the open the forms of domination obscured by Leninist conceptions of class and nationalist conflicts. Comradeship in struggle creates new identities for the agents of change.

3. Gorz and the Non-Class

It is appropriate to discuss the theory of Gorz at this point because he, like the anarchists, also rejected the authoritarianism of Third International marxism (Leninism). In his book *Farewell to the Working Class*, Gorz argues against 'Marx' (a Marx understood through a Leninist reading).[74] This text, originally published at the start of the 1980s, sought to find an appropriate agent for libertarian transformation that acknowledged the changes wrought upon society. The growth in production due to microelectronics and information technology is considered to have fundamentally derailed the socialist project.[75] Gorz outlines Marx's account of capitalist forces of production developing particular forms of class and class antagonism.[76] He identifies the key features of Marx's proletariat as immiseration, functional capability, nascent organisational strength and prefigurative habits. The multi-skilled proletariat was the unique revolutionary class for Marx, because it had the complex competencies to operate the technology of modern capitalism but was denied sovereignty over the machinery by capitalist relations of production.[77]

Gorz points out that the proletariat no longer has the historically specific features ascribed to it by marxists. De-skilling caused by automation and the wide distribution of the workforce co-ordinated by heteronomous management has meant that the features ascribed to a uniquely revolutionary class no longer apply. Technical expansion has permanently affected the role of the marxist subject. The skilled hand employed in large-scale industries (the mass worker) has become dispersed into smaller, replaceable units, and is less prone to union discipline. The western industrialised workforce have a relatively high standard of living and thus for those who accept the immiseration thesis, the proletariat are no longer in vital need of revolutionary change.[78] Instead Gorz recognises the characteristics of the revolutionary subject in a new neo-proletariat, 'the non-class'.

Automated capitalism has produced a new non-class. The non-class results from the transformation in the labour market. They are a group of individuals who have acquired interchangeable skills through the necessity of flexibility in the new economiy. However, this group has also experienced long periods of unemployment and has not been domesticated by the industrial process. They are a 'non-class' because they no longer have class allegiance to the production process and consequently, for Gorz, no class identity.[79] This increase in leisure time means that the non-class is not marked by capitalist modes of production, and as a result they maintain their autonomy and creativity. As such, they prefigure a new society liberated from alienated labour.[80]

There are a number of criticisms to be made of Gorz's thesis from a libertarian perspective. Firstly, by designating the non-class instead of the industrial proletariat as the revolutionary agent, he repeats the Leninist (or in Gorz's view 'marxist') problem of relying on a purely economic category and consequently seeing resistance in strategic terms. Secondly, Gorz merely inverts Marx's hierarchy. Marx classifies the long-term jobless as part of the lumpenproletariat, a reactionary sub-class rather than a vanguard non-class. By contrast, Gorz creates a taxonomy in which the mantle of revolutionary vanguard goes to those capable of the refusal to work. A lower place is given to those positioned for industrial militancy.[81] While some anarchists regard dropping out as the primary site for activity,[82] others reject this prioritisation.[83] Anarchists, unlike Marx, do not dismiss the unemployed as part of the working class but similarly, in accordance with the ideal, reject identifying one section as the universal class.[84]

The working class (including the pool of surplus labour) in the economic sector are the only ones in this context who can reject work. In the context of other struggles the unemployed are those best suited to act. In the campaigns against the further harassment of social security claimants through the invasive Job Seekers Allowance (JSA), anarchists saw the unemployed as the primary agents of change. Disagreements grew between libertarians and the Leninist left in the anti-JSA campaigns because the latter still regarded the unionised staff who were instrumentally applying the new regulations as the agent of change, rather than the unemployed who were directly affected by the benefit changes.[85] Like the proletariat, the unemployed are subjected to a role predetermined by capitalism, so they too can find methods of resistance in which they play the leading role. As there are similarities of experience and interest with other economically oppressed groups the unemployed can find links of solidarity. But it is not only the unemployed or the industrial manual working class who are the potential agents of change. Transformations in technology create new types of workforce subject to their own forms of oppression as well as those shared by other employees.

4. The Processed World

The revolutionary agent of anarchism extends beyond the Leninist model of the proletariat and Gorz's non-class. Recent class struggle libertarians from America, such as those behind *Processed World* magazine, and those in Britain such as Aufheben, have acknowledged that oppressive circumstances and resistance to these conditions occur in a wide range of economic activities, not only in large scale heavy industries.[86] No oppressed group is the universal vanguard; that is to say that there is no central struggle of the working class that can be universalised across all contexts. Meaningful opposition is not specific to particular groups of the oppressed but can include the service and information sector as well as the unemployed and the industrial workforce.

Further, like the anarchist ideal, *Processed World* illustrates the importance of local context. As technical advances are made in pursuit of surplus labour, occupations within the technological industries alter in their abilities to infringe on the lives of others. As oppressive practices extend or are contained so too new subject identities are formed and these new subjects discover their own innovative methods. A universal distinction between clerical and manual labour or between rural and urban worker is unsustainable when they are both subject to alienating conditions that result from qualitatively similar dominant practices. Although employees in different areas face their own particular forms of oppression, there can be as many areas of similarity between different sectors as within them. For instance, a manual labourer unpacking goods in a bookstore may be subject to the same managerial surveillance as a clerk or computer operator in the same (or even other) employment front(s).

The restructuring of capitalism has altered class positions, but while there has been a well-documented embourgeoisement within certain occupations (such as the increasingly managerial role of Employment Service staff mentioned above) and in trends in consumption, there has been a countervailing process of proletarianisation. Technical and white collar work, which previously had high degrees of autonomy and high status, has been reduced in standing. Increased surveillance and control of such work, abetted by technological change which makes such labour open to a wider section of the labour market, has brought many technicians into the general pool of labour.[87] Certain occupations are constituted by more chaotic power shifts, combining, momentarily, managerial and workers' roles, in what Class War identify as a 'grey area'.[88] *Processed World* describes the subtle graduations in office hierarchy, combined with informal networks of influence that affect the power roles of individual employees. These networks are in a constant process of change.[89] An employee can be carrying out managerial ('order-giving') and working class ('order-taking') roles, depending on context, with hierarchies that constantly readjust and reform. Libertarian confrontations with repressive practices aim to resist the creation of other structures of dominance. In a particular location, different heteronomous powers combine, such as sexism and class oppression. To confront only one form of oppression may assist the expansion of the other. Proletarian Gob declares that efforts to create equal representation of genders for High Court judges would be an assault on a specific manifestation of patriarchy, yet would leave class (and other managerial) divisions intact, if not strengthened. Those who would still be oppressed by the amended judiciary would not be behaving prefiguratively in assisting the revision of their domination.[90]

The fluidity of managerial power is illustrated by changes in the status of the teaching profession. The authoritarianism of many aspects of education has long been a subject of libertarian critique stretching back to such influences on anarchism as Godwin and Rousseau, through to Ivan Illich and Paulo Friere. Contemporary libertarian revolutionaries, such as the Andersons, condemn teachers as part of the dominant class and denounce the professional elite status of its practitioners. Teachers, the Andersons explain in an article originally published in 1988,[91] have a high degree of autonomy which is exercised in the disciplinarian control of children in order to train them for work.[92] However, teaching has undergone substantial changes, as Subversion note. They recognise that while teachers do play a repressive role, the lowering of their status due to less autonomy in the class room over course topics and materials (with the introduction of the National Curriculum in England and Wales) and greater surveillance of their activities, has proletarianised certain fundamental features of their work.[93] Consequently, unlike the Andersons, Subversion accepts that there are aspects of the teachers' employment struggles that can be supported as they represent, in specific contexts, aspects of a libertarian class struggle.

The archetypal anarchist position also considers significant those sections of the workforce dismissed by Leninism as extraneous to the revolutionary struggle. Rural, white collar workers and the unemployed are not only capable of resisting oppressive practices, but in certain localities they are the only ones capable of carrying out libertarian direct action. The ideal paradigm also extends beyond economic relations. However, before examining this aspect of anarchism's conception of the agents of change, it is important to show how consistent anarchists' understanding of the revolutionary identity extends outside the realm of immediate production and labour.

5. Extension of Class: The social factory

The autonomist critique of Leninism concerned the latter's concentration on production in the workplace, whereas for autonomists the point of production is not the sole site for the extraction of surplus labour. All aspects of social life are commodified in pursuit of greater profit. Consequently not only the factory worker, but also those who prepare the worker for production, through housework, education and upbringing, are part of the production process.[94] All those subjected to capital's need for greater consumption constitute the working class ('the socialised worker').[95] Maria Dalla Costa includes all those involved in productive labour from which a surplus can be drawn. Class struggle therefore also extends beyond employee/employer struggles in the industrial setting.[96] As areas of leisure become subject to capitalist relations and priorities of profit, culture itself becomes an arena for class struggle. This extension of capitalist relations has altered the terms and terrain of the conflict between the classes, but has not eradicated it.[97] The situationists refer to the subjection of leisure and communication to capitalist modes of production, distribution and exchange as 'the spectacle'.

The tendency by Leninists is to regard class as being primarily located at the industrial or productive sites. Writers like Gorz also regret that the industrial workforce is no longer the vanguard capable of eradicating the basis for repressive social relations. By contrast, anarchists ascribe a pre-eminent role to proletarians only when facing specific types of oppression within the industrial context, whilst in different circumstances they regard other types of worker or subjugated group to be potential agents of change. The anarchists' notion of struggle does not rely on a centralised strategy, but conceives of the arena of conflict more tactically, as one arranged along multifaceted, interconnected webs of oppression.[98]

Castoriadis (also known as Paul Cardan and Pierre Chaulieu), whose group and journal *Socialisme ou Barbarie* had a large influence on contemporary British libertarians, especially Solidarity,[99] reformulated the class question not in terms of ownership of the means of production, but in terms of control of production, thereby switching the focus from exploitation to alienation. The central contradiction was of workers being objectified by bureaucratic capitalism although the system of administration requires worker participation in order to renew and develop such management. Castoriadis's reworking of the dynamics of capitalist oppression revolved around the notions of bureaucratic management ('order-givers') and the executants ('order-takers').[100] The tension manifests itself in production but increasingly penetrates into all aspects of social life, as described by autonomist marxists. For Aufheben, Castoriadis's revision was not an overhaul of Marx. These critical marxists interpret Marx as having detected that capital accumulation requires the transformation of people into objects, thus reducing their autonomy, and that profitable production needs the active participation and ingenuity of the workforce. Castoriadis's modification of Marx does not replace capital's drive to accumulate but is just another aspect of it.[101] The autonomist interpretation of Marx differs from the Leninist readings favoured by Gorz and Harman.

For Castoriadis, what links the working class is not the same experience of industrial work, as in Harman's revolutionary subject, but the same feature of being reduced from subject to an object by capitalism.[102] Thus, Gorz's non-class is not uniquely privileged, as all order-takers are potential revolutionary subjects. So too in Class War's analysis, those who are 'told what to do', those subjected to power, are the working class.[103] 'Order giving' is contextual, an employee in one situation can be subjected to managerial control, yet in another situation the same person might use and maintain such routines of bureaucracy against others.

Similarly, the economic well-being of sections of the industrial working class does not prevent them from participating in a potentially revolutionary position. Their status as skilled workers makes them essential to the success of the social transformation, along with other sections of the working class, while the shared experience of alienation, even if of an increasingly spectacular kind, still provides the vital need for change. The Situationist Raoul Vaneigem satirises the type of argument put forward by Gorz:

> We hear from some quarters that in the advanced industrial countries the proletariat no longer exists, that it has disappeared forever under an avalanche of sound systems, colour TVs, water-beds, two-car garages and swimming pools. Others denounce this as a sleight of hand and indignantly point out a few remaining workers whose low wages and wretched conditions do undeniably evoke the nineteenth century.[104]

This is not to say that the material conditions of the working class are unimportant. Capital and wealth provide one form of power and as John Casey, then of Class War, notes, this is one reason to support pay rises for the working class.[105] More important than actual wealth is the nexus of interrelated forms of power, of which wealth is but one, where people can influence the lives of others or impose heteronomous forms of governance, such as that of capital. Class War refer to this network of forces as 'social power'.[106]

The revision of marxism offered by Castoriadis and the situationists concerns itself with how economic oppression leads to the extension of capital relations into all aspects of life, creating servitude amongst abundance. Heteronomous power is now identified throughout a bricolage (intertwined sections) of social relations rather than directly through economic relations. The historical context which led to the development of the Castoriadis-Situationist thesis of growing wealth of the working class (especially in the West) has altered in recent years, with evidence showing that in Britain from 1979-93 the economically disadvantaged became significantly worse off.[107] Despite the change in economic circumstances, the relevance of the extension of oppressive forces into all aspects of social life remains pertinent.

Traditional marxism assigned strategic importance to the workings of the economic base over the ideological superstructure (politics, law, culture) whereas anarchism perceives a reciprocal relationship between them.[108] The class struggle extends into the community and cultural arenas as well as the economy. This expanded notion of capitalism also extends the category of the working class, and therefore the potential revolutionary subject. For anarchists, all those who are subjugated by capitalism, who contribute to the extraction of surplus labour in the whole of the social factory, are working class, whether they are located in the industrial sector or preparing and reproducing capital relations in domestic, social and cultural life. Consequently, the working class includes the proletariat but also the non-class, domestic labourers, white collar employees and school students.[109]

The central feature and problem of this form of analysis, as May submits, is that capital still remains central and anti-capitalist conflict the key struggle, even if the sites of this warfare extend beyond the industrial and workplace arenas.[110] The weakness is that this analysis risks reductivism. The ACF acknowledge this flaw and suggest that some forms of oppression, such as gender and racial power, pre-date capitalism. Groups that maintain a strategic conception of struggle, with one source of oppressive power, namely capitalism, consider divisions of race, gender and sexuality to be superstructural. These struggles threaten to lessen class unity and therefore should be rejected on those grounds alone. This can lead to three types of responses. The first two are strategic – either to be concerned about discriminatory practices only when they affect the working class (like Proletarian Gob),[111] or to regard any sexist or racist behaviour as encouraging class divisions.[112] A third response, compatible with the ideal, regards capital relations to be dominant in most contexts, but not the sole organising force. This third response recognises that capitalism interacts with other forms of oppressive practices that may not be wholly reducible to economic activity. Here different subjugated identities are formed and it is these agents that must take the leading role. However, as capitalism is still a significant factor, economic liberation must also be a necessary feature.

The criticisms of class analysis are a feature of the wider anarchist movement who have often commented on what is excluded from these formulations, in particular those agents who do not identify with, or fall outside of, the subject class. McKay cites those activists who consider themselves middle class as examples of those excluded.[113] He holds that environmental activism exceeds the remit of class, where wider social movements hold sway. As will be seen, other explanatory traditions, feminism and postcolonial studies, also maintain that their explicatory frameworks are not reducible solely to class terms.[114] However, the anarchist view of the revolutionary subject has fluid, multiple identities. Liberation involves avoiding reductivist uniformity and instead frees non-hierarchical differences.

6. Ethnicity, Gender and Sexuality

The anarchist concept of the revolutionary subject extends beyond the proletarian categories of Leninism: it includes those in mass production, other forms of industry and preparatory labour, and those subjected to capitalist demands in their leisure and living conditions. Nonetheless, these accounts, shared by some class struggle anarchists, have been strategic in that the oppressive forces are thought to emanate from one source, namely capitalism. The question of whether all forms of oppression, such as racism, homophobia and patriarchy, have a single origin in capitalism has been a difficult question for anarchism. It has often been dealt with in a contradictory manner, or ignored. However, a position is discernible within many contemporary class struggle groupings that reject a strategic position and are close to a poststructuralist position.

Early British radical publications such as the *The Worker* portrayed the traditional anti-semitic caricatures associated with such luminaries as Fourier and, allegedly, Proudhon and Bakunin.[115] However, British anarchists past and present have been active in campaigns against discrimination, whether in groups dominated by refugee East European Jewry, led by Rocker, or more contemporarily Anti-Fascist Action (AFA) and other anti-racist networks. Similarly, the complementary influences of anarchism and feminism were due to the recognition by anarchists that self-organisation is required to prevent paternalism. This meant support for autonomous women's and black groupings, for where racism and sexism existed it was primarily, but not exclusively, up to those excluded to determine the appropriate forms of resistance. In the 1970s and 1980s there were close working relationships between women's and anarchist groups, as well as the formation of active anarcha-feminist sections.[116]

Some British anarchists differ from the ideal as, although they recognise that wage-labour is not the only form of oppression, these other forms of hierarchy are often seen as still emanating from a single source, the economic modes and relations of production. Earlier groups, such as the Anarchist Workers Association (AWA) in 1977, had explained in their 'Aims and Principles' that sexism and racism were results of capitalist forms of production and exchange: 'The class nature of society is reflected in all the dominant philosophies: class, race, sexual, social and personal relationships. The class relationships are expressed through all social relationships and generate attitudes such as racism and sexism.'[117] The dynamics of capitalism initiate the other forms of oppression. These are sometimes seen as epiphenomenal (by-products) of capitalism, as having a separate dynamic to economic forces. Big Flame, for instance, cite the way racial and sexual ideologies, generated to protect the economic interests of an elite, adversely affect the drive for surplus which they were originally brought about to promote.[118]

Nonetheless, the strategic strands of anarchism see economic forces as the primary cause of sexism, and this single site is the strategic place for confronting oppressive powers:

> The struggle against sexual oppression is integral to the struggle against the whole of this society, i.e. the class struggle. There is little class unity, while sexism is a force in the working class.
>
> [....] Feminism seeks to emphasise the common interests of women of all classes at the expense of their class interests. Unless the working class develops and maintains a *class analysis* of their position in society then they will remain the dupes of the ruling class.[119]

The Andersons share a similar explanation for the development of racism. They regard it, straightforwardly, as a product of capitalist administration: 'In a depraved attempt to justify their atrocities against Africans, several of the middle class managers of the [slave] trade widely publicised the profound lie that Africans were sub-normal heathens with an inherent inferiority.'[120] According to this analysis, racist ideology is simply a superstructural by-product of class domination.

The radical feminist Valerie Solanas also saw social conflict as a simple strategic one between two distinct opposing forces: in her view, a battle between male and female. Maleness, which is incomplete, inferior and biologically inadequate, clashes with female attributes, as these are the ones that essential masculinity lacks, both genetically and psychologically.[121] In this form of feminism, which is not unique to Solanas, other expressions of exploitation are extensions of this gender opposition.[122] Class and gender binary oppositions have been subject to a number of fierce critiques because of their reductivism (disparate, complex events being given the same simple, foundational account, and thus ignores differences). Ryan, writing in Class War's magazine *The Heavy Stuff*, for instance, indicates the authoritarian character of assuming there is a single source of oppression.[123] Such attempts to impose on diverse social struggles a single political determinant applied universally, regardless of context, assumes a metaphysical belief in a singular source of power: an origin which is fundamentally unknowable. In addition, the imposition of this single dominant (and epistemologically unchallengeable) viewpoint on struggles leads to dictatorial forms of organisation.

Dalla Costa's attempt at resolving the division between gender and class opposition through extending the definition of the agent of change from the industrial worker across to all those involved in production and reproduction, nevertheless still remains reductivist. This is because 'feminist struggle [...] is assimilated within the working class movement'.[124] The stretching of the category 'class' to reapply it to feminist concerns is considered by Kathi Weeks to lose the specificity of its explanatory force as well as reducing feminist analysis to a sub-set of marxism.[125] Weeks is right to be wary of attempts to subsume other identities into economic classifications. The efforts of Leninists to contain other agents of resistance are part of their strategy of directing opposition. The autonomist critique of Leninism does not avoid the ascription of pre-eminence to the economic, yet Dalla Costa's work does indicate the multiplicity of class identities without reducing the importance and precision of class analysis.

Many anarchist activists become aware of oppression through direct experience of capitalist authority. As a result, there has been a tendency to continue to use terms like 'class' to identify the origins of oppression even when they may not be wholly economic or when the structures of reification are too well hidden to be accurately articulated. The domination of Leninism has meant a foreshortening of the vocabulary of explanation. Terms such as 'class' are used to describe forms of domination that may not be wholly (or predominantly) economic in origin. The use of a singular category (and one with its origins in economic analysis) leads to an inadvertently inaccurate designate of the agent of change and the imposition of the direction of solidarity, a situation incompatible with anti-representation.

Figure 3.1. Working Class Fights Back, front cover of *Class War*, 1985.

Yet the category is meant to indicate multiplicity. A poststructural reading of the anarchist notion of 'class' propounds a positive reclamation of urban conflict from the exclusive categories of 1980s identity politics that saw Black struggles as distinct and separate from other forms of conflict (fig. 3.1.).[126]

It attempts to avoid analysing events through a singular category of oppression as this leads to missing important specificities, as recognised by Gilroy. Conflicts, such as the urban riots of 1981 (which included Brixton, Handsworth, Moss Side, Southall and Toxteth) and 1985 (most notably Brixton and Handsworth (again) and Tottenham), are represented as racial in character while empirical evidence suggests that the main participants were not distinguished by racial origin.[127] An anarchist analysis, like Gilroy's criticisms of the reports of the riots, indicates how the uprisings were misrepresented as resulting from a singular (racial) source of oppression.[128] Urban conflicts whose actors were predominantly from ethnic minorities, such as the Los Angeles riots of 1992, were popularly caricatured as race riots. Anarchists interpreted these clashes differently. Libertarian analyses of these incidents, which were sometimes in the form of reports by participants,[129] described the disturbances in terms of class conflicts against capitalism, rather than in terms of race. Analysis using a single universal determinant, whether of ethnicity or economics,are critical approaches rejected by the ideal, as consistent anarchisms hold that in different contexts different forms of oppression operate.[130]

Rosemarie Tong identifies a system of analysis that avoids reducing one form of oppression to another. Tong's 'division of labour' account has the same attributes as the archetypal anarchist (but not the Leninist) description of the revolutionary agent:

> [A Leninist] class analysis aims to scan the system of production as a whole, focusing on the means and relations of production in the most general terms possible, a division-of-labour analysis pays attention to the individual people who do the producing in society. In other words, a [Leninist] class analysis calls for only the most abstract discussion of the respective roles of the bourgeoisie and the proletariat, whereas a division-of-labour analysis requires a detailed, very concrete discussion of, for example, who gives the orders

and who takes them, who does the stimulating work and who does the drudge work, who works the desirable shift and who works the undesirable shift, and who gets paid more and who gets paid less.[131]

Tong's analysis applied originally to the division of labour in and around the workplace, but her technique can equally be applied across the social factory. Tong recognises that society is a complex web of interacting forces that cannot be disentangled entirely and whose compositions differ between locations. As a result, her micro-analytical method is pertinent for locations where race and ethnicity, as well as class and gender, are significant.[132] Tong's technique is concordant with approaches identified as specifically anarcha-feminist by Carol Ehrlich, in which localised power relations, whether of class or gender, are examined in their particular context.[133] Tong's method is not complete, for different methods may be relevant to different contexts. For instance, on other terrain it may be necessary to take account of not only the giving and taking of orders, but also of the degree of latitude that the order-givers have in issuing their directives. Such an analysis would require an investigation into the structural processes that promote one individual or group over another. But Tong's approach indicates that there are multiple processes at work in creating a repressive social practice and that these alter according to domain.

A subjugated class within a specific context may have many different causes; as a result, methods of analysis and forms of resistance must be cognisant of the ways that capital relations extend beyond the site of production, and recognise that in some contexts other forms of oppression operate. The phrase 'working class', in some writings within the class struggle tradition, refers to the myriad oppressed subject positions formed from the nexus of forces that constitute social space. The potentially misleading use of the phrase 'working class' is akin to the employment of the term 'capitalism' to forces which are not solely economic or reducible to the economic but refer to the historical period when the dominant forms of production, distribution and exchange were based on capital accumulation. Ideal anarchist class analysis lies in its ability to recognise, locate and contest the forms of power that operate within given situations. Contemporary anarchisms recognise that diffuse forces operate and consequently different subjects take to the fore in opposing these constraints.

The archetypal anarchist analysis of oppression is distinct from the singular oppositions of class proposed by some libertarians such as Proletarian Gob. The libertarian ideal regards other struggles as having separate dynamics, with sets of relationships which are not reducible to capital relations alone (and in some circumstances capitalism may not be a dominant factor). The ACF, for instance, notes that patriarchy is not reducible to capitalism as the former predates the latter:

> Equally important is the division between the sexes, which first appeared before history and was the blueprint for later forms of oppression, such as class, race and disability. The ideology of hierarchy is practised in the home, the workplace, the school, indeed in all relationships, for example sexual harassment at work, male violence, women's unpaid domestic labour and exclusion from all major areas of decision-making. Many racial groups also experience intolerable discrimination as seen in apartheid, anti-Semitism and everyday experience of racial minorities in Britain.[134]

The ACF and Attack International recognise that gender divisions are not the result of capitalism, even if these boundaries are manipulated by dominant economic classes.[135] *Green Anarchist,* too, is critical of other anarchists for trying to reduce all forms of oppression to a single origin: '[A]lthough capitalism has deepened certain forms of oppression such as racism and sexism it's a complete lie to see it as being their sole cause.'[136] Recognition of other forms of oppression as well as class conflict is not to reject or relegate class to other determinants, nor to propose simply a dual system of patriarchy and capitalism. Instead, the ideal affirms a multiple system in which different oppressive practices may be situated depending on location, although in certain contexts (maybe most) capitalism is dominant.

Class War, because of its wide membership, has writers promoting contradictory views. On the one hand there are those in the group who share Proletarian Gob's view, which relegates racism and sexism to epiphenomena of capitalism: 'anti-racism has to be anti-capitalist by it's [sic] very nature – because that is the source of racism.'[137] On the other hand there are those who consider other forms of oppression, such as patriarchy, as pre-capitalist; thus sexism occurs across all classes. 'Sexism means the oppression and putting down of women just because we are women, implying we are of lesser importance than men. All women experience this to varying degrees according to what class they live in.'[138] A reconciliation between these two positions is possible, as Class War goes on to explain, in that the economic overcodes pre-capitalist hegemonic practices: 'While this division predates capitalism and came from religion, it has been used by capitalists for their own end.'[139]

The lack of clarity over whether sexism and/or racism is a product of capitalism or existed prior to capitalism and has been subsequently overcoded to suit its (capital's) requirements is repeated throughout anarchist writings. The former Black Panther Lorenzo Kom'boa Ervin is one of the few contemporary libertarians to attempt a critique of anarchism from a Black perspective. He, however, also fails to resolve this apparent contradiction. Like the Andersons and Gob he believes that Black oppression has its roots in capitalism. '[I]t is the capitalist bourgeoisie that creates inequality as a way to divide and rule over the entire working class. White skin privilege is a form of *domination* by Capital over White labour as well as oppressed national labour.'[140] Yet he also suggests that 'the capitalist used the system of White skin privilege to great effect',[141] signifying that racism pre-existed and was incorporated into capitalism. Near the end of his tract Ervin posits another hypothesis that, rather than racism being a product of capitalism, capitalism is a product of racism: 'The Capitalist system was created by and is maintained by enslavement and colonial oppression.'[142]

Such confusion is hardly surprising, for activists like Ervin are more concerned with identifying how, and in what forms, racism and class oppression are experienced in the present context than about discerning their origins (tracing origins might be a task which is impossible). Regardless of whether racism has its roots in capitalism, has been generated separate to it or been overcoded into a form of capitalism, what matters for Ervin are the methods for dealing with oppression. Carol Ehrlich determines that the purpose of analysis is to assist in the 'thousands of small battles which go into daily living (and the not so small ones as well)'.[143] It is less the origins of subjugation but how it manifests itself in particular terrain and how it can be effectively conquered that is important.

The oppression affecting the Black working class in the West is often different to that of the White working class. Consequently, as the appropriate agents are identified through oppressed subject positions, the agent for change against racism and capitalism is, in this context, the Black working class. Ervin encourages Black working class groups to take the lead in resisting predominantly racist phenomena and the oppressive forces operating in Black localities, but promotes a wider confederation of libertarian working class organisations to deal with forms of class oppression.[144] In the setting of anti-patriarchal actions, women are the agents of change;[145] in anti-racist movements, those in subjugated ethnic minorities are the appropriate subjects.[146] However, in most contexts discriminatory practices are rarely made up of only one form of oppression, especially as capitalism extends further into all aspects of social life. Black anti-racist struggles have reciprocal relations, in many contexts, with anti-capitalist and White workers confronting state restraints. Black Flag reported on Newham Monitoring Project (NMP), whose main activities were in confronting organised fascists (groups such as the British National Party and – prior to that – the National Front) and institutional racism, primarily in the local police. Although the NMP was mainly a Black organisation it took on the case of a White working class family who had also been subject to police harassment. NMP began to combine concerns of race with those of class.[147]

Rather than concentrate upon a single locus of repression, anarchist writings see oppression as a result of the wider nexus of power. For example, Sean Reilly of Class War explains that merely dropping out of middle class employment, or squatting in a working class neighbourhood, does not fundamentally alter one's position. The squatter's social power may remain high due to connections with other informal coalitions of influence such as family background or old school connections.[148] So too feminist struggles or Black resistance that fail to take class into account will merely reform capitalism for the benefit of a particular section of that oppressed group. A rising bourgeoisie is created to the detriment of working class women and men, White and Black.[149] The tendency in class struggle anarchism, especially amongst the autonomists, is to see capitalism as the most powerful factor, with economic concerns having greater priority in almost all contexts.[150] The disposition towards a strategic conception of capitalism, in contrast to the tactical approach of the anarchist ideal, is partly a hangover of the influence of Leninism and partly a result of the contexts in which contemporary British anarchists have operated. Managerial structures to further extend the search for surplus value are a dominant factor in most contemporary British situations, especially those where anarchists have been active, such as in strike support and anti-Poll Tax campaigns.

The phrase 'working class' is a potentially misleading synonym for the oppressed. Such a phrase should not suggest that there is a romantic vision of an essentially moral set of industrious individuals, straining to create the revolution on behalf of others, although there are occasionally such sentimental images in Bakunin and Kropotkin.

Nor is the frequency of the term standing for 'the oppressed' in anarchism a commitment to an economically reductionist account. The repeated occurrence of the 'working class' is probably due to the fact that anarchists themselves are located in contexts where economic oppression is the main form of domination so consequently workers are the main group(s) capable of making social transformation of a libertarian kind. It is through the oppressed recognising and acting to overthrow hierarchical structures and create in their place egalitarian social relations that anarchism takes place. In the process of contestation avenues of solidarity open up which provide opportunities to create prefigurative relationships with other subjugated agents.

7. Antagonisms and Solidarity

For the anarchist archetype not all social antagonisms are determined by class oppositions, a view endorsed by Laclau and Mouffe. They reject what they consider to be an essentialist hegemony in which all subjected positions are unified under production and class.[151] In its place Laclau and Mouffe attempt to rebuild a socialist praxis out of the multitude of subjugated positions, whether these are based on class, race, age, sexuality, ethnicity or gender. As there is no irreducible single contradiction, such as that between worker and capital, there is no universal revolutionary subject. Just as forms of power and their intersections are in continual flux, often responding to countervailing forms of resistance, so too arenas of antagonism and identities of radical subjects are also altering. A form of democratic solidarity is proposed by Laclau and Mouffe where there are temporary equivalences, rather than fixed identities of conflict.[152]

These new socialisms, embodied in social forms by the likes of solidarity networks, have been promoted by Laclau and Mouffe and, latterly, moulded by May into a 'poststructuralist anarchism'. This recognises a multiplicity of forces, not reducible to a single unifying cause – that of capitalism for Harman or gender for Solanas, although both are recognised as major, but not sole, determinants. This poststructural libertarianism also warns against the imposition of solidarity from without. Political programs that predetermined which groups should combine in struggle recreate hegemony, as they suggest that subjects capable of resistance have fixed identities whose interests can be directly known by others. Instead, the anarchist archetype suggests that those in the localised subject position discover and create links. *Subversion*, for instance, criticise the Leninist group Militant for rejecting autonomous organisations of Blacks and gays on the grounds that they should subsumed under a single class-based organisation.[153]

A strategic analysis imposes links of solidarity. Where economic class is seen as the sole determinant the working class victims of homophobia are expected to join a proletarian party, which may not be the most appropriate structure for confronting this particular form of oppression. So too Black nationalists urge oppressed non-Whites to unite into a single organisation, regardless of class differences, even though economic oppression may be, in many contexts, the dominant disciplining force. The situationist-inspired Larry Law in his analogy warns against making inappropriate links, such as when superficial similarities are confused with mutually discovered shared interests and desires: "'Don't worry", said the trees when they saw the axe coming, "The handle is one of us".'[154]

The archetypal anarchist accepts that in some social forms the economic is subservient to other practices, but this is not to say that it falls to the same criticisms which have been made against Laclau and Mouffe. Best and Kellner noted that Laclau and Mouffe fail to raise the question of whether certain practices and forces are more central in forming the political hegemony and therefore in creating the political identities of those who will transform capitalist society.[155] For class struggle anarchists, the reply is still that it depends on context, but that as capitalism extends into more areas of social life, overcoding other oppressive forces, it is this which appears as the dominant power. Correspondingly, even in those contexts where other oppressive practices are dominant, without the inclusion of a critique and response to capitalism the project would not be libertarian as other oppressive forces would remain and become primary.

Similarly, the grounds for solidarity for Laclau and Mouffe are far from transparent. For anarchists, all forms of oppressive power must be confronted. To concentrate on just one root of the rhizome would allow others to flourish unchecked. Consequently, anti-sexist struggles which failed to take into account capitalism would merely reform the economic order, ensuring traditional class domination.[156] Similarly, anti-capitalist activity that did not recognise other forms of oppression would recreate hierarchy.[157]

Poststructuralism concentrates on the micropolitical, where converging local struggles create new forms of resistance. Such opposition is irreducible to a single strategy. As May points out, this coheres with many anarchist practices, in particular with direct action, in which the actors affected are the main agents of change. By rejecting a universal, original determinant, anarchists cannot universally identify an appropriate agent without recourse to the context. The category 'class' is not reductive in the Leninist sense as it refers to multiple oppressed subject positions, including those where the economic is not dominant. However, contemporary British anarchists would maintain that there were few contexts where capitalism was not a factor, and possibly even the major determinant.[158] Oppressed agents are subjugated in more than one location. Recognising areas of similarity in these hierarchical practices as well as sharing experiences with other oppressed groups assists in recognising grander forces of domination and methods of resistance.

The notion of 'class' in contemporary British anarchism has expanded. In the past its use was restricted. 'Class' referred to agents in predominantly male, occidental environments. The anarchist category of 'class' has extended beyond the proletariat – a specific agent located at the point of production, in a particular socio-historical era. Gorz recognised that the 'proletariat' as a revolutionary subject was specific to industrialism, and that new agents were being formed as a result of technological development. Nonetheless, Gorz's new revolutionary subject, the non-class, was still identified primarily in terms of a static relationship to production. *Processed World*, by contrast, avoids the limitations of Gorz's non-class, as it recognises that power relations in the workplace are more fluid and contingent; even so, it still concentrates on the arena of production. The Situationists and autonomists expand the analysis of class beyond the immediate sphere of production. The search for surplus labour extends managerial relationships into all aspects of social life, embroiling domestic, social and cultural activity into the arena of class struggle. Nevertheless, the autonomists still maintain that the economic has a universal, strategic role. Learning from Black peoples' and women's struggles, the anarchist concept of 'class' recognises that other forms of oppression have priority in some contexts. In these locations different subjugated identities have precedence, as liberation requires the oppressed themselves to overthrow their oppression.

The persistence of 'class', a term associated with economic determinism, is due to anarchism's origins in industrial struggles. Self-identifying anarchists tend to be in social terrain where economic oppression dominates. However, the four principles of anarchism on which the *ideal* form of anarchism is constructed recognise that subject identities are fluid and irreducible to a single hegemonic identity. Recognising one's subjugated position, as Tong points out, assists in developing tactics to resist oppressive power, but the search for origins of oppression is not always possible. Like Ervin, Tong suggests that investigation into oppression is far less important than the attempt to overcome and supersede these hegemonic forces without recreating hierarchy.[159] Organisation is required to create anti-hierarchical social relations that are self-affirming as well as resistant to oppressive power. In order to be consistent with the anarchist ideal these structures must be prefigurative.

Chapter Four

Organisation

A revolutionary organisation rejects any reproduction within itself of the hierarchical structures of contemporary society.[1]

Introduction

The previous chapters portray contemporary anarchisms as fluid, polymorphous movements. They are comprised of interweaving sets of temporary groupings that lack specific origins and are without a single, central, universal goal. This makes linear narrative accounts of anarchism, such as those encouraged by traditional academic strictures, particularly problematic. Special difficulty arises in the case of organisation because (as raised in the previous chapter) anarchist methods vary according to the identity of the agents in question. Nonetheless, the types of relationships formed by oppressed subjects are an essential feature of anarchism. The types of social interaction that are developed in accordance with the four criteria of the anarchist ideal are part of the process of the class in itself becoming the class for itself. The development of organisations as prefigurative acts is explicitly stated by the ACF. 'Creating organisations that have a revolutionary structure is an act of revolution itself. [....]. Only through the dynamics of working together can we achieve the unity of activity and theory necessary to bring about a free and equal society'.[2]

There is an intimate connection between formal structures, the identity of agents, tactics and aims. There are different organisational systems, such as centralism, federalism and cellular, which have distinctive co-ordinating and governing principles. There are also different types of anarchist organisation; these are often based on their primary function or location. This chapter divides these organisational types into workplace and non-workplace ('community'). Whilst different systems might be associated with particular organisational types – centralism with the revolutionary party, cell structures with terrorist groups and affinity groups – these sorts of organisation can be governed by other systems.

In turn there are particular methods associated with these different organisational systems and types. Workplace structures based on formalised systems of co-ordination (such as trade unions or revolutionary syndicates) tend to be associated with industrial tactics like strike action. Groups based in the community are more frequently connected with methods such as propaganda by deed, squatting and social theft. Organisational structures are conditional on context, methods and agents involved. Individuals who believe they are an elite group will create a vanguard organisation and will tend towards centralised, secretive bodies that use methods which do not require mass support. Bodies that favour legal methods, such as propaganda-by-word, may tend towards more open structures.

Anarchist groupings have used both flexible, dispersed associations, and more centralised, rigid systems with prescribed structural blueprints. Thus, there are examples of hierarchical local anarchist campaigns as well as those based on a more adaptable federated form. Just as some libertarian groups have adopted a Leninist analysis of the revolutionary subject so too they have adopted similar forms of organisation. As the autonomist-influenced Red Menace points out, many anarchists, like orthodox marxists, have made the mistake of wanting a more equitable form of management instead of the more consistent libertarian ambition of abolishing all forms of hierarchy.[3] However, although certain anarchist structures are inconsistent with the archetype, the most significant contemporary movements have created structures that are consistent with the prefigurative ideal.

The ideal stresses the importance of regarding organisation as pragmatic and contextual, embodying the desires of those constructing and utilising it.[4] Many of the most innovative libertarian actions have come about through organisational methods consistent with the ideal. Local activist networks, and the J18, N30 and Mayday 2000-3 co-ordinating bodies involved different groups coming together where interests coincided without attempting to impose a single agenda upon all those attending.

While Mayday 1998 saw anarchist activities centred on just one location (Bradford), others like J18, N30 and the later Maydays saw events taking place in many more locations. British protests on N30 were concurrent with the larger scale ones in Seattle, USA where the World Trade Organisation (WTO) was attempting to meet to further expand neo-liberal policies both on western and non-occidental populations. The British activities were not just in support of the larger Seattle demonstrations but also advanced local concerns. Anarchist organisation, in its ideal form, is de-centred and federal in nature. Participating anarchist groups use a variety of anti-hierarchical organisational methods; in their ideal form they are temporary and fluid. The anarchist archetype recognises that different types of organisation appeal to different types of agent, and promote and support distinctive forms of tactic.

As the forces of decomposition attempt to restrain liberatory movements, so too contrary phenomena occur such as the development of new alliances and the evolution of novel forms of confrontation. Multiple organisation is required to overcome diverse forms of capitalist forces. These fluid structures encompass and construct different and changing identities. To use a commonplace example, the miners in the 1984-5 confrontation with the second Thatcher government used both their trade union organisation and also informal community structures. The latter sometimes took a covert and informal form such as the hit squads that sabotaged NCB and police property. This communal resistance created new active agencies, such as the groupings run by women from the coalfields who became increasingly influential throughout the strikers' campaign.[5] Class struggle anarchist organisations are likewise multiple, changing, reactive and proactive. The membership of appropriate anarchist movements must also be responsive to and constituted by the appropriate agent of change.[6] As a result of the micro-political identification of the working class (see previous chapter), the forms of organisation have to be flexible and multiform. This was a characteristic of anarchism as far back as the mid-1880s[7] and is still maintained today: 'Organisations [...] will be fluid and flexible': they 'have the ability to change or cease as circumstances dictate'.[8]

Although organisation, tactic and agent are intrinsically connected, for ease of explication this chapter deals predominantly with the organisational structures in isolation from their tactical connections as these are discussed in the next chapter. It will show that commonly held views conflating anarchism with the rejection of organisation (sometimes referred to as 'anti-organisation' or 'dis-organisation') or with any single particular formal structure are misplaced. While certain types of organisation are incompatible with an ideal tactical libertarianism, such as the vanguard party, there is no single universally appropriate method of organising.

The perception of anarchism as antipathetic to formal structures is not entirely inaccurate. Certain types of anti-organisation are consistent with a prefigurative libertarian ethic: so too are arrangements which are flexible and de-centred, which have been confused with disorder. However, other anarchists who have witnessed the apparent success of Leninist and social-democratic organisational arrangements have either wanted to imitate them or reacted against them. Various types of formal structure are adopted by anarchist groupings. The different centralised, federated, networked, democratic or dictatorial forms are examined in terms of their prefigurative content. Some are shown to be incompatible with anarchism, while the ideal types are those that are flexible, multiform coalitions created by oppressed subject groups themselves.

The final sections deal with the locality of the anarchist organisation, whether based in the workplace or in the community, and the types of agent involved and excluded. This includes consideration of whether, like anarchist syndicates, organisations are open for any person (employed in a particular sector) to join regardless of their ideological consciousness, or whether, like revolutionary groups, only those already committed to a particular set of principles may join. This will demonstrate that structures that are most adaptable, tactical and de-centred are the most appropriate to libertarians' prefigurative ethic.

1. Anti-Organisation

A common misconception, feverishly contested by contemporary libertarians, is that anarchism is identical to a lack of, or even antagonism towards, organisation and a concomitant approval of chaos.[9] Like the identification of anarchism with violence, the efforts at disassociation merely help to reinforce the general stereotype, although there are strands of anarchism that are explicitly and uniquely anti-organisation. The impassioned statements in favour of strong, but particular, forms of organisation suggest that only groupings with a reputation for the opposite would need to make such overt declarations. Consider, for instance, the pronouncement by Malatesta, endorsed by the ACF, that, 'Anarchism is organisation, organisation and more organisation'[10] and Class War's announcement: '*Why do we need Organisation?* The short answer is that if people are to achieve any objective involving a number of others then some kind of organisation is necessary.'[11]

Part of the explanation for this perception that anarchists are anti-organisation was the pre-eminence of Leninism in radical circles, which had strict interpretations concerning appropriate industrial and revolutionary structures.[12] Because of the tightly-defined formal structures normally associated with the term 'organisation', there is a tendency for many critics to believe that libertarians have rejected organisation even when they have formal, if somewhat more flexible, guidelines. Anarchists reject the rigid hierarchies and centralism of Leninist revolutionary organisational practice[13] as such methods are incompatible with their prefigurative principles of the abolition of hierarchies and the promotion of autonomous, creative power.[14]

Multiple and flexible organisation, concordant with the anarchist ideal, is not the same as the rejection of association. Nor is the rejection of organisation the same as inadequate or inappropriate structures. Promotion of diverse organisation is not the sole cause of the (mis-) association of anarchism with anti-organisation. There are currents within the libertarian tradition that are suspicious of not only the familiar organisational arrangements based on hierarchy and coercion, but also of any formal structures. Activists and theorists regard the lack of a clear organisational arrangement as one of main frailties shared by all the anarchisms. Liberal critics, too, have associated anarchism with anti-organisation. The historian F. G. Clarke comments that the 1905 Russian Revolution failed to take a decisively anarchist direction not because there was inadequate support for libertarianism but because its mode of operation made it difficult for them to act effectively. 'There were many sympathizers with the libertarian philosophy espoused by the anarchists, but by its very nature it was a belief that made tight organisation and activity almost impossible.'[15] Joll, also, proposes that anarchists failed to take a decisive role in revolutionary situations because: '[T]heir principles made organisation so difficult.'[16] However, in the instances that Clarke and Joll cite, it was inappropriate co-operative structures, not a rejection of organisation, that was responsible for anarchism's historical failures.

There are three types of anti-organisation. The first rejects all organisation on a supposedly prefigurative basis. The second rejects all forms of organisation prior to the revolutionary period, but supports spontaneous revolutionary structures, such as the self-managed soviets of 1905 or the Hungarian workers' councils of 1956. This type of anti-organisation is found most clearly in the council communist tendencies (referred to as councilists). The final form of anti-organisation only rejects any formal structure which is imposed on the revolutionary agent. This latter type of anti-organisation is the most compatible with the micropolitical anti-representational characteristics of contemporary British libertarianism. As the revolutionary agent is context-dependent, it has different organisational requirements that promote multiple, flexible structures.

1.1. The First Form of Spontaneity: Chaosism

Anti-organisational tendencies associated with anarchism are not solely the result of malicious misrepresentation, as there are sections of anarchism that appear to celebrate the rejection of any form of organisation. The anonymous writer of the early 1980s tract *Oh No Not Again* proposes examining relationships in order to cut down dependency, whether mutual or otherwise.[17] One of the reasons for this popular connection with disorder may be due, according to Daniel Guerin, to the fact that anarchism is defined as 'absence of authority or government'.[18] The generally held correlation of anarchism with chaos is considered by Guerin and class struggle anarchists to be inaccurate and inappropriate. The rejection of organisation extends only to hierarchical and heteronomous control. This may lead to a 'complete disorganisation' of present society but it will also lead to 'a new, stable and rational order based on freedom and solidarity'.[19]

A further reason for the link between anarchism and disorganisation may be evinced in the correlation of the term 'anti-organisation' with 'chaos'. Some anarchists also seem confused by the association, on the one hand celebrating chaotic, spontaneous moments,[20] while also recognising that organisation is necessary for action.[21] On the one side are contemporary anarchists like Booth and tendencies in Subversion who follow Nechaev and envision wholly ordered societies, albeit of differing types.[22] On the other side there are those influenced by situationist thinking, such as Hakim Bey, who dream of a wholly unstructured future society, in which there is still the possibility for the unpredictable, the unfamiliar, and even the sinister.

Anarchism, like Bahktin, celebrates the chaotic features of the carnivalesque, with its associations of participation, unpredictability, excitement, rejection of norms and mockery of heteronomous authority. These include the band of drummers and the masked and costumed participants on the Mayday carnivals (2000-3), March Against the Monarchy (31.10.98), the festival sound systems used in the anti-

Criminal Justice Bill antics in 1994 or Reclaim the Streets road parties (1996-9). Such revelry subverts the traditional motifs of political action, allowing greater individual participation less constrained by the normal conventions of protest.[23] Carnival has authoritarian features which cannot be overlooked: its provision as a safety-valve to contain revolt, and the subverted norms which can become either a reinforcement of the existing laws by their obvious parody, or in turn become established ceremonies secured into the existing symbolic order. These chaotic celebrations nevertheless hold out the promise of unrestrained, individual free-play. It is this possibility of breaking out of prescribed roles and the opportunity to create new associations, rather than the abandonment of all alliances, that makes carnival attractive to anarchists both as means and end.

'Spontaneity', associated with the carnivalesque, has many differing and competing interpretations. For some class struggle anarchists its meaning lies closer to 'autonomous' organisation,[24] while for Leninists it is seen as anti-organisation, such that rational structures are replaced by instinctive relationships. This latter interpretation has connotations of conditioned responses promoted by capitalism which are prone to the turmoil of the market place, whilst for Lenin freedom was the result of appropriate planning.[25]

The order/chaos distinction does not map precisely on to the organisation/anti-organisation distinctions. A strong authoritarian organisation, such as the German National Socialist government of 1933-45, is often hugely chaotic. Anti-organisation may itself lead to the creation of hierarchy and authoritarian social order, as political thinkers both ancient and modern have made clear.[26] It has also been a strategy of authoritarian movements to produce situations of great disorder so as to create popular desire for a strong central authority.[27] This situation of anti-social turmoil is identified with 'anarchy',[28] although it has little to do with the egalitarianism of class struggle libertarianism. This is not to say that rare examples of support for disruption that adversely affects the oppressed as well as the oppressor cannot be found within the

203

broader anarchist movement. Booth of *Green Anarchist*, for instance, praised the fascistic bombers at Oklahoma and the theocratic cult which used sarin gas to murder commuters on the Tokyo underground, because these assaults interrupted the smooth functioning of an oppressive society (termed 'the machine').[29] Class struggle anarchists, such as Black Flag, rightly denounce Booth for his elitism, in which he demarcates between a predetermined vanguard of 'revolutionaries' on the one hand, and the passive masses on the other who can be harmed at any cost.[30]

In addition, social chaos is not a society of equals indulging in free interplay. The types of societal turmoil supported by Booth, such as the civil wars in Somalia (1991-) and latterly Bosnia (1992-95) and Kosovo (1995-99), are ones in which hierarchically-organised gangs acquire dominance by force alone.[31] Phenomena viewed as social chaos are almost never equivalent to anarchism. Consistent class struggle anarchists argue that the strongest form of organisational rejection does not avoid hierarchy but creates a situation which allows those already existing in the wider oppressive social setting to continue to dominate. The object of organisation, as Malatesta explained, was to enable co-operation by the oppressed groups without which people were 'subject to the general organisation of society'.[32]

Just as authoritarian groups devise conspiracies of confusion to allow the most heavily armed and disciplined forces to dominate, so too situations of informality may unintentionally allow the strongest to gain command. Anarcha-feminist writer Jo Freeman describes how the leaderless, structureless groups common to the radical women's movement of the late 1960s and 1970s came to be controlled by the most powerful and charismatic as there were no formal structures to prevent their domination.[33] With no adequate system permitting the less confident to participate, a situation develops which members of Class War in the 1980s used to refer to as the 'dictatorship of the big-mouths'. However, leaderless groups, criticised by Freeman and supported by Cathy Levine, need not degenerate into informal hierarchies. Safeguards such as chairing rotas, randomised agendas (agenda points picked by lot rather than by first-in or by order of the chair) and techniques for egalitarian participation can be temporarily installed without creating permanent formal structures.[34] Temporary multiform organisation, while capable of being hierarchical, can also resist such formations. Anti-organisation is not a rejection of structure, but the replacement of formal structures with informal ones. Whilst the latter may replicate the worst excesses of some constituted bodies as described by Freeman, neither type of organisation must take this form.[35]

The creation of new types of social relations requires co-ordination. These relations and co-ordinating principles can remain egalitarian

if the group dynamics encourage flexibility and non-elitism and thus do not contradict the prefigurative principles of libertarianism. Similarly, modern chaos theory demonstrates that even in unconstrained systems a spontaneous order can be created, a phenomenon that has been recognised by free market liberals such as Adam Smith and Hayek. The concept of spontaneous harmony negates the supposed opposition between order and chaos and is captured in the symbol of anarchism

Figure 4.1. Anarchist symbol in Derby, 2000 (photograph by Julie Bernstein).

– the circled 'A' (fig. 4.1.), which identifies anarchy with order.[36] Contemporary anarchists are aware of the anti-social connotations of 'chaos'. As a result, many anarchists revile the term, wishing to associate it with oppressive economic conditions which bring about unplanned (although foreseeable) famines and destructive behaviour. 'Neither is anarchism chaos. The present system *is* chaos. An anarchist society would be infinitely more ordered and sane: Chernobyls and vast food mountains in Europe alongside starving millions in Ethiopia would not be allowed to exist.'[37] The ACF, aware of Leninist and liberal critics who regard anarchism as disorganised and anti-social, overreact and overlook libertarian interpretations of chaos that are compatible with spontaneous, equitable, flexible social structures.[38]

One of the few class struggle publications to acknowledge the possibilities inherent in chaos was *Proletarian Gob*.[39] The subtitle of its first issue proclaimed: 'Only when the working class is completely out of control will we be able to take control of our lives.'[40] Gob seems to suggest that it is only in circumstances of unplanned disorder that freedom can be developed, a view which borrows specifically from Bakunin who similarly maintained that it was through breaking the restraining ties of existing organisational forms, products of oppressive societies, that the masses would be liberated. *Proletarian Gob*'s delight in disorder is more rhetorical than programmatic. Although Gob does indicate that certain types of chaotic event are compatible with a liberatory ethic, elsewhere he tends towards the second and third interpretations of 'anti-organisation'.

1.2. Second Form: Organisation only in revolutionary epochs

The second form of anti-organisation rejects all forms of organisation prior to the revolutionary period. This form of spontaneity has a strong influence on contemporary British anarchism, although it is rarely adhered to rigorously. This trend comes predominantly, but not exclusively, from within the council communist (councilist) tradition. This revolutionary movement, one of the targets of Lenin's tract *"Left-Wing" Communism: An Infantile Disorder*, was influenced by incidents such as the formation of Russian soviets of 1905 and was strengthened by the examples of the German workers' and soldiers' councils of 1918-9. Proletarians in times of immense social conflict succeeded in building their own institutions external to the trade unions and socialist parties.

The councilist tradition includes figures such as Anton Pannekoek, Herman Gorter, and more contemporarily, François Martin and Jean Barrot (who sometimes writes under the name Gilles Dauvé). The councilists at the start of the twentieth century supported working class and labour groupings such as trade unions as these bodies prepare the revolutionary class and help the proletariat to advance revolutionary demands.[41] Gorter and Pannekoek even accepted the legitimacy of Leninist revolutionary parties in contexts such as those that applied in Eastern Europe in the first two decades of the twentieth century, but felt they were inappropriate to the West.[42]

The early councilists, such as Pannekoek, started as members of social democratic parties,[43] yet they witnessed how these organisations replicate the hierarchical features of capitalism through a process of integration into the functioning of that society. Trade unions and even revolutionary parties, once the possibility of revolution has passed, become reified. These structures are co-opted into the system they sought to overthrow. Rather than encouraging autonomous activity by the working class trade unions, reformist and revolutionary parties impede the autonomy of the revolutionary class.[44] Trade unions exist predominantly to assist in selling labour for commercial exploitation and thereby maintain that system of production and exchange.[45]

The free one-off British journal *Anti-Exchange and Mart*,[46] which accepted the councilist critique of trade unions, describes how other forms of workplace organisation soon face the pressure of being co-opted into assisting management, as will be discussed later in this chapter.[47] The only alternative is to create a group that allows entry only to revolutionaries who share a tightly defined ideological position and to participate in other broader organisations in times of overt industrial conflict.[48] Dauvé (Barrot) explains that as 'revolutionaries do not organise themselves outside the organs "spontaneously" created by the workers'[49] all they can do is organise contacts with other revolutionaries but without carrying through any program.

The belief that revolutionary moments are characterised by the revolutionary class creating new modes of autonomous organisation separate from existing integrated structures is a central conviction of council communism, and one which is developed by the autonomist marxist tradition. Capitalism tries to incorporate the working class and its organisations into its system of production and exchange in order to extract surplus value (profit).[50] In order to retain any independence and develop its autonomy, the oppressed subject has to break with these absorbed organisations and recompose itself through new organisational forms.[51] It is this feature of abstention from participation in organisations such as unions or revolutionary syndicates that is the main cause of disagreement between councilists and other libertarians. Furthermore, councilists stand accused of elitism for their advocacy of separate groups for revolutionaries.

Pannekoek and Gorter are clearly libertarian in proclaiming that the subjugated must overthrow their oppressors themselves rather than wait to have it done on their behalf:

> A small party or leadership clique cannot rule over the mighty proletariat: neither during nor after the revolution.
>
> Who must rule here, during and after the revolution? Who must exercise dictatorship?
>
> The class itself, the proletariat. At least the great majority of it.[52]

Gorter and Pannekoek, while proclaiming the autonomy of the proletariat, maintain a distinction between those who recognise the need for revolution in the period prior to the revolutionary situation ('revolutionaries') and those who overthrow the conditions of capitalism ('the masses' or 'proletariat').[53] The are two Leninist strategic implications of this. First, they posit one universal revolutionary class regardless of context, determined by a single source of power. Second, they presuppose that the appropriate responses and states of consciousness required by the oppressed to liberate themselves can be known independently of that class. This latter consequence, ironically, was recognised by the councilists as characteristic of the counterrevolutionary authoritarianism of Leninism.[54]

As explained in the previous chapter, the anarchist ideal recognises that oppressive power occurs variably and is not confined to locations such as the workplace. Different practices create different changeable oppressive power relations. There is no single fixed set of individuals who can be universally identified as the subject able to resist such forms of domination. There is no objective position from which a revolutionary section can be identified. Nor is it possible to make clear-cut distinctions between revolutionary and non-revolutionary periods. Pannekoek himself realised, when criticising Kautsky, that there is no distinction between 'day-to-day action and revolution'.[55] For those not involved, an incident between one oppressed group and its oppressors may appear to be unimportant, but to those involved it marks a fundamental shift of power.

The council communist view of spontaneity nevertheless is an important contribution to contemporary poststructural anarchism. Its belief that subjugated agents can rise against oppression in a libertarian fashion without a revolutionary organisation to guide them is certainly accepted by more formal anarchist organisations, for instance in Class War and the ACF's support for rioters,[56] but they maintain that not all anarchist tactics can rely on spontaneity of this sort. Universalising independent organisation restricts certain forms of libertarian action.

The solution, consistent with the prefigurative ideal, is multiple forms of organisation constructed by the oppressed group themselves, which evinces unmediated social relations.

1.3. Third Form: Organisation by oppressed subject groups

The third form of spontaneity, which is most consistent with the anarchist ideal, is the dominant type of anti-organisation in contemporary British libertarianism. Unlike the councilist approach, this method of co-ordination recognises that organisation is not specific to revolutionary epochs (however defined) or for a predetermined elite of revolutionaries. However, like the councilists, it rejects any formal structure which is imposed on the revolutionary agent. 'What we mean by working class spontaneity is the ability of that class to take direct action on its own behalf and to develop new forms of struggle and organisation.'[57] Anarchist means of co-operation are in contrast to orthodox communist methods as the former embody the egalitarian social forms that they seek.

In *Like A Summer With A Thousand July's* (sic.), a libertarian analysis of the 1981 urban riots, the authors report approvingly the response of a heckler to the interventions by Claire Doyle, a member of Militant:

> Doyle [...] was constantly heckled by the youth of Brixton and Toxteth when she tried to hustle in on their action by calling for the setting up of a Labour Committee (euphemism for the Labour Party) for both neighbourhoods. She was rightly accused of trying to make political capital out of the riots. When she told a Brixton meeting, 'You have to organise to defend yourselves', the reply came back, 'We will defend ourselves'.[58]

Any external political organisation, whether calling itself marxist, Leninist or anarchist, is condemned by the authors as an external imposition on the oppressed. Any form of political organisation not directly of and by the particular groups subjugated is regarded as an attempt to re-introduce hierarchies, in this case with political leadership at the top and the locals of Toxteth and Brixton as clients at the bottom.

Subversion explain their organisational ideal in similar anti-Leninist terms: 'If some bunch of fascist thugs is harassing black workers then they deserve a good beating and we should support those workers *organising themselves* to sort the fascists out, in whatever way we can.'[59] The anarchist ideal is that no organisation, including libertarian groups, can represent the multifaceted nature of resistance to oppressive power. Consequently, anarchist groups are not leading the oppressed but acting for their own emancipation from economic oppression. 'We exist not as something separate from the working class, not as some leadership for others to follow, but as part of the working class working for our own liberation.'[60] The basis for action has to be the autonomous organisation of those affected, with solidarity arranged on the basis of self-identified and reciprocal shared interests.

The emphasis on self-organisation undirected by external groupings can be found in the earliest British anarchist periodicals. The newspaper *Freedom* reported autonomous strike action and Welsh anti-tithe (church tax) agitations.[61] Contemporary anarchist sheets continue to give prominence to radical actions organised by the working class, regardless of whether an anarchist group was formally involved. This is in contrast to many Leninist groups. They give prominence primarily to the campaigns in which their particular organisation is active.[62] Anarchist groups, ideally, are made up of those in oppressed subject positions and, unlike the councilists, they do not make a significant distinction between revolutionaries and the mass. 'Class War is not just another party seeking to gain power or a new way of telling people what to do.'[63] Although this is consistent with the anarchist ideal, in practice many libertarian groups have tended to replicate the features of Leninist organisation, which was hegemonic in revolutionary circles for over 70 years.

2. Formal Structures: Leninist organisation

The primary political structure which anarchist groups define themselves against is the Leninist political party, although, as will be shown, certain features of Leninism reappear in libertarian organisation. Considerable amounts of anarchist propaganda have been directed against these repressive structures, especially prior to the fall of the Berlin Wall when orthodox communist groupings were more popular and influential.[64] The critique of the party has three main features. The first is that the party has strategic weaknesses, identifying just one central location of power, which is known primarily by a privileged elite, rather than by those subject to it. The second critique follows from the first, in that it concerns a paternalistic attitude towards the revolutionary subject, and the promotion of an elite to guide the already subjugated group. Finally, the party's magisterial structures restrain autonomous activity and create hierarchical and oppressive relationships.

2.1. Strategic Weaknesses

Although Lenin recognises that the revolutionary struggle will take place not just at the point of production, he did maintain that there is one identifiable source of oppressive power: the economy.[65] The economic battle determines all other forms of conflict including the political struggle for governance of the state. The proletariat establishing control through the abolition of the economic power of capital ensures that the state becomes a non-repressive power and withers away.[66] This primary source of oppressive power is knowable independent of the experiences of those who are subject to it. The oppressed, rather than being the primary movers in resisting their oppression, are secondary; they require first and foremost a revolutionary elite to guide them. Without the vanguard, the working class can only assist 'bourgeois democracy'.[67] By contrast, the anarchist archetype has a more tactical approach to power. There is no dominant central power, so there is no vanguard who can articulate the true nature of oppression.[68] Consequently, there is no single group who can represent the oppressed group but the subjugated group itself, hence anarchisms' prefigurative rejections of representative bodies.

Lenin, however, considered the class struggle to be understood as an objective social science. Intellectuals properly versed in appropriate study would be fully able to appreciate the correct strategies for combating autocratic and bourgeois democratic rule. Socialism, argued Lenin:

> [H]as grown out of the philosophical, historical, and economic theories that were worked out by the educated representatives of the propertied classes – the intelligentsia. The founders of modern scientific socialism, Marx and Engels, themselves belonged by social status to the bourgeois intelligentsia.[69]

The dependence on the dominant elite for leadership was not a matter of regret for Lenin, for the working class was incapable of developing adequate political consciousness, as they did not have the time for sufficient study.[70] The working class requires leaders properly versed in marxism to educate the masses and raise their consciousness.[71] Anarchists, by contrast, are critical of this view that intellectuals and the middle classes are more able than the oppressed themselves to represent the interests and desires of oppressed groups. 'To the Left the working class are there to be ordered about because we are too thick to think for ourselves.'[72] This is not to say that the anarchist ideal demands that the expressions of every section of the working class in themselves present the most suitable form of action. They are well aware that subjugated groups often replicate forms of domination, such as anti-social crimes against other economically deprived citizens. Certain forms of resistance can be equally, or more, hierarchical,[73] but anarchists also recognise that no group is capable of liberating others. The rejection of vanguards does not mean that those anarchists and others who are members of an oppressed group must follow the majority view: they can chose to act prefiguratively for themselves and in doing so provide opportunities for others to act likewise.

2.2. Paternalism

Lenin and his anarchist critics agree that the economically oppressed do not create political parties autonomously as their main weapon. As Lamb points out, the revolutionary party was never a method of organisation that erupted spontaneously from the industrial working class. In fact, in revolutionary situations the workforce spontaneously developed other organisational forms, such as Pannekoek and Gorter's favoured workers' councils.[74] For Lenin, this was merely evidence of the backwardness of the oppressed group and of the necessity for trained revolutionaries to provide leadership.[75] A revolutionary elite or cadre is required who have the appropriate training and social background. Only these people are in a position to direct appropriate action.

Leninist paternalism met bitter criticism from libertarian socialists. Castoriadis indicates that the official working class organisations built on Leninist lines act as a restraint on working class involvement:

> The [official] working class organisations have become indistinguishable from bourgeois political institutions. They bemoan the lack of working class participation but each time the workers attempt massively to participate, they shout that the struggle is 'unofficial' or against the 'best interests' of the union or the party.

> The bureaucratic organisations prevent the active intervention of workers. They prostitute the very idea of socialism which they see as a mere external modification of existing society, not requiring the active participation of the masses.[76]

As Ken Weller, a member of the Castoriadis-influenced Solidarity group explained, such paternalism reduces the working class to 'actual or potential clients' while the party is an 'elite'.[77] The party replicates the order-giving managerial role of capitalism that revolutionary socialism is supposed to supersede.

2.3. Authoritarian Structures

Lenin's *What Is To Be Done* provides the blueprint for traditional Communist organisation. It was written before working class parties were finally legalised in Russia in 1905, although Lenin still maintained much of the organisational detail after this date. Ernst Fischer defends Lenin by arguing that tightly controlled party discipline was necessary after this date because of the possibility that legal sanctions would be reintroduced.[78] Lenin certainly acceded to some democratic changes after 1905 which did not risk the survival of the Bolshevik Social Democrats (precursor to the Communist Party), yet even after Lenin's faction had seized power and their legality was secured, the requirements for party discipline remained in place. In *"Left-Wing" Communism, An Infantile Disorder*, written in 1920, Lenin maintains that the membership of the party must be subservient to the will of the leadership in order to reach the objectively knowable ends.[79]

To avoid infiltration and wasteful theoretical disagreements, the revolutionary party was to be directed by a small group of dependable and hardened revolutionaries who would influence the organisations of the working class along the appropriate predetermined communist lines.[80] The minority elite were to 'centralize all the secret aspects of the work – preparation of leaflets, the drawing up of rough plans, the appointing of leaders from each district'[81] without the intervention of the subjugated class. The pivotal position of the party in the process of emancipation resulted in underplaying of autonomous actions. By definition, for Leninists, if the subjugated acted without the guiding hand of the revolutionary elite their action must be bourgeois.[82] Hence the constant stress on the importance of maintaining the party, not just in Lenin's writings but also by his followers.[83] As Lamb maintains, the result of giving precedence to preserving the party is that, in true Hegelian fashion, the interests of the instrument start to dominate over those the instrument is supposed to serve (see Chapter Two). The revolutionary party, which was supposed to be the tool for the oppressed to meet their interests, instead comes to dominate over the working class.

Leninism is driven by hypothetical imperatives, where predetermined ends impose particular forms of action. Lenin outlines the form of revolutionary structure which will ensure firstly its own organisational survival and then further the 'political struggle'.[84] Lenin's programme for revolution requires the most efficient form of organisation in order to reach these ends. Leninists consequently propose a centralist form of organisation that can act effectively, without wasting time on democratic accountability, which rarely operates efficiently. As Lenin proclaims: [85]

> [T]he revolutionary socialist party must also be *centralised*. For it is an active party, not a debating society. It needs to be able to intervene collectively in the class struggle, and to respond quickly, so it must have a leadership capable of taking day-to-day decisions in the name of the party.[86]

The SWP, of which Harman is a leading propagandist, deliberately follows Lenin. The leadership of the party has to be a professional corps, able to efficiently direct the subject class to its desired end. The division of labour within revolutionary groupings is essential for its effectiveness.[87] Against this method of separation and specialism, anarchists attempt to create structures that limit dependence on leaders and encourage greater participation, by promoting the transfer of skills, rather than the maintenance of distinctions.

Leninist centralism and elitism, with its correspondingly paternalistic view of the membership and the subject class, often results in brutal treatment of those at the lower end of the hierarchy. Accounts are legion. Solidarity in the 1970s and '80s, and Trotwatch in the '90s, have provided detailed accounts of the behaviour of party officials towards their lower-ranking members. These have included an almost cultist brainwashing of members, threats of violence against party-dissenters and complete absence of democratic control of the leadership by the membership.[88]

2.4. The Invisible Dictatorship

While anarchists have been vocal in criticising the major revolutionary socialist tradition for constructing repressive structures, it is another irony that the main originator of this critique, Bakunin, appears to propose a structure even more repressive than the specialist party.[89] Like much of Bakunin's theorising, his ideas on the invisible dictatorship are not only ill-formed, but also frequently contradictory.[90] Many contemporary libertarians who are sympathetic to Bakunin, drawing on him as a thinker and an icon of rebellion, have tended to ignore his more dictatorial leanings. The ACF, for instance, in their booklet on Bakunin,[91] make no mention of his collaboration with Nechaev (see below), and benignly interpret his conspiratorial organisational strategies, culminating in the invisible dictatorship, as just aiming to influence the revolution not to direct it.[92]

Left-wing opponents certainly tend to be less forgiving. Red Action, for instance, portray Bakunin as being 'the enemy of all official dictatorships – he wanted an unofficial one'[93], an interpretation for which there is plenty of evidence. For instance, in a letter to Nechaev, in which Bakunin extricates himself from his young, former comrade's plans, he lays out his own preferred revolutionary organisational scheme:

> [T]otal destruction of the framework of state and law and of the whole of the so-called bourgeois civilisation by a spontaneous people's revolution invisibly led, not by an official dictatorship, but by a nameless and collective one, composed of those in favour of a total people's liberation from all oppression, firmly acting in support of a common aim and in accordance with a common programme.[94]

There are two main inter-related features that make Bakunin's organisational project inconsistent with the libertarian ideal. Firstly, like Lenin, he believes that the oppressed require a vanguard who can best understand their oppression and lead their emancipation, a stance which contradicts with libertarian advocacy of liberation (self-emancipation) over mediation. Second, Bakunin holds that the link between the masses and leadership should be kept secret.

Bakunin had a passion for the clandestine, a not unique characteristic in revolutionary circles in the early nineteenth century.[95] It is this conspiratorial feature alone that is often considered incompatible with prefigurative principles. Yet, secrecy itself is not necessarily incompatible with anarchism, as will be discussed below. Certain revolutionary organisational tactics supported by contemporary libertarians, such as the miners' hit squads, were hardly models of free, open organisation. What makes Bakunin's invisible dictatorship unacceptable is that the oppressed agents are excluded from the conspiracy. Secretive organisation aimed at excluding government and other interventions are common within anarchist circles. Security precautions in contacting libertarian groups are often recommended because of the interest (real and imagined) state security services take in activists.[96] Similarly, the Anderson's Splat Collective aims to exclude the order-giving middle classes while trying to be inclusive of the working class, so as to increase the latter's autonomous power.[97] The aim, however, unlike Bakunin's invisible dictatorship, is to be open and accessible to the oppressed subject groups. There is a problem when secrecy intended to exclude only oppressive agents starts to proscribe the group who wish to overcome their subjugation as well, a point discussed in further detail below.

Just as theorising was dismissed by Bone as discourse directed at a privileged group at the expense of the wider potential revolutionary subject, so too Bakunin's invisible dictatorship, as Debord points out, restricts the design of liberation to a universal vanguard.[98] It is not secrecy per se, but the type of groups that are excluded, which makes Bakunin's conspiratorial plans incompatible with its commitment to prefigurative direct action.

3. Contemporary Anarchist Structures

There are many different structures used by anarchist organisations, from the formal centralised grouping with a clear strategy and political programme, to the diffuse temporary network. They appear in a variety of contexts from the industrial setting, community groups, social centres, cultural venues, and environmental protests to direct confrontations with forces of economic and state oppression. A libertarian grouping may take one form in one context: for instance, a non-aligned, informal anti-Poll Tax union might become a more permanent, stable but limited legal defence campaign. In this section, organisational structures are examined in terms of the diffusion of power within these bodies, across them and between the libertarian grouping and the oppressed subject. The following two sections (4 and 5) examine these structures in the context of specific contemporary groupings in the workplace and the community.

Anarchist movements have often been differentiated from Leninist ones on the basis of their organisational differences. The more localised, informal structures favoured by libertarians are often a consequence of previous flirtations by members with Leninist and other centralist groupings. After alienating experiences within traditional political bodies, activists who go over to anarchism try to avoid recreating repressive, hierarchical structures.[99] Nonetheless, there are features of Leninist organisation which have been overtly and covertly incorporated into anarchist structures. The most obvious attempt at Leninising anarchism was the *Organisational Platform of the Libertarian Communists* (henceforth *The Platform*). Supporters of *The Platform* (Platformists) are not the only ones from the anarchist tradition who superimpose an identity onto subjugated groups. Many anarchist critics of *The Platform* also share strategic weaknesses with Leninism which are incompatible with the libertarian paradigm.

3.1. Centralism and *The Platform*

The Platform was written by a group of exiled Russians including Nestor Makhno (the commander of the Ukrainian insurrectionary force that fought both the White and Red Armies during the Russian Civil War), Ida Mett, Piotr Archinov, Valevsky and Linsky. Together they printed an organisational blueprint in 1926 under the name of The Dyelo Truda Group. This document responded to the failure of the libertarians to prevent the Bolshevik reaction after the success of the October Revolution. In Britain, various groups have embraced the main tenets of *The Platform*, amongst them the AWA (Anarchist Workers Association) and the short-lived AWG (see Appendix One). In the 26 Counties of Ireland, the WSM (Workers Solidarity Movement) has taken up the organisational plan outlined in this document. The main features of *The Platform* are shared with Leninism, namely criticisms of past shortcomings of libertarian modes of organisation and a proposed centralised structure as the solution. *The Platform* identifies the cause of anarchist failure to be the fault of 'disorganisation' and 'chaotic' organisation.[100] *The Platform*'s other shared characteristics with Leninism are a paternalistic attitude towards subjugated groups, which designates a universal vanguard, and the repressive character of this representative body, the centralised Anarchist Union, which is to lead the social revolution.

In common with Lenin, *The Platform* identifies just one source of repression, the class struggle, which is a product of capitalism. 'The social enslavement and exploitation of the working masses form the base on which modern society stands, without which this society could not exist' and this 'generated a class struggle' which has 'general, universal scope [....] in the life of class societies'.[101] Oppression can be determined objectively as emanating from one source. Unlike Lenin, Platformists believe that the working classes can, and do, develop sufficient awareness of their social position without the necessity of the intervention of bourgeois intellectuals.[102] However, the Platformists still give priority to the leadership of a vanguard. *The Platform* recognises that some workers, prior to periods of social upheaval, developed revolutionary ideas before other sections of the subjugated class. This advanced group are the self-identified Anarchists who are to join the General Union of Anarchists.[103] These individuals, as Joe White (a member of the AWG) explains, are the 'vanguard'.[104]

The AWG, who used *The Platform* as its organisational basis, make a distinction between their interpretation of the 'vanguard' and that of Leninism.[105] The AWG argue that Lenin's advanced group had organisational priority over the subjugated class, while they maintain only a 'leadership of ideas'. Lenin saw the party as 'the most advanced expression of proletarian rule' which leads to the 'substitution of party rule for class power'.[106] In contrast, argues White, his group proclaimed no organisational or individual priority, but that anarchist principles should be regarded as the most advanced.[107] White's distinction is an insufficient ground for claiming an adequate differentiation from Leninism. Followers of *The Platform* still maintain that there is a strategic, objective, anarchist science, according to which libertarian tactics can be prescribed irrespective of context. This view contradicts the libertarian principle of self-emancipation, in that *The Platform* accepts that a vanguard knows the best means to achieve goals. Second, this separation of a select group of revolutionaries off from the uneducated masses is reminiscent of Lenin's party, as it recreates a hierarchy between the 'conscious' minority and subjugated classes. Thirdly, as in the revolutionary party, there is a hierarchy within the vanguard group.[108]

Consistent libertarians do not deny that certain groups are most in conflict within the prevailing sets of powers and in this sense take a lead. However, *The Platform* conflicts with the ideal because it jumps from the particular to the universal, for it assumes that those who are the most militant in one section represent the most appropriate anarchist response overall. The AWG aspired to an organisational structure that was based on cadres, a group of highly-knowledgeable militants who would be the core of a central body which promulgates anarchist ideas to the general revolutionary class.[109] As *The Platform* explains, the General Union co-ordinates scattered local groups and drives the whole movement towards a strategic 'clearly recognised goal':[110]

> Although the masses express themselves profoundly in social movement in terms of anarchist tendencies and tenets, these

tendencies and tenets do however remain dispersed, being unco-ordinated, and consequently do not lead to the organisation of the driving power of libertarian ideas which is necessary for preserving the anarchist orientation and objectives of the social revolution.[111]

There is a set of predetermined ideas to be applied by the vanguard faction into other various working class organisations such as the trade unions. The General Union not only claims the ability to speak better for others than the subjugated group itself, but also attempts to use the subjugated class for its predetermined aims, reducing the autonomous subject to objects. As a Liverpool-based anarcho-syndicalist pointed out, the aim of intervening in all workers' struggles to guide them in accordance with predetermined objectives is 'edging very close to the idea of a party leadership: an anarchist vanguard controlling a wider labour movement'.[112]

The repressive feature of the General Union is the imposition of 'Theoretical Unity', 'Tactical Unity' and 'Collective Responsibility'.[113] The first two principles are based on the supposed universal nature of anarchist economic and social analysis that makes it possible to determine others' methods. This strategic approach, which leads to the creation of a cadre organisation directing operations and tying its membership to centrally-determined decisions, is approvingly described by the AWG-member Joe White:

> The actual implementation of tactical unity is more problematic. General tactical positions must of course be decided by the whole membership through national conferences. However, general positions cannot anticipate all the questions that the class struggle throws up....
>
> Thus the executive committee would not simply serve an administrative role but would be delegated with responsibility of deciding tactics in between conferences.[114]

White makes more explicit than *The Platform* itself the centralising feature of the General Union, i.e. the pivotal role of the Executive Committee. It is thus organisationally similar to the revolutionary party described earlier by Harman of the SWP. The structure of the Executive Committee has other parallels with the Leninist party's 'central committee'. The leadership is regarded as being in advance of the followers and this leads to hierarchical relationships within the group. *The Platform* stresses the 'theoretical and organisational orientation' determined by the Executive Committee of the General Union over the whole organisation. Executive and democratically-determined decisions are binding on all members, although it accepts both the right for dissenters to debate and attempt to change policy, so long as they adhere to decisions, or to withdraw from the General Union.[115] The relationship of the member to the General Union is a contractual one, and it differs little from the forms of Kantian, binding obligation approved by minimal-statists and anarcho-capitalists. These agreements are rejected by the anarchist ideal as merely another form of constraining exchange which is incompatible with the free, spontaneous associations of communism (see Chapter Two). *The Platform* posits a contractual obligation that is contrary to the aims of anarchism and therefore its organisational structures are not prefigurative.

Other class struggle anarchists have condemned the AWG's organisational approach. The ACF, for instance, maintained that the anarchist organisation must be prefigurative: systems of co-ordination should be based on the same principles as those desired for a post-revolutionary society including 'complete autonomy, and independence, and therefore full responsibility, to individuals and groups'.[116] The ACF claim that because the centralised committee holds power 'the AWG froze the relation between the anarchist militant and the mass'.[117] A minority who was most conscious in one context was considered able to represent the interests of others from different contexts. Consequently, the AWG concentrated their efforts on developing the enlightened cadre rather than participating in direct action against their own immediate oppression, in the same way that Leninists concentrate on the party.[118]

In place of *The Platform*, the ACF advocate the organisational principles found in *The Manifesto of Libertarian Communism* (henceforth *The Manifesto*) written by George Fontenis.

3.2. Federalism and the Manifesto

The ACF recognise that the centralism recommended by the AWG was inappropriate as an anarchic social arrangement. '[N]o organisation can be anarchist without total freedom to take part in the formulation of goals, aims and methods plus, ultimately, the right to withdraw from this process.'[119] However, the proposal found in their organisational recommendations and *The Manifesto* in particular differs only slightly from that in *The Platform*. Like the Dyelo Truda Group, Fontenis recognises that the Leninist method of imposing tactical and theoretical views from outside is repressive. Yet his solution is similar to *The Platform*, in that it too stresses the need for 'Ideological Unity', 'Tactical Unity' and 'Collective Action and Discipline'.[120] *The Manifesto* also identifies a vanguard who can best represent 'the experiences and desires of the masses'.[121] There are important differences, expanded on below, between *The Manifesto* and *The Platform*, which are indicative of the first's more prominent libertarian attitude: (1) *The Manifesto* stresses federation rather than the central committee as the final arbitrator of authority; (2) Internal structures are less dependent on the contractual relationships that are characteristic of Kantian liberalism.

(1) The ACF supporters of *The Manifesto* applaud its greater stress on the autonomy of local groups. They promote federalism, in which: 'Political power flows from the base to the summit'.[122] Local units have ultimate responsibility for the tactics in their regions and therefore allow for tactics, organisations and agents that respond to the micropolitical. Although *The Platform* also proclaims an adherence to federalism, the binding nature of the Executive's decisions permits only small degrees of latitude in the manner of execution.[123]

(2) The contractual obligations of members to the group are less rigid in *The Manifesto*. Constituent sections may dissent from the

majority decision yet still retain membership of the federation without being forced to carry out the obligations. However, this only goes so far as abstention; they may not perform acts contrary to the central decision, so are still contractually restricted. Like local groups in *The Platform*, each unit has the freedom to secede at any time.[124] Anarchist-communists are not the only libertarians who favour federalism over centralism. SolFed and other syndicalists such as Tom Brown espouse the diffusion of power to localised autonomous groups federating into larger groupings as both the means and ends of anarchism.[125]

3.3. Networks

The network makes more explicit what is implicit in the federalist proposal of the ACF, namely that authority lies in localised groups that come together on the basis of mutual self-interest. No agreement ties them into tactical unity. Where groups wish to carry out separate actions they are free to do so, unbound by the decisions of other local groups. Some have proposed a network model but called it a 'federation'.[126] One example of the network is Reclaim the Streets (RTS), which brought together interested individuals and groups on environmental themes. Participants joined up on various projects placing their own emphasis on planned actions. Another version based on the co-ordinating model of RTS was the 'Carnival Against Capitalism' on June 18 1999. Different groups voluntarily came together for mutual interest in pursuing the oppressive forces that directly affect them. The event was used by MA'M to confront the totems of deference to a sovereign; by environmental groups to oppose businesses which harm their communities; by class struggle communists to challenge the institutions of banking and finance (such as the LIFFE building) and by workplace activists to attack the reformist TUC headquarters. These targets intersected, providing avenues of solidarity and co-operation.

In a network, if a particular activity is considered by a participant to be inappropriate they are free either to abstain or even undertake opposing action outside of the network. It would still be possible for them to rejoin in other events that did meet their interests. This method of organisation has prefigurative elements favourable to anarchists. It employs a free contract and allows for greater flexibility of operation. It does not involve a universal vanguard, offers free and equal access to any wishing to participate and does not, ideally, have a centralised leadership. There are a few provisos. Some bodies calling themselves 'networks', such as Globalise Resistance, are considered to have either an official centralised leadership, or a covert de facto one. Additionally, following the success of J18, members of state socialist groups such as Workers' Power and the SWP have tried to join libertarian networks, such as those around N30 and Mayday 2000 (fig. 4.2.). Attitudes to such interventions have varied according to locality and the people who are members of these parties. In some locations, individual orthodox marxists have been provisionally accepted as they have, in practice, behaved in accordance with the network's principles and have not tried to impose Leninist methods. In other places Leninists who joined attempted to dictate a strategic politics and, as a result, were excluded.

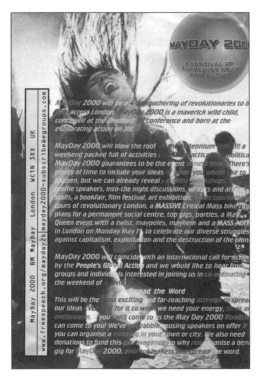

Figure 4.2. Mayday 2000 flier.

Networking is not a universal organisational method. It is only suitable for certain forms of (anti-) political action. It cannot be applied to all libertarian action, or to all contexts. In particularly oppressive circumstances, where free association is extremely difficult or impossible, or where tactics require little formal discussion, networks are not a suitable form.

3.4. The Closed Cell

If the free network embodies many of the features that prefigure the anarchist ideal, the closed cell is regarded as its antithesis. However, notable anarchists have advocated and supported it, the most infamous being Nechaev. The disapprobation towards this organisational structure is partly a result of its close association with terrorist tactics, a method normally regarded as incompatible with prefiguration. Although the use of extreme coercive harm against civilians is generally disapproved of in anarchist circles, especially the academic ones, certain types of cell-structure can be justified as concordant with a prefigurative ethic.[127] It can be the most appropriate organisational form to carry out certain tactics in specific circumstances. Before examining these exceptions, it is necessary to elucidate why this form of structure is considered to be outside the anarchist ideal.

The cell structure for revolutionary organisation was first fully formulated by Nechaev in his 1869 work *Catechism of the Revolutionist*, a work which many commentators consider to be abhorrent and has caused its author universal denunciation.[128] The particular features of the cell organisation proposed by Nechaev include the worst characteristics of the most authoritarian institutions. The starting point is that the cell is to be comprised of a few individuals, who form a vanguard of committed revolutionaries. 'The revolutionary is a dedicated man (sic.). He has no interests of his own affairs, no attachments, no belongings, not even a name. Everything in him is absorbed by a single exclusive interest, a single thought, a single passion – revolution.'[129] This specialisation and distancing from one's community is out of step with contemporary anarchism, where the revolutionary is not an expert, but someone undivorced from the everyday.[130] For Nechaev, the revolutionary is concerned only with insurrection and socialises only within the cell.

Each cell would be arranged so that only one person, the 'organiser', would be in contact with other cells, providing this person with unchecked power within the cell. The organiser would also be the sole contact with the 'committee', the co-ordinating body of the cell network.[131] It is no surprise that Nechaev set himself up as the central figure in his own gang, *Narodnya Rasprava*.[132] The insularity and the hierarchy of the organisation had two purposes: first to ensure unity and second to protect the group's internal security.

Nechaev's aim was to create a united, disciplined, revolutionary organisation under one person's control.[133] His strategic response prefigured his totalitarian ambition of a thoroughly directed utopia in which the revolutionary leaders manage the masses. The new harmonious society was under threat from the organisation's enemies and required tight control to prevent breaches in security, as Clarke explains:

> Under this plan, no member, save the co-ordinator ['organiser'], knew the names of more than a small selection of his [sic.] comrades. Thus, if a cell was infiltrated by an Ochrana spy [tsarist secret police], or if one of the comrades turned traitor, he could only destroy his own group and not the entire operation.[134]

Nechaev felt that such organisational arrangements were vital for the tactics necessary to achieve his aims, such as bombings and assassinations. Open revolutionary activity risked long prison sentences, extra-legal summary execution and extradition.

The central objective of the conspiracy of cells was to worm its members into all parts of capitalist social life including, if possible, 'the houses of commerce, the church, the mansions of the rich, [....] the Third Section (the Secret Police) and even the Winter Palace'.[135] The cells were to use all and every means at their disposal to subvert and destroy state institutions, especially those responsible for repression and torture.[136] Nechaev's strategy recommends revolutionary cells as the best method for revolutionaries to avoid detection for as long as possible and promote through their leadership an uncompromising war of destruction against society.[137] Cell organisation offers internal unity and consequently many different political movements have used it. In the British Isles the most notable are the Provisional Irish Republican Army (IRA) and their predecessors the Irish Fenian Brotherhood.

For libertarians, the main weakness of cell organisation in general (and not just Nechaev's particular version) lies in its elitism both between the leaders at the centre of the cell organisation and the lower ranking minions, and between those in the conspiracy and those excluded. The hierarchical nature of the cells makes it a suitable form of organisation for those who wish to impose an authoritarian form of society. Eldridge Cleaver, who was at one time the Minister of Information for the Black Panthers, was so impressed by Nechaev's work that he considered *The Catechism of the Revolutionary* to be his political Bible.[138] Leninists approve of the organisational division because it replicates their strategic difference between the vanguard (co-ordinators) who are at the centre of directing operations and the ordinary cell members who do not even know the leadership. Repressive practices from cell-based 'liberation movements', argue anarchists, 'are not simply a result of regrettable but unavoidable "errors". Rather they flow from the politics of organisations steeped in the Leninist tradition and the separation of "the (armed) vanguard" and the "masses".'[139]

The cell also acts as a representative of the oppressed by carrying out actions which, because of their illegality, the 'clients' can know little about, nor influence. The claustrophobia of the cell structure means that the membership loses connection with the community that they live amongst. Even for social, and sometimes sexual, relations, the cell was to be the centre of the individual's life.[140] The closed organisation of the cell is intended to block the gaze of oppressive power, but it also obstructs the cell from the view of the oppressed and prevents them from participating in (anti-)political action. Attack International, in *The Spirit of Freedom,* criticise the IRA on the grounds that the members of the cell are separate from the class they wish to inspire, a point that is repeated by the A(C)F and Subversion. The terrorist cell is a vanguard elite with the monopoly of armaments and equipment, thereby restricting the autonomous activity of the oppressed.[141]

Although cell organisation is supposed to be immune to state intrusion it is particularly prone to the activities of *agent provocateurs*. The habit of obeisance and subservience to organisers and co-ordinators make it easier for the spy to persuade the lower members of the cells into committing acts which could turn public opinion against libertarianism. The necessarily disparate nature of the cells makes it hard to distinguish rogue groups from legitimate ones.[142] Cells are not in direct contact with each other, so do not know whether a particular act was performed by one of its allied cells or a false one set up by state agents. Thus, as the former SI member Gianfranco Sanguinetti argues, in reference to the Italian Red Brigades: 'Any secret service can invent "revolutionary" initials for itself and undertake a certain number of outrages, which the press will give good publicity to, and after which, it will be easy to form a small group of militants, that it will direct with the utmost ease.'[143] The gaps in responsibility and co-ordination that result from highly entrenched secrecy and hierarchy provide exploitable opportunities for the state. Thus, anarchists argue, cells cannot be used for libertarian ends, as they are hierarchical organisations that claim to act on behalf of the oppressed and impose one strategic co-ordinating structure. Structures that fix unequal distributions of power are suitable only for elite actions and prefigure autocratic ends.

Despite the origins of secretive cell structures and their general approbation, class struggle anarchists have supported some organisations based on this system. In the first dozen years of the century, Lettish social revolutionaries, often described as 'anarchists', were organised in cells and carried out politically motivated crimes, the Siege of Sidney Street being their most infamous event. In the 1970s and early '80s, the distinctly anarchist Angry Brigades' (AB) and Animal Liberation Fronts' (ALF) cell-based groupings were active. Class War during the 1984-5 Miners' Strike proclaimed 'Victory to the Hit Squads', which were groups of miners who carried out secretive acts of sabotage.[144] Such advocacy need not contradict prefigurative principles, for there are certain subtle distinctions between these cells and the closed cell groups modelled on Nechaev's principles.

3.5. Open Cell

To avoid the possibility of an elite force mediating between the masses and their liberation, contemporary libertarian terrorist groups have attempted to evolve new forms of organisation. Although they are intended to be different from the formal structures used by statist freedom fighters, in many cases the types of tactics they have used have led to insularity of the cell structure. The effort to avoid the elitism of traditional terrorist methods has prompted clear distinctions between authoritarian and libertarian cell structures, which will be referred to here respectively as closed- and open-cells. These differences have often been overlooked. Marshall, for instance, places the cell groups of the Angry Brigade (AB) in the same category as Leninist and Nationalist cell groups.[145]

According to Sadie Plant, an expert on the Situationists and their successors, there are significant differences in organisational practices and objectives that make the AB more powerful and threatening to the ruling class than the elitist urban guerrilla cells:

> They promoted a sense of anonymity and ubiquity which earned them an inflated notoriety and side-stepped all attempts at easy definition, and although the majority of the attacks for which they claimed responsibility only involved the destruction of property, this was a strategy which also ended in long prison sentences.[146]

The AB was structured such that its membership was open. Anyone could be a member and no one was responsible for recruitment. People not in contact with each other but sharing political aims were encouraged to commit acts of violence, primarily against property. There are four organisational differences between this cell-structure and that of the Nechaevian original. First, it does not require a vanguard but depends on local activists. Second, it avoids centralised hierarchical structure. Third, this grouping is contingent on other organisations and tactics and does not have strategic primacy. Finally, as state security forces themselves admit, this structure makes it hard for a locus of opposition to be identified and controlled. [147] Given these advantages, groups with authoritarian and hierarchical politics, such as Christian and Islamic theocratic movements, have also used them.[148] It should be stressed that these latter groups have employed the open cell for completely different ends and employed entirely different tactics to those of consistent anarchists.

The open organisation dissolves distinctions between a revolutionary elite and 'the masses', allowing agents to act on their own behalf. An indication of the success of this organisational tactic is recognisable in the large number of outrages that have been committed: Bunyan cites 123 attacks on property between March 1968 and August 1971.[149] Class War admired the miners' hit squads because they were localised groups of the strikers themselves.[150] The provisional, informal nature of the open cells, made up of friends, colleagues and neighbours, required no hierarchies. The mining communities' support of the hit-squads' actions, and the wider and larger libertarian milieu in which the AB first operated, made the stress of clandestine activity unnecessary. At first no distance opened up between an active elite and the wider oppressed community, especially as all could carry out their own actions.[151] The hit squads took place against the background of a general insurrection in the coal-fields. These gangs were a minor, albeit useful, supportive feature of a larger set of conflict. In Attack International's graphic novel *Breaking Free*, the hero Tintin (satirically based on Herge's original) and his friend Charlie are striking labourers who secretly burn down the site where scabs (replacement workers) have been bussed in.[152] The book also contains sympathetic characters who are involved in physical assaults on the organisers of strike-breaking labour.[153] These small, flexible groups are set up in support of a wider set of liberatory acts, which sabotage assists rather than replaces or leads and as a result they are viewed favourably in the novel.[154] The hit squads encourage others to undertake other forms of action: none are regarded as pivotal nor are the structures designed to represent the views of others. The closed cell-based structures, by contrast, see their organisations and their acts as the vanguard and as the mediating force between the client class and their emancipation.

The accessible nature of the open cell, in which membership is based on acceptance of principle rather than on formal recruitment means that anyone, regardless of location, could participate. As one AB communiqué put it: 'The Angry Brigade is the man or woman sitting next to you.'[155] This clearly inspired a large number of people to perform anti-political acts. The police had great problems in trying to discover the perpetrators due to the anonymity and fluidity of the groups. Alongside the AB, there were others involved in the informal network: 1st May Group, Lotta Continua, the Wild Bunch, Butch Cassidy and the Sundance Kid and, on the continent of Europe, groups such as the Hash Rebels. These, too, were loose autonomous networks of friends and colleagues bent on damaging the state, by carrying out acts of violence on property. The AB recognised the multitude of sites of power within contemporary society, and consequently attacked and supported action on a variety of fronts, such as blowing up the homes of industrialists during strikes or machine-gunning Franco's Spanish embassies in co-operation with Spanish anti-fascists.

Yet, even open cell groups can become rigid and, as circumstances change, move towards a closed cell structure. Bommi Baumann, a member of the (West) German Hash Rebels, points out that when the group became more embroiled in illegal acts it became isolated and replicated the party-class distinction of Leninism:

> Because you are illegal, you can't keep your contact with the people at the base. You no longer take part directly in any further development of the whole scene. You're not integrated with the living process that goes on....

> Consequently, the group becomes increasingly closed. The greater the pressure from the outside, the more you stick together, the more mistakes you make, the more pressure is turned inward.[156]

The insularity necessary to a small group bent on illegal actions, without mass popular support, tends towards elitism. As a result of the separation between elite and mass, the actions of the terrorist group can only be interpreted through the medium of the mainstream, capitalist press, which is always hostile. Faced with this hostility, the movement begins to reciprocate the animosity back onto the oppressed group from which they came but are now separated. The once open, flexible group becomes more insular and static. AB members who committed criminal acts had to leave or hide from the community they lived amongst:

> Under the onslaught of police raids, the conspirators began to stick together, seeing other people less, but using their houses clandestinely. "Your ideas start to be shared by a smaller and smaller group of people. You become isolated from mainstream actions and from socialising with other people".[157]

The police response to illegal actions and the desire to evade capture leads to the band becoming alienated from the people they wish to interact with.

Open cells were most suitable when combined with other forms of organisation rather than acting as the vanguard movement. Similarly, so long as they were temporary enough to avoid the creation of new criminal elites, small cells made up of the oppressed agents themselves in a context of general community support were able to act in a libertarian manner. However, historically, small anarchist militant groups have become distanced from the oppressed classes.[158] In an effort to reconnect to the revolutionary classes of peasants and industrial workers, anarchists supported the building of structures based at what they considered the primary site of oppression: the workplace.

4. Workplace Organisation

One of the great schisms within class struggle anarchism has been between the libertarian communists and the anarcho-syndicalists, a disagreement which is said to date from the late nineteenth century.[159] Many contemporary anarchists, from both sides, still maintain this demarcation. Bookchin, for instance, complains that anarcho-syndicalism appeals to a 'marxist' agent – the industrial, employed workforce alone, a group which is too select for his municipal anarchism.[160] The anarchist-communist ACF is critical of permanent workplace groupings because they become integrated, like unions, into the running of capitalism.[161] The anarcho-syndicalists retort that their libertarian opponents have no effective revolutionary organisation and have consistently appealed to very few compared to the tens, sometimes hundreds, of thousands who have been in anarchist syndicates.[162]

While there are differences between these two groupings, it is possible for workplace and community organisation to be mutually consistent. Syndicalism, as communists such as Kropotkin recognised, can be a tactic compatible with anarchism.[163] As will be discussed, some anarcho-syndicalists still consider their organisations to be the necessary and key structure for creating the post-revolutionary world. Strategic workplace activists are incompatible with the anarchist ideal. However, some syndicalists today, such as SolFed, resist elevating their organisation as a universal form and as such are consistent with the prefigurative ethic (see Appendix Two). Multiple responses are a feature of contemporary anarchist movements (and are evident in previous anarchist movements); they are consistent with the anarchist ideal, as there is the need for diverse organisational forms to confront numerous complex oppressions.

4.1. Syndicalism, Anarcho-syndicalism and Trade Unionism

Revolutionary syndicalists, such as Bill Haywood, tended towards 'economistic' theories, namely that the agents who would bring about change are primarily workers at the point of production. These organisers stipulated that industrial organisation and workplace tactics would provide the basis for a future just society. In this strategic 'economic' form, syndicalists believed that political action was epiphenomenal and that, as a result, members were free to pursue whatever political action they wished.[164] Variations on this form of syndicalism were commonplace.[165] Some revolutionary syndicalists, such as Daniel De Leon, held that a political party was necessary to support the industrial movement. In other variations, industrial organisation began to play a secondary role to the political party. In order to gain influence in parliament to protect the gains they had made, the British trade unions founded the Labour Party, but the structure set up to serve the unions, in Hegelian fashion, began to dominate them.

For anarchists, the attractions of syndicalism were clear. It had a distinct, comprehensible organisational aim: the uniting of the working class into federated militant industrial bodies, hence the Industrial Workers of the World (IWW or Wobblies) slogan of 'One Big Union'.[166] Syndicalism also had a simple revolutionary tactic tied to this singular organisation, the general strike. Such a method also clearly identified the revolutionary subject, the worker at the point of production, where exploitation and class divisions were most evident. 'Anarcho-Syndicalism applies energy at the point of production; its human solidarity is cemented by the association of people in common production undiluted by mere groupings of opinion'.[167] The workplace is a site where a myriad of effective tactics could be used against the oppressing class. The arsenal includes sabotage, strikes, occupations and boycotts. The great appeal of syndicalism, as Pierre Monatte, a turn of the twentieth century advocate, proclaimed, 'can be summed up in two words: *direct action*'.[168] Workplace organisation provides the opportunity for effective prefigurative tactics.

In Britain, anarcho-syndicalism started as a variation on the purer form of revolutionary syndicalism. British anarcho-syndicalism also concentrated on economic activity, but this is not because it considered constitutional party politics to be uninfluential. As sociologist R. J. Holton and historian Richard Price suggest, even in their early twentieth century form, syndicalists did not neglect the state, but considered that constitutional practice would only lead to the development of new hierarchies, whilst industrial practice provided possibilities for alternative experiments in social organisation.[169] As a result, the structures of anarchist syndicates try to reflect anti-hierarchical aims. DAM, citing Rocker, proposed that there should be no professional union officials and no central direction for the industrial union but that decision-making should be participatory. Paid leaders have interests separate from their electorate and as result, settle for deals that protect union representation rather than meet employees' needs, so instead:

> The organisation of anarcho-syndicalism is based on the principles of federalism, on free combination from below upward, putting the right of self-determination of every member above everything else and recognising only the organic agreement of all on the basis of like interests and common convictions.[170]

Anarcho-syndicalists recognise that it is necessary to have a number of people performing particular duties such as writing minutes, chairing and publicising meetings and negotiating with other groups, yet believe it is possible to operate without creating new elites. In SolFed (formerly DAM)[171] officials are temporary and almost always unpaid. Those in co-ordinating positions remain alongside the workforce and are not in an advantaged economic position. Even in very large syndicalist bodies, such as the CNT, where full-time paid positions could not be avoided, elected positions could not extend beyond one year and wages were tied to parity with the workers.[172]

The creation of workers' associations that have distinctive participatory structures is partly a result of an overt rejection of existing trade unions. Trade unions mediate between worker and employer and thus have to police any agreement and have a responsibility to assist in disciplining rebellious members. Unions have an interest in maintaining capitalist relations as their position is based on their mediating role and they therefore become part of the machinery of control. At the top end, general secretaries and presidents of trade unions are financially, geographically and socially distinct from their members and are part of the social networks of the state.[173] Anarcho-syndicalists not only have different aims – the eradication of the current system of production and exchange, the domination of the state, and their replacement by free co-operation between workers' bodies – but also distinctive organisational and tactical means.[174] Anti-representational structures and rejection of constitutional activity are at their core.[175]

There are two further differences between unions and anarchist syndicates. First, unions are organised predominantly on the basis of trade while syndicates are based on industry. For instance, in hospitals white collar staff might be in UNISON, medics in the Royal College of Nurses and the British Medical Association, delivery drivers and domestics in the Transport and General Workers Union and technical staff such as radiographers in AMICUS. Anarcho-syndicalists try to unite staff within industries into a single union.[176] The other major difference is that in Britain currently seven million people are members of trade unions affiliated to the TUC, whilst members of specialist anarchist syndicates are counted in the dozens. Efforts to create an anarcho-syndicalist union for previously unorganised dispatch riders collapsed in the early 1990s after just a few years. This failure consequently has led to a change in organisational approach amongst contemporary syndicalists. Instead of creating their own separate unions, SolFed are concentrating their efforts on creating networks of workers inside and outside of unions on an industrial basis to propagandise and to participate in struggles within those industries.[177] As a result, there is little organisational difference between contemporary anarcho-syndicalists and anarchists who operate through trade unions, such as the short-lived TUNA, resurrected in 2003 as the Anarchist Workers Network. Each recognises that multiple methods are required rather than a single organisational form.

Douglass, himself both a trade union militant and a supporter of radical action through specific anarchist workplace tactics, identifies the advantages of multiform structures. He explains that employing manifold methods is not contradictory, but based on employing whatever structure works best in resisting oppression in a given situation:

Workers [...] will drive the trade union bus in whatever direction they want to go, no matter what it says on the front. And while it wasn't constructed for, say, charging police roadblocks, from time to time it is the nearest thing to hand and will do until something stronger comes along. This bus may not take us as far as we want to go... but in many cases we can take it as far as it will go, at which point we'll adapt it or change it for something else.[178]

4.2. Against Workplace Organisation

There are three main criticisms of revolutionary workplace organisation. The first is that it is necessarily reformist. The second picks out an apparent vanguardism, with one site for organisation and those who are located within it prioritised over all others. Finally, rather than unifying the working class, as the aim of 'One Big Union' suggests, it divides it between industries and between workers and non-workers. It will be shown that while these criticisms do carry critical weight against particular forms of syndicalism, the ideal type of poststructuralist anarchist organisation avoids these faults. It *can*, and in certain contexts *must*, support industrial organisation.

4.2.1. Workplace Groups as Reformist

Libertarians, especially from the council communist tradition, have been particularly critical of trade unions and consequently anarchist syndicates. As seen in Section 1.2., councilists argue that pre-existing organisations become co-opted into capitalism. Any grouping, whether it is a trade union or revolutionary syndicate, that negotiates with management helps to settle the price for wage-labour and thereby assists exploitation. As a result, it is inherently a structure that assists capitalist domination.[179] While trade unions nowadays are keen to show that they are non-radical organisations, concentrating on constitutional pressure, legal support and selling services to members, anarcho-syndicalists by contrast are explicitly revolutionary. However, anarcho-syndicates also arbitrate with management; as a result they too will be integrated into the structure of administration or else fail in their function as negotiating bodies. Consequently, no matter how radical the union or syndicate, it would have to behave in the same way as trade unions, disciplining the workforce into accepting managerially agreed decisions, as the councilist *Anti-Exchange and Mart* explain:

> A steward who is a revolutionary cannot last, either they will be drawn into the union apparatus through the day-to-day accommodation with management that they have to negotiate for – or they will 'go too far' for the members and lose the ability to do a good job as a steward.[180]

Both trade unions and syndicates are identical in that, once they start negotiating a fairer rate of exploitation, they are open to the risk of incorporation into management. Any deal has to be patrolled to ensure that future bargains can be entered into. Radical groupings change into order-making and enforcing roles, supporting hierarchical arrangements.

The councilist criticisms are valid: if groups represent and accept, through negotiation, the rules of capitalist domination then they are behaving hierarchically. Nonetheless, some workplace groups will not negotiate with management and will hence avoid having to discipline other employees.[181] Similarly, as Douglass has pointed out, even reformist trade unions, when their rank-and-file members are radicalised, can ignore the leadership and engage in consistent anti-hierarchical activity. Such radical behaviours can be carried out both through their existing trade union structures, such as the defeat of the 1972 Industrial Relations Act, and by acts outside of the unions such as the hit squads.[182] Autonomous workers' struggle may start in trade unions or existing syndicates but, through use of direct action, the oppressed groups create new organisational structures that in their ideal forms embody anarchist principles.

4.2.2. The Vanguard

The prefigurative characteristic of the anarchist syndicate is twofold. First, its non-hierarchical federalist structures, which are replicated in SolFed's current industrial networks, are supposed to be synecdochic (a small example of the wider whole) of social relations after the revolution. The second characteristic is more important, for not only does the workplace organisation embody the principles of the future revolutionary community, but it is also the proposed controlling body for future society. As the preamble to the IWW Constitution explains: 'By organising industrially we are forming the structure of the new society within the shell of the old'.[183] There are considerable problems with the classical syndicalist view of the IWW. It assumed that the syndicates had an ahistorical form. Critics rightly point out that the conditions that bring about revolutionary organisations are a product of alienating conditions; reifying that form would preserve those conditions. New methods of struggle might need to supersede the syndicates, just as Douglass recognised they might (necessarily) outgrow the unions. As Miller correctly points out, to be genuinely liberatory, 'syndicates, therefore, must disappear along with the society that had given birth to them; otherwise they would become a force of stagnation'.[184] Revolutionary struggle involves superseding and developing new forms of social relations, not freezing them.[185] Hence, syndicates would not be the basis for the new society.

Like the Communist Party bureaucracy having strategic centrality in the reorganisation of post-revolutionary society, syndicates are seen as being core institutional forms, rather than fluid examples of anarchist principles. The Leninist's strategy of a party directing the proletariat is not abolished by strategic versions of anarcho-syndicalism, but merely replaced by workplace federation, as in evidence in the DAM slogan: 'The union not party'.[186] One vanguard is substituted for another. This criticism equally applies to trade union anarchists who would see these organisations as having strategic primacy. Yet contemporarily, there has been a move away from such organisational arrangements. There have been many syndicalists who regard workplace organisation as the primary necessary means for waging the class war, amongst them the Hull-based Syndicalist Alliance and the British section of the IWW.[187] The latter states: 'The sooner we get one big industrial united front in or out of the existing unions, the bloody better. [... T]he workplace is the only place where workers have any real economic power.'[188]

Most contemporary anarcho-syndicalists and trade union anarchists do not consider that their organisations should have strategic primacy at all times and under all conditions. The anarcho-syndicalist Meltzer, in his final article before his death in 1996, accepts that 'the struggle to achieve workers' control is not the whole answer'.[189] Syndicates and other work-based organisations are not universally appropriate methods though they can play a leading role in struggles against oppression in particular circumstances. The anarchist ideal involves diverse organisational approaches. Different forms of workplace structure are responsive to distinct contexts, counteract local repressive practices and are established by oppressed groups in specific situations.

The activities of the Liverpool Dock-strikers (which began in 1995) and the Zapatistas rebellion (reaching public prominence at the start of 1994) are good examples of the multivaried approach. The docks dispute originated when the employer's, Mersey Docks and Harbour Company, sacked trade unionists for refusing to cross a picket line. Although links with the union were not entirely broken, despite the Transport and General Workers Union (TGWU) officers abandoning their members, the dockers sought lines of solidarity which stretched beyond the traditional routes of organised labour.[190] As the Secretary and Chairman of the Mersey Docks Shop Stewards Committee wrote:

> We are now proud to be joined by the thousands of people throughout the country who want to safeguard the world against the evils brought by exploitation for profit: deforestation, poisonous land, rivers and roads, infected animals and crops and dangerous dumping of toxic waste.

And the thousands leading the fight against the government's Criminal Justice Act, Anti-Asylum and Job Seeker's Allowance legislation.

We thank Reclaim the Future (RTF) organisers for their patience and respect towards our committee, and towards all the sacked dockers and their families.[191]

The dockers linked up with environmental protestors and those whose freedom was further restricted by government legislation brought in to protect and enhance neo-liberal economic policies.[192]

The Zapatistas also created new frameworks of solidarity, establishing networks of support amongst and between different oppressed subject groups. These alliances have been multiform and unpredictable, but came about partly in reaction to similar economic policies that led to the Merseyside dockers' radical responses, as John Holloway describes:

> Neoliberalism is not an economic policy but an attempt to reorganise every aspect of human life. Neoliberalism destroys everything, but at the same time there arises new forms of resistance and struggle. They are no longer the struggle of the masses, but a new rainbow of different struggles, the struggles of women, the struggles of the gay movement, struggles to redefine the relation between people and nature, struggles for the rights of people in all phases of their lives, as children, adolescents, old people, struggles just to survive, struggles that are not perceived or recognised as struggles, struggles that, taken individually, are partial but that, seen all together, point towards the construction of human dignity.[193]

There is no objective position from which to predict precisely which categories of people will be oppressed by the expansion of free market practices and what subject identities will be created. Neither is it possible to foretell what forms of resistance will be adopted or which groups will coalesce in networks of solidarity.

4.2.3. Privileging the Industrial Worker

The aim of uniting the working class through federated unions, a feature of both anarcho-syndicalists and revolutionary syndicalists, is criticised by Malatesta as divisive. Strategic industrial organisation segregates by either trade or industry. Additionally, syndicalists are accused of prioritising the industrial worker.[194] As noted in the discussion of the 'social factory', surplus value is created not just in the industrial setting, but also in the wider community. Further classical syndicalism of 'one big union' assumes that capitalist economics is the sole locus of subjugating power.

These criticisms, especially the latter two, would suggest that syndicalism and trade union based anarchist currents have not thrown off Leninist views of power, and consequently retain a strategic organisational approach. However, developments in contemporary anarchist workplace organisation which are close to the anarchist ideal manage to avoid these weaknesses. SolFed recognise that interests extend beyond particular industries, thereby attempting to combine organisations of different sectors into networks of support. So too, as even critics of anarcho-syndicalism, such as the WSM, point out, syndicalists organised beyond the productive setting:

> Critics who reject syndicalism on the grounds that it cannot organise those outside the workplace are wrong. Taking the example of anarcho-syndicalism in Spain it is clear that they could and did organise throughout the entire working class as was evidenced by the Iberian Federation of Libertarian Youth, the 'Mujeras Liberes' (Free Women), and the neighbourhood organisations.[195]

Similarly, SolFed attempts to set up 'locals'. These are community organisations that concern themselves with struggles based on local interests, not just on the basis of production. 'A *Local* is also a base for action on a wider social agenda, not simply for supporting workplace activity.'[196] Neighbourhood groups are necessary because 'the class war also takes place on the working class streets and housing estates'.[197]

Likewise, the 'Aims of the Solidarity Federation' suggest that there are other forms of oppression which require their own forms of localised organisation, although SolFed does suggest a single location from which these oppressive forces originate:

> [N]ot all oppression is economic, but can be based on gender, race, sexuality, or anything else our rulers find useful. Unless we organise in this way, politicians – some claiming to be revolutionary – will be able to exploit us for their own ends.[198]

The original strategic organisation of syndicalism and other forms of anarchist industrial organisation has been replaced by a multiform approach compatible with the anarchist ideal. Criticisms of anarcho-syndicalism have been overcome by recognising that certain forms of oppression require distinctive, flexible responses not amenable to industrial organisation.

4.3. Syndicalism and Other Forms of Organisation

The standard explanation of the supposed split in anarchist ranks lies in the historical background that led to the development of anarcho-syndicalism. The 1880s saw a growth in individual acts of violence carried out by small groups of anarchists, acts which prominent libertarians, such as Pouget, believed did not further the emancipation of the working classes.[199] In their place new practical responses were considered: the most desirable, at that time, was the move towards industrial organisation.[200] This development is presented by Marshall as the creation of a new (anti-)political hegemony within western anarchism, a shift from the small groups of insurrectionists associated with the early anarchist communists (such as Malatesta) to a broader popular organisation promoted by the syndicalists.[201]

The development of syndicalism amongst anarchists is regarded as a product of the failures of cell-based movements. As discussed earlier, cells were thought to cause an elitist division between the revolutionaries and the subjugated class, which was far from the prefigurative archetype.

The hierarchical relationship between the active terrorist agent and the passive 'client' class occurs predominantly when propaganda by deed becomes the main method of struggle at the expense of other tactics. For some anarchists, particularly in France, for example the Bonnot Gang, propaganda by deed did become the central strategy, fixed at the top of a hierarchy of methods.[202]

It has been suggested that new industrial methods were advanced to replace the exclusivity of small groups operations.[203] However, this view is mistaken, as it is not a matter of either/or (cells or syndicates), but of different combinations of organisational tactics applying according to the legal and social practices pertaining in each context. In France, after the murderous repression of the Paris Commune, in which an estimated 30,000 communards were executed, and the consequent legal restrictions on workers' movements, mass organisation was impossible. It was not until the Waldeck-Rousseau Law in 1884 that even trade union activity was decriminalised in France.[204] In Britain, because trade unions had been in existence for longer – the Miners' Association (the forebear to the NUM) was formed in 1844 – there had been less need for propaganda by deed and the groupings associated with it.[205]

Workplace activity was not simply a reaction against other organisational forms. As Clifford Harper argues, the 'whiff of dynamite' furnished by the propagandists by deed gave the workers the confidence to develop workplace organisations based on direct action and motivated the government into liberalisation.[206] Even after the legalisation of syndicates, propaganda by deed continued, and after the Francoist victory the mass anarcho-syndicalist movement in Spain had to mutate into secretive 'underground' bodies to survive the fascist reaction.[207] Consistent with the anarchist ideal, libertarians have used multiple organisation rather than awarding strategic priority to one structure or method. Rather than mass workplace organisation being a reaction to smaller cells, there are clear parallels between them. As the historian of French syndicalism B. Mitchell indicates, they both promoted direct action at the site of oppressive circumstances by the subjugated themselves.[208]

5. Community Organisation

Anarchists have shifted away from the traditional anarcho-syndicalist strategic concern with creating prefigurative alternatives in the workplace. In Bone's words, the 'physical community [.... is] the main focus of resistance rather than the workplace'.[209] This change in direction was in part a result of the effectiveness by successive governments, starting with the Thatcher administration of 1979, in restraining class conflict at the point of production. The economic restructuring of Britain during the 1980s, marked by the eventual crushing of the militant miners, prompted a search for other areas of confrontation.[210] Such zones of conflict have in recent years been largely, but not exclusively, based on environmental issues. Changes at the sites of resistance can lead to the creation of a new strategic location outside of the workplace and a new vanguard. In the ideal form, however, anarchist community structures are flexible and multiform. They often combine with, or are partly constituted in, industrial organisation and other forms of struggle.

There are a number of problems in discussing 'community organisation', because of ambiguities about what is meant by the term. For Tom Knoche, an American activist, community organisations are specific types of structures based on geographically peculiar terrain, which are run by the people resident in these areas.[211] For many British anarchists, such as Class War, the community organisation appears to be any grouping which is not based in the workplace.[212] Community action might appear to be privileging non-occupational based organisation. Bone placed stress on organising outside of the workplace, although such emphasis on non-workplace activity was due to specific, historically contingent and localised conditions, and not a universal rule.[213] Other anarchists, such as older anarcho-syndicalists, have regarded community groups as only subservient adjuncts to the more important workplace-based revolutionary union. Tom Brown suggested that those members of the working class who had left the workforce and did not wish to return (identified in his day as married women) could support workplace agitation through communal work.[214]

Libertarians such as autonomists widen the function of the community. Just as the search for surplus value involves various types of informal labour not normally identified as work, so too the pay for such toil comes in more forms than a formal salary. Consequently, battles such as non-workplace struggles against benefit cuts or wages for housework are considered an equal part of the wider economic battle for the 'social wage'. Benefits, National Health Service and various legal rights are part of the informal negotiated social wage wrought by previous class struggles.[215] So community groups created to enhance or, more recently, just protect the post-war welfare settlement are engaged in a section of the economic struggle, albeit in a wider set of contexts than traditional industrial battles.[216]

Although Aufheben ascribe equal importance to community-based action, they still consider it as auxiliary to the wider economic battle. 'The revolutionary movement is grounded in the basic contradictions of wage labour as the essence of capital.'[217] Other conflicts, such as those community or 'cultural' forms of social movements like the hippies or punks, are only important for Aufheben when they oppose the commodity form, as did the squatters movement.[218] The strategic centrality assigned to the economic base is understandable as it is the dominant oppressive force in most contexts, at least in most contexts that Aufheben members operate. Even these critical marxists suggest that all subjugated identities are reducible to economic ones; consequently all liberated forms of organisation must be economic in character. As shown in Chapter Three, in different locations different combinations of power operate which may not be wholly determined by the economic.[219] Blacks, gays and lesbians and women face differing subjugating practices.[220] The anarchist ideal, according to which groups are formed by the oppressed subjects themselves and co-ordinate amongst themselves, has been evident in a variety of local campaigns and most significantly in the anti-Poll Tax movement.

5.1. The Structure of Community Based Groups

Community structures are as diverse as those based in the workplace. They can be centralised, small cell or federated. They are often in flux, changing their structure depending on the scale and enthusiasm of participants and types of oppressive practice they seek to undermine. As the ACF recount, the campaigns they are involved in can include:

> squatting, opposition to the Criminal Justice Act, unemployment issues such as the Job Seekers Allowance, anti-Poll Tax work, opposition to council and government collaboration with big business – wrecking our environment by building roads through where we live and giving land to supermarket chains to build yet more superstores – housing projects, resistance to the closure and under funding of community facilities as well as in creative and cultural projects.[221]

As Class War's Darren Ryan stresses, the main activists must be the locals rather than interlopers coming in to run it on others' behalf.[222] Different campaigns will involve distinct structures and varying participants, although there may be an overlap in agents or aims, and it is through these shared interests that co-operative solidarity develops.

The practicality and flexibility of community action in overthrowing the Poll Tax contrasts with Leninist groups such as the SWP, who maintained that only action based in the workplace could be effective.[223] The autonomy of community bodies in which the people in each locality control their campaigns was also opposed by another orthodox marxist party, Militant, who believed that an objective strategy should be determined and applied paternalistically to all local anti-Poll Tax unions (APTUs). Consequently, the flexible and informal, participatory nature of the non-aligned APTUs differed from the hierarchical structures of Militant-based anti-Poll Tax groups.[224] In areas where an APTU could have been successfully set up, but would not assist in party recruitment, Militant withdrew its support.[225] Through greater local involvement, without being wedded to a predetermined strategy, groups were able to create informal networks of support and tactics determined at the local level, which were more suitable for creating neighbourhood support.[226] These groups assisted in the maintenance of the successful non-payment tactic and proved, despite their smaller scale and lack of finance, to be more successful than Militant's groups. An example of the success of the non-aligned groups was the assistance provided to the Trafalgar Square Defence Committee (TSDC) controlled by those arrested during the March 31st 1990 riot.[227] The TSDC provided legal and financial assistance to anti-Poll Tax detainees long after the community charge was abolished.

The success of the APTUs in co-ordinating local actions and creating networks of solidarity inspired the creation of informal networks of community activists based in regions. The first of these groupings, Brighton's Rebel Alliance, links a host of local campaigning groups from environmental, animal welfare, unemployed, anti-racist and formal anarchist movements. The network allows groups to meet up, share information and collaborate in action without any collective having to compromise its autonomy. This local network system has been replicated, with regional differences, in London, Manchester, Nottingham and Norwich.

5.2. Environmental Groups: Tribes and communities

There is insufficient space to provide a thorough examination of British environmental movements during the period of the study. Groups as diverse as CND, Earth Liberation Front (ELF), EF!, Friends of the Earth (FoE), GenetiX Snowball, Greenpeace, Green Party, London Greenpeace, Hunt Saboteurs Association and RTS have all been influenced by, and inspired, libertarians to a greater or lesser degree. A wide range of political and anti-political philosophies are advanced in anarchist environmental movements, from the social ecology of Bookchin to the primitivism of Fredy Perlman, John Zerzan and Steven Booth. Some environmentalists reject the pertinence of capitalism and class as dominant explanatory factors.[228] A separate study would be required to do justice to these groups, the many other informal networks of ecological activists and their varied analyses and doctrines. This section just touches upon some of their different organisational methods.

Although not all anarchists recognise environmental concerns as important sites of struggle, regarding these issues, at best, as a peripheral consideration in relation to more pressing class conflicts,[229] other class struggle libertarians have been involved in ecological campaigns. Class War, for instance, although critical of the professional elitism and liberalism of established environmental groups, have supported actions such as the mass trespass to open up land to ramblers.[230] Radical environmental groups have been, in recent years, the most sophisticated in adapting their organisational methods according to the repressive threat they are combating, the local context and the appropriate tactic. In areas where there is a large local presence directly under threat, such as in the anti-roads campaign in Pollok, Glasgow, residents have taken prominent roles in the campaign. Thousands went on marches, hundreds were involved in tearing down construction site fences and pupils at a local comprehensive demanded the right for time off school to protest the road development.[231] Elsewhere campaigns have been based almost entirely on environmental camps because there is no large local populace, such as at the Nine Ladies protection site in Derbyshire (1999-2000 and 2004-5).

On other sites there has been conflict between the inhabitants of the sites and local residents. The relationship between environmental protestors and locals is an instance of the general problem between self-identified 'radicals' and those with other identities. Often the problem manifests itself in an elitist division between the 'specialist' campaigners whose interests dominate over local residents. The creation of a vanguard group, whose tactics dominate and who identify themselves as having superior knowledge and consequently tactical priority over other subjugated individuals, has been a phenomena noted by radical environmentalists themselves. These differences are often exacerbated by the distinctive dress of the fully committed activist in contrast to those housed in threatened neighbourhoods. At Newbury, site-based activists (as opposed longer established residents) claimed a tribal identity, 'Donga'. What started as a way for a loose coalition of people to unify under the name of a tribe that resisted Roman rule became reified. It became a badge of commitment, placing those in a position to organise their whole lives around the campaign over local activists and those with other responsibilities.[232]

Even veterans of environmental camps recognise that the state and media responses have assisted in spectacularising radical protests. The most dedicated, 'long-haired' individuals and those who perform the most televisual stunts gain the most coverage and kudos. An informal hierarchy inside the group is created which reflects that between the camp members and those subjugated groups outside the tribe.[233] Yet such hierarchies are not inevitable, after all 'tribal' identities are rarely fixed. In addition, those who are capable of dedicating themselves to one campaign do not necessarily create closed 'tribal' identities; many in such long-running campaigns try to avoid practices that place the more permanent campaigners in primary or elite positions, at the expense of irregular attenders. Neither is the solution to prioritise the desires of local residents, nor expect solidarity from them. A member of South Downs EF!, in an article reprinted in *Aufheben*,[234] points out that in the case of the M3 redevelopment, wealthy inhabitants around the area of the contentious Twyford Downs project had interests which were diametrically opposed to those of the protestors. Many of Winchester's citizens had no direct contact with the land and supported the extension of the car economy. The roads programme would enhance their access to rural pleasures as the new throughways would speed up the journey to Heathrow Airport and their Provençal retreats.[235]

Dedicated environmental activists are not necessarily divorced from class struggle; nor do they come from privileged sections of society. The types of coalition developed will depend on the types of shared concerns, outlooks, dreams, fears and aspirations. As the Liverpool dockers coalition demonstrates, links of solidarity can be found between environmental and workplace groups with apparently different projects, and common interests and inspiring co-operative alliances can be forged. Douglass, partly in jest, explains that the prefigurative, alternative social arrangements created by travellers are attractive to many individuals left unemployed by industrial decline. The travellers' example offer a positive, confrontational, alternative to grimly surviving redundancy in decaying mining communities.[236]

5.3. Internet Co-ordination – the Global Community

Much has been written concerning the expansion of global communications.[237] The internet[238] as a significant form of communication was a phenomena that (bar for some specialist research groups) arose in the mid-to-late 1990s. It appears to embody many of the key features associated with anarchism. The Poll Tax was probably the last major UK campaign to be largely uninfluenced by the internet. Nearly every event with an anarchist following is advertised on at least one web page. All the major class struggle groups in Britain run a website (see the website section in the bibliography) on which the association's meetings and actions are advertised.

The internet also permits dialogue through email newsgroups, chat-rooms and guestbooks, in a way that normal printed propaganda finds difficult. Participatory forms of communication are more congruent with the prefigurative ideal than the monologue of much printed propaganda (see Chapter Five). The freedom of expression offered by internet technology, and taken up by contemporary libertarians, has fed mainstream newspaper fears concerning the organisation of anarchist activities, especially J18.[239] The cross-continental nature of J18 co ordination, replicated by N30 and Mayday 2000, helped to encourage these fantasies. Certainly many subjugated groups are in a minority, and anarchists, especially those in geographically isolated regions, find that electronic communications can increase bonds of solidarity. A global action like J18 allowed small groups in places as diverse as Belarus, Uruguay and Pakistan to participate in a co-ordinated event.[240] The Zapatistas realised computer-based information distribution provides gateways of solidarity with similarly subjugated groups in geographically diverse areas. As *Time* magazine acutely relates: '[T]he Web was supposed to be globalism's great tool, not a forum for its enemies. The Web was supposed to weld together markets into one enormous worldwide trading floor, not organize thousands into picket lines.'[241]

For Cleaver, it is the internet's ability to create links of solidarity across national frontiers without subsuming one organisation or campaign into another that is one of its key liberatory characteristics. The internet does not just support existing organisations, but also creates new structures and tactics.[242] These organisations may just operate in the sphere of electronic civil disobedience using tactics specific to this arena (hacktivism). Hacktivists can be legal, electronically-linked individuals, who may never meet directly, but co-ordinate in running independent web-based radios and news periodicals to counteract established channels of propaganda. Hacktivity can be more immediately transgressive, for instance entering and subverting government and corporate websites by swapping their texts for oppositional propaganda or swamping email addresses (spamming) so that the ebusiness can no longer operate.[243] Computer activism can also create new structures which are distinct from capitalist modes of interacting, as the DiY software Linux demonstrates: geographically disparate programmers have voluntarily collaborated and created an operating system that is free to anyone who wishes to use it. Relationships are formed which are largely unmediated by capital.[244]

The Zapatistas provides another example in which technological developments have altered methods of struggle. The indigenous population of the Chiapas region created their own autonomous structures outside of the repressive, partially authoritarian state and sought support that went well beyond the borders of Mexico. Linking up through computer communication networks with other radical movements opposed to globalised neo-liberalism, the Zapatistas were influential in creating international networks concerned with human rights, indigenous struggle, labour organisation and women's rights.

By being connected electronically, groups could respond rapidly to counter governmental manoeuvres. The flow of communication was so great that the Zapatista National Liberation Army (EZLN) proposed an international gathering to compare notes on successes and failures. Radicals who had originally met through the internet gathered in the Chiapas in the summer of 1996. This international gathering (or Encounter) was repeated in Spain in 1998.[245]

Martin, an advocate of hacktivism, suggests that it provides a means for international co-operation and involvement in (anti-)political activity:

> Electronic protesting these days is a simple matter of downloading easy-to-use software from the Web, or of visiting a protest site where you can set up your browser to bombard a target site with requests for information. Anyone can be a hacktivist.

> The global G8 protests of 1998 and 1999 and the WTO protests of last year were successfully organised by email and mobile phone – creative (but not illegal) use of information technology by protest groups has confounded law enforcement worldwide.[246]

Yet it is easy to overstress the importance of the internet and to ignore problems with hacktivism. The flow of information from newsgroups and e-lists can make it difficult to track down significant information, although some newsgroups offer an edited version. Second, as Cleaver describes:

> We bring to cyberspace our habits acquired in other spaces and many of those have been counterproductive and continue to be so in the new terrain. Personality conflicts, arrogance, sexism and racism and all other behaviour patterns that have tortured or destroyed other kinds of political efforts have been reproduced on the "Net". Few are the activists who have

not abandoned a discussion or unsubsubscribed from a list or avoided returning to a newsgroup because of flame-wars [abusive emails], unbridled antagonisms or endless dialogues of the deaf...

Anyone with activist experience in cyberspace is familiar with the frustrations of being confronted not only with detailed reports but also with urgent pleas for action on the part of those struggles and situations that we know little or nothing about and feel incapable of evaluating.[247]

Generally accepted rules for dignified behaviour that adapt according to site ('netiquette') are often developed to prevent the worst excesses of anti-social behaviour, and demonstrate the ability for groups to govern themselves, but Cleaver's point still stands: 'Cyberspace is no privileged arena' in terms of creating purer organisation.[248]

Martin's contention raised earlier that 'anyone can be a hacktivist' is also somewhat problematic. The spread of computer networks in the Americas is not yet matched by similar developments in Africa, where 'vast areas not only lack any kind of internet backbone, but even telephone lines'.[249] Martin's other claim is also contentious, i.e. that the major anti-globalist actions organised primarily on the internet. While the protests against the WTO, IMF and World Bank at *J18* (June 18th 1999), N30 in Seattle, USA (November 30th 1999), A16 in Washington USA (April 16, 2000), Mayday protests in London 2000-3, Prague's S26 (September 26, 2000), Genoa (July 21, 2001) and Gleneagles (6-8 July, 2005) did have a presence on the Net, and email lists did create links of solidarity prior to the respective events, other forms of communication were also of importance. Whilst *Time* also concentrates on the more spectaular use of the internet in its report on the N30 protests, it does note that they were not primarily co-ordinated by email and website. Standard methods of organisation were fundamental to their success. So too the protests from J18 to Gleneagles were often planned in public, using traditional forms of communication such as leaflets, stickers and posters, which were plastered throughout the main UK's main conurbations and beyond.[250] Dependence on computerised communications would be incompatible with the anarchist ideal because, as anarchists are aware, access is available only to 'a small fraction of people in the West outside of government, academia and business, and a much tinier fraction in the developing world'.[251] Nevertheless, the internet does provide additional possibilities for international solidarity, creating its own flexible cyber-organisations as well as influencing those not wholly dependant on the microchip and modem.

5.4. Community and Workplace Organisation

The division between community and workplace has been superseded. Contemporary British anarchists rarely advocate the traditional syndicalist proposition that community groups exist to support organisation at the site of immediate production. For many oppressed people it would be impossible, and indeed irrelevant, to distinguish between oppression experienced through employment and oppression in the wider social factory. Although in some contexts the oppressive practice is directly related to managerial control of labour, not all sites of heteronomous administration are based at the point of production or exchange. Some subjugating practices take place across many different contexts. In some areas of employment the forms of oppression experienced might be more comparable to those in an area of the community than to those of another workplaces. Thus, whether at work or in the community, responses to shared forms of disciplinary power would be similar.

Community-based struggles often have shared interests with labour conflicts, and often the two are intimately interweaved. In combating the Poll Tax, APTUs combined with workplace activity. In Derby, for example, the unions assisted Poll Tax rebels financially without trying to influence the decisions of the independent APTUs.[252] Unions recognised that they and community-based groups had common interests, with neither having universal priority over the other.[253]

Local community groupings are often linked to workplace groups. Nottingham Association of Subversive Activists (NASA), a variant of the Bristol Rebel Alliance, includes the Anarchist Trade Union Network and SolFed. In these bodies links of solidarity are formed between environmental, community and workplace groups. Different tactics may be specific to certain localities, such as strikes in a factory or deliberate undercharging by sales assistants, and these methods might not be immediately available to those active on other terrain. Similarly, community groups can employ tactics not available to those under the managerial gaze, yet through co-operative collaboration new tactics are developed. Transposing methods and adapting them to other settings provides for new forms of solidarity and techniques for self-emancipation. Workplace and community groups are increasingly working together, with neither demanding strategic hegemony.

6. Summation

The disagreement between anarchist communism and syndicalism has largely been overcome as neither now assumes that community- or workplace-based organisations are exclusively appropriate for libertarian politics, and as such both are consistent with the anarchist ideal. Industrial organisation and community-based groups are pragmatic responses to specific oppressive practices. No form of organisation is applicable irrespective of context, just as no category of people is the appropriate agent of social change under all circumstances. Anarchist organisation is not necessarily spontaneous. Non-planning may be consistent with certain forms of libertarian action, but formal structures, even outside of revolutionary situations, can still be consistent with the prefigurative ideal. In their ideal form, the subjugated groups themselves form anarchist structures and combat their oppression through methods that prefigure libertarian principles.

Anarchist organisational principles do not prioritise one particular form, but do rule out certain representative and hierarchical modes of operation, such as the invisible dictatorship and the vanguard party.

Modes of organisation should be synecdochic of the social relations that anarchists wish to achieve. Like desirable, mutually-beneficial relationships, they cannot be predicted beforehand. Just as friendships cannot be imposed, and just as it is impossible to predict how deep or how long a love affair will last, so too no one can externally will the forms of solidarity between subjugated groups. In the same way that relationships can become romances, life-long partnerships or develop into transitory but intense liaisons, so too groups and collaborations can be continuous, occasional or temporary, depending on context and the requirements, desires and identities of the subjects.

Multiform types of oppression, which are not necessarily economic alone, require and create heterogeneous responses, as Jean Grave suggested well before the First World War:

> Society teems with abuses; against each abuse, there must rise up that group of those who suffer most from it in order to combat it.... Not only groups struggling against that which exists, but attempts to group together along the lines of the future, with a view to producing faith, well-being, solidarity, among like-minded individuals.[254]

Multiple organisational tactics confront the diversity of oppressive practices and seek to develop solidarity along autonomous, locally-decided lines. Frequent, diverse, local acts of resistance that combine with other micro-oppositional forces can create a critical mass which initiates change. Particular types of structure are associated with certain types of tactic. The interrelation of structure and tactic and appropriateness of various forms of resistance and confrontation are examined in the next chapter.

Chapter Five

Anarchist Tactics

Introduction

Ideal types of contemporary anarchism reject the strategic and unitary responses of Leninism and instead propose varied and flexible tactics. The previous chapter described and evaluated the many different organisational methods that can be consistent with the anarchist ideal. In – and through – these structures, subjugated agents practise reciprocal social relations that prefigure the characteristics of a liberated society.

The variety of organisational arrangements inspires a multiplicity of tactics that prefigure anarchist objectives. These practical methods, as discussed in Chapter Two, are often classified as 'direct action'. They make sense in relation to prefiguration through an examination of the identities of the oppressed subjects who use them, contextual characteristics such as the links (and limits) of support, as well as the aims they prefigure.

There are libertarians who favour one particular method or programme. Such radicals regard one strategy as being central and essential to the programme of liberation. Nonetheless, whilst these Leninist forms of anarchism are not ignored, the ideal type anarchist response that is tactical and multiform is also shown to be a significant and effective constituent in contemporary libertarian movements. A strategic politic is based on a hypothetical imperative. It sees one central struggle with one fundamental aim, which is regarded as 'the revolution' (or sometimes 'Revolution'), a temporally distinct and identifiable event. All actions are assessed, in the final analysis, in terms of whether they foment or distract from this momentous occasion. Consequentialist approaches have a clear separation of means from ends. Chosen methods, whether they be a particular form of hierarchical political organisation or a vanguard approach to tactics, are justified through appeal to the benevolence of the eventual ends and the effectiveness and efficiency of these methods in achieving the prescribed desirable goals. Such consequentialist approaches are rejected by the prefigurative analysis of consistent, class struggle anarchism.

The rejection of instrumentalist approaches does not mean that anarchists are non-revolutionary, although their conception of 'revolution' differs significantly from that of their opponents within socialist traditions. All the major class struggle anarchist groups repeatedly stress that social and economic relations require fundamental alteration, and that this radical transformation is achieved only through non-constitutional methods. Whilst the Leninist model sees the revolution as an event which validates all the acts leading up to it, contemporary tactical anarchists view the revolution less as a unified moment, and more as a continuous and developing process of situations and enchanting instances of liberation.

The first section of the chapter discusses the specific nature of the anarchist ideal of revolution as a non-unique event. Revolution is not a single phenomenon but the accumulation of ever expanding and growing incidents of prefigurative anarchist actions. 'Rebellion' and 'insurrection' refer to less frequent, more geographically contained, incidents of libertarian resistance. In a later section, localised forms of rebellion, such as sabotage and criminality, are identified and assessed in terms of their prefigurative characteristics.

The forms of direct action considered in this chapter are divided contingently into industrial and community actions. Workplace methods including the mass strike and sabotage have been seen as archetypal of anarchism. In the community category are tactics such as squatting and theft that also have a long association with anarchism. Other approaches, such as constitutional activity, are often regarded as antithetical to libertarianism, yet these too have been used by class struggle anarchists. Alternative techniques, derived from poststructuralism, such as hyper-passivity and disengagement, are also critically assessed with regard to prefiguration.

1. Revolution

Despite the universal acceptance, in contemporary class struggle anarchist writings, of the need for revolution,[1] there is a lack of clarity concerning its constituents and characteristics. While the term 'revolution' is widely evoked, it is rarely defined or explained.[2] 'Revolution' indeed has contradictory meanings, suggesting both drastic change, and the notion of a full cyclic sequence returning back to an original position.[3]

Anarchists consider that increasing liberty is the aim of revolution and that altering political practice is insufficient to achieve this end. Other oppressive forces such as the economic modes of production and exchange need to be confronted and overcome. Marx and Engels' definition of revolution as 'the most radical rupture with traditional property relations',[4] is approved of by class struggle anarchists. As Ray Cunningham of the WSM explains: 'We are not interested in exchanging one set of rulers for another; when we speak of revolution we do not mean a coup d'etat. Anarchist revolution is a fundamental change in the way society is ordered.'[5] Anarchists conforming to the ideal type reject the political revolution but in doing so are not merely suggesting its replacement by an economic one. The paradigm of prefigurative libertarianism recognises that the ambition of social revolution requires a transformation of the whole nexus of intertwined practices.

In rejecting political revolution, anarchists are in agreement with Hannah Arendt who, in order to demonstrate its inadequacy, repeats Plato's definition of revolution as the 'quasi-natural transformation from one form of government to another'.[6] The cosmological character of revolution still has residues in the modern era, but it is not the supernatural feature of Plato's definition that is criticised but the fact that it is too wide. Changes in government do not require wider social or economic changes.[7] For anarchists, as well as Arendt, these latter oppressive powers have to be challenged in order for a process to be truly 'revolutionary'.

Confusion arises as sometimes only libertarian forms of social change that are in agreement with anarchist principles are described as 'revolution'. On other occasions those uprisings that change social relations but reintroduce hierarchy are still recognised by anarchists as revolutions, although as undesirable ones. There are yet other instances where the demarcation between one conception of revolution and the other is ignored, so a critic may appear to be discussing one type of uprising while it is being interpreted as another. Even those revolts that do not have libertarian aims are discussed in terms of their revolutionary potential, irrespective of the eventual result and intentions of their main actors. For instance, John Casey of Class War makes a distinction between the mutiny against the Shah of Iran, which is designated a 'revolution', and the theocracy that followed ,which is regarded as counterrevolution.[8] Similarly, anarchists from an earlier era supported the October Revolution which they considered to be distinct from the Bolshevik takeover.[9] Meltzer, in the context of the Bolshevik Revolution, suggests that such a distinction between means and eventual ends is not feasible, as it is not possible 'to defend the gain of the Russian Revolution while not accepting Lenin's triumph'.[10] Casey and Meltzer have different interpretations of 'revolution'. For Casey, it refers to the series of events that culminates in the overthrow of the leadership. For Meltzer, it is a more elongated process, extending into the creation of new social relations after the expulsion of the original hierarchy.

1.1. Anarchist Ideal of Revolution

The anarchist conception of revolution, in its ideal form, requires multiple successful confrontations of oppressive powers, rather than a single determining conflict. Revolution needs agents of change who are conscious of their role in wishing to create more egalitarian social relations. Struggle takes place across a variety of terrains and

263

is carried out by the oppressed subjects themselves, who, through their self-organisation, prefigure forms of libertarian social relations. Acts of resistance and the types of alliances that these create are sometimes temporary, but always strive to be non-hierarchical. In different locations revolutionary action will take different forms and involve distinct tactics, with no single method being regarded as either universal or sufficient. As such, revolutions are both means and ends. They are on-going adventures, that generate non-hierarchical processes.

For libertarian marxists, as discussed in Chapter Three, the acts of the agents of change are the pivotal determinants in changing social relations. The anarchist concept of change differs from Leninist orthodoxy that sees revolution as being economically determined.[11] The modes of production determine the structure of social relations. As capitalism develops, the classes, which are produced by the developing forces of production, grow in antagonism. The increasing alienation of the oppressed class, the proletariat, raises their consciousness of their subjugation and heightens their desire for revolution.[12] The determinist account is rejected by libertarian marxists, who recognise that the various factors in the political-economic description are not mechanically related in a relationship of cause and effect, but are mutually interdependent.[13] Revolutionary class(es) create their own social structures, some separate to, others in conflict with, existing heteronomous forces. These relationships provoke changes in economic conditions as well as being produced by them.

Revolutions, according to the anarchist ideal, are not unique acts, being indistinguishable, except in scale, from more localised anarchist tactics from which revolution materialises. The ideal avoids the problems associated with the Leninist model. Orthodox marxists regard 'revolution' as having a temporally specific location, differing in its social relations to the movements which create it and the emancipated society that comes after. The uprising produces in its first instance a transitional society, which for Lenin and Trotsky is identified as socialism, while the eventual goal remains communism. Anarchists recognise that this distinction between methods and aims led to the transitional period becoming the objective rather than the means. Oddly, Trotsky confirms this. He observes that it was the transitional period and the 'temporary' state apparatus, a bureaucracy Trotsky and the Bolsheviks helped to create, which assisted in the repression of Soviet citizens. The transitory administrative regime came to be identified with the Soviet Union and Communism itself.[14]

The anarchist model regards revolution as emerging from escalating, diversely-located acts that interact and interweave. Such a paradigm is illustrated in novels like *Breaking Free* and *The Free*. The growth of intertwining libertarian actions, rather than one heroic, centrally-organised assault, leads the existing order to crisis.[15] Class War describe the prelude to the overthrow of heteronomous rule in similar multiple tactical terms. Communities come together to expel state, bourgeois or other oppressive instruments and create liberated spaces or 'no go areas' which are matched by similar acts in production, where workers impose their own desires onto distribution and creation.[16]

The size and frequency of these libertarian acts, rather than any millennial or 'quasi-natural' trait, characterises the ideal type anarchist revolution. Wide-scale subversive tactics so disrupt the existing social and communicative order that existing categories of explanation and understanding dissolve and new forms of communication appear. The events of May 1968 were transmitted, often via graffiti, in quasi-poetic forms. Revolution, as the SI described in their 1960s free magazine, becomes a succession of miracles, rather than a unique, isolated wonder.[17] Revolutions as singular events would be reintegrated into the already established symbolic order and hence become counterrevolutionary. The spontaneous, unending progressions of these wonders may avoid such recuperation. When revolution ceases, it has failed.

1.2. Temporary Autonomous Zone

The preference for these immediate insurrectionary moments led some anarchists, especially Americans such as Bey, Black and Zerzan to favour the Temporary Autonomous Zone (TAZ) as preferable to revolution. The concept of the TAZ, influenced by poststructuralism,[18] is contrasted favourably to a very specific pre-modern version of revolution, interpreted as part of a cyclic return to heteronomous power.[19] This is not a depiction of revolution shared by contemporary anarchists. The TAZ, although sharing many features with the libertarian ideal revolution, as many class struggle proponents recognise, has flaws that the latter avoids.

Bey's concept of the TAZ appears in many contemporary anarchist discussions. It was, for instance, taken up by the Alder Valley Anarchists,[20] by *Do or Die*, in their critical discussion of social centres and squatted spaces,[21] and by Ian Bone, previously of Class War then of MA'M, where he identifies TAZs in a variety of tactics:

> [T]he Autonomous Zone was the place where you were in control and they weren't! It might be Tristan Da Cunha in 1928, a barren rock off Ireland in the '60s or 300 yards of rioter controlled roadway in the stand-off with the cops.[22]

The similarities between the TAZ and the anarchist conception of revolution are that the methods of their realisation are non-hierarchical, creative and stimulating.[23] The TAZ does, however, differ from the revolution, in that it does not confront oppressive forces, but hides or flees from them. 'The TAZ exists not only beyond Control but also beyond definition, beyond gazing and naming as acts of enslaving, beyond the understanding of the State, beyond the State's ability to *see*.'[24] The TAZ does not aim to defeat or subvert the State but disbands, when confronted, and re-forms elsewhere, like the Peace Convoys of the 1980s, the New Age travellers or the House music ravers, that melted away and reformed on another site.[25] The TAZ is always fleeting and fleeing.

Class struggle anarchists support acts of liberation that may be short-lived, such as riots, but do not hold that state power will exist forever. The TAZ co-exists with oppressive power as it exists in the empty spaces that have escaped the gaze of the state and is distinct from the lived experience of the everyday.[26] Consequently, while such tactics of evasion might well be appropriate, especially where the alternative methods of conflict can only be symbolic due to the strength of opposition, prioritising the TAZ discriminates against those forms of resistance that can successfully confront oppressive force. The anarchist ideal of revolution allows for greater, wider and more flexible forms of opposition than the TAZ.

Bey's partiality for nomadic methods privileges a vanguard. He diminishes the role of those economically constrained from itinerant drifting, such as those involved in more mundane, but necessary, acts of rebellion.[27] Bey, like Deleuze, regards change as not simply reactive. Yet, in common with Deleuze, Bey's nomads are specific only to those practices and oppressed subject positions that are capable of drifting. This unspoken assumption leaves Bey open to the criticism that he ignores the specificities of various forms of oppression by reducing responses to a singular form of response.[28] The nomad, at least as described by Deleuze, assumes an equivalence between genders that overlooks their different socio-historical constructs.[29] The nomad is little different from the abstract, liberal moral agent of Freedom Press and Baldelli, as it is gender-, race- and class-blind. Bey's liberalism extends to regarding the band, the organising force of the TAZ, as being capable of forming under contractual obligation. Bey's version of the TAZ reinforces the anarcho-capitalist position, as against class struggle anarchism, that contractual obligations are a form of social arrangement free of compulsion.[30]

In contrast to Bey's version of the TAZ, the consistent anarchist recognises that the subjects of change have many different identities and that methods will correspondingly take disparate forms. These methods can be confrontational as well as evasive, while it is their continuity and frequency that constitutes revolutionary change. The similarities between the anarchist ideal of revolution and the TAZ are clear. Camus, quoting Bakunin, calls the revolution 'a feast without beginning and without end'.[31] The revolution is an amalgamation of prefigurative rebellious acts whose frequency and intensity creates a critical mass that fundamentally alters a multitude of interdependent repressive practices and powers. Unlike the TAZ, revolution is not dependent on the lacunae in state relations, but can create its own values that challenge dominant practices.

1.3. Rebellion

'Rebellion' has been interpreted in many, often incompatible, ways. For class struggle anarchists, the term 'rebellion' is compatible with revolution, but indicates smaller scale interruptions of oppressive practices. Burns, for instance, titles his analysis of the campaigns against Thatcher's changes in local government finance, *Poll Tax Rebellion*.[32] The book describes the confrontations with constitutional political institutions, judicial powers and penal disciplines. Burns ends with a description of how the multiplicities of defiant tactics led to the successful eradication of an important, iniquitous piece of legislation. The multiple acts of resistance to the Community Charge led to the fall of Prime Minister Thatcher, but did not undermine these wider, grander, singular oppressive practices. Rebellion, nevertheless, holds out the promise of extension into revolution.

Others, such as Woodcock, interpret 'rebellion' in terms of *individual* defiance and consequently as distinct from revolution. Quoting Camus, as supporting a Stirnerite evocation of the individual ego, Woodcock declares that rebellion is different to revolution as the latter demands the overthrow of the existing order while rebellion, by contrast, is individualist and egoistic.[33] Rebellion for Woodcock is identified with a strategic preference for individual liberty. Yet Woodcock's description of Camus is inaccurate, and his analysis of rebellion is also open to doubt. Camus dismisses the notion that such rebellion is purely self-centred: 'rebellion is not, essentially, an egoistic act'.[34] In frustrating the imposition of heteronomous values the dissenter is affirming other values.[35] These ethical principles cannot be wholly personal, for in the most extreme cases the rebel may be willing to die to affirm these values: the rebel 'considers that the latter are more important than he [sic] is. He acts, therefore, in the name of certain values which are still indeterminate but which he feels are common to himself and to all men'.[36] Consequently, Camus's version of rebellion, as opposed to Woodcock's interpretation, is essentially humanistic, regarding it as the basis for solidarity. Revolution differs from rebellion for Camus, not on the basis of collectivity, but because he considers revolution in statist terms, as being the (re-)imposition of law while rebellion remains impermanent.[37]

Confusion in definitions is indicative of the different types of anarchism and their disparate aims. Woodcock's version, tied to a supposed atomised revolt, is compatible with 'lifestyle anarchism' as it 'foster[s] ideas of individual autonomy rather than social freedom'.[38] Class struggle anarchists such as the AWG by no means approved of Bookchin's municipal anarchism but shared his disdain for individualist rebellion that sought 'personal solutions to social problems'.[39] They consequently rejected Stirnerite rebellion as it ignores oppression and neglects to create social relations such as networks of solidarity. Fox of the AWG, for example, disapprovingly assessed tactics like the 1980s Stop the City demonstrations, which made little attempt to broaden out beyond the 'anarchist ghetto', and the refusal, by some anarchist currents at the time, to assist workers' struggles, preferring 'isolation by the anarcho elite'.[40] Such an individualism not only narrows avenues for necessary solidarity but permits only a restrictive form of freedom. As Thomas notes in his critique of Stirnerite revolt, the liberated ego has little choice in what forms of social relationship it can engage in.[41] When class struggle anarchists promote rebellion they are not doing so in individualist terms, as they do not consider such action to be appropriately prefigurative. The term 'rebellion' from hereon refers to the social version preferred by Burns (and Camus) and class struggle anarchists.[42]

1.4. Insurrection and Riot

There are two interpretations of 'insurrection'; the first defines it as the armed period of a general revolution;[43] the second as a localised, often spontaneous, uprising. It is the latter definition that has long been associated with anarchism. Bakunin and his followers are often portrayed as 'insurrectionists'[44] on the basis of their activities in Lyons in 1870 and Bologna in 1874. Bakunin's supporters are not the only class struggle libertarians to support regional uprisings.[45] The insurrectionary strategy of promoting local revolts involved the setting up, by force, of zones liberated from local and national law. These risings were intended to encourage, by example, neighbouring areas to also rise up. They are popularly identified with spontaneous rather than organised movements, although Bakunin and others did attempt to contrive them.[46] Orthodox marxists, in particular, have been critical of such tactics, on two grounds.

First, insurrection was based on a non-specific revolutionary agent, 'the masses', rather than the proletariat.[47] This objection prioritises the proletariat as the only legitimate revolutionary agent and has been dealt with in Chapter Three. The second criticism is that insurrection is too localised to oppose more general oppressions. These grander powers are thought to require a wider, more stable organisation,[48] a view that seems to be supported by the abject failure in which Bakunin's insurrectionary attempts ended. For the anarchist ideal, however, insurrection can be acceptable and need not be restricted to Bakunin's domino theory of strategic revolution. Insurrections are permissible so long as the following conditions are met: that the agents primarily involved in the uprising are the oppressed themselves; that the social relations the riot promotes are consistent with anarchist ethics;[49] and finally, that the uprising must be seen as tactical rather than strategic, reaching out beyond the confines of specific localities to promote, assist and be superseded by other forms of tactic. There is certainly a prefigurative feature to insurrection, which the historian Roderick Kedward admires, as it is a method that is consistent with principles of federated local control.[50]

The consistent anarchist would not regard the local, physical uprising as sufficient either as means or end, but as a useful tactic. British class struggle libertarians maintain that a major change in economic conditions would require substantial acts of force, occurring across a range of localities. But the fact that anarchists, such as Class War, defended and encouraged rioting made them a suitable scapegoat for the urban unrest in 1985.[51] Class War was delighted to be considered so influential, although they acknowledged that radical sections of working class communities themselves should take the credit. Class War was willing to be associated with the urban insurrectionists in the hope that the media interest would boost anarchism, which indeed it did. It should be noted, however, that their influence in the widespread disturbances that year was minimal.[52]

It was not just the mainstream media that misunderstood Class War's support for insurrectionary uprisings. An article in *Here and Now* inaccurately portrayed British anarchists, and Class War in particular, as regarding riots as 'the highest expression of class warfare'.[53] If anarchists did assert a hierarchy of activities, then this would be inconsistent with the ideal, but libertarians, even in the early 1980s, proposed multiple responses. During the Miners' Strike of 1984-5, Class War proposed a programme of 'minor insurgency as the real anarchist contribution' to an effort to open up a 'second front' in non-colliery neighbourhoods so as to draw 'police out of the mining areas'. Such a tactic was proposed in support of, not to replace, other forms of revolt. Rioting would take advantage of and support industrial action, hit squad attacks on scabs and nearby police stations, and conventional propaganda.[54]

Riots, a form of insurrection, have long marked the distinction between anarchists and Leninists. The incendiary wave of spontaneous riots which hit urban, suburban and rural areas alike in 1981 were dismissed by the traditional marxist parties, the main complaint being that, although these uprisings voiced grievances about capitalist oppression, they were not a suitable method for resolution.

For the orthodox revolutionary left, the appropriate method was the proletariat seizing political power through the revolutionary party, not the (largely) urban poor acting for themselves.[55] Leninist attitudes persist, for example, in their response to J18, the large scale multi-site convergence of direct action, demonstration and street-party of June 18, 1999.

J18, the 'carnival against capitalism' metamorphosed from festival and rave into a riot and back again. Revelry and insurrection sometimes co-existed, making it hard for the authorities to distinguish the dangerous mob from the joyous (but apparently unthreatening) dancer. As the police intervened, one identity would be tactically swapped for the other, or merged into a confusing but liberating hybrid. The event was co-ordinated by an amalgam of environmental, anti-Third World debt and anarchist groups.[56] The action demonstrated the difference between the anarchist ideal and Leninism. The J18 campaign deliberately avoided central representation; no one mediated with the police, as there was no formal leadership who could represent the diversity of groups. Prior to the event, J18 was considered an irrelevancy by orthodox marxist groupings who took no role in the planning or in the day itself. The SWP, at the time, rejected the methods and organisation of the J18 events, considering them to be 'inadequate'.[57] The SWP also dismissed J18 as 'not enough to challenge the system', yet on this basis every action – including strikes or voting for the Labour Party, methods the SWP support – should be dismissed.[58] J18 was also considered illegitimate because its means and structure were not based on prioritising the industrial working class at the point of production; for the SWP this is where 'real power to change society lies'.[59] The successful method of co-operative, decentralised co-ordination not only left 'vanguard' parties bewildered, but also confused most mainstream reporters, as without a spokesperson or leader, with no single locus of confrontation, the J18 fell outside of their experience and interpretative abilities.[60]

Anarchists do not believe that singular localised insurrections will completely alter power relations, but that they can assist in the process and strengthen oppressed subject groups:[61] they can provide instant moments of solidarity, breaking down divisions between and within oppressed groups.[62] Urban uprisings also provide opportunities to demonstrate different forms of distribution. The restraints of commercial norms and the process of commodification are subverted. As Plant describes, when bricks break the spell of the shop window, commodities are shorn of their false properties and can be seen anew. Riots provide opportunities for the oppressed to create fresh forms of exchange themselves, rather than having a 'radical' blueprint for the replacement of private enclosure imposed upon them. It is through the process of contesting private property relationships that new forms of social relationship are formed, and these, as Plant acknowledges, cannot be predicted, as there is 'no possibility of distinguishing between the "good" values of the revolutionary consciousness and the "bad" ones of spectacular reification in advance'.[63]

With the breaking down of the rule of capital, new subjectivities emerge which take many forms. Pillaged household goods piled up and burnt are turned into bizarre avant-garde sculptures.[64] Social services are recreated with deliveries of milk made to every house from a looted milk float.[65] Co-operative plunder creates new social relations away from state observation and other quasi-state hierarchies.[66] British anarchist descriptions of the Trafalgar Square riot of 1990 during the anti-Poll Tax campaign also report the creation of imaginative social relations.[67] The uprising had many consequences that could not have been predicted beforehand. It confronted the conspicuous consumption of London's West End and terrorised the government into reversing its local taxation initiative (fig. 5.1.).[68] The large-scale unrest also played a significant role in removing the apparently impregnable Conservative leader, something that the SWP originally believed rioting could not achieve.[69]

The brawling affray in central London in 1990 cannot be divorced from the range of campaigns, confrontations and organisations that came before and followed it, including work-based activity. Paul Gilroy's observations on the earlier urban riots of 1981 add credence to the notion that community uprising and industrial activity are interrelated, rather than separate. The aftermath of the 1981 revolts influenced the structures and composition of trade unions and subsequently the Health Service strike the following year.[70] Yet, despite such achievements, riots are, rightly, not prioritised over other forms of libertarian struggle.

Rebellions take many forms; they can be riots, TAZs, or other liberatory moments in themselves. Such revolts against hierarchical authority are prefigurative processes in which creative forms of libertarian social organisation can be realised. Unlike Bey's TAZ, however, most rebellions seek out areas of confrontation and encourage other forms of contestation. As these events grow in frequency, the social formations that form these dissident acts dissolve heteronomous

Figure 5.1. Poll Tax Riot, 1990, from ACAB's book of the same name.

power. Thus the term 'revolution', rather than identifying a separate phenomena, such as a single millennial rupture, might signify the greatest frequency and impact of such acts of rebellion, insurrection and riot. Challenging oppressive economic conditions and practices, which divide production and consumption, pleasure, play and labour, is a feature of prefigurative, liberatory action, and also leads to other forms of confrontation against heteronomous control.

2. Industrial Activity

As discussed in the previous chapter, many contemporary anarchists do not make a critical strategic distinction between community and workplace activity. They follow the autonomist marxist argument that capitalism operates in all aspects of social life seeking out surplus labour, not just at the point of production. Nevertheless, there are tactics that are customarily described as specific to the point of production, the most prominent and disruptive being the general social or mass strike. While this chapter segregates workplace and community actions, it does not endorse the division but simply reflects their frequent differentiation. Many of the tactics described in one form can be used in the other arena. Such features of contemporary employment as home-working, commuting and in-service training, that encompass environments beyond the immediate location of production, further undermine the legitimacy of the division. Forms of oppression in a particular office may have more in common with demeaning practices in a household than with another, apparently similar, occupation.

As seen in Chapter Three, some contemporary activists, such as Meltzer, wrongly place a strategic emphasis on the workplace:

> It is not because we think that 'the industrial proletariat can do no wrong' that we advocate action by the industrial proletariat; it is simply because they have the effective means to destroy the old economy and build a new one, in our type of society at least. The Free Society [...] will come about through workers' councils taking over the place of work.[71]

Meltzer in 1986 gives pre-eminence to the industrial, based on a version of economic determinism in which altering modes and relations of productivity directly cause radical change in social relations. Destroying the economic base is akin to building a new society. Meltzer's reductive account rules out the possibility of oppressive powers that may not be wholly determined by economic forces. Rejecting strategic centrality for industrial methods does not imply a repudiation of these tactics, only that they are not exclusive or sufficient.

Historically, the tactic most associated with anarchism was one classified as an industrial method, namely the mass strike (see Fig. 5.2.). However, whilst the mass strike is an important form of direct action, it is not the only one. The most appropriate forms of anarchist action (ideal ones) are compatible with variants of sabotage. Sabotage is a category of anti-political activity that includes more than just machine-breaking, which is how it is normally understood by orthodox marxists. Before examining how the concept of 'sabotage' embraces the key features of direct action, it is first important to consider the mass strike, in order to appraise its prefigurative strengths and weaknesses.

Figure 5.2. From the cover of *Direct Action in Industry*, 1980e.

2.1. The Mass Strike
In 1832 William Benbow promoted the idea of a grand national holiday, in the form of a mass strike.[72] This form of direct action would allow the

productive classes to wrest control of the manufacturing apparatuses from their owners. Practical efforts at its realisation impelled the tailors of Derby during the Silk Mill Lock Out and prompted the formation of the Grand National Consolidated Trades Union (GNCTU) as the organisational structure to support this proto-syndicalist strategy.[73]

As seen in the previous chapter, revolutionary syndicalists such as the American, pre-First World War IWW had a clear strategy. The revolution would be made by building one big union, and this would co-ordinate the general social strike.[74] The weaknesses of 'One Big Union' was recognised by Malatesta, who argued that one structure could not represent all interests.[75] The strategic centrality of industrial activity found in the early forms of anarcho-syndicalism, and in the writings of Rocker,[76] can also be discovered in contemporary anarcho-syndicalists in the key role given to the mass strike as the critical tactic in creating revolution. For instance DAM stated: 'The social general strike is the weapon with which the working class will make the social revolution'.[77] However, most contemporary anarchists, including many anarcho-syndicalists, do not have such a strategic view of the mass strike, but regard it as one tactic amongst others which can assist in contesting oppressive practices.

The general strike was considered to be so effective on its own that it was even approved of by more pacific anarchists.[78] Johann Most contests the understanding of the general strike as sufficient and nonviolent. For Most, the general strike is the millennial method which would destroy the old order but would not be a peaceful tactic because 'the strike-breakers will loot, burn, dynamite, and assassinate. Beginning in anticipation of social revolution, the general strike thus becomes social revolution itself'.[79] Although Most, like many other syndicalists, recognised that the mass strike would require other tactics, he still considered the workers involved in the industrial dispute to be the central agents and that the general stoppage held principal importance.

The mass strike is closely associated with anarchism because it is an example of libertarian direct action. For example, Rocker views the basis of anarcho-syndicalism to be the eradication of managerial control of industry through the generalised refusal to work and the replacement of such control by workers' self-management. 'The great importance of the general strike lies in this: At one blow it brings the whole economic system to a standstill and shakes it to its foundations.'[80] So associated is the tactic of the general strike with anarchism[81] that revolutionaries from other socialist traditions, such as Rosa Luxemburg, had to distance themselves from anarchism, by denouncing it, in order to advocate this method.[82]

Poststructural anarchism would be in agreement with Luxemburg as she does not regard the mass strike to be a method solely applicable to the organised worker. '[T]he class instinct of the youngest, least trained, badly educated and still worse organised Russian proletariat is immeasurably stronger than that of the organised, trained and enlightened working class of any other Western European country.'[83] Luxemburg's observation conflicts with Lenin who considered that the mass strike required such organisational preconditions that it presupposed the political ascendancy of the working class, and was hence unnecessary.[84] Luxemburg recognised that the political strikes, those favoured by Lenin, which are arranged and controlled by parties, tend to be rare, small and limited in scope. These disciplined political strikes, Luxemburg explains, at best play only a minor role in preparing workers, or can act only as initial sparks for greater conflagrations.[85] The mass strike is libertarian in form because it cannot be commanded as it is too large and multifaceted to be under political control. It is 'the indication, the rallying idea, of a whole period of the class struggle lasting for years' which no structure is capable of dictating.[86]

Luxemburg and the anarchist ideal do, however, differ. For Luxemburg, the economic battle is, in the final analysis, central and strategic. Luxemburg reduces revolutionary activity to the role of a

278

single, vanguard agency, the proletariat, albeit one free of Leninist control.[87] Contemporary anarcho-syndicalists, like SolFed, breaking with the strategic centralism of their predecessors, argue that a multi-tactical disposition is required:

> Anarcho-syndicalism involves recognising the essential need to remove *all* forms of hierarchical power relationship in order to create a better society. The call for the Social General Strike/Social Revolution has to be more than a call for the end of capitalism. It cannot be limited to workers opting out of capitalist control; either because other oppressive control is not recognised, or because 'the end of capitalism means the end to all oppression'. Neither should it be the overthrowing of capitalism and then it is time to get on with all these other problems. Those 'other problems' need to be addressed (along with economic control) both now, at the time of the social revolution, and no doubt afterwards as well.[88]

The general strike would involve conflict not just within the economic arena but also in other areas. These battles would require the engagement of actors far wider than the subsection of the 'industrial worker' as the strike led to conflict within communities.[89] The types of oppression countered would not only be those reduced to the economic, but would also extend into other practices.

2.2. Sabotage

The term 'sabotage' has its roots in the industrial sector and either refers to the clumsiness of the step when wearing a wooden clog (*sabot* in French)[90] or to using the hard footwear to destroy machinery. Engels speaks of sabotage only in terms of machine-breaking and associates sabotage with the pre-industrial Luddites. He considers Luddism to be a form of protest that is easily crushed and which should be replaced with a more appropriate organisational method.[91] As such, Engels places sabotage very low down a hierarchy of proletarian action, just above criminality.[92] Such a limited view of sabotage is shared by some anarchists,[93] but is wrong on three grounds. Sabotage is not necessarily unplanned, although it may be more covert than other forms of action.[94] Second, when carried out by the oppressed, such activities can involve self-creative confrontation to oppressive practices.[95] Finally, sabotage is not only limited to machine-breaking.

The orthodox marxist parties and social democratic trade unions have historically been suspicious, and often downright contemptuous, of machine-breaking. The industrial sociologist Pierre Dubois, writing in the aftermath of the Paris uprisings of 1968, relates how the different trade union organisations in France can be distinguished according to their stances on sabotage which reflect their ideologies. The professedly 'marxist' post-1914 *Confederation Generale du Travail* (CGT) opposes sabotage, while the *Confederation Francaise Democratique du Travail* (CFDT) takes a less strict line. Anarchists, who dominated the pre-1914 CGT, approved of sabotage, as do 'Maoists', according to Dubois; however, Dubois suggests the latter 'marxist' position of the CGT opposing sabotage can be traced back to Engels.[96]

The low status Engels awards sabotage is partly due to his definition of the term, regarding it as simply machine or product breaking. This is too narrow. It will be interpreted here as 'the conscious attempt to reduce the profitability of the organisation through the subversion of managerial authority'. As such, it shares similarities with Antonio Negri's concept of the 'refusal of work', which he describes as: 'the most specific, materially given, foundation of the productive force reappropriated to serve the process of working class self-valorisation'.[97] 'The refusal to work' encompasses a range of direct action that obstruct sthe processes by which surplus value is extracted and creates instead social relationships based on different values. This concept is akin to anarchist direct action, a multifaceted form of prefigurative behaviour performed by subject groups themselves. Thus, 'the refusal to work' and its synonym 'sabotage', like 'direct action', usefully encapsulate the anarchist revolutionary ambition.

2.3. Machine and Product Breaking

Accounts of sabotage, such as the description by Solidarity's Ken Weller of General Motor's Lordstown (Ohio) car plant 1971-72,[98] also described by Lamb in his introduction to Flynn's treatise,[99] uncover an array of sophisticated structures and communication between workers. Even less overt forms of sabotage rely on the networks of workplace friendships, the sophisticated signs of a nod and the wink, rather than the formal administrative structures of official labour organisation. Machine-breaking and product destruction is not often amenable to central administrative control. The oppressed agents themselves are better located than a revolutionary leadership to recognise how a loose screw, or a mis-hit computer key, can cause maximum inconvenience for their employers. As such, sabotage is much more acceptable to anarchists than strategic politicians. Sabotage is no more an act of powerlessness than striking (an activity that is higher up Engels' hierarchy). It is through acts of machine manipulation that workers can hit immediately at their bosses, create networks of support and, as part of a wider industrial campaign, gain reforms when other tactics have not succeeded. Flynn provides an example, describing how Copenhagen print-workers at the start of the twentieth century sabotaged the newspaper they produced, such that the news stories and advertisements were humorously distorted. The loss of revenue, as well as the embarrassment this caused the owners, forced the paper's management into making concessions to the workforce.[100]

Dubois correctly recognises that sabotage can take many more forms including arson, theft, vandalism, strikes, go-slows and absenteeism.[101] Nonetheless, he still defines it inadequately: 'that done by workers, individually or collectively, to the manufactured product or the machinery of production, that results in lowering the quantity or quality of production, whether temporarily or permanently.'[102] The problems with this definition are twofold. The less important is that it seems to exclude those service sectors that might not have a tangible product or machinery. Flynn gives an example of service-sector sabotage, when New York waiters at the start of the twentieth century informed customers of the kitchen's poor hygiene, thereby dissuading patrons from remaining and as a result reducing the restaurant's profits.[103] The more important problem with Dubois' definition is that some sabotage can increase the quality of the product at the expense of the owners, rather than decrease it. Flynn described how in silk manufacture the product was routinely adulterated with tin and lead to increase the weight and thereby company profits; similarly, milk distributors would regularly dilute their product with water. In these cases, Flynn recommends that the workers exclude the impurities which would increase quality and cut the factory owner's profit.[104] The 'good work strike', as McFarlane argues in *Here and Now*, is prefigurative in that it affronts the current system and partly invokes a new social system: production under a non-capitalist ethic.[105]

Sabotage is a direct attack on the extraction of surplus labour through either ignoring or subverting managerial dictate. While some class struggle libertarians interpreted 'sabotage' in Engels' limited sense, the wider interpretation is one that is most compatible with the anarchist ideal. As E.P. Thompson demonstrates, from communal riots to political agitation and from propaganda by word to more murderous propaganda by deed, tactics often went hand-in-hand, rather than viewed as mutually exclusive options.[106]

2.4. Strike

Anarchism, because it rejects parliamentary reform, has been represented as being only interested in immediate change.[107] Yet contemporary anarchists are active in participating and supporting smaller scale strikes. Industrial disputes, which appear to consist of action against minor grievances, for instance the reduction of a tea-break by five minutes, are often the result of cumulative frustration with managerial practices.[108] Anarchists, while extending the range of autonomous activity, regard any concession, such as the lengthening of paid breaks that strengthen the revolutionary subject, as partly prefigurative. But strikes are not the only method. If withdrawal of labour is not possible, then harming oneself, or sacrificing sections of the proletariat for a political reason (a technique which anarchists accuse Leninists of) is counter to the prefigurative concept of recomposing oppressed subjects, as Douglass reminds us:. 'Striking is not a principle, it is a tactic.'[109]

Although Engels places strikes higher up the hierarchy of proletarian action, their effectiveness relies on the exact same features as sabotage, such that Dubois correctly classifies the withdrawal of labour as one of its forms.[110] The shared characteristics are the withdrawal of profitable efficiency and the replacement of managerial authority, bourgeois rule in its most direct sense, with different forms of social structure. In a very few cases, the social arrangements created by the working class in conflict with management are even more repressive than those they are resisting. A rare example would be the Whites-only strike organisation of the Billingsgate fish porters or the anti-Black workers' group at Imperial Typewriters in 1974.[111] Anarchists reject support for these actions. Likewise the replacement of management by a hierarchical union structure, whose leadership have interests distinct from those of the workforce, means that contemporary libertarians, when involved in industrial action, aim to create other structures in which control remains with the workforce.[112] This often manifests itself in preference for wildcat or 'unofficial' stoppages.[113]

Strikes may flare into a greater conflagration and erupt across contexts. Large scale strikes create new links of solidarity, forming new types of identity for those involved, replacing those of the 'happy worker' or 'contented consumer', and creating new forms of social relationships, as Luxemburg recognises: 'peaceful wage struggles and street massacres, barricade fighting - all these run through another, run side by side, cross one another, flow in and over one another....'[114] Strikes are not only a form of sabotage because they reduce managerial control or stored surplus value but also because they provoke other forms of self-organisation in conflict with bourgeois rule. As a result, no meaningful distinction between strikes and product destruction is sustainable. The Miners' Strike of 1984-5 necessarily involved destruction of mines, as without maintenance the work-heads flooded. This passive form of sabotage is morally indistinguishable (assuming the level of intent is the same) from active destruction of the coal stocks and is an inescapable part of the workplace conflict whether in the industrial or service industries.

Many forms of striking can encourage worker passivity. The union representatives try to take control of the negotiation process by maintaining a monopoly on information gathering and distribution to its members, and by speaking to the established media on their behalf. As secondary and mass picketing is illegal, there seems to be little role for the workers themselves. To overcome this potentially passive role, anarchists prefer other forms of action which place the resisting agents in a position where they are not dependent upon a mediating force.

2.5. Industrial Boycott

There are two versions of the boycott. The first is where wage-earners, as consumers, are encouraged to avoid buying the products of companies in dispute with their workers, an action carried out in support of other industrial methods.[115] The second is when workers 'black' or prohibit the importation or distribution of goods produced by such companies; Employees refuse to carry out labour for businesses that have caused special offence. This second form differs from a strike, because the withdrawal of labour is much more selective.

One of the most recent examples of the second form of boycott was during the Liverpool dockers' dispute with the Mersey Docks and Harbour Company and that company's major user, Atlantic Containers Limited (ACL). Dock-workers throughout the world, especially in the USA, refused to deal with ACL cargoes in order to put pressure on the sacked dockers' former employers to re-instate them.[116] The globalisation of capital places workers in competition with each other in a world-wide market place. Resistance to capitalism, such as the boycott, builds international links of solidarity and resists managerial rights to determine the beneficiaries of dockers' labour. Sabotage is not necessarily individual, nor covert (although it can take those forms), but can be open and collective. Its multiple forms can be prefigurative of new forms of social relation.

2.6. Occupation

Anarchists often consider the occupation of the workplace to be a more effective form of sabotage than strikes. In the 1990 ambulance drivers' dispute, the pickets, rather than strike, occupied their stations and ran an ambulance service taking instruction from the public rather than through their management.[117] Class War suggests that this form of action, in the context of this period and this service, is preferable to the total withdrawal of labour, for three interrelated reasons. First, it maintains workers' control over those who wish to represent them. Second, occupations effectively resist managerial counter-strategies and expand the arena of solidarity. Finally, occupations have a far greater prefigurative character both in their relationship with others (i.e. still assisting the sick) and in their self-organisation.

Possessing the workplace makes it easier for the workers (who in the industrial setting are the predominant agents of change), rather than the union leadership, to remain actively involved and to control the action.[118] DAM argued that it should be no surprise that workplace occupations are preferable because in order to develop they require a greater level of workers' autonomy than strike action: '[O]ccupation implies positive action actually to take over a plant and to deny access to the management. [This ...] needs a high level of militancy and solidarity as well as rank-and-file organisation.'[119] Yet DAM's argument is contentious. It overlooks strikes that also require significant workers' self-organisation. DAM risk creating a hierarchy of industrial action, which freezes methods according to their predetermined position (in the same way as Engels' hierarchy of tactics).

The occupation at the Lip watch factory strike in France in 1973 was part of a wider industrial dispute that had started with go-slows, machine-breaking and product seizure, as well as withdrawal of labour.[120] DAM's hierarchy of industrial action wrongly assumes that in every case sit-ins require greater organisation: sometimes co-ordination occurs spontaneously, developing out of strike activity. Similarly, the opportunity for a successful occupation is often dependent on disorganisation by management rather than the self-creative abilities of the workforce.

The second argument for preferring the occupation appears to be a purely practical reason: namely, that occupying a workplace prevents replacement labour (scabs) from being brought in.[121] Yet underlying this apparently pragmatic ground is the wider implication that the sit-in provides the opportunity for the workforce to control their immediate environment, determining questions not only of access, but also subverting productive and managerial practices.

The third reason for preferring occupation is its prefigurative character. For an occupation to function successfully, workers must create a social network that is independent of managerial structures. 'This dispute has demonstrated how ordinary workers can run an essential emergency service without bureaucratic management. It has been a shining example of workers' control.'[122] Occupiers, such as those at the Lip watch factory, or the ambulance drivers, continued their labour albeit under different social conditions.

There are two types of criticism of Lip-style occupation as a prefigurative response. The first comes from Gorz. He argues that self-management is not only impossible because of the reconstitution of the economy with geographically diverse manufacturing units, but is also undesirable because such rearrangement of production has de-skilled manufacture.[123] The production process is wholly unfulfilling. Attempts to engage the workforce in determining output targets are not only futile but a further repressive restraint on workers' time.[124]

To reduce production time requires heteronomous management, and the goal should be diminishing work time rather than autonomous production, according to Gorz.

The other criticism questions whether self-managed occupations prefigure a desirable aim. It assesses the reconstitution of hierarchy that accompanies such protest when occupations reintroduce capitalist relations of exchange. This evaluation comes from the French autonomist-influenced Negation group following the events at Lip. The take over of production of watches to supplement strike pay was considered a spectacular tactical breakthrough. This tactic not only confronts liberal property rights by the producers reappropriating the product, but also demonstrates the ability of workers to manage themselves. Managerial authority is shown to be redundant.[125] Yet Negation argue that, for all its positive features, such self-management is nevertheless non-prefigurative as it is self-alienating. Production is performed as wage-labour, and so the strikers become a 'collective capitalist'.[126] The aim is still to protect the business enterprise rather than to bring about its overthrow.[127]

Occupation, however, does not necessarily have to replace managerial capitalism with self-managed capitalism (as characterised by Gorz). As Negation themselves point out, the occupiers also rediscovered the art of living. This, however, soon came into conflict with the ethos of commercial manufacture necessary to provide strike pay.[128] Occupation and workplace autonomy can subvert factory production for a more liberated ideal. Lamb presents examples where self-management of the factory did not reinstate commodity production but replaced it with carnivalesque creativity:

> In the violent struggles against intensive production at the US car plant at Lordstown in 1970 there was an attempt to turn the workshops into swimming pools with high pressure hoses. There were even sabotage competitions to see who could blow an engine up so as to send the bits furthest away.[129]

Occupation can replace the productive with the ludic ethic (one which promotes free play). Sabotage is a threat to political movements that just want to replace control of industry and distribution rather than to fundamentally alter the terms by which creativity takes place. The orthodox marxist CGT rejected sabotage because it wanted to take over the means of production and redistribute its commodities, not destroy commodity production.[130]

The possibility that occupiers could be reconstituting a hierarchy also occurs to Class War. During the ambulance dispute, Class War were critical that the drivers did not take the opportunities available to open up the stations to even broader sections of the community.

> [A]t the grass roots level, ambulance workers have failed to capitalise upon the support of the working class communities they serve. They should be trying to get people to help with the running of occupied stations, helping maintain vehicles, getting supplies in and so on.[131]

The writer in *Class War* appears to be taking a Leninist position, commenting on a strike from a supposedly objective position, external to the conflict. However, assuming that the writer is in the community that is being excluded by the strikers, these comments are legitimate. The failure to make connections with other groups could lead to isolation and the reification of identities between a 'key group' and a largely passive set of supporters.[132] Occupations do not necessarily create elitist divisions; the students who took over the universities in Paris in 1968 opened up spaces to the workers who had been previously prohibited or inhibited from entering.[133]

Many forms of occupation can be prefigurative. One of the aims, as Tom Brown explains, 'has always been to persuade workers to keep on holding the factories and other plants, never to return them for promises'.[134] However, this objective is too narrow for the anarchist ideal: the aim is not to alter the management, but to undermine the very divisions between production, consumption, distribution, adventure and play.

2.7. Go-Slow and Working Without Enthusiasm
Engels disparaged other forms of unofficial action as being a sign of political naivety, as he thought that they were individual moments of protest that were unplanned, disorganised and rare. Yet, on the contrary, they are so frequent that it is often forgotten that they do constitute forms of industrial resistance.[135] Unofficial action takes a range of forms from the overt wildcat work-to-rules with quasi-official trade union-backing, to the more everyday responses to managerial control such as apparent tardiness in responding to the ringing telephone and the obviously uninterested delivery of sales pitch on answering and the unauthorised extra time taken for a break.[136] Although such actions seem to be individual acts of rebellion (in the sense used by Woodcock), such sabotage is more likely to occur if workers can count on mutual solidarity. The reassurance of knowing that a protective excuse will be proffered or sly signal given should managers become inquisitive provides a basis for greater incidents of autonomous activity.

Flynn describes the nineteenth century tactic of the 'ca-canny', when work was purposely performed badly in order to irritate managers and restrict profitability. The ca-canny was used as an immediate response to unsuccessful pay disputes.[137] Such go-slows date back to the earliest days of proletarianisation, in which merchant seafarers were amongst the first recorded group to have employed the tactic.[138] Peter Linebaugh presents a list of early eighteenth century sailors' terminology for loafing. The specialised vocabulary had the effect of keeping conversation from the ears of interfering authority. 'Manany' and 'King's bencher' were terms which covered the people involved in shirking, while 'Tom Cox's Traverse', 'two turns around the longboat' and a 'pull at the scuttlebutt' were the phrases for work avoidance itself.[139] As such they indicate that resistance to managerial control has never depended on the approval of a revolutionary party; such methods are already features of the survival tactics and humanising routines against work discipline. Go-slows may be prompted in reaction to different oppressive practices. They can be an individual desire to work at one's own pace, or a general reaction against managerial authority.[140] They are methods of working class autonomy which are not just of immediate benefit to the agents themselves but also assist in building up networks of trust and hence lead to other tactics.

2.8. Work-to-Rule

A version of the go-slow recommended by anarchists is the work-to-rule. In literary form Jaroslav Hasek's Good Soldier Schweik, whose overly assiduous obedience to the orders of his superiors brings them to ruin, exemplifies the work-to-rule. Practical examples are cited by Brown and Flynn, who recount how French railway workers won industrial victories through apparent obedience. The management devised a long list of directives, such that, if any accident occurred, responsibility would be placed on the employee who had not kept a particular rule, yet if workers fully implemented every safety directive, the service would grind to a halt. After an accident, management shifted the blame on to the stationmaster on the grounds that he had not followed the regulations. As a protest, fellow employees worked to the letter of the rules and by pursuing the explicit orders of management 'within three days the railroad system of France was so completely demoralized that they had to exonerate this particular stationmaster'.[141] Such tactics have immediate advantage over activities like strikes in that there is little cost to the worker. Indeed, strikes may benefit employers, as they save on wages while in most instances production quickly recovers and the shortfall is soon made up.[142]

The work-to-rule subverts managerial authority through immanent critique. Rather than demonstrating the inadequacy of managerial control through appeals to another ideal, the work-to-rule demonstrates the inherent contradictions within this form of administration. Such a method leaves authority baffled and appears far beyond the industrial setting. It can be seen in the actions of children of strictly religious parents who rebel by becoming even more zealous. The work-to-rule pushes authority to the limits and in the confusion establishes room for greater autonomy.

Such tactics are criticised by Gorz, as the work-to-rule replicates capitalist values and norms. Citing the cases of British workers 'who stop work as soon as the siren goes, no matter how much waste and damage is caused', he reports their attitude:

> This sort of resentment is the only form of freedom left to proletarians in 'their' work. They're expected to be passive? Well then, let's be passive. Or more exactly, let us use passivity as a weapon against those who impose it. Since 'their' aim is to create active passivity. This behaviour of resentment which, by overacting the role the worker is expected to play, robs the oppressors of the desired results of their orders, is the last refuge of 'working class dignity'. [....] 'Screw the Bosses!' 'The Gaffer can sort it out!' 'What about our bread!' 'Shit work for shit wages!' The language of proletarian resentment is also the language of impotence.[143]

For Gorz, the work-to-rule advances no positive ideals like 'the abolition of wage slavery'. It has no positive ambition, nor does it create values outside of those created by capital.[144] Gorz's criticism overlooks fundamental features of the work-to-rule. First, the appearance of passivity hides the active autonomy of those involved. Workers are actually making complex choices. They are choosing which ordinances to obey. Some guidelines may be discriminatory or anti-social, such as the hospital porter refusing entrance to a patient who arrives by taxi rather than ambulance, but they may be more socially minded, such as applying the strictest implementation of food hygiene or safety standards.[145]

Second, all rules require interpretation and there is no final determinant for the way these dictates are understood. The work-to-rule involves employees rejecting both the existing meanings of regulations, and the authority of those who create those definitions. The choice to undertake work-to-rules against the pressures of management, as well as the choice and interpretation of the regulations employed as a block to executive command, indicates neither passivity nor impotence but creative resistance. The structures of support that lie beneath the undermining of managerial authority can be prefigurative.

2.9. Refusal to Work

The term 'sabotage' has been used in this chapter to cover direct action in the industrial arena. To describe similar methods Negri uses the expression 'refusal to work': *'The refusal to work is first and foremost sabotage, strikes, direct action.'*[146] In this chapter, however, 'refusal to work' has been used to refer to a particular form of sabotage, namely resistance to entering the labour force at the point of production. Negri and other autonomists recognise this mode of contestation as a liberating form of industrial direct action, which can be prefigurative, producing innovative forms of social interchange and creative identities.

The conscious withdrawal of the workers' efficiency through resistance to managerial authority need not be limited to those who are already employed. As businesses plan production years ahead, so too they have strategies for recruitment. Frustrating these corporate policies through impeding the flow of workers by encouraging the refusal of work can be viewed as a form of resistance. Such obstructive tactics can include, as Flynn argued, birth-control. She viewed it as a form of sabotage that deliberately restricts the supply of potential proletarians.[147] Autonomists have considered the tactic of job refusal a legitimate mode of working class resistance.[148] The time freed from work can be used for autonomous activity. As with all the other tactics discussed as sabotage, the refusal to work is contingent on certain social and historical factors. Paid non-work, such as welfare benefits, allows for greater refusal of work.[149]

During the 1980s in Britain, the refusal to work was often not an autonomous choice for millions of people. The circumstances of mass unemployment, although encouraged and tolerated by the Thatcher governments as a tool for reducing labour costs and trade union discipline were also subverted, as Aufheben notes, by potential proletarians who used the benefits system and free time to 'be creative and to please themselves.' They also created 'collective antagonistic tendencies [...] most notably anarcho-punk, a movement that expressed itself well in the Stop the City demos and the trouble-making elements on the CND demos'.[150] The refusal tactic was repudiated by liberals, who considered this an abuse of the welfare state, and by Leninists, who considered 'laziness' incompatible with communism.[151]

The refusal to work, described by Negri, is, however, a set of legitimate tactics. It is:

> [F]irst and foremost, the refusal of the most alienated - and therefore most productive work. Secondly, it is the refusal of capitalist work as such - i.e. of exploitation in general. And thirdly, it is a tendency towards a renewal of the mode of production, towards an unleashing of the proletariat's powers of invention.[152]

The refusal to work attacks the profits of capitalist enterprises and evolves alternatives to the social factory by creating new forms of fulfilling endeavour. Rather than necessarily being a response by indolent individuals, it can be a means for greater activity, as the peace convoys, the eco-warriors and the road protestors demonstrated.

The refusal to work is provocative. It rejects the role of the worker, which state- and reformist-socialists wish to maintain through restructuring capitalism to 'preserve work'.[153] The refusal also opposes the identification of the unemployed working class as passive victims. It spurns the few, but spectacular, rewards of disciplined proletarian existence. The trade union based anarchist Douglass correctly notes that what upsets critics who condemn the convoy, such as Labour MP Terry Fields, is their self-creativity and fulfilment.

> They're fucking enjoying themselves! *How dare those Hippies have fun when they're not working.* Your (sic) supposed to be all defeated and desperate and hung up and grateful to smug gits like Fields. Instead, here are people who've accepted it's a waste of time trying to find work, grovelling along to petty tin gods, they've actually gone to try and live their lives another way and have fun.[154]

There is a danger that the refusal to work (in the limited, non-Negrian sense) comes to be thought of as *the* technique of the revolutionary vanguard. Certainly there have been tendencies in overtly lifestylist anarchism which concentrated their interests on 'dropping out'.[155] Some class struggle groupings, like Attack International, also promote a similar strategy and view those who act in this way as being, potentially, the advanced vanguard class:[156]

> They say "get a job". A job? More like slavery. So you can stuff your crappy jobs. If we want money, then we will just have to find ways of getting some. It can be done – and it's a damn sight better than working for a living.[157]

Yet for many, there is no welfare state, and the commons, another potential source of 'free goods', have been enclosed. In Britain, 16 and 17 year olds can no longer claim Income Support and a system of work-fare has been increasingly implemented. Housing benefit rights have been severely curtailed for those under 25, while disability benefit and other forms of welfare have also been reduced, making it more difficult to opt out of employment.[158] Even where a basic benefits system does exist, it is often so inadequate that it is necessary to sell one's labour for a wage (whether in the formal economy or on its fringes) in order to meaningfully participate in social life.

2.10. Absenteeism and Sick-In

As the globalisation of the economy forces nation states to cut social costs, the total rejection of work becomes increasingly difficult, as the social wage is reduced. However, the temporary refusal to work through such practices as taking a sick day or sneaking off home has been approved as a method for gaining some autonomy from the regimentation of capitalist production (fig. 5.3.).[159] It can be traced back to the pre-industrial epoch when artisans would organise their time rather than having their labour regimented. Festivities and holidays were the norm and included the practice of celebrating 'saint Monday' (an unofficial extension of the Sunday rest day into the start of the working week).[160]

Phoning in sick has been strongly advocated by the more individualist, art-provocative, Decadent Action group,[161] but it has also been used by less self-consciously avant garde subjects ('subjects' being the individuals/ groupings that are central to a project or ideology). Due to the employment conditions at British Airways, strike action was near impossible, so in 1997 when staff had a grievance they all arranged to telephone in sick on the same day. Such action was successful as part of a purely industrial campaign. The sick day was also part of the J18 events. It was suggested that taking that Friday off as paid absence would

Figure 5.3. Anti-work poster.

be a protest against work, and would also allow participants to fully engage in the day's events.[162]

Contrary to Engels' taxonomy, sabotage or direct action in the workplace is a multifaceted approach to repressive conditions. It encompasses many diverse but complementary tactics, including the withdrawal of labour, one of Engels' more favoured methods. Sabotage does not necessarily imply anti-organisation (in the 'chaotic' sense), as even apparently spontaneous acts can take place in a background of friendship networks and non-formal support. Although some anarcho-syndicalists give strategic precedence to the mass strike, contemporary anarchists recognise that no single form of industrial method can be acontextually advanced. Despite the fact that some revolutionary syndicalists still give primacy to industrial workers and hence their methods, even contemporary anarcho-syndicalists like SolFed place an increasing emphasis on forms of resistance and self-activity outside of the workplace.

3. Methods of Propaganda

The division of workplace from non-workplace is entirely provisional. The continued use of the distinction is pragmatic, reflecting, in part, current usage rather than a commitment to this distinction. Some methods, like propaganda, sabotage and theft, have direct counterparts at the point of immediate manufacture. Others, like the consumer boycott, appear to complement industrial tactics, but can be significantly different. Propaganda is a method that bestrides even the supposed division between industrial and community action. As touched upon earlier, the industrial/communal distinction, with regard to tactics and subjects, is contextual and not universal. The creation of communication is common to no particular sphere and often interweaves the two. Propaganda by deed expresses dissatisfaction and identifies causes of torment. It is used both within and outside the point of production. Berkman's unsuccessful attempt on the life of Henry Frick, for instance, was in support of murdered strikers. So too propaganda by word, and the creation of situations and stunts (discussed below), is not particular to any specific domain.

3.1. Propaganda By Deed

As seen in the discussion concerning organisation, syndicates associated with workplace activity, and the small groups identified with propaganda by deed, are not competing forms of organisation; neither has universal preference over the other. Such organisational techniques are used interchangeably and inter-dependently rather than mutually exclusively. It is not a matter of either one or the other, but different choices and combinations of tactics, which depend on the social practices and judicial constraints being contested at the time.

Propaganda by deed is most often associated with individual terror, and in particular assassination,[163] but its origins lie in Carlo Priscane's belief that the deed promotes the idea.[164] 'Propaganda by deed' as a result refers to a much wider variety of actions than solely (anti-) political execution, being almost synonymous with 'direct action'.[165] It was Auguste Valliant's and Francois-Claudius Ravachol's activities that encouraged the conflation of propaganda by deed with murder and the lesser crimes of theft and arson.[166] The terroristic version of propaganda by deed may rightly be denounced when it recreates hierarchy, but these objections are contingent, not necessary, features. In some circumstances propaganda by deed, when allied with other tactics, or when other alternative tactics are denied, is consistent with the model of direct action. It can be prefigurative, engaging the subjugated agent in a manner congruent with anarchist anti-hierarchical goals.

The main arguments denouncing terroristic propaganda by deed have originated from pacifists, predominantly using the argument from prefiguration, which has already been examined (see Chapter Three). It states that if anarchism demands that the means must be in accordance with the ends, and the forms of social relations they desire are non-violent, then their methods have to be peaceful. As noted earlier, this argument is inadequate as 'violence' is a flexible term which is often used pejoratively to describe forceful actions that the speaker has already prejudged as unacceptable, rather than found unacceptable because of the use of brute power. Pacifism may be less prefigurative than a violent act. Others have criticised propaganda by deed for hitting random or inappropriate targets. French illegalists, for instance, followed the anti-semitism of Fourier. Richard Parry, the historian of the French anarchist bandits the Bonnot Gang, recounts the list of acceptable victims for illegalists: 'pawn shops, *bureaux de change* and post offices [...] bankers, lawyers, Jews(!).'[167] Yet other propagandists by deed were not so prejudiced and were selective in their targets.[168] Even the attack on the Cafe Terminus by Emile Henry, which Woodcock presumed was indiscriminate,[169] was in fact carefully chosen.[170] The AB and ALF were similarly discerning in their targets.

As discussed in Chapter Four, Leninist and statist terrorist groups, such as the IRA or ETA, tend to regard their actions as the central strategy for liberation, and this has been true of some anarchist groupings who committed outrages to support a wider cause (illegalists).[171] Their acts were to emancipate the subject. As a result, as Attack International described, terrorist organisations see themselves as a benign vanguard acting on behalf of others. Their paternalism, however, suppresses autonomous agitational activity by the client group, recreating hierarchy.[172] The separation between terrorist and supported subject group still occurs even with the open cell system, as illegal acts, especially spectacular ones, require the perpetrators to act in great secrecy and isolation.

Parry illustrates that illegalists were far more individualist, and rejected any collectivist intention. 'Illegal acts were to be done simply to satisfy one's desires, not for the greater glory of some external "ideal".'[173] These egoist anarchists avoided the paternalism of strategic propagandist by deed, but regarded liberation in terms of Stirnerite rebellion. These individualists, who rejected class struggle and collectivist methods, had nothing but disdain for other subjugated subjects and other methods of revolt. The actions of the individualist *Übermensch* (superior man) took precedence over those of the common mob, thereby further reducing the autonomy of the oppressed.[174] The social relations the individualist terrorist created within the gang, as well as those established with non-illegalist anarchists and other oppressed subjects, lacked comradeship and reciprocity.[175] They were not synecdochic of the New Left's 'beloved community' that embodied the values of liberation.

Both individualist and collectivist propagandists by deed tend to regard their targets as being central. A strategic view of struggle is conceived where one set of targets will bring about a millennial revolution. Terrorist actions, as well as being occasionally necessary, carry a symbolic meaning. Those carrying them out expect that the oppressed groups who observe the act will understand the metaphors embodied in the radical action. The Baader-Meinhoff Gang hoped that their act of blowing up a German based Zionist organisation would be recognised as part of a wider struggle against imperialism. As the bombing took place on the anniversary of Kristelnacht it was unsurprisingly interpreted somewhat differently. Those carrying out the attacks, however, are in a different position to other oppressed agents, including those they wish to help. As a result, the symbolic meaning of this form of direct action can be differently read. Many of the Protestant working class in the Six Counties interpret particular bombings differently to their Catholic counterparts. As Gregor Kerr of the WSM points out, such vanguard examples of 'armed struggle', rather than resolving sectarian conflict, which is often how the guerrillas want them to be read, act to reinforce the division.[176]

The dominant powers, such as the British state, will attempt to impose their meanings onto the symbolic features of individual terror. Such manipulations of interpretation can be more successfully resisted when the readers of the symbolic feature are also the ones carrying out the act, as they already understand the tactic and what it prefigures. The smaller the involvement, such as acts of individual terror, the greater the dependency on the symbolic power for its effectiveness, and the greater the potential that heteronomous powers can apply 'spin', re-integrating the metaphor into its own symbolic order.

Some acts of individual terror can still be consistent with the ideal, as these are not the primary tactic, they are aimed at supporting wider struggles and are carried out by oppressed agents themselves in order to equalise disproportionate power relationships. They do not impose a single specific interpretation, nor take a central role or replace other methods. In most major disruptions, where myriad local actions interact and coalesce, incidents occur which may appear to be propaganda by deed. The targeting of a Mercedes showroom for violent assault during the J18 in 1999 or the arson attacks on the Apartheid South African embassy during the Poll Tax riots of 1990, could be represented as propaganda by deed. They are compatible with ideal types of anarchism as they are not vanguard actions.

3.2. Propaganda By Word

'Freedom of the press belongs to those who own one.'[177]

'Propaganda' has connotations of 'brainwashing' and 'distortion', information imparted to have a prescribed effect. It has additional undertones of hierarchy and coercion. This is due partly to the instrumental character of propaganda, so that even the messages intended to have benign ends are regarded as manipulative and demeaning. The term, however, is often used in a less pejorative way by radicals. Anarchists admit that their news-sheets are propaganda, as they have explicit aims, namely 'putting over a revolutionary message'.[178] Yet whilst having a message to impart is true of any form of communicative act, anarchists are explicit about their goals. Critics of the more mainstream media, such as Chomsky or the Oxford-based Institute of Social Disengineering,[179] indicate that network (corporate) news also have explicit and implicit political aims, although not of the revolutionary variety.[180]

The message is only one part of the operation of propaganda. Other factors are also pivotal: the choice of media for the bulletins, their style, tone, choice of images, mode of production and distribution, the intended constituency and the audience's relationships and involvement with these communications are also integral aspects of the role of propaganda. For consistent anarchists, their propaganda must be compatible with direct action. Relations of production, for instance, must be non-hierarchical and the images, format and relationship with the readers must be prefigurative.

The established media, identified as that which is either state-controlled (such as the BBC) or owned by large, wealthy corporations, or funded through advertising revenue, have interests which are antipathetic to anarchism.[181] As a result, separate organs of communication are necessary, as SolFed explain:

> The current mass media is a creation of those in control, those who hold the purse strings and power. We as individuals oppose all this, and we can and must change it by our deeds. So don't hate the media, *become* the media of the future.[182]

Most anarchist groups organise predominantly around the production of their propaganda, and for many it remains their main method. In this respect there appears to be similarities between libertarians and Leninists, as orthodox socialist movements are based around the production and distribution of their respective journals. Bob Drake, a former member of the British Communist Party, reports how in the 1950s much of the Party's organisational structure and events were based on and around the propaganda sheet. The SWP and the Socialist Party also lay great emphasis on the importance of their respective publications: *Socialist Worker* and *The Socialist*.[183]

There are, however, differences between anarchist and orthodox marxist papers. Chris Atton, in his analysis of revolutionary propaganda, uncovers significant differences between the production methods and internal structures of anarchist magazines, in particular *Green Anarchist* and those of the *Morning Star* and *Socialist Worker*. Whilst *Green Anarchist* is not a class struggle magazine, in the 1990s the personnel behind its production and distribution co-operated with such groups, participating with them on AEA and MA'M activities. The analysis provided by Atton does, therefore, provide a useful indication of the differences between libertarian and orthodox marxist propaganda. *Morning Star* and *Socialist Worker* replicate the hierarchies of capitalist media businesses, with editors overseeing reporters, staff writers and specialist technical staff, while *Green Anarchist* creates structures to dissipate power.[184]

The arrangements for production and distribution of propaganda reflect and often form the formal organisation, because the production of propaganda is considered one of the most influential methods for any revolutionary movement. So important is the distribution of information and analysis that it was proposed that one of the identifying criteria for a healthy active group is that it publishes its own material.[185] The American CIA (Central Intelligence Agency), reportedly, also judges the vigour of the radical movement through the vitality of the available alternative press.[186] Propaganda production is intricately and intimately bound to anarchist organisation.

Written propaganda remains one of the main tactical-cum-organisational methods for British anarchists. Even MA'M, one of the few predominantly anarchist groups which has no ambition to produce a regular bulletin, newspaper or journal, advertised their irregular events through a steady stream of fliers, stickers and posters. They have a flexible organisational structure to encourage independent production and distribution. CWF became increasingly centralised as the imperative grew to standardise publication and increase the quality of their eponymous tabloid. The organisation of the group and the publishing of propaganda are indistinguishable: Green Anarchist's 'self-definition [is] as movement and magazine'.[187]

Anarchists' stress on the micro-political has often resulted in their preference for local publications over national ones.[188] Regional magazines and newspapers can, because of their smaller scale, more easily experiment in organisational methods and avoid the hierarchies associated with Leninist publications. Lenin, by contrast, favoured the national, rather than regional, agitational newspaper.[189] The intrinsic link between the propagation of information and organisation is deliberate. Anarchist publishing, in its ideal form, should prefigure the desired social and organisational structures. As Atton describes: 'The alternative press will exhibit the primary characteristics of the new protest: direct participation and local, grass-roots decision-making where resources are diffused and shared within and between groups.'[190] He argues that Green Anarchist is successful in dispersing power and resources and creating opportunities for developing new skills, to a far greater degree than traditional Leninist publications or underground magazines such as *Oz*.

The hierarchical divide between the producers and audience for anarchist publications is dissolved. Readers have considerable access to influencing the contents of anarchist magazines and many take advantage of this. Nearly half of *Green Anarchist* is composed of articles written by the readership (excluding the large letters section which is almost entirely free of editorial control). Approximately a quarter of the content comes from the editors, with a smaller percentage emanating from known thinkers in the anarchist milieu (people like Bob Black, John Zerzan and John Moore).[191] In anarchist papers the creation of propaganda is open to all; indeed, almost all the main anarchist publications invite not just letters but articles as well.[192] Some offer opportunities for greater participation from the readership.[193] In Leninist publications, by contrast, the readership is essentially passive, while the newspaper disseminates the message of the party leadership. Neither membership nor readership are involved in dialogue with the newspaper.[194] Readers' contributions are confined to small sections such as the 'letters page'.

Contemporary anarchists, consistent with the ideal, open up the opportunity to their readership to develop the skilled jobs of publishing, such as typesetting, proof-reading, lay out and design, with some groups offering training sessions.[195] This open approach helps extend the opportunity to learn skills, and ensures that publication is not dependent upon one person or clique. The downside is the notoriously amateurish appearance of anarchist publications, especially *Green Anarchist. Animal,* also the product of non-media professionals, boasted its amateurism with the sub-heading on one edition, 'The magazine whose content is better than its layout (sic)'.[196] Circulation of the location for editorial control and printing has also been a factor in libertarian production. *Here and Now,* for instance, would alternate editorship between groups in Yorkshire and Scotland and other national anarchist groups such as the pre-1990s CWF had similar arrangements.[197]

The importance of presenting anarchist arguments has long been considered a key tactic. William Godwin, regarded by Rocker, Marshall and Woodcock as a precursor to British anarchism, felt that reason alone is a sufficient tool for creating a liberated society:

> Coercion has nothing in common with reason, and therefore can have no proper tendency to the cultivation of virtue.... Reason is omnipotent: if my conduct be wrong, a very simple statement, flowing from a clear and comprehensive view, will make it appear as such; nor is it probable that there is any perverseness that would persist in vice, in the face of all the recommendations with which virtue might be invested, and all the beauty in which it might be displayed.[198]

Contemporary anarchists are critical of such a liberal approach. Godwin's agent, the abstract individual, and singular view of rationality are divorced from economic conditions and material practices. Contemporary libertarians would also reject his preference for reform rather than insurrection.[199] Yet they would also see reasoned argument as a part of their propaganda, although not the only part.

Critics of British anarchists have looked at their printed output and concluded that the movement lacks rigour and is suffused only with a naive instinctive rebellion. Class War's approach, in particular, is targeted for its 'anti-intellectualism' (figure 5.4.). Their provocative, populist propaganda marked them out as an irrational group who 'never achieved [an] adequate theory'.[200] Class War is certainly professedly anti-academic, but British anarchism does have a sophisticated analysis of appropriate actions. Even *Class War*'s 'retarding influence', diagnosed by Aufheben, of colloquial, rather than theoretical complex propagandising is a result of a particular anti-representative, prefigurative approach.[201]

Liberal anarchists follow Leninists in believing that they have to instruct the masses, and this results in the pedagogic tone of their propaganda. Thayer, in his account of the British libertarian movement, then dominated by non-class struggle groupings, says that they 'take

themselves far too seriously; they also think that satire is decadent.'.[202] Class struggle anarchists, by contrast, have long addressed their readers in a more familiar tone. From the earliest periodicals, Johann Most used irony and ridicule in his newspaper.[203] His engaging hyperbole was partly responsible for his imprisonment in Britain (see Chapter One).

In the anarchist movement abrasive humour is not unique to Class War (fig. 5.5.). The ACF, during the 1990-1

Figure 5.4. Best Cut of All, cover of *Class War*, circa 1985.

Gulf War, parodied Leninist support for Saddam Hussein's Ba'athist authoritarian regime in a satirical front cover. Regional groupings in particular continue Most's tradition of having an authorial accent that is coloured by abrasive humour.[204] This is deliberate. The use of humour and everyday vernacular eliminates the division between (anti-)politics and 'everyday life' and helps, prefiguratively, to make resistance enjoyable.[205] Bone describes how the newspaper kept altering its presentation to avoid reification. Staid propaganda can be assimilated into the dominant symbolic order, restricting its participatory audience and limiting its possible meanings:

> After a while it became obvious that the paper in its particular form had its limitations. Whilst it had been successful [...] in putting Class War on the political map, and developed a loyal following amongst many otherwise unpoliticised working class people, it still only appealed to a relatively small section of the working class.
>
> We had, in effect created a new 'Class War Ghetto' and it was obvious that a new-style, even more 'populist' paper was required to break out of it.[206]

Class War continued to evolve, and when the majority of its producers felt it could no longer reinvent itself they unsuccessfully tried to end it. Whilst it was occasionally predictable because of its self-conscious image as 'the mob with attitude', its galvanising humour was well considered and pertinently directed. By mocking and abusing the powerful, *Class War* 'tries to encourage and increase the confidence, the autonomy, initiative and solidarity of working class people'.[207] This was in contrast to the established Left which 'emphasized victims, [whilst] Class War emphasized fighting back',[208] hence their regular photo-slot of 'hospitalised coppers'[209] (fig. 5.6.).

Humour is an important feature of anarchist propaganda whether it be *Class War*, *Evading Standards*, regional publications such as

Where's My Giro or campaign-centred propaganda such as striking Wapping printers' version of *The Sun*. The light-heartedness suggests a lack of didacticism. For the comedy to work there has to be a sharing of values with the readership. The reader is complicit in considering the butt of the joke as deserving denigration. The spoof page three, 'hospitalised coppers', is knowingly unappealing to law-and-order authoritarians and this adds to the readers' pleasure. Discriminatory and authoritarian groupings and individuals also use comedy for their ends but there are important differences, in particular in the choice of the target.

For anarchists, ridicule is aimed at two types of target; firstly it is directed at those who wield greater heteronomous power, in order to encourage the readership to see through the dominant group's aura of power. Secondly, the writers of the propaganda themselves are ridiculed. This latter target may occasionally lead to the creation of in-jokes that alienate the general reader, reducing the potential effectiveness of the ridicule. The primary impression, nonetheless, is to demonstrate the provisional nature of the group or publication. Mockery undermines authority.[210] By laughing at themselves, anarchists indicate, and encourage others to recognise, that their grouping is contingent and not strategically necessary. The publication

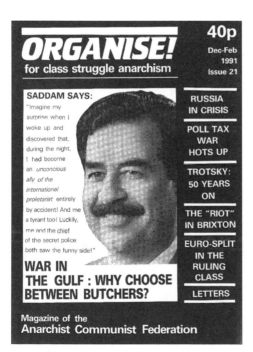

Figure 5.5. Why Choose Between Butchers, cover of *Organise!*, 1991.

of propaganda written in a colloquial form, a characteristic of British anarchism from before the twentieth century, also undermines vanguard organisation which considers that an elite educated in the appropriate theory is a prerequisite. Class War's informality implies that the hierarchies of party leadership, with its specific roles for instructive theoreticians, are unnecessary.[211]

Critics argued that anarchists', and in particular Class War's, populist approach is patronising, as its self-conscious parodying of tabloid humour 'reduced all the individual and collective diversity of real people down to a convenient lowest common denominator'.[212] The populist journalism which Class War adopted 'was an invention of middle class tabloid hacks which claimed to speak for and represent the working class - but like all media representatives, the real function was to pacify and manipulate'.[213] There is also the suggestion that Class War's use of the populist approach is indicative of a desire to create a vanguard body. 'Underlying this populism were certain patronizing assumptions about what the "average prole" was capable of comprehending and what projected image of Class War would make them most popular to the largest number of "average proles".'[214]

Figure 5.6. Hospitalised Copper from *Class War*, No. 28, circa 1987.

Class War's response is to accuse critics of jealousy on the basis that tens of thousands bought their paper in comparison to the tiny circulation of the theoretical texts produced by their antagonists[215] and, by implication, that their readers were unlikely to support the publication if they felt patronised by it. Yet, while Class War is right to celebrate the accessibility of their propaganda, given that it had reached a constituency beyond a small arena of activists, this is not an adequate reply to the charge of being patronising. The red-top, mainstream tabloids have circulations thousands of times higher than *Class War* yet, although more entertaining than their broadsheet partners, they still stereotype and demean the identities of their working class readers. One defence of *Class War* is that it was written in the language of the pub and the football terrace, because this is where the writers hailed from, and is merely the discourse of working class conversation. Another reply is that alongside the newspaper they also produced thought-provoking theoretical publications. The journal *The Heavy Stuff*, as well as their book *Unfinished Business*, indicate that they did not perceive their readers as unenquiring. A critic of Class War, William Dixon, in the journal *Radical Chains*, notes: 'behind their paper there was indeed not just careful thought but also knowledge of what needed to be fact'. Their objective was 'to make everyone an intellectual' rather than have a 'Dictatorship of the intellectuals'.[216]

Aufheben's hypothesis that Class War's rhetoric is just a middle class fabrication, an effort by do-gooders to purposely talk down to its readership, is worth raising as, if true, it would indicate that Class War is paternalistic rather than liberatory. As Chapter Three demonstrated, the anarchist ideal notion of class is much broader and contextual than that offered by orthodox marxism. However, even if the narrow Leninist measure of class is used as a guide, the evidence suggests that Aufheben's appraisal is questionable (at least for the period up to the early 1990s). Although there is no comparable breakdown of the writers of *Class War* to that provided by Atton for *Green Anarchist*, a speculative, sociological analysis of the class backgrounds of two of the three Class War members who edited an anthology of the paper, *Decade of Disorder*, does suggest that Class War was written by members of the (orthodox marxist) revolutionary subject, the working class. Ian Bone is the child of domestic servants,[217] and Alan Pullen is a plumber[218] while only the shadowy Tim Scargill's origins (and motivations) are open to question.[219] The journalist Rob Yates describes others associated with Class War as 'labourers, clerical workers, unemployed'.[220]

There were certainly tendencies within Class War,[221] which grew as time went on, which suggested that it regarded itself as a vanguard organisation. The desperation to keep their federation going[222] suggests that some regard the organisation as necessary and pivotal. Nonetheless, the efforts to create a popular, entertaining and engaging paper which encourages self-education[223] as well as autonomous participation indicates that these strategic, vanguardist elements are more often subordinate than dominant.

One of the problems with anarchist propaganda has been its inadvertent role in the commodification of revolt. The SI described the phenomenon whereby radical activity is denuded of its ability to contest by being turned into a product that can be bought and sold alongside other goods and services (which the SI termed 'recuperation'). Alienation, the product of a specific form of society (class-based), actually appears to be all-embracing. The individual remedy for this isolation seems to be through embracing spectacular roles, consuming products of ersatz rebellion. The merchandising, whether of T-shirts or golf-umbrellas emblazoned with 'radical phrases', packages discontent as another form of commodity.[224] Rather than destroying market relations, it simply extends the range of goods on offer. This is not to be blind to the two-sided nature of the 'radical' product, namely that it can be used to promote anti-hierarchical social relations. Indeed, seeing an inspiring piece of radical art, or an everyday product emblazoned with the logo of radical protest can reduce the sensation of isolation that radicals are encouraged to feel by dominant powers. Yet the method of such promotion, the commodity form, is not a synecdoche of its ambitions, and the revolutionary object only develops a truly radical character when it undermines the economic rationale behind its creation, such as when the Class War cigarette lighter is used to light Molotov cocktails in an urban insurrection.

In an effort to counteract the process of the commodification of revolt, some radical groups distribute their products for free. *Anarchist Theft, ContraFLOW, Counter Information, Evading Standards,*

Pink Pauper, *Proletarian Gob*, *Resistance*, *SchNews* and *Subversion* have all been distributed without charge. The SI's own journal was also potlatched.[225] Such methods of distribution and exchange are prefigurative. Contemporary class struggle anarchists are against all forms of market economy and consider that free distribution helps prevent recuperation. Gifts dispensed without obligation, created for the pleasure of producing and the delight of giving, applies not just to propaganda. Free food is distributed at festivals and demonstrations; other 'senseless act[s] of beauty' are features of the TAZ, the riot and the prank. Non-obligatory gifts stand as an alternative to capitalism. Despite anarchists' attempts to encourage new forms of distribution, based on pleasure rather than profit, recuperative processes have intervened. Even potlatched revolutionary tracts have been subsumed into the order of commodities. An original complete set of the SI's journals now changes hands for hundreds of pounds.

The internet, as discussed in Chapter Four, also provides an opportunity for free communication, although accessing information requires a substantial initial outlay in computer hardware, if one does not live close to a well-resourced library or have a job which provides such access. The drawback, as the A(C)F acknowledge, is that the readership is predominantly, although not exclusively, occidental and specific to certain professional positions.[226] Nonetheless, by the early years of the twenty-first century, all the main British class struggle groups, even the techno-sceptical Green Anarchist movement, had a presence on the World Wide Web.[227] Harry Shlong, writing in *Green Anarchist*, has pointed to the positive possibilities opened up by 'these new forms of communication' which are 'outside traditional institutions of state broadcast and communication control'.[228] The internet and email news-groups provide media for expression, allow for ease of communication between groups and assist in the co-ordinating of activities, as well as engaging new participants. Like all libertarian revolutionary action, electronic propaganda seeks to extend the scope of participation.

Contemporary anarchists do not just propagandise through texts (newspapers, magazines, books and pamphlets). The 1994 ten-day 'Anarchy in the UK' festival that took place in London (October 21st-30th), was organised by Bone, and included a significantly cultural input, including bands, film, cabaret, comedy and poetry, as well as more traditional (anti-)political demonstrations and meetings (fig. 5.7.). For Davies, 'Anarchy in the UK' is evidence of British anarchism's appreciation of a 'connection between anarchist politics and popular culture'.[229] However, anarchists have long recognised that diverse social practices interweave in constructing functional control. Whitechapel's Jubilee Club, supported by *Der Arbeiter Fraint*, housed theatre, poetry and musical events to create a culture of resistance. Class War, amongst others, has reviewed films and used popular cultural icons in their propaganda. The ACF, over a series of issues of *Organise!*, considered how periodical-based propaganda is not the only form for promoting anti-representative tactics and ideas. Poetry, film, music and theatre can also be used, both in terms of content and as a method of constructing prefigurative social arrangements.[230]

Other cultural forms are also used. Cinema, music and theatre have been vehicles for anarchist sentiment. They also attempt, through their dramatic structures, to critique the hierarchy inherent within artistic practices. In the comedic play

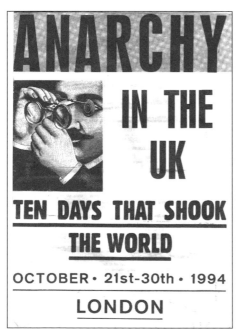

Figure 5.7. Front cover of programme of *Anarchy in the UK: Ten days that shook the world* festival 1994.

Accidental Death of an Anarchist, the autonomist-influenced author Dario Fo has his characters stand outside of the narrative of his drama, to comment on the conventions of theatre, such as the paucity of roles for women. In Situationist forays into cinema the aim was to provoke the audience out of their passive consumer role.[231]

As mentioned in earlier chapters, anarchist cultural tactics involve using techniques to uncover the manner in which varieties of media mould opinion and create susceptible, passive audiences. For the Situationists, this cultural tactic of *détournement* involved intervening in the symbolic order, either through graffiti or collage.[232] A frequent form that was radically altered by the SI, but has also been the target of other libertarians, are the conventional comic strips. These traditional formats, with their linear narrative structures, containing simplistic morality tales and with characters who were designed as role models for upstanding citizens, were widely parodied[233]. In the 1960s, Mickey Mouse was shown as a junkie, *Oz's* Rupert the Bear became a decidedly sexual being, Olive Oyl gave powerful speeches on Women's Liberation to Popeye and Superheroes debated marxist cultural theory.[234] In the 1980s, Tin Tin and Captain Haddock became class struggle heroes concerned with issues of race, gender and sexuality whilst in the 1990s The Teenage Mutant Ninja Turtles and The Flintstones appeared in anarchist literature spouting revolutionary slogans rather than homely reassurances.[235] The unorthodox adventures of old cartoon characters draws attention to the absences of issues of class and gender and the presumptions of liberal imperialism within mainstream comics.

As a writer for Class War describes, other methods such as graffiti are also used to mark out territory, to warn and to inform:

> To re-raise awareness of the other areas of working class culture we are interested in, and also to make unfashionable and smother the other ideas, our slogans, ideas and our symbols should confront our class every day. Every day they

are faced with pro-capitalist and racist media, sexist and reactionary graffiti and conversation. It must be the job of all of us (sorry if this sounds melodramatic) to take up pens and spray cans and reclaim the walls of our areas.[236]

Such interventions also question property rights. Billboard pitches are *détourned*, to mock the product advertised. Such intercessions uncover the means by which promotions attempt to seduce and pacify and the oppressive presuppositions that underlie the product and its representations.[237]

To return to a more British phenomenon, punk not only had confrontational lyrics, but also, through its subversion of commercial rock-and-roll, drew attention to the spectacular function of the band and the quiescent function of the listeners. The punk movement also critically attacked hierarchical constructs such as 'talent', 'skill' and 'originality' in order to promote greater participation.[238] Groups like Chumbawamba use their music to espouse anarchist ideas and help fund various ventures. Crass displayed through the content and style of their lyrics and album designs a radical alternative to multinational record labels, which highlighted how mainstream leisure industries sought to control and profit from youthful discontent. Crass attempted to develop, albeit in a liberal fashion, alternative means of production and distribution to counter these corporations. However, as the final issue of the unified *Class War* self-critically points out, too frequently the culture they helped generate was often exclusively White, unintentionally inhibiting involvement from other oppressed agents.[239]

3.3. Situations
The SI define the 'constructed situation' as: 'A moment of life concretely and deliberately constructed by the collective organisation of a unitary ambience and a game of events'.[240] Creating situations involves using the technologies and practices developed under capitalism in order to overcome these repressive conditions. Just as

the apparent oppositional forces to capitalism can be recuperated into the dominant ideology, so too 'everything which appears within spectacular society can be reclaimed by the consciousness which seeks to subvert it'.[241] Rather than being constrained by the conditions of capitalism, which create alienating situations, the agent should act to overcome these restraints.[242]

The creation of situations is pivotal to the Situationists. Their tactic has a twofold character. 'Our central idea is that of the construction of situations, that is to say, the concrete construction of momentary ambiences of life and their transformation into a superior passional quality.'[243] The first point is that the situation involves contesting forms of oppressive power. The second characteristic of the situation is that it creates temporary, immediate moments of autonomy.[244] Situations are a form of TAZ. Taking part in situations carries a synecdochic message to the participants. The Situationists explain that the role of creators of situations must be temporary in order to prevent the recreation of hierarchy.[245]

Temporary and playful situations take many forms. They can be a gathering of people for some emotional event or an intervention into other formal spectacular cultural activities, such as interrupting a film show, or disrupting the planned city.[246] Groups such as RTS have constructed contemporary situations. The priority given to the transportation of commodities over the desires and safety of residents is challenged by locals taking over the highways.[247] Stop the City demonstrations and even, claims Plant, (anti-)political riots, such as the 1990 Poll Tax uprising in Trafalgar Square, are examples of a situation.[248]

3.4. Pranks and Stunts
Stunts are very similar to situations but have an additional characteristic, namely that the imaginative interaction is aimed at the mainstream media, the intention being that they broadcast the prank to a wider public. The established media may not be aware that

it is being manipulated. Unlike situations and orthodox anarchist propaganda, the stunt interrupts and undermines the symbolic order through the dominant means of communication.

The 'Spectacle' is not just the amalgamation of arresting images but refers to the social relationships created through these images.[249] To interrupt such hierarchical symbolic orders is in itself an assault on repressive practices that threatens to expand into other forms of direct action.

> The Spectacle has so successfully infiltrated Everyday Life that an attack upon the Spectacle appears to be an attack upon Society. When attacked the Spectacle threatens us with the Spectre of Anarchy [...]

> We start to dismantle the Spectacle by seizing back from authorities the power to run our own lives. Once again to take control of the organisation of everyday life ourselves.[250]

Situations may inspire mainstream media coverage but, unlike the stunt, this is the foreseeable result, although it is not the main aim.

Amongst the most famous examples of a prank is the Yippies disruption of Wall Street. Abbie Hoffman and other pranksters threw dollar bills into the trading pit, causing the brokers to break off from their work to scramble and fight amongst themselves for the free greenbacks floating down. Dealers brawling over dollars was a dramatic metaphor for the single-minded rapaciousness of the market economy.[251] It was an act carried out to be transmitted through the mainstream media. In Britain, Class War were at the forefront of attempting to manipulate the mass media to gain attention for anarchist ideas. They initiated pranks that encompassed a multitude of tactics:

Stuntism included the *Henley Regatta*, the *Bash the Rich* marches, the *Rock Against the Rich* tour, the Notting Hill by-election campaign, disruption of CND and Labour Party rallies, the *anti-yuppie* campaign, the *Better Dead than Wed Royals* record.[252]

The effectiveness of some of the acts Bone describes can only be assessed by the amount of media attention they gain, rather being based on their immediate transformatory and ambient qualities. It is this publicity-seeking feature that is most frequently criticised, and was part of the debate surrounding the split in Class War in 1997.

Bone's stunt methods were regarded as successful as they raised the profile of anarchism in Britain. Home, a critic of Bone and Class War, suggests that stunt tactics had helped make anarchism a 'perceived [...] threat to the British establishment'.[253] Yet Bone's stunts were criticised because this media attention also had a downside, the group eventually becoming reduced to caricatures established by the same institutional processes.[254] Even when the tabloids are duped into portraying an image of anarchism which scares the bourgeoisie, it does not measure up to the reality and therefore disappoints those who become interested.[255] Rather than confront and subvert the media's power to represent, the stunt too frequently accepts the media's legitimacy and panders to the imperatives of the multinational communications industry.

Stunts create an aggrandised image through a sophisticated manipulation of mainstream media, and thus reveal the most serious problem with this method, i.e. its dependence on corporate communications for its effectiveness.[256] Unlike anarchist-produced propaganda, the message has to be mediated through organs and institutions which are hierarchical and a ruling part of the hegemony. The critical role is not played by the subjugated agent, and as such is incompatible with anarchist direct action. For stunts to succeed, all that matters is that the media reports them, thereby using participants instrumentally.[257] Dependence on the capitalist media strengthens their power to represent others, fixing radical acts into a repressive social order.[258]

One of the weaknesses of propaganda by deed was that it relied on mainstream media to broadcast the rebel's spectacular message through press reports of the heroic act. Media, however, are integrated into the dominant structures of power so either misrepresent or ignore the prefigurative features of anarchist propaganda, turning a synecdochic act into a metaphor. Radical squatting, rather than being seen as a form of prefigurative action that challenges property rights, is reported in terms of elitist and/or anti-social behaviour.

The machinations of the media also affect the aim of creating non-hierarchical social relations. The desire for publicity can create a system of leadership and elite roles:

> For who's the best person to go and do an interview – the best talker, the most photogenic, the person who did it last time? It's all too easy for the comrade with personal contacts to the media, a way with oratory and previous knowledge to make themselves indispensable. TV people lap it up, it creates individual stars of previously collective movements and makes their job of coverage so much easier.[259]

As a result, the authors of *Test Card F* suggest refusal to co-operate with mainstream media. To engage with the media would be to acquiesce in a hierarchical relationship with a dominant and domineering partner, and to encourage the creation of leadership within the group.

Despite the necessary shortcomings of the stunt, such media-dependent actions have been a prominent feature of more recent anarchist activities. There are two reasons for this development. Firstly, there are immediate advantages as media coverage extends the range of audience for anarchist ideas. Most anarchist propaganda, because of financial constraints, runs to just a few thousand copies. More ambitious attempts such as the transitory (but largely Bristol-based) Committee of Public Safety's effort to print up and distribute half a million anti-election posters in 1997, reportedly fell well short of their target.[260] Tabloid newspapers, by contrast, are read by millions and reach into areas where there is no anarchist presence. Opening up to the media therefore assists in circulating anarchist ideas, even if they are in a distorted form.[261]

The second reason for the continued popularity of stunts is that any event may become subject to the gaze of the non-sympathetic mass media and consequently manipulated. The proposal made in *Test Card F* that efforts should be made to avoid media representation is impractical.[262] The attempt to escape the gaze of the cameras is itself a use of the media. Attacking photo-journalists and subterfuge to avoid representation, tactics favoured by the Institute for Social Disengineering, are themselves responses to the media.[263] The aim is not to avoid representation, for that is impossible, but to limit and subvert the way in which one is depicted, so as to constrain the power of the mediators.

There is no clear-cut distinction between stunts performed for the media and situations that may be reported by them but are not based on creating representation. While prefigurative situations are created which are not directly intended to attract the media, it would be disingenuous to claim that those involved did not alter their behaviour because of the presence of journalists and photographers. J18 activists were well aware that there would be attention from the media. The wearing of carnival masks not only provided a disguise against unfriendly cameras but also a more benign image to viewers than the more traditional balaclavas or bandannas. It is consequently not possible to make absolute distinctions between the non-mediated situation and the stunt. To act as if the media does not exist is unfeasible and possibly dangerous to individual liberty, not least as reporters hand over their footage to the police.[264] To ignore the mainstream media is to remain oblivious to sets of interfolding oppressive practices, which constitute part of the material conditions of subjugation.[265] The media is integrated into the state, corporate and military networks. To overlook corporate and state media operations is to disregard hierarchical forms of surveillance and control.[266] The point is not to neglect the media, but to uncover its oppressive practices and attempt to undermine them: in other words, to avoid playing by their rules, and instead act prefiguratively, creating anti-corporate groupings whose internal structures and methods reflect values of equality and reciprocity rather than those of the market place.

Tactics to demonstrate the means by which the media manipulate and misinform can often involve using, through *détournement*, mass media. These methods are as diverse as 'placing guerrilla ads, doctored billboards, TV jamming, anti-ads and spoof commercials through to full-blown TV slots' in order to show who 'owns the spectacle' and how it operates.[267] Stunts are unacceptable when they are not in themselves prefigurative situations, indicative of anti-hierarchical adventure, but act to reinforce the role of the media rather than subverting it. In some instances, stunts use participants instrumentally and recreate a bureaucracy of organisers and an elite of spokespeople. Pranks are unacceptable when their criteria for success are those of dominant media practices, such as whether they attract sufficient attention from corporate news organisations.

To confront distortions, and the integration of anarchism into the established order, it is necessary for anarchists to create their own communicative processes, to uncover the strategies of corporate repression and to challenge them through direct action. Anarchist propaganda, whether through its newspapers, free-sheets, journals, leaflets, stickers, internet sites or pirate radio, provides this role. It also extends into cultural practices such as theatre, film and music. The aim is to create social arrangements that prefigure the multifaceted, multi-identitied characteristics of the anarchist ideal.

The social influence of the media is dissipated through the creation of temporary, experimental interventions. The avant-garde artistic movements associated with anarchism break down elitist divisions between audience, creators and subjects, especially the privileged position of artists.[268] Anti-representation undermines those procedures that encourage people to transpose their aspirations onto others. The democratisation of the mass media, by opening up the means of communication to all, requires abandoning distribution on the basis of profit. The results of such assaults involve the creation of new forms of egalitarian expression, which dissolve specialist divisions, such as those between art, reporting and narration.

Contemporary anarchists' engagement with other oppressed groups and individuals is difficult to determine. An examination of the letters page of *Class War*, for instance, suggests an overwhelmingly male readership.[269] British anarchist periodicals do fail to create substantial relationships with other oppressed groupings such as those within the ethnic minorities. This is regrettable but not devastating, as libertarians believe that no publication is pivotal to the struggle, including their own. Some oppressed groups prefer to engage in propaganda through their own magazines or other media. Participatory and egalitarian patterns of communication have successfully avoided creating an anarchist 'star'. Despite the relative fame (or notoriety) of Alice Nutter of Chumbawamba, Ian Bone and Stuart Christie, none represents, nor seeks to embody, anarchism, in the way that Tony Benn, Derek Hatton or Ken Livingstone have personified the Labour Party left.

4. Community Sabotage and Criminality

As discussed earlier, the division employed here between communal and workplace action is one employed by activists and theorists rather than one that is compatible with the anarchist ideal. Malatesta and many of the anarchist communists are thought to favour specialist local organisation. Bone, for instance, places greater emphasis on community struggles,[270] while Tom Brown, Rocker and many anarcho-syndicalists tend to take an opposite view.[271] Yet a blanket preference for one location of action over the others is contrary to the anarchist ideal. It suggests that there are objectively identifiable and totalising oppressive forces that can be superseded only in specific locations. It would accept that the oppressed subjects in these particular sites, or those in a position to distinguish the 'correct' strategic location, constitute the revolutionary vanguard.

The progressive search for surplus value, and the preparation of the workforce for production under modern capitalism, means that no institution or activity is free from commercial inspection and interference. As discussed earlier, the distinction between workplace and community seems even harder to justify when they can be on the same geographical site.

Conflicts which may appear to start in one location on closer examination have their origins in resistance in another area and extend into yet more. Bone himself, when discussing the Miners' Strike of 1984-5, refers to the community-based riots, not only in mining areas but also beyond, that were intended to support a dispute which originated in the workplace. The division of workplace from non-workplace is entirely provisional. The crossover in tactics is apparent in the term 'sabotage', which has its roots in the industrial sector, but also applies to forms of action that extend beyond the point of immediate production. The search for profit and the imposition of practices based on control of subjugated groups for reasons of financial efficiency extends to locations beyond the workplace. Consequently sabotage, as the means of resisting these disciplines and creating social relationships which are not determined by the dictates of surplus value, occurs in the community as well as in the factory. Such forms of resistance are exemplified in tactics such as vandalism, theft, the consumer boycott, squatting and other types of non-hierarchical social interaction.

As social crime theorists such as Peter Linebaugh and E. P. Thompson have indicated, illegality through theft and destruction of property has long been part of working class protest.[272] Marx himself note that assaults on bourgeois property relations not only bring about stimuli for new products and new modes of production, but also produce new laws, new academic disciplines (criminology, deviant sociology) and social actors (juries, barristers, social workers, detectives, prison wardens) to restrain and subjugate the criminal.[273] The process of criminalisation is one of the legitimised ways for the state to discipline (potential) miscreants and re-order their structures of domination, through the open use of coercion. Classifying acts as criminal, and thereby fit for punishing, is a response to class conflict. Crime is consequently a category whose embrace is in constant flux depending on the strength of dominant classes and the types of resistance they face. Such a view of crime as having the possibility for anti-hierarchical action is distinct from the characterisation of lawbreaking by Engels. He considered criminality to be the lowest form of working class resistance.[274]

Thompson's concept of the moral economy is useful to the understanding of villainy. Autonomous actions that are the product of values created by the oppressed agent rather than those imposed by heteronomous forces are often in conflict with bourgeois standards. Acts that transgress the values of the dominant class are declared to be criminal. Linebaugh presents examples of the moral economy. The early eighteenth century imposition of capitalist priorities on the carriage of goods in the industrialising West, meant emphasising efficiency and maximising profit at the expense of custom. Thus there were conflicts between the new port authorities protecting transported private property and the long established dockers' tradition of taking a sample of all goods they unloaded.[275]

There are a number of reasons why anarchism is associated with criminality. Partly it is because of Bakunin's and Nechaev's admiration of banditry, their recognition that constitutional forms are inadequate and that direct action, which is often illegal, is required.[276] The association is also a result of class struggle anarchists' recognition of a more expansive, and contingent, definition of 'the working class agent of change'. This multi-form subject, depending on context, can be both worker and criminal. As the reconstruction of capitalism involves deploying different forms of hierarchy, employees too enter into unlawful activities and offenders enter into business arrangements. Sympathetic strike action is now criminalised where before it was officially tolerated. As oppressive practices constantly intersect, so too resistance to hierarchy and heteronomous discipline appear in multiple contexts. The structure of drug-dealing gangs often replicates those of mainstream business. There is a small, permanent, highly rewarded elite at the top with a larger group of temporary associates underneath contracted for less well-rewarded, riskier tasks. A variety of methods are used to reduce the extraction of surplus labour by those at the top of the supply chain from those at the bottom (from stealing and adulterating product to, in extreme cases, murdering those in ascendant positions). Forms of class struggle can take place within criminal groups and can legitimately be supported by libertarians, whilst Leninists would ignore them.

4.1. Vandalism and Hooliganism

Although criminal activity may be antisocial (that is to say, further disadvantaging the least powerful) there is no necessary connection between the two. The antagonistic caricature of criminality is the portrayal of the irrational, destructive vandal, who craves only self-fulfilment through desecration. The victims are the equally poor (or poorer) near neighbours. Such individuals exist, and their misanthropic behaviour is widely condemned by class struggle anarchists as it weakens the power of the subjugated class materially and through mutual suspicion erodes networks of social support.[277]

Yet, while certain forms of vandalism are indiscriminate or anti-social, many other forms of direct action (criminalised under this category) are social as they combat heteronomous power. Recent environmental campaigns have used creative vandalism as parts of their activities, whether against the ecological risk of genetically modified crops (GMC), or the imposition of new roads on to 'poor people's communities'.[278] The environmental protests identified and publicised a category of vandalism called 'monkey-wrenching' in which mechanical deforestation equipment is disabled using predominantly low-tech methods. 'Monkey-wrenching' covered a multitude of tactical possibilities, breeding other sub-genres. One such sub-category of environmental vandalism is 'pixieing':

> Equipment, materials, structures, offices, vehicles, fences and machinery at link road sites were damaged all the time, sometimes by a large crowd who would outnumber security and disappear when the police arrived, but more often by small groups who operated out of view of security.[279]

In campaigns against GMC, direct action has been equally unequivocal, with mass trespasses onto test-sites and destruction of crops before they pollinate and potentially cross-fertilise with non-GM species. Such action is portrayed by agri-business as vandalism, but it is (also) a form of prefigurative action consistent with the anarchist ideal.[280]

These activities and the campaigns they are connected to encourage a range of constructive-disruptive tactics. The people involved come from a variety of backgrounds and have a range of complex identities. They create links of solidarity across a range of subjugated groups. The anti-M11 link road campaign of the early 1990s is an example that used creative vandalism and involved a wide variety of groups. Amongst the opponents were local residents whose health was at risk and whose social networks the road would sever. There were, amongst the anti-road protestors, those who regarded the new highway as an example of rapacious capitalism that had already marginalised them. Also included were collectives whose forms of autonomous communal organisation had already been threatened by legislative changes, such as the 1994 Criminal Justice Act.[281] Vandalism is not the sole tactic, but it provides links for intense communal relations, as the sociologists Welsh and McLeish identify: '[T]he fear and exhilaration born of danger and companionship in the collective obstruction of "progress" [... creates] direct action movements [which] are not easily "destroyed" by the crude exercise of power and continue to have unforeseeable effects.'[282]

4.2. Theft

For classical liberals, who regard the market as a non-coercive mechanism, the right to private property is sacrosanct. Yet, as we have seen, anarchism rejects the abstract notion of contractual obligation, regarding these agreements as coercive (see Chapter Two). The anarchist ideal rejects any form of market arrangement which depends on such contractual conventions and their enforcement for its survival.

In the environmental campaigns, as well as in other forms of protest, 'pixied' items are not only destroyed, but are also often (re-) appropriated:

> [L]ots of material was stolen from link road sites and other sites in the area. This material was then used for *our* purposes - using fencing for barricading, for example. This process had a beautiful roundness and economy about it: turning the enemies' 'weapons' against them! In devalorising these materials from capital's point of view, we revalorised (or autovalorised) them from our own.[283]

Theft strengthens the agents of change, weakens the practical capacities of oppressive forces and leads to further challenges to larger oppressive forces such as those that support private property rights.

It is not just in recognised campaigns that selective theft is accepted. Mere survival, or experiencing some degree of fulfilment, often requires minor acts of illegality.[284] According to *Anarchist Theft* shoplifting is a form of resistance that is available to many oppressed subject groups: 'Shop lifting is *more accessible* than the world of big business: anyone can do it, and many of the people whom big business usually shits on (parents with prams and wheelchair bound, for example) have a positive advantage'[285] (fig. 5.8.). Such activities strengthen oppressed groups at the expense of subjugating powers and also help to undermine the spectacle of commodification.

As Marx describes in *Capital*, goods are imbued with false properties through their relationships in commodity exchange. Once disrobed of their price-value, goods are perceived in a new light as Sheffield's Black Star explain:

> [B]ecause you gave nothing to get the things you shoplift, mealy [merely] owning them means nothing. Shoplifting removes the glamour from goods, it devalues them so that their worth is measured only by how useful they are. And, as the things that you've shop lifted become truly price-less, you see more clearly than ever before. That no amount of books, records, drugs, clothes, food and drink could ever compensate for the misery this society creates.[286]

Critics claim that stealing recreates hierarchies, where the finest thieves, rather than the best entrepreneurs, gain hegemony. Attack International is aware of this risk and indicates that shoplifting should be a part of creating equitable social relationships: 'shoplifting should not become just another individual consuming. We should share out our freebies and help other people (as well as encouraging them to join in).'[287]

This is not to say that all acts of theft are legitimate. Targets should, as Class War explain, be selective, ensuring that those robbed are not from subjugated groups:

We're totally favour in mugging the rich, shoplifting, burgling posh neighbourhoods, looting, assaulting the police and putting the boot in whenever we can [sic]. We're totally opposed to crimes against our own class. Mugging old ladies for a fiver, stealing TV's from council houses – the fuckin' bastards who do this have to be dealt with – and dealt with by local people not the police.[288]

Choosing selectively is a prerequisite, but the evaluative criteria are not based only on the relative material deprivation of victim and assailant. Burglary reduces the target to the status of a 'victim', who is robbed of autonomy. Responses to anti-social crime, just as to any other oppressive practice, must be prefigurative. The victims of the violation should be directing the operation against the transgressor, so as to regain control over their lives.[289]

Selective theft demonstrates self-valorisation, where subjugated groups rather tah dominant powers, determine how goods should be distributed and exchnged. Berkman describes how anarchist-communism involves creating different forms of distribution based on individual use and collective access rather than financial contract.[290] Distribution through socially-concerned theft is prefigurative if the burglary is carried out by an oppressed group, the target has greater social power and the result of the act does not create a new hierarchy by harming the victim to such a degree that they have less autonomy than the perpetrators and beneficiaries of the crime. The proceeds should be distributed socially. For instance, land seizures allow for free and equal access.[291] When riots and other localised uprisings grow more frequent and increasingly inter-relate, there is an escalation of acts which appropriate the means of production.[292]

4.3. Boycott
The refusal to handle goods from marked firms and industries has long been a form of industrial action which has been supported as a selective tactic by anarchists.[293] In the community, the boycott

is slightly different, in that the tactical agent is the consumer who refuses to buy particular wares because of some unacceptable features. Boycotts have been a popular tactic by those opposing state-racist countries (such as the Anti-Zionist and anti-Apartheid campaigns against Israel and pre-1994 South Africa respectively); goods manufactured by slave- or prison-labour (for companies such as Wilkinsons, Nike and Joe Bloggs); and goods produced or sold by firms that refuse to recognise trade unions (Body Shop) or have a poor environmental record (Shell). The aim of such a tactic is to pressurise the marked firm (or country), stemming its income and directing business to its competitors.

Anarcho-capitalists, such as Nozick, consider the boycott and concomitant methods of ethical consumption to be consistent with liberal theory. For instance, argues Nozick, if a customer considers workers' control of a business to be of primary importance, this can be incorporated into a free market society. Customers may be willing to forgo, or boycott, cheaper goods from hierarchically-managed firms and choose to pay a little more for supporting the product of self-management.[294] Niche marketers, such as ethical businesses, explore these possibilities.[295] The boycott recuperates working class rebellion from the practices and consequences of the

Figure 5.8. Let's Go Shoplifting, from
Do or Die, no 7.

existing processes and relations of production and consumption. Capitalists undermine radical assaults by transforming their practices whilst maintaining hegemony. The consumer boycott is one such method, preserving capitalism by reinterpreting discontent into choices between 'ethical' and 'unethical' commodities.

Class struggle anarchists are critical of the boycott tactic and the class of 'ethical' entrepreneurs. Attack International, for instance, are hostile to the boycott on the same grounds that Nozick admires it, i.e. it does not challenge, and indeed supports, the precepts of free market capitalism. 'The act of boycotting is an inherent part of consumer choice. Whenever we participate in the consumer market, we exercise our "right" to boycott by choosing a particular product'.[296] The boycott accepts the legitimacy of the free market as a suitable vehicle for creating progressive change, a position which is incompatible with anarchism's anti-capitalism. A boycott 'merely transfers the profit margins from one product to another'.[297] The industrial boycott might also transfer profits from one producer to another (unblacked) manufacturer, but here it is the economically-oppressed agent that is in control, not the well-meaning, but often paternalistic, consumer.

The tactic of the boycott also gives pre-eminence to the wealthier consumer. For a boycott to be successful it becomes more important to influence the buying decisions of the extravagant – normally wealthier – customer, than the poorer buyer whose economic strength is less significant (the boycotts organised by Gandhi may provide a rare exception). The agent for bringing about change is not the oppressed but the benign paternalist. As a result, Attack International recommend stealing the offensive product as this hits directly at the profits of the producers. The strength of this argument is that the boycott, in the form described by Attack International, is insufficiently prefigurative and cannot be considered an ideal type anarchist tactic. Nonetheless, there are three important caveats. First, there are occasions where the oppressed group is not the worker but the consumer. In the campaigns against the health risks of various foods (British beef for example), it is the dangers to the customer which is highlighted. The boycott in these circumstances is not paternalistic, but it does fall foul of other criticisms, namely that it places greater emphasis on wealthier consumers and does not undermine capitalism as a mode of production and distribution.

A second caveat is that it is conceivable that liberal practices can be less repressive than other prejudicial ones. The use of boycotts against goods produced in Apartheid South Africa may be such an example. For strategic anarchists, for whom all struggles are reducible to anti-capitalism, such an argument does not hold. For contemporary anarchists who recognise a multitude of oppressive practices, not all of which are wholly reducible to capitalism, it is possible that a boycott regime that successfully rewarded a liberal exploiter at the expense of an authoritarian one would be considered legitimate. Yet, even here, as capitalist relations increasingly extend and dominate all contexts, such occasions are increasingly rare.

The most important caveat is that not all boycotts are a matter of choosing commodity X instead of commodity Y. An alternative may be a non-market relationship. In the Montgomery bus boycott of 1955-6, famously sparked by the arrest of Rosa Parks, following her refusal to vacate her seat for a White passenger, the Black citizenry rebelled against discrimination and abandoned the segregated public transport system although no alternative service was available. This type of boycott avoids prioritising richer consumers, and creates new relationships not based on commercial transactions. A similar example would be students boycotting school lessons or lectures (whether because of a discriminatory curricula or in protest at an unjust war); here too relationships are not mediated by the market, so Attack International's legitimate criticism of consumer-led embargoes does not apply. Nor would it apply to rent boycotts that aim to hurt the owners of unearned income and do not assist another landlord. These actions remain anti-market tactics rather than arrangements in selective consumption. As a participant in the Glasgow rent boycott of 1915 points out, the boycott joined up with other working class tactics and organisations, such as anti-war and industrial protest. It also gave opportunities for women to play a dominant role in radical action.[298] Greater diversity of tactics inspires a larger set of agents and creates more complex links of solidarity.

4.4. Squatting

Squatting is a form of rent boycott that has been associated with anarchism since the 1960s,[299] as it demonstrates the main themes of libertarian direct action. The method intends to resolve the problem of homelessness and as such is synecdochic of the wider vision of anarchism, while the persons affected are those involved in the process of resolution. Squatting frequently leads on to other forms of class struggle so it is not merely an end in itself.

In 1968 the London Squatters Campaign was formed. The founding members came from New Left backgrounds, either anarchist and libertarian-socialist groupings or the International Socialists (a forerunner of the SWP). Although its first activity was largely symbolic, a brief demonstration outside the Hollies, a luxury private housing development in Essex, it began to move into practical direct action, assisting homeless families in taking over empty properties in the Redbridge suburb. Those directly affected by the failure of the paternalistic state and the market in housing took action to resolve their situation. The actions of the squatters won substantial support from the local community.[300]

The London squatters gained substantial press coverage because of their resolve in dealing with the legal and extra-legal measures taken by the council and bailiffs. Squatting campaigns flourished throughout London, Nottingham, Birmingham and Glasgow as homeless and inadequately-housed individuals, families and friendship groups discovered empty properties to re-appropriate. Others who resented paying large percentages of their income to landlords and those who found the squatters' communities a congenial arena for other forms of resistance also endorsed the tactic.[301]

The squatters' targets were the symbols of the failure of capitalism to fulfil its consumer promises. Centrepoint, a vacant London office block, was squatted in 1974 as was Biba Boutique, a former target of the Angry Brigade.[302] Squatting subverted the intended meanings of these buildings and their place in the geography of capitalism. Offices became communal homes for the dispossessed and residential properties were transformed into workshops and community centres. The tactic of appropriating land remains one of the most immediate tactics for class struggle anarchists, as it also develops into and interacts with other forms of action.

The difference between reformist and radical squatters was based on whether the expropriation of space was the ultimate objective. Within the Redbridge squatting movement, there were two distinct camps. The first, personified by Ron Bailey, saw squatting and the reform of the housing system as the aim; the other regarded squatting as a base for other forms of struggle.[303] Bailey accused his 'anarchist' opponents of using squatting instrumentally. Chris Broad countered the allegation. He considered squatting as an action that encouraged other tactics through example. Squatters themselves tried to extend liberatory social relations. Robert Goodman in *After the Planners* also distinguishes between reformist and 'guerrilla' architects. The latter, like anarchist squatters, believe that the 'successes and even failures [of their actions] lead to the kind of political consciousness which in turn leads to further political acts and the creation of a larger movement'.[304] Challenging civil law and acting directly boosts confidence and encourages ever more radical possibilities.[305]

Even reformist squatters challenge the inviolability of private property rights, and aim to formulate distribution in terms of use and social need. As a result, squatters stress that it is a prerequisite that empty properties are appropriated rather than those already inhabited by others.[306] Yet squatters like Bailey sought only to ameliorate property relations, ignoring other oppressive social practices that are linked to the capitalist determination of ownership and control. By cauterising possible links of solidarity, reformist squatters embrace free market relations rather than opposing them.

Squatting has been used for entrepreneurial advantage, providing cheap rent to create new markets and supply novel goods. Squats have housed vegan cafes, creators of primitive jewellery, wholefood suppliers and 'alternative' music shops.[307] Thus, squats in these contexts, rather than challenge market-relationships, have initiated the creation of new commodity forms and thus assisted in the gentrification of economically deprived areas. The guerrilla squatters, by contrast, sought to extend the conflict with oppressive powers. Speculation was identified as a cause of homelessness. Campaigns were launched against housing entrepreneurs, such as the estate agents Prebble & Co. in Islington.[308] Brixton squatters opposed the gentrification of part of South London, which saw the introduction of repressive by-laws as well as council action against undesirables. Earlier squatters from the same area had participated in the riots of 1985, fortifying links with other local oppressed groups.[309] In the environmental campaigns against the Newbury by-pass, in Pollok against the M77 (1994-5), and in 1994 at Claremont Road against the M11 link road, less than two miles from the original Redbridge campaign, squatting was itself used as a barrier against the highway developments. The physical possession of space through the occupation of buildings and trees (as well as using legal, constitutional manoeuvres in order to slow down clearances) not only impeded the contractors, but also helped to create communities of mutual support. Ali Begbie, an activist in Pollok, describes their protest as succeeding on two grounds: disrupting environmentally destructive construction but also creating 'a place of beauty and hope where energy is directed from the heart towards respecting the earth and each other'.[310]

The Pollok Squatters tried to break down the separation between themselves and other local residents in order to avoid elitism and to find avenues of effective solidarity (see Chapter Four). In an effort to counteract this separation of roles and the fixing of oppositional identities, contemporary anarchist squatters reject a vanguard approach and, as a result, intend many of the squatted properties to have a wider community use. Appropriated buildings such as the Autonomous Centre in Edinburgh or the Brighton Courthouse squat are used by community groups and for local bands to have gigs. These co-users of the space also share in the management of the space.[311]

Squatting provides opportunities for experiments in communal living arrangements, which often seem to non-participants to be at the expense of personal privacy and dignity. Such experiments offer a chance to develop wider, prefigurative social arrangements within the squatting group and beyond. The buildings and structures often reflect this diversity, including temporary partitions, communal sleeping dormitories, and rooms with multiple transient uses.[312] Squatting is a useful multiple tactic. It conforms to the pattern of anarchist direct action. The prefigurative response to specific repressive conditions not only engages the squatters themselves but also assists in the development of new modes of protest and different types of protestor.

4.5. Communes
The term 'commune' is used often as a synonym for 'squats', but another interpretation sees them as close to specialist communities with limited access from outsiders. The latter version aims to create a liberated society, a 'beloved community', complete in itself, within capitalism, providing opportunities for experimentation in social relations and forms of production. Examples include the Whiteway Colony, to which the survivors from the original *Freedom* retired in the 1930s, and the Crabapple community, whose aims are suitably prefigurative: to create a mini-society which is co-operative and consensual and which eradicates the sexist division of labour and other forms of hierarchy.[313] Creating new communities has been a tactic advanced by a variety of political ideologues as well as by an assortment of anarchists.[314]

Communes are, however, subject to considerable criticism from class struggle anarchists on four grounds. First, they are often elitist, open only to those with sufficient wealth or desirable skills. Second, for all their anti-hierarchical motivations, their relationships with non-commune members are patronising and tend towards isolation and inertia. Third, relationships within communes, between their members, fail to live up to their egalitarian principles, with informal and persistent leaderships and unreformed, sexist behaviour. Finally, in building and sustaining the commune they are too acquiescent towards capitalism and neglect other avenues of solidarity with oppressed groups.

The first of these weaknesses are exemplified not only by Fourier, who famously targeted the wealthy to support his phalanxes, but also more contemporaneously by a proposal in *Green Anarchist* to build a 'primitivist community in Zimbabwe or Mozambique for US$66,000'.[315] This proposal not only raises questions about which individuals are in a position to leave family, friends and other responsibilities and afford their share of the initial set-up fee plus the substantial transport cost to the commune, but also raises the question, from whom are they buying the land (and how did the sellers initially acquire it)?[316] And what sorts of relationship will these European incomers have with the African authorities and especially the citizenry? It would seem that the proposers of the commune are aiming their publicity at an Occidental, independent, relatively wealthy, elite.

In keeping with their anti-hierarchical views, communes often desire free admittance, but those with such an open policy frequently fail. John Vidal and George Monbiot describe in their accounts of the Pure Genius encampment in Wandsworth set up in 1996 the problems of communes based on uninhibited access. Vidal describes how the free site attracted the victims of the Conservative government mental health reforms. Individuals with severe psychiatric problems, without adequate social support, and having few other avenues, drifted towards the site:

[U]topians and protestors had no training in dealing with the mentally disturbed, beyond common sense and sympathy (of which there was a lot). 'How do you deal with people on heroin? People with guns and knives? We have no support network. Some of these people need hospital care, many needed professional help'.[317]

Monbiot elucidates:

[T]he tragedy of open access [... is] that where there are no constraints on exploitation everyone who makes use of a resource will overexploit it, as the gain accrues only to himself [sic], while the loss is shared by the whole population. Resources used in this way inevitably will be eroded until they disappear.

In Wandsworth, the resources in question were not land, which on the whole was well-tended but the more ethereal commodities of peace and good-will.[318]

Monbiot concludes that experimental communities should be built only on common interests excluding those whose concerns do not coincide with these predetermined priorities.[319] For Monbiot's commune to persist it must recreate capitalist divisions, between those who are deemed to be an asset and are thus permitted entry and those who are deemed a liability and consequently excluded. Bey and ideal type anarchists propose more transitory and multiple modes of protest in order to avoid fixing such discriminatory identities.

Communes are often geared towards escape, a refuge from repressive social structures. Other proponents of a radical commune, appealing for supporters in *Green Anarchist*, describe their aim as being to 'swim sideways out' of capitalism.[320] As critics of such avoidance point out, dominant social relations still influence even a solitary individual's reality.[321] Communes do provide useful prefigurative moments, but as a class struggle visitor to Crabapple describes, they do so inadequately: 'I found the community lacked a political angle as it was not challenging the state although it was tackling related issues - junk food, consumer culture, animal welfare.'[322] By ignoring other forms of action, and concentrating only on the commune, roles and social identities become fixed. Identities of commune members (defined against those excluded) become reified and that leads to the reconstruction of hierarchical practices. Other, more transitory, communes, which do not impose a rigid division between their 'perfect' community and the rest of the world, and act in a similar way to the guerrilla squats, might avoid such an elitist separation.

5. Atypical Anarchist Tactics

Anarchist tactics depend on context and agency. As seen with categories of action such as propaganda by deed or industrial sabotage, these terms cover a multiplicity of methods whose consistency with the prefigurative ethic depends on the subject identities and the particularities of the specific location. Generalised approval or disapproval of classes of (anti-)political behaviour is indicative of a quasi-scientific approach that permits an elite vanguard outside of these contexts to make this decision and dictate action. As a result, even acts that appear to conform to categories of behaviour normally accepted as being incompatible with the prefigurative archetype, on occasions can be legitimate.

In Chapter Two certain classes of social action, such as constitutional activity, were assessed as irreconcilable with anarchism as they involve mediation. Other forms of radical behaviour such as encouraging capitalism and conformity appear to be utterly inimitable. Nonetheless, libertarians have propounded these methods because of their apparent anti-elitist forms. These manoeuvres deserve closer examination. Even when, bar a tiny minority of occasions, they are irreconcilable with the prefigurative ethic, they illustrate the continual attempt to innovate, and the tensions in trying to create effective tactics whilst avoiding the problems associated with consequentialist strategies.

5.1. Constitutional Activity

Opposition to representative democracy has been part of British anarchism since the late nineteenth century. *Der Arbeiter Fraint* split from *Der Polishe Yidl* on the basis of the latter's support for a parliamentary candidate. Yet there have been rare incidents of anarchists participating in elections. In Australia, where voting is compulsory, anarchists have stood as candidates to provide their supporters with an opportunity to avoid being fined as well as to mock the electoral process.[323] In Britain in May 2003, the Bristolian Party, heavily influenced by anarchists, stood candidates in the local council elections and in some wards scored a significant percentage of votes (although without coming close to threatening the winning party). In 1988, Class War stood a candidate in the Kensington by-election and writers for the anarchist influenced *Alarm* were candidates in the 1979 Swansea Council elections.[324]

Anarchists, however, have tended to reject constitutional means, so these albeit rare instances of involvement in state and quasi-state elections require some examination. The anarchists' own justifications for these constitutional methods are distinct from those advanced by anti-market socialist groups such as the SPGB who also stand representatives. The SPGB rejected all other forms of struggle in favour of parliamentary methods, considering the democratic mandate as necessary and sufficient for revolutionary change.[325] Other socialist groups such as the Socialist Party claim to use parliamentary politics much more tactically, as opposed to the SPGB's strategic response; however, in practice, as Trotwatch point out, the result is often similar. Socialist electoral parties, because they participate in the constitution process (either independently or through active support of the Labour Party) end up in a contradiction, namely supporting the legitimacy of the institutions they claim to oppose.

Class War's intervention into constitutional politics is distinct from that of the SPGB. Class War's participation in the political process is provisional, not as the main route to liberation, as Tim Palmer of Class War explains:

[W]e haven't suddenly come to the blinding realisation that there is a parliamentary road to anarchism, socialism or whatever, or even having Class War's MP wandering the corridors of Westminster would be in any way a particularly good thing – all the way through the 'campaign' we always stated in no uncertain terms exactly what we thought of the parliamentary system.[326]

Class War used the opportunity to attack parliamentary activity in a similar way to that of the anti-elections campaigns, but 'by getting in the thick of it [...] people actually heard it for once'.[327] This tactic was classified by Bone as a stunt, as it relied on the media for its effectiveness.[328] It was successful, as stories appeared in the national newspapers, yet as a stunt it could not be repeated too often: 'things are never as good the second time around [...] but as a tactic we hope it played a part'.[329] With the multiplicity of fringe parties the opportunities for a CWF candidate to gain attention is restricted. Intervention into politics is a qualified tactic designed to undermine through subversion rather than to reaffirm the legitimacy of constitutional authority.

There are still problems with Class War's electoral stunt, including its dependence on the established media that has already been discussed. However, the reliance on constitutional methods does reaffirm electoral tactics as an effective and legitimate mode of protest. For all of Class War's attempts to condemn parliamentary activity and to advocate working class self-activity instead, the medium remains that of constitutional politics. With little or no chance of winning, the criticisms of electoral methods, and the heteronomous power they legitimise, might be read by the non-anarchist (the agent Class War was aiming to reach) as the cries of a sore loser. Participation in the Westminster system reaffirms Parliament's liberality in allowing oppositional voices to stand. Furthermore, rather than encouraging action, the agent remains the passive voter, looking on at Class War's subversive intervention. Additionally, there are pragmatic considerations, for instance the cost in terms of time and effort, for relatively little lasting publicity and even fewer votes (60) that might suggest that other tactics might be more appropriate.[330]

The SPGB's criticism of anarchism remains that, without the democratic mandate provided by the electoral system, anarchist actions are elitist and paternalist as they do not have the agreement of the people.[331] But this is to misunderstand communism. For class struggle libertarians, liberation is not the imposition of a set of absolute, scientifically determined rules (whether with or without democratic agreement), but the struggles of the oppressed subjects themselves in defetishising the social conditions of capitalism.[332] Consequently, the methods have to be prefigurative. The use of constitutional means, if they reaffirm representative democracy, would not be synecdochic of non-hierarchical social structures. Nonetheless, there can be occasions where constitutional means can be used to subvert and diminish representative power. This may happen, for instance, when candidates conform to the principles of anti-representation by promising not to take their seats in the legislature. In such circumstances, electoral methods prefigure less hierarchical social organisation, although such campaigns must be provisional and steer clear of creating an unofficial hierarchy of candidates and voters, and the tactic should avoid taking strategic centrality.

5.2. Over-Production

Jean Baudrillard's poststructuralist tactics are also motivated by avoidance of vanguard actions. It is not the intention here to give a comprehensive account of Baudrillard's postmodernism, nor to trace his development from ultra-leftism with links to the SI to the alluring pessimistic nihilism of his more recent writings,[333] but to concentrate on the features of his work that posit a different tactic. Baudrillard engages in sketching the contours of phenomena that will bring about a new society without providing new forms of domination.

Marxism since Lukaçs has been concerned with reification and the decline of subjectivity, as people are increasingly treated as objects and become enthralled by commodities, in particular the hierarchies of status ascribed to these goods and services. Radical proposals from libertarians such as the Situationists sought to reawaken the subjective desires of the oppressed, whilst Baudrillard instead proposes the fatal strategy of embracing objectification and giving up the illusion of subjectivity. Objects, according to Baudrillard, pursue trajectories of going to extremes,[334] like 'cells in cancer'.[335] Pushing the logic of capitalism to its extreme would cause a crisis leading to its transformation. Consequently, Baudrillard promotes consumerism as a means of forcing capitalism into collapse where debts do not have to be paid ('amortisation'). He proposes a form of deficit spending without the hangover of repayment or the consequences of bankruptcy:

> [A] system is abolished only by pushing it into hyperlogic, by forcing it into an excessive practice which is equivalent to a brutal amortisation. 'You want us to consume - O.K., let's consume always more, and anything whatsoever; for any useless and absurd purpose.'[336]

The avowedly anarchist Decadent Action follow Baudrillard in arguing that capitalism can best be forced into a fatal crisis by stimulating it further. Through encouraging the desire for goods that the economic system is unable to meet, it will reach a critical point. Decadent Action demand greater and better commodities and embrace the benefits of further consumption: 'Abstaining from the trappings of capitalism won't make it go away. But if it is fed to excess it will burst.'[337]

The development of capitalism, as productive forces extend, certainly brings about traumatic changes in social relations. The restructuring of the British economy by successive Thatcher governments, such that market mechanisms were given freer rein, unleashed a mass of chaotic drives. Yet, as Best and Kellner point out, such a strategy of encouraging grander oppressive forces (capitalism) in itself 'hardly caused capital any hardships and obviously [... was] not going to subvert or transform the system and by the 1980s Baudrillard gave up postulating any specific goals or political projects.'[338] It was the countervailing forms of resistance and self-valorisation that were a threat to dominating power, not the extension of market relationships. Baudrillard's method of over-production is rejected by the anarchist ideal on three grounds. First it prioritises economic strategies as the main method of defeating heteronomous forces, second it reifies existing oppressive practices and third, it makes historically-specific practices of late capitalism appear totalising and universal.

Decadent Action's fashionable anarchism bears remarkable similarities to Leninism.[339] For this group, it is capitalism that is determinant, whereas the actions of the oppressed are secondary. Decadent Action share with Lenin the view that the forces of production must be developed until a point of crisis is reached, and they thereby prioritise a distinct class of people as being most capable of bringing about liberation: namely, those in the most advanced capitalist countries. This tactic of advancing capitalism so that it collapses, as proposed by Decadent Action, is not only incompatible with the prefigurative ideal which rejects vanguardism, but is also inconsistent with Decadent Action's industrial campaign of sabotage through absenteeism ('phone-in sick') which encourages a rejection of productivism.

5.3. Hyper-Passivity and Disengagement
Baudrillard considers the Situationist notion of the spectacle to be problematic as it posits a set of real meanings that capitalism has overturned, and to which the revolutionaries aim to return. Yet such essentialism, evident in the Situationist search for authenticity, does not apply to the poststructuralist anarchisms developed here. For Baudrillard, there is no reality below the surface. In a world of ever-expanding production, of greater and greater media of communication and expansion of signs, simulation becomes more real than reality. The grammar of advertising and entertainment enters that of politics

and art.[340] Not only do soap-opera villains require bodyguards, but presenters on real-crime programmes, where villainy is reproduced to entertain the masses and assist the police, also become victims of murderous crime themselves (more than likely as a result of their media role). The assassination of the TV personality is then recreated on the same 'real crime' programme that thrust them into public prominence. Hyperreality blurs the distinction between the real and unreal. Intervention only increases the production of signs whilst also promoting an authoritarian notion of authenticity.

A result of the explosion of signs, and ever increasing bombardment of messages exhorting the masses to act, react, consume, produce, vote and opine, is that the rabble refuse and become, in Best and Kellner's words, 'a sullen, silent majority'.[341] '[T]he masses scandalously resist this imperative of rational communication. They are given meaning: they want spectacle.'[342] The masses choose watching football over participating in protest and this shocks the radicals who demand that the working class reacts in an appropriate manner, or at least appears to care.[343] The masses, for Baudrillard, defy the authoritarianism of imposed meanings by rejecting engagement. Through apathy, the masses resist developing the process of creative dissent that is used to further spectacular production. According to Plant, there are similarities between Baudrillard's method of total disengagement and Stewart Home's 'Art Strike' advanced in his Art Strike propaganda and in the Situationist-inspired *Here and Now*.[344] By refusing to engage in critical art, the artist resists the creation of artefacts for galleries, museums and dealers.[345]

Ideal type anarchism, partly through engaging with poststructuralism, rejects the metaphysics of claims to knowing or believing in a human essence and is not predicated on objective, primary, or authentic relationships. Green Anarchism, liberal forms of anarchism and some parts of the classical anarchist canon were based on notions of 'authenticity' and 'naturalness' between subjects or between subjects and 'nature'.[346] Poststructural anarchism nonetheless recognises that the present symbolic order is not indispensable, that it can be replaced with different systems. As a result, it is in conflict with Baudrillard's and the Art Strikers' tactic of disengagement. Passivity of this form celebrates quiescence (and even death).[347] The Art Strike's inactivity may, like Baudrillard's hyperpassivity, argues Plant, leave nothing for capitalism to recuperate, but it also disarms opposition.[348]

By ignoring the subjectivities of 'the masses', reducing them to a single identity, Baudrillard fails to recognise that even in watching sport the opportunity for subversion occurs and is grasped. Baudrillard argues that the spectacle of televised sport, like the artwork deposited in a museum for mass consumption, represents a flight from engagement.[349] Yet viewing television need not be a wholly passive recreation. Watching a match on the big screen at a pub can involve a myriad of social behaviours: meeting friends, conversing, conspiring, celebrating and commiserating. Although the locations for mass spectating have moved from the direct arena of the pitches and the stadia to the mediated environments of the brewery-sponsored giant televisions, new forms of social disruption have arisen. The theft of signal from pay-TV is commonplace. The over-policing and mass-surveillance of the football ground have long prevented the development of an environment for congregation and conflict. Technological advances and capitalist restructuring of sport have dispersed the mass spectating environment into multiple locations. Disorder is no longer situated in one site, namely the football stadium and its immediate environs. Following England's games in the 1996 European championship and 2002 World Cup, riots took place in numerous locations throughout that country,[350] while Newcastle town centre witnessed substantial anti-police disorder following their team's defeat in the FA Cup final in 1999, although Wembley, where the game was played, was unaffected.[351]

6. Summation

Contemporary anarchism embraces a diversity of tactics and agents, with no approach or domain taking universal precedence. In the past, such multiplicity was considered to be confused or chaotic, yet diverse and polymorphous (changeable forms) tactics are appropriate to the range and complexity of different oppressive practices. Thieves, hooligans, vandals and saboteurs are not an underclass of naive rebels but are some of the identities imposed on and assumed by those engaged in struggle. Multiform agents can form part of a wider coalition of creative liberation.

There are no universally appropriate strategies, or organisational forms. Some tactics are only suitable within certain contexts aimed at particular forms of oppressive force and carried out by specific agents. When they meet constraints, such as the commodification of roles or integration of opposition into the dominant order, new identities form and corresponding methods and organisational forms emerge. Reactions and responses to repressive practices cannot be determined from an objective position, as no such location exists, nor can the precise forms or identities of solidarity be prescribed. For anarchists, however, certain forms of organisation and particular groupings will be ruled out as their intervention would be paternalistic and their methods antipathetic to their prefigurative ambitions.

The divisions between community and workplace tactics have come to an end. Some networks and organisations, by the nature of the subjects, will concentrate on issues at the workplace and develop methods to overcome bureaucratic rule. In other contexts, distinct oppositional networks will form which may contain the same agents in different organisations using disparate methods. Each victory creates a modification of the strategy of control by the dominant class. The miners' victories in the early 1970s resulted in new procedures in policing to destroy industrial tactics. Autonomous workers' groups found imaginative means of countering the mass policing of workplace hot spots, such as hit squads and spontaneous road-blocks. Agents of capital (either private or state) reacted by finding methods to control disputes and keep them within containable routines.

Innovative types of organisation encourage imaginative tactics and produce new subject identities. The anti-roads protests created novel networks of co-ordination; others, such as the squatting communities, developed fresh allegiances with more conventionally-housed neighbours. The criminalisation of their actions and policing of their protests led them to take on strong, mutually supportive (almost tribal) groupings and as such they celebrated the primitive. Tactics develop in response to ever-altering circumstances and encourage resourceful forms of solidarity. For contemporary class struggle anarchists, the revolution is not a single event that heralds immediate new social relations, but is the culmination of extending creative, collaborative social relations. The brave, magnificent experiments in living which transform everyday life are both the means and the end.

'Resistance is fertile'[1]

In May 2000, for the third time in less than twelve months, anarchism was the subject of enormous media interest.[2] Invective screamed from the front pages of national newspapers following the anti-capitalist demonstration in London on Monday May 1st, 2000. All the major newspapers led with denunciations of the day's events: 'Riot yobs desecrate Churchill Monument', 'This was their vilest hour', 'MAY DAY MAYHEM'.[3] Once again anarchism was conflated with irrational violence, and there were calls for groups to be subjected to greater state and quasi-state investigation.[4]

Mayday 2000 was a weekend of activities based on the theme of 'anti-capitalism'. It was loosely co-ordinated by a network comprising many of the groups that are the subject of this book, including AF, EF!,

Figure 6.1. Winston Churchill statue, Mayday, 2000.

Class War, MA'M, RTS and SolFed. The operational core was an assembly based at the Resource Centre on Holloway Road in North London. Talks ranged from practical advice on direct action and de-schooling to highly theoretical exchanges on situationist theory, the challenge of globalisation and debates between Trotskyist and autonomist interpretations of marxism.[5] The ambitious programme of events concluded with an RTS-inspired 'guerrilla gardening' project. Parliament Square opposite the British legislature was replanted with bushes, flowers and shrubs. The torn up turf carpeted the roads. To the horror of *The Daily Mail*, the statue of Churchill was redecorated with a grass mohican (figure 6.1.).[6]

Quoting an unnamed source, *The Guardian* gives an indication of the size of the threat anarchists are supposed to present. 'Millennium eve apart [...] the police operation to deal with the demonstration was "the biggest in 30 years"'.[7] The high-level reaction was so intense it often seemed absurd. An educational walking tour examining the anarchist history of the East End, arranged for the Friday night on the eve of the conference, was attended by 50 participants but was met by five mini-vans of riot police. Those entering the Resource Centre were video-taped, and a special surveillance unit recorded anyone leaving the nearby tube station. The intrusion of the state and the preceding hysterical press coverage impeded the very spontaneity that had marked events such as J18.[8]

Following the guerrilla gardening, the impromptu march up Whitehall to Trafalgar Square led to the all too predictable attack on McDonalds. The ensuing mini-riot was little more than a showcase for the police to use well-practised crowd control and harassment techniques. Unlike J18, when the destruction was predominantly discerning and a useful addition to the diverse alliances and creative propaganda, the forms of contestation at Mayday 2000 had become formulaic. Activist roles had been frozen into a symbolic order that was easy for both the police and media to manipulate. Targets, such as the graffiti on the cenotaph or the statue of Churchill, were represented as assaults on the anti-fascist dead.[9] The vengeful Metropolitan police easily outnumbered the 2000 protestors they interned in Trafalgar Square for four hours. Likely suspects were picked out, individually photographed, questioned and humiliated. 97 were arrested.[10] A similar scenario developed on Mayday 2001, when the police successfully contained the carnival of protestors in a section of Oxford Street. Whereas J18 had been an exercise in extending autonomy and participation, later anti-capitalist demonstrations, by contrast, were becoming tainted by frustrating paralysis.

Reactions to anarchism have been as complex and provisional as the liberation movements. The class struggle anarchism of over a century ago faced religious and press investigation of its clubs. Political interventions included legal restrictions on immigration.[11] The first chapter traced not only the development of the formal anarchist groups in Britain but also responses to them. Legislative assaults are a feature of more recent times. Margaret Thatcher in the 1980s criminalised many industrial tactics; the Major government introduced the 1994 Criminal Justice Act that prohibited major aspects of the rave culture; and Blair's Labour government has steered through parliament several new acts to 'prevent terrorism', and in September 2005, was promising further initiatives that will curtail civil liberties even further in order to 'protect freedom'.[12] This legislation targets not just reactionary Islamic terrorists but also direct action organisations. Counter-measures provoke new subjugated groups and are one of the impulses for innovative, emancipatory manoeuvres.

The framework of evaluation, the subject of the second chapter, was constructed from portions of contemporary anarchist texts that critique the tactics of competing movements and those fragments that appraise their methods. An ideal type of anarchism was created by which to assess the actual techniques of contemporary groups. The ideal is not a fixed archetype, but a collection of principles whose manifestations change according to localised circumstances. The multitudes of, and transformations in, libertarian tactics nevertheless share key characteristics. One particular trait is a commitment to non-hierarchical participation by those directly oppressed. The identities of the agents of change, discussed in Chapter Three, demonstrated that liberation requires that the primary agents of change are those in subjugated positions. In different contexts a distinctive oppressed subject appears; in the nineteenth century East End of London these would be the

Jewish immigrant sweatshop employees; in the same geographical area in the twenty-first century a different subjugated agent appears. Different contexts have distinct agents with no single oppressed group taking universal priority. Oppression is irreducible to a single source, although for contemporary anarchists economic oppression is often (although not always) primary in the locations in which they operate.

Many contemporary libertarians explicitly identify prefigurative, anti-hierarchical and participatory characteristics as being key features of their organisational and tactical praxis (chapters four and five), even though their critics do not. The multiplicity and impermanence associated with contemporary anarchism means that libertarian trends share similarities with politically-engaged poststructuralisms. Nonetheless, some contemporary class struggle anarchists share their critics' confusion surrounding methods and tactics. Consequentialist approaches still abound; the long shadow of the grand modernist designs still obscures the more elaborate and temporary textures of the contemporary radical movement. Bewilderment, however, is more evident amongst those whose purpose is to control libertarian action than those who are involved.

In evaluating anarchist tactics one area of analysis is that concerning propaganda by word. This raises the question of where this text, which is based on an university thesis, is located? What are its aims, and what relationship does it hold to the prefigurative criteria it uses to assess anarchist tactics? There are a number of misgivings that are legitimate concerning research projects such as this. No analysis, especially those on the self-creativity of oppressed groups, can claim to be objective. Specific prominent events provoke partisan emotions. Additionally, my selection of materials and choice of incidents is influenced by my (perhaps tenuous) position within an elite institution (a university), as well as my social and cultural background, just as the social position of the reader will affect her/his interpretation of this text. The decision to dedicate time and resources to this project already implies a pre-existing attraction to the subject. There is also a contrary tendency in which prolonged proximity leads to frustration and disenchantment. The aim, nevertheless, has been to provide a convincing, documented account of contemporary anarchism and to critically evaluate its tactical and organisational forms through an appropriate framework. In carrying out these tasks, movements have been classified under various categories such as 'anarchist communist', 'syndicalist', 'autonomist', 'workplace' and 'environmentalist'. These, often provisional, divisions are especially problematic for movements that aim to break through the reifying restraints of categorisation.

The acts of accumulating and collating information on rebellious social movements are often precursors to the control of these groupings. Thus, codifying material carries the risk of assisting those bodies that police and discipline revolt. As a result, steps were taken to provide interested individuals from relevant anarchist groups an opportunity to review the enterprise prior to publication, to at least minimise the risk to individuals and groups named herein.

The fluidity that characterises contemporary anarchism makes analysis of their groups and alliances particularly problematic. Anarchist associations are as complex as relationships themselves. Just as no one can impose camaraderie, or predict in advance how deep or how long-lasting a friendship will be, so too no one can externally will the forms of solidarity between subjugated groups. In the same way that some liaisons become intermittent amicable acquaintances or life-long romances or brief but intense affairs, so too the groups and collaborations can be permanent, occasional or temporary, depending on context. This research has concentrated on texts or semi-prominent activities, and as a result it has tended to concentrate on those groups that achieve(d) a degree of permanence. The consequence of concentration on the more constant organisations is that there is the risk that a deceptive impression of anarchism is created: one that implies greater solidity, or that intimates that the formal groups are the sole vehicles for libertarian action. This potentially misleading perception of libertarianism would be stronger if the reader's attention is not drawn to the considerable degree of change that takes place within these apparently stable groups. The Black Flag, Class War, DAM/SolFed or EF! of 15 years ago are considerably different from those operating after the turn of the millennia. The successes of the Poll Tax campaign, environmental campaigns and J18 each provided new stimuli for change within and across groups. Similarly the failures of the miners' and printers' industrial actions, or, more modestly, the shortcomings of more recent anti-capitalist actions, provoke new adaptations. The vibrancy of liberatory movements depends on their abilities to respond inventively to constraints as well as new freedoms they, in part, help to create. The strengths and weakness of anarchism can be assessed by how quickly they adjust and the degree to which these new tactics correspond to the prefigurative ethic.

Introduction

1   See for instance, Waterman, 2001, vii-viii and Sheehan, 2003, 7-12. Nobel Prize winning economist Joseph Stiglitz too begins his critical account of globalisation with the riots in Seattle and Genoa (Stiglitz, 2002, 3).

2   Other protestors had been shot but not killed at the earlier anti-capitalist demonstrations in Gothenburg, 'Sweden defends EU summit policing', (BBC News Online, Sunday, 17 June, 2001, 02:26 GMT 03:26 UK, <http://news.bbc.co.uk/1/hi/world/europe/1392839.stm>).

3   'Libertarian and 'anarchist' are used synonymously. In this book, 'anarchist' and 'libertarian' are used to stand for the class struggle movements, unless the context indicates otherwise.

4   Karen Goaman makes a division between the earlier anti-summit events and those which are 'Post-11 September' (Goaman, 2004, 167).

5   'Blair: Anarchists will not stop us' (BBC Online, Sunday, 17 June, 2001, 06:02 GMT 07:02 UK, <http://news.bbc.co.uk/1/hi/uk_politics/1392957. stm>). Blair's insult was reappropriated, as Goaman describes, by the anti-capitalist May Day Collective in 2002 (Goaman, 2004, 163).

6   I follow Todd May's approach of looking at marxism, or rather marxisms, rather than Marx (or a Marxism). As he comments, this may be unfair on Marx's own writings but his:

> fate will be determined less by what he said, and by what he meant by what he said, than by what others said he said. That is why his legacy is of more moment for our purposes than the exegesis of his writings (May, 1994, 18n).

Consequently, throughout the book, I refer to 'marxism' to avoid demarcating one particular version as the single correct 'Marxism', especially as so many versions are in conflict. For instance, the autonomist marxist tradition of Harry Cleaver, Massimo de Angelis, John Holloway, Toni Negri et. al. has more in common with class struggle anarchism than with Leninism. Although there are differences between the various Leninisms, the main issues for debate in this work, such as the central role of the Party and the strong versions of economic determinism, are fundamental features of all Leninists. 'Leninism', as a result, retains its capital letter.

7   Miller, 1984, 3.

8   Capital letters are used to describe formal members of groups and lower case letters are used for writers or activists in a particular tradition.

Guy Debord, therefore, is a 'Situationist' (as he was a member of the SI) but the magazine *Here and Now* is 'situationist'. Movements called after an actual person retain an upper case, for instance 'Bakunist' and 'Leninist'. The exception is for those named after Marx, see endnote 6.

9   Quail, 1978, x.

10   Reprinted in the *Anarchist 1992 Yearbook*.

11   These are similar to the main features of traditional anarchism drawn up by Bookchin (Bookchin, 1995, 60).

12   See, for instance, Organise! No. 33, 19 and *Class War*, No. 39, 13; 'Who is Solidarity Federation?' (sic.), Solidarity Federation, <http://www.solfed.org.uk/>, last accessed September 2, 2003.

13   Anderson & Anderson, 1991e, 3.

14   *The Anarchist*, March 1885, 2.

15   EF!'s US roots were originally in the often conservative environmental movements such as the Sierra Club and Wilderness Society. 'Some founding EF! (US) activists initially advocated a set of conservative naturalist beliefs, drawn from a misanthropic reading of deep ecology' (Wall, 2000, 44).

16   Morland, 1997, 12 and 20-21.

17   David Morland, in his analysis of conceptions of human nature in the classical libertarians, traces a similar distinction between individualist anarchists and social anarchists (Morland, 1997, 3-6).

18   These desires are 'often socially engineered today in any case' (Bookchin, 1995, 16).

19   Bookchin, 1995, 16 and 57.

20   Wolff, 1976 and Nozick, 1984.

21   Also influential has been Saul Newman's (2001), *From Bakunin to Lacan*. The main websites discussing postanarchism are Postanarchism Clearing House, <http://www.geocities.com/ringfingers/postanarchism2.html> and Postanarchism discussion archive at <http://lists.village.virginia.edu/cgi-bin/spoons/archive1.pl?list=postanarchism.archive>. An excellent introductory talk by May on postanarchism, 'Renewing the Anarchist Tradition: A poststructuralist approach to Anarchism', is available at A-infos, <http://www.radio4all.net/proginfo.php?id=2725>, last accessed September 2, 2003

22   May, 1994.

23   The construction (anti-)politics is used because 'politics' in anarchist literature is often construed in terms of statecraft, strategems that are at variance to anarchism. A wider interpretation of 'politics' such as the 'ability to influence other peoples' realities' still places anarchism as an 'anti-political' movement, as such heteronomy is contrary to anarchism. Nonetheless, in confronting political behaviour, anarchism is not always successful in avoiding recreating political relationships.

24   WSM is the acronym of the Workers' Solidarity Movement. A full list of abbreviations is found in the key to the histogram (figure 1.1).

25   One member of the WSM recalls traveling to Britain 'on over 20 occasions specifically to attend anarchist events' (Andrew, 1998, 40).

26   The AWG, who also advocated this structure, lasted just four years and disbanded in 1992.

27   These Jewish groups were omitted by the ACF in their history of British anarchism, and were barely mentioned by John Quail in his otherwise extremely useful account..

28   Cores, 1992, 6.

29   Taylor, 1993, 23 & Bernstein, 1976, 69. As Richard Bernstein points out: 'To understand human action – one must understand how language and action are grounded in inter-subjective practices and forms of life' (Bernstein, 1976, 23).

30   Melucci, 1996, 15.

31   Gorz, 1983, 30.

32   McKay, 1998, 11-12.

33   Bone, 1997, 8-9 and N and Others, 1997, 12-14.

34   See, for instance, Bone's comments on how the first 'March Against the Rich' in Kensington and the incidents at the Henley Regatta helped to alarm the more powerful residents of London (Bone, 1997, 9). Similar activities took place at the 'Lets Ruin Their Party For a Change' demonstration against the 'Queen Charlotte Debutantes Ball' (Grosvenor Park Hotel, London, September 14, 1992) and 'A Night at the Opera' (Royal Crescent, Bath, June 28, 1992). The acerbic banners and shouted slogans served to intimidate as well as to inform.

35   Morris Beckman describes how rallies organised by British fascists in the East End caused Jewish families to stay indoors. The 43 Group challenged the followers of Oswald Mosley over the control of East London streets (Beckman, 1993, 96).

36   *Class War* No. 54, 7.

37   *Black Flag*, No. 203, 30.

Chapter One: Histories of British Anarchism

1   Later editions include a brief update of post-war events such as Paris 1968 and the Angry Brigade, possibly to correct his earlier hypothesis that anarchism had died out and would 'never [be] born again' (Woodcock, 1975, 443).

2   George McKay, in his survey of British anarchism in the *New Statesman*, talks of the academics interested in the subject and the

environmental protestors but fails to include a reference to any anarchist group (McKay, 1996b, 27). Marshall gets biographical details wrong: see, for example, his description of Ian Bone (Marshall, 1992, 494).

3   Christie, 1980; Christie, 2004 and Meltzer, 1996b.

4   Meltzer, 1976a; Meltzer, 1976b and Meltzer, 1992e.

5   Dangerfield, 1997; Fountain, 1988 and Hewison, 1986.

6   Communist Party, 1957, 28.

7   Lindsey German, 1996, 25.

8   McKay, 1996, 11-12.

9   There is a tendency, as Richard Porton vividly describes, 'to lump anarchists, socialists and communists into a monolithic subversive threat' (Porton, 1999, 64).

10   The Welsh Socialists (Cymru Goch) whose roots are in the Welsh Socialist Republican Movement, a splinter from Plaid Cymru, a parliamentary party, admit that their works are influenced by Class War's introductory tract *This is Class War*. Cymru Goch are viewed with suspicion by some within the wider libertarian camp (The Welsh Socialists, 1996, 3 and *Do or Die* No. 8, 1999, 335).

11   Morland, 2004., Mueller, 2003, May, 1994, Newman, 2001.

12   Everett, nd, 3.

13   Woodcock, 1975, 443.

14   Quail, 1978, xi.

15   Marcus, 1989, 91-92 and Cohn, 1961, 285.

16   Marshall, 1992, 133-39, 74-85.

17   Proudhon, 1994, 204-05.

18   Proudhon, 1994, 205.

19   Thomas, 1980, 249.

20   *The Anarchist: A revolutionary review*, Number 1, March 1885, 1.

21   Woodcock, 1975, 415.

22   Quail, 1978, 5.

23   Mike Lipman, the son of immigrant revolutionaries, reports that his parents had portraits of both Marx and Bakunin hanging in their house (Lipman, 1980, 17).

24   *Organise!,* No. 42, Spring 1996, 11.

25   *Organise!,* No. 42, Spring 1996, 12.

26   Cores, 1992e, 3-4 and McCartney, 1992, 8.

27   Meltzer, by contrast, cites the *Cosmopolitan Review* dating back to the 1850s as 'the first anarchist paper' (Meltzer, 1976a, 9).

28   Q. Most, Trautmann, 1980, 52.

29   Powell, 1989.

30   Diamond, 1994, 72.

31   See, for instance, David Nicoll, 1992.

32   Marshall, 1992, 629.

33   Clarke, 1983, 50-53; Fishman, 1975, 291. Darker interpretations of Paiktow's role are suggested by Bunyam, 1983, 154 as well as in Clarke, 1983, 55.

34   Clarke, 1983, 40.

35   Jacobs, 1995, 36.

36   Marshall, 1992, 255, 257.

37   Tillett later came to support the rights of immigrants.

38   Fishman, 1975, 77.

39   Fishman, 1975, 247.

40   Fishman, 1975, 104 and 131.

41   Fishman, 1975, 231.

42   Douglass in Ablett, Hay, Mainwaring and Rees, 1991e, 2.

43   Q. *Jewish Chronicle*, Fishman, 1975, 279.

44   Dangerfield, 1997, 194.

45   Q. Rocker, Fishman, 1975, 295.

46   White, 1990a, 101.

47   Challinor, 1977, 48.

48   Ward, 1987, 7.

49   White, 1990a, 104-05.

50   Dangerfield, 1997, 191.

51   Meltzer, 1976a, 38.

52   White, 1990a, 108-09.

53   Dangerfield, 1997, 120.

54   ACF, *Organise!*, No. 42, Spring 1996, 11.

55   Quail, 1978, 43.

56   *The Anarchist*, Number 1, March 1885, 2-3.

57   Woodcock, 1975, 419.

58   Quail, 1978, 19.

59   *Freedom* Vol. 1, No. 2, November 1886, 8.

60   Luminaries such as Kropotkin, William Morris and Eleanor Marx spoke at a meeting 'to protest against the inhuman treatment and persecution of Jews in Russia' organised by Workers Friend (*Der Arbeiter Fraint*) (Fishman, 1975, 197). See too Quail, 1978, 269.

61   See Malatesta, 1984, 310-11.

62   Hyams, 1979, 139 and 142.

63   Hyams, 1979, 122.

64   Kropotkin, 1980, 353-57.

65   Berkman, 1987, 29-30.

66   Berkman, 1987, 19.

67   *Freedom*, April 1888, Vol. 2 No. 19, 75.

68   Marshall, 1992, 438; Kropotkin, 1997e, 26.

69   Joll, 1964, 128 and Woodcock, 1992, ix.

70   Rocker, 1956.

71   Meltzer, 1992, 23.

72   Aldred, 1943, 83; Lipman, too, reports that the war forged a unity between marxists and anarchists (Lipman, 1980, 15).

73   *Organise!,* 42, Spring 1996, 13.

74   *Freedom*, October 1918, 55; Narodnik, 1918, 165.

75   Aldred, 1943, 82.

76   Meltzer, 1996, 48.

77   Marx, 1967, 110-11.

78   Lenin, 1976, 73.

79   Lenin, 1975, 6; Kendall, 1969, 249.

80   Quail, 1978, 287.

81   Aldred, 1943, 82.

82   Shipway, 1987, 106-8.

83   Walter in Berkman, 1989, xi.

84   Berkman, 1989, 297-303.

85   Berkman, 1989, 303.

86   Aldred, 1943, 7.

87   The Communist Unity Convention from which it developed was held in 1920.

88   Ken Weller, *Flux*, Issue 5, Autumn 1992, 10.

89   Quail, 1978, 305.

90   Meltzer, 1976a, 8.

91   Meltzer, 1976a, 8.

92   Meltzer, 1976a, 9.

93   Richards, 1989, 3.

94   Meltzer, 1976a, 14.

95   Meltzer, 1976a 15-18.

90   Meltzer, 1006, 54.

97   Meltzer, 1976a, 15-16.

98   Meltzer, 1976a, 15.

99   Meltzer, 1976a, 19.

100   Meltzer, 1976a, 18.

101   Meltzer, 1976a, 19-20.

102   Libertarian in Richards, 1989, 21.

103   Meltzer, 1976a, 29.

104   Comfort became famous as the author of *The Joy of Sex*.

105   Meltzer, 1976a, 24 and 33.

106   Meltzer, 1976b, 5.

107   Meltzer, 1976b, 5.

108   Marshall, 1992, 492.

109   Meltzer, 1976a, 28.

110   Ward, 1987, 8.

111   Weller, 1992, 9; Meltzer 1976a, 35.

112   Fountain, 1988, 2; the free marketeer Mike Mosbacher cites the CP's own figures that indicate that 'membership fell from 33,095 in February 1956 to 24,670 in February 1958', a drop of 8425 (Mosbacher, 1996, 4).

113   See 'The Leninist Left in Britain', *New Statesman*, December 17, 1993.

114   This has no connection to either the right-wing grouping in the Labour Party or the British fascist movement ran by Lady Birdwood, which both had similar names.

115   Parkin, 1968, 105.

116   Parkin, 1968, 17.

117   Meltzer, 1976b, 13.

118   Hewison, 1986, 15 and Christie, 1980, 25.

119   *Organise!* No. 42, Spring 1996, 15.

120   Meltzer, 1976b, 64.

121   Christie, 1980, 34-69.

122   Banham, Barker, Hall and Price, 1969.

123   Breines, 1982, 53-55.

124   Breines, 1982, 48-49.

125   Ward, 1987, 8.

126   Meltzer, 1976a, 32.

127   Christie, 1980, 31.

128   Christie, 1980, 8.

129   Woodcock, 1975, 462.

130   Meltzer, 1976b, 8.

131   Penguin, London, 1968.

132   Cohn-Bendit, 1968, 220-32.

133   Cohn-Bendit, 1968, 234-45.

134   Cohn-Bendit, 1968, 218.

135   Cohn-Bendit, 1968, 244.

136   Knabb, 1989, 63, 84, 133, 275, 289 and 345; see also Vague, 1997, 13.

137   Willener, 1970, 3.

138   Christie and Meltzer, 1984, 41.

139   Lefebvre, 1988, 77.

140   Willener, 1970, 201.

141   Knabb, 1989, 323.

142   See, for instance, Goldman, 1969, 195-211.

143   Kropotkin, 1970.

144   See, for instance *Organise!*, No. 49, Summer-Autumn 1998.

145   Solidarity, 1986.

146   For instance, *Sunday Telegraph* 19/5/68, *The Guardian* 23/5/68, *The Observer* 19/5/68. When Hoffman asked himself, 'what is the way of the future?', he replied, 'The National Liberation Front, the Cuban Revolution, the young here and around the world' (Hoffman, 1968, 38).

147   See, for instance Solanas, 1991 (available in 1968) and Malcolm X and Alex Haley's *Autobiography of Malcolm X*.

148   Fountain, 1988, 101-06.

149   Kornegger, 1996, 159.

150   Freeman, 1984 and Levine, 1984.

151   Dalla Costa and James, 1975.

152   Kornegger, 1996, 162.

153   *Class War* printed a mocking article about Liberal Democrat councillor Liz Penn which pilloried her for her sexual activity in a manner which would not be considered derisive if applied to a man (*Class War* No. 74, 5).

154   See, for instance, 'The struggle against sexism in the left-wing movement is a women's issue and they [leftist men] don't want to be involved' (*Bad Attitude* No. 5, Oct/Nov 1993, 24). See too *Class Whore* (woman with two angels front cover 1987e), 23 and 27.

155   PNR, 1992, 2.

156   See 'Agricultural Anarchism', *Merseyside Anarchist*, April 1991, No. 26, 11-12 and *Merseyside Anarchist*, June 1991, No. 28, 18.

157   Miller, 1987, 122.

158   Price worked with the Communist theatre impressario Joan Littlewood on the design for a Fun Palace for London, and with Alexander Trocchi on plans for a situationist university.

159   Broad, 1978.

160   Bear, 1988, 8.

161   Debord and Wolman, 1989, 8-14

162   Vague, 1997, 131.

163   Vague, 1997, 8.

164   The total number of anarcho-syndicalists was estimated, in 1965, at 150, 50 of whom were in the SWF and 100 of whom were associated with the CNT (Thayer, 1965, 154).

165   Marshall, 1992, 493 and 558.

166   See Vague, 1997, 29-30.

167   Communique 1, The Angry Brigade, Weir, 1985, 24.

168   'The Brigade is Angry', in Jean Weir, 1985, 37; Vaneigem, 1983, 19.

169   Communiqué 7, Weir, 1985, 30.

170   Communiqué 5, Weir, 1985, 25, See also Communique 14, Angry Brigade, Geronimo Cell Q. Vague, 1997, 122-23.

171   The Brigade is Angry, Weir, 1985, 37.

172   Communiqué 6, Weir, 1985, 26.

173   Barker, 1999, 101-02.

174   Fountain, 1988, 145.

175   Vague, 1997, 67.

176   Angela Weir (now Mason) later joined the gay rights group Stonewall and was, in 2002, appointed as head of the Blair Government's Women and Equality Unit at the Department of Trade and Industry. She was awarded an OBE in 1999 (Bright, 2002, 27).

177   Barker, 1998, 103 and Vague, 1997, 113.

178   Bunyan, 1983, 42.

179   Fountain, 1988, 179-80.

180   Gray (ed), 1974, 16.

181   Barker, 1999, 103-05.

182   Freedom: Supplement Vol 40, No. 16, 8 September, 1979, 9-17

183   Q. Widgery, Fountain, 1988, 214.

184   Q. Vague, 1997, 26. The working class militant Martin Wright reports his disappointment at the Grosvenor Square riot. He had hoped for a Paris-style insurrection and left disappointed when the students and police joined together, after a little pushing and shoving, to sing 'Auld lang syne' (Martin Wright 'Enemies of the State', May 1, 1998, 1 in 12 Centre, Bradford). Wright's recollection may seem an exaggerated parable of working class hatred for the pathetic pretensions of middle class student activists, but Paul Byrne also repeats the story using an article from *The Times* newspaper as his source (Byrne, 1997, 32).

185   Widgery, 1989, 11.

186   Fountain, 1988, 61.

187   *Organise!* No. 42, Spring 1996, 16-17.

188   *Organise!* No. 42, Spring 1996, 17.

189   Vague, 1997, 130.

190   Reid and Savage, 1987, 35 and 45.

191   Reid, 1987, 55.

192   The Sex Pistols' 'Anarchy in the UK' went to the top of the charts and the best selling single in the week of Queen Elizabeth II's Silver Jubilee was the Sex Pistol's 'God Save the Queen'.

193   Bone, 1997, 9 and Home, 1988, 95.

194   Home, 1995, 19.

195 Home, 1995, 96, and the London Class War leaflet, 'Andy Reeves: Royal Lickspittle' November 1997.

196 Marcus, 1989, 37-40; Burchill and Parsons, 1978, 79.

197 Crass, 1982, 15; See too Reid's 'Never Trust a Hippie' graphic (Reid, 1987, 43).

198 Fox, 1989, 6.

199 Q. Simon Reynolds, McKay, 1996, 98

200 McKay, 1996, 78 and 19; Rimbaud, 1998, 127-29 and 219-20

201 McKay, 1996, 131

202 *Organise!* No. 42, Spring 1996, 17-18

203 Big Flame's brand of revolutionary politics was not easy to categorise: 'some call themselves anarchists, some Maoists, and some "third worldists"' (Brinton, 2004, 117).

204 *Organise!* No. 42, Spring, 1996, 18.

205 Longmore, 1985, 20 and Fox, 1989, 8.

206 Smith, Speed, Tucker and June, 1982.

207 Smith, Speed et. al., 1982, 4-5, 9-10, 20, 25n. Paul Gilroy also highlights the fact that rioters came from a variety of ethnic backgrounds in contrast to the media representation of the events as racial uprisings (Gilroy, 1991, 32).

208 Smith, Speed, et. al., 1982, 21 and 23.

209 See *The Guardian,* Section 2, August, 4, 1993, 7 and Toczek, 1991.

210 For instance, in an article in *Xtra* in 1980, Martin Wright associated anti-sexism with middle class liberalism (*Xtra* No. 3, 2).

211 *Solidarity* No. 13, 11-13.

212 Home, 1988, 95.

213 *Class War*, 'The Best Cut of All' issue 1985e, 2.

214 Hugo Young, *The Guardian* December 14, 1993, 22.

215 MacGregor, 1986, 116.

216 MacGregor, 1986, 170.

217 MacGregor had asked for the National Guard (troops) to assist the police but uncharacteristically Thatcher had declined the request, perhaps because she thought they were unnecessary (MacGregor, 1986, 193).

218 Douglass, 1992e, 14.

219 Fox, 1989, 8.

220 *Class War* Issue 73, Summer 1997, 2.

221 Class War, 1991e, 4; *Class War* Issue 73, 2.

222 Home, 1988, 95.

223 See, for instance, David Rose blaming Class War for encouraging the Brixton riots in *The Guardian*, September 30, 1985. Home, 1988, 95.

224 *Class War* No. 28, 3.

225   Home, 1988, 99 and Bone, 1997, 9.

226   Bone, Pullen and Scargill, 1991, 9.

227   John Cunningham, 1990; Rosie Waterhouse and David Connett, 1990, 4.

228   O'Brien, 1992*e*.

229   MacGregor, 1986, 117.

230   *Class War*, No. 59, 13.

231   *Class War*, Issue 73, Summer 1997, 1.

232   *Class War*, Issue 73, 2 and 16.

233   Public Meeting, Conway Hall, London, 17/7/97.

234   *Direct Action*, No. 77, 4.

235   *Direct Action*, Spring 1997, No. 2, 35.

236   Dual strategy involves participating in existing trade unions and revolutionary syndicates.

237   AWG, 1988a, 2.

238   AWG, 1988b, 23.

239   Homocult, 1996, 21.

240   Homocult, 1996, 30.

241   *Virus*, No. 5, 2.

242   *Virus*, No. 7, 16, See also *Virus*, No. 12 and No. 13.

243   *Organise!*, Issue 42, 19.

244   Economic League, 1991a, 11.

245   *Anarchist 1993 Yearbook*, 1992e, 4.

246   *The Red Menace,* No. 2, March 1989, 2.

247   *Wildcat*, No. 17, Spring 1994, 9-21.

248   PNR, 1992, 14.

249   Booth, 1996, 67.

250   Bill Bryson, a former Murdoch journalist, noted that the print unions at the centre of the dispute were exclusive and elitist, 'without once showing collective support for any other union, including, on occasion, provincial branches of their own NGA' (Bryson, 1996, 61).

251   Booth, 1996, 74.

252   McKay, 1996, 33-34.

253   Booth, 1996, 72.

254   PNR, 1992, 16.

255   *Alternative Green* No. 3, Summer 1992, 10-11

256   Green Anarchist distributed the Unabomber's 'Industrial Society and Its Future', *Green Anarchist,* No. 40-41, 21; see too the interview with Kazcynski in *Green Anarchist* No. 57-58, 20-21.

257   Sheehan, 2003, 44.

258   *Green Anarchist* No.47-48, 1.

259   Green Anarchist, <http://www.greenanarchist.org.uk/Split.htm>, last accessed 15, September, 2003.

260   Byrne, 1997, 130.

261   Byrne, 1997, 22 and 27; Booth, 1996, 84-86.

262   *Class War*, No. 41, 8-9.

263   *Aufheben* No.3, 11.

264   *Do or Die*, 2003, 23.

265   *Do or Die*, 2003, 25.

266   *Do or Die*, 2003, 27-28.

267   Lull, 2000, 41-44.

268   Beynon and Dunkerley, 2000, 20.

269   Miyoshi, 2000, 50-1; Hardt and Negri, 2000, 9.

270   De Angelis, 2001, 112.

271   Hardt and Negri, 2000, 45.

272   White and Gordon, 1990, 24; AWG, like NWBTCW, also expressed support for the Iraqi opposition to Saddam Hussein (White and Gordon, 1990, 24 and White, 1991, 23).

273   See the Aufheben article 'Lessons From the Struggle Against the Gulf War' found on <http://jefferson.village.virginia.cdu/~spoons/aut_html/auf1gulf.htm>, last accessed 31, March, 1998), also appeared in *Aufheben* No. 1.

274   This was the figure reported by Vicky Hutchings writing in *The New Statesman* (Hutchings, 1992, 14). Others present that day estimated the size at just over half that amount.

Chapter Two: The Anarchist Ethic

1   The terms 'ethics' and 'moral theory' are used interchangeably in this section.

2   Similar arguments have been raised against anarchist art and aesthetics (Sheehan, 2003, 140).

3   For examples of these approaches see Alan Ritter (1980) and David Miller (1984), or from the liberal anarchist traditions, Giovanni Baldelli (1971), Marshall (1992), Woodcock (1975), and, more recently, Randall Amster (1998).

4   Carling, 1992, 231-35.

5   Cleaver, 1979, 12-16.

6   Rejections of ethical considerations as irrelevant or bourgoise mystifications might be indicated in slogans from Class War where they claim to endorse all tactics: 'by all means necessary'; or their claim that, 'We have no time for middle class moralism'. However, it is more likely that the latter

statement is aimed at particular forms of moral discourse that support bourgeois rule. Indeed, Class War do distinguish between different forms of struggle and are critical of those which fail to meet libertarian principles (Class War, 1999, 3 and 10-13).

7   Flood, 1994, 7.

8   Cleaver, 1979, 3 and 7.

9   Woodcock, 1992, xix.

10   Bakunin, 1984, 7.

11   Avrich, 1987 7-8 and 29.

12   *Organise!*, April-June 1992, No. 26, 20. See also the writer in *Black Flag* who writes of Argentina's popular uprisings against IMF policies: 'means and ends are linked, with direct action being the means of generating combative working class organisations and preparing people to directly manage their own personal and collective interests' (*Black Flag,* No. 221, 20). See, too, Paul Kingsnorth's account of anti-globalisation movements. He identifies 'anarchic, in the best sense of the word' actions as those 'in which means matters as much as ends' (Kingsnorth, 2003, 74).

13   May, 1994, 11-12 and 20. May's synthesis with politically engaged poststructuralism is also endorsed by Lewis Call, who identifies an anarchism shorn of humanism and scientific rationalism in the works of Debord, Baudrillard, Deleuze and Foucault (Call, 1999, 100).

14   For instance, Free Information Networks such as *SchNEWS, Counter Information* and *ContraFLOW*, the development of Internet-based media such as Indymedia, <http://www.indymedia.org/>, and the Anarchist News Service, A-Infos, <http://www.ainfos.ca/>, last accessed September 23, 2003, discussion boards on Urban75, <http://www.urban75.net/vbulletin/> last accessed June 25, 2003 and general anarchist discussion at: <http://flag.blackened.net/wwwthreads/postlist.php?Cat=&Board=cwdiscuss>, last accessed September 23, 2003.

15   Lenin, 1976, 74.

16   Hardie, 1968, 15; Hursthouse, 1992, 222-24.

17   Aristotle, 1963, 15.

18   Grayeff, 1974, 27 and 42.

19   Mill, 1987, 278.

20   Weber, 1995, 29.

21   MacDonald, 1980, 52.

22   Lenin, 1975, 21-22.

23   Lenin, 1975, 31; Lenin, 1963, 144.

24   Lamb, 1997, 12.

25   It is important to note that anarchist rejection of instrumentalism does not imply that people never use others to reach their goals – even catching a

bus requires treating the driver as an instrument in reaching one's destination – but one should not treat the driver *solely* as a means.

26   Lenin, for instance, justified the strict discipline of the party on the grounds of its efficiency in guiding the proletariat to the desired revolutionary state (Lenin, 1975, 31).

27   Lamb, 1997, 13.

28   Kropotkin, 1992, 241.

29   Q. Most, Trautmann, 1980, 99.

30   Nechaev, 1989, 4-5.

31   Such as CWF's previously mentioned, in endnote 6, endorsement of waging class conflict 'by all means necessary' (*Class War* No. 45, 1).

32   Nechaev, 1989, 9.

33   Prawdin, 1961.

34   Prawdin, 1961, 48-49.

35   Other forms of anarchist fiction portray not the ideal end state but the manner in which the revolutionary society might come about through the application of libertarian tactics. Gilliland's *The Free* and Daniel's *Breaking Free* (the latter published by Attack International) follow the narrative themes of Emile Pautaud and Emile Poget's *How Shall We Bring About The Revolution* in presenting accounts of ideal forms of social change.

36   Sargisson, 1996, 87.

37   Humphrey, 1951, 171-73.

38   In this context, Ursula Le Guin's *The Dispossessed* is another important text that explores fictional alternative communities based on libertarian principles; as Sheehan notes, Le Guin's fiction acknowledges the way hierarchy might recompose informally even in future anarchist societies (Sheehan, 2003, 51-52).

39   Harvey, 1996, 9, 14 and 43; See too May, 1994.

40   Baldelli, 1971, 19 and Marshall, 1992, 38.

41   Kant, 1959, 12.

42   Kant, 1959, 17 and 21.

43   Kant, 1959, 30.

44   Kant, 1959, 32.

45   Kant, 1959, 39. For a discussion of whether there is just one categorical imperative see Beauchamp and Childress, 1989, 38-39.

46   See, for instance, Wolff, 1976, 12-14 and 72.

47   Hayek, 1973, 35-54.

48   Cooper, 1989e, 1.

49   von Mises, 1949, 258.

50   Hyams, 1979, 186-87.

51   Graham, 1996, 71.

52   Trautmann, 1980, 110.

53   Pengam, 1987, 72.

54   Berkman, 1987, 64 and 69.

55   Cohen, 2002, 429-30.

56   Kropotkin, 1970, 98.

57   See, for instance, Kropotkin, 1992, 221.

58   Baldelli, 1972, 74.

59   Kant, 1959, 73.

60   See, for instance, Nozick's criticism of social justice, Nozick, 1988, 185-86.

61   Class War, 1992, 44 and 47; Kropotkin, 1972, 48-49.

62   May, 1994, 63. See also Morland, 1997, 3; Call, 1999, 100.

63   Melucci, 1996, 23.

64   Class War, 1992, 125-26.

65   Dauvé, 1997a, 17 and 36.

66   Cardan, 1975e, 5-7.

67   See MacDonald, 1987, 9.

68   Carter, 1973, 137. The connection between anarchists and direct action was recognised by the Economic League (EL), a privately funded surveillance body responsible for politically vetting existing and potential employees. EL categorised disparate groups, anarcho-syndicalists, animal liberationists and libertarian-communists as 'anarchists' on the basis that all described their preferred tactics with the identical phrase (Economic League, 1986, 50-2; Economic League, 1991b, 14). The EL was wound up in 1994 (Hencke, 2000, 7).

69   Although, as will be seen, there is considerable confusion surrounding this term, with some, like the activists Corrine and Bee, quoted by McKay, who use 'civil disobedience' in a sense that neither rules out violence, nor accepts legal consequences, and is more akin to direct action (McKay, 1998, 5-6).

70   *Freedom*, June 1917, 27.

71   The forerunner of DAM, Syndicalist Workers Federation (SWF), and its precursor, the Anarchist Federation of Britain (1944-50), had named their newspapers by the same title. Hunt saboteurs, who include considerable numbers of anarchists in their ranks, have used the term in the titles of their propaganda:, e.g. *Direct Action Against All Bloodsports*.

72   Carter, 1983. It was initially published in 1962, but later re-printed in the early 1980s in support of the then sizeable anti-nuclear peace movement.

73   See, for instance, *Class War* No. 52, 8-9 on constitutional versus direct action.

74   Carter, 1973, 3.

75   Ian Welsh, amongst others, has argued that the criterion for civil disobedience is accepting arrest and other consequences of law breaking. He cites the Clamshell Alliance who employed the tactic of accepting arrest and imprisonment as a way of overburdening the criminal justice system (Welsh, 2000, 154 and 164). However, most acts of civil disobedience do not involve acquiescing to the state; the destruction of genetically-modified crops which some, such as the French radical farmer's leader Jose Bove, consider 'civil disobedience' often involves protestors actively avoiding arrest (Jones, 2001). *Do or Die!* No.8 illustrates how activists wear protective masks to avoid recognition and often attempt to flee capture by the police rather than announce themselves to the authorities (*Do or Die*, No. 8, 89-90).

76   The BBC television programme 'Heart of the Matter' (BBC1, 23.3.97 23:10 - 00:00) is another case in point. It included a film by Merrick Goodhaven and a panel discussion in which 'direct action' and 'civil disobedience' were used interchangeably.

77   Carter, 1973, 3.

78   Carter, 1973, 3.

79   Carter, 1973, 17.

80   Carter, 1983, 3-4 and 22.

81   Carter, 1973, 19.

82   Ward, 1982, 23.

83   Carter, 1973, 25.

84   Debord, 1983, para 93.

85   See, for instance, the ACF who vary between a practical, transient view of organisation and a vanguard view (ACF, 1997, 21 and 27-28). Class War, too, contains tendencies that propose a specialist role for a distinct political elite who should not face the same risks as others:

> [L]ike the IRA learned in the seventies, there must be a separation between the political wing and the military wing which led to the birth of Sinn Fein. Of course we all know there is overlap but our opokoopoople must not jeopardise their liberty (*Class War* No. 78, 9).

86   Carter, 1973, 19 and 6-7.

87   *Subversion*, No. 9, 6.

88   Smith, 1972, 310.

89   *Think Global Act Local* was also the name of a newssheet produced by North East England based anarchists, socialists and Greens in the late 1990s. See also *ContraFlow* No. 24, Jan-March 1998, 2; Routledge and Simons, 1995, 479.

90   McKay, 1996.

91   For instance, increases in workers' pay and conditions are welcomed (Brown, 1990, 110 and DAM, 1984, 3).

92   Chan, 1995, 52-3.

93   *Class War* No. 46, 4; Burns, 1992, 177.

94   See, for instance, DAM, 1984, 8.

95   It should be noted, however, that the road protests at Newbury, Pollok and Wanstead, did encourage the British government to restructure its road building plans.

96   Burns, 1992, 190-202.

97   'State' is used to mean the final arbiter in the use of force in a particular geographical region and the institutions that operate to ensure its legitimacy and enact its commands. These are the judiciary, legislature, executive, and constitution (written or unwritten) and the formal and informal rules that operate between and within these bodies. This definition also includes the conventions (covert and overt) which mediate between these institutions and the wider civic and economic realms.

98   Marcuse, 1969, 98.

99   Bakunin, 1953, 221.

100   The Anti-Election Alliance is an umbrella grouping 'largely energised by the Class War Federation [....]. Those backing the [1992 Anti-Elections] rally are London Greenpeace, the Anarchist Communist Federation, the Direct Action Movement, the 121 Centre, the Anarchist Black Cross and Affiliates and Harringey Solidarity Group' (Hutchings, 1992, 14).

101   Lenin, 1976, 55; Donald Rooum, the cartoonist for *Freedom*, based his estimation of support for anarchism in the United Kingdom on the numbers of voters abstaining in general elections, on the assumption that non-participation is a necessary, albeit insufficient, condition for being a libertarian (Rooum, 1992, 20-21).

102   Dauvé and Martin, 1997, 79.

103   Stirner, 1993, 108-09.

104   See, for instance, Palmer, 1988e, 2.

105   *Situationist International*, No. 1, para. 16.

106   ACF, 1997e, 2.

107   Rousseau, 1983, 240.

108   Rousseau, 1983, 242.

109   There are numerous examples of anarchists taking part in some forms of representative democracy. For instance, Proudhon stood and was elected to the French parliament as well as advocating support for left-wing candidates (Guérin, 1970, 18). Similarly, Daniel Guérin points to the anarchists who ignored the CNT's electoral strikes and Durruti's biographer

Abel Paz mentions those comrades who voted in the November 1933 elections (Guérin, 1970, 19 and Paz, 147). Other examples are discussed in Chapter Five.

110   Paine, 1983, 199-202.

111   Locke, 1993, 343.

112   *Virus*, No. 1, 8.

113   Parry, 1978, 128.

114   Chomsky, 1986.

115   *Virus*, No. 11, 14-15.

116   See too *Anti-Mass: Methods of Organisation for Collectives*, 1988 and Christie, 1983*e*.

117   Paine, 1953, 8 1 31-32.

118   Hegel, 1987, 271-72 and Hegel, 1977, 118.

119   Bakunin, 1953, 218.

120   White, 1998, 4.

121   Bakunin, 1953, 216.

122   ACF, 1997e, 2; See too Subversion who approvingly reports Sylvia Pankhurst's comments: 'Women can no more put virtue into the decaying parliamentary institution than men: it is past reform and must disappear....' (Q. Pankhurst, Subversion No. 9, 8).

123   Bakunin, 1953, 219.

124   Headline of *Workers Solidarity*, Number 51, Summer 1997, 1.

125   Class War, 1992, 45.

126   Marx and Engels, 1977, 37-38.

127   Carter, 1989, 183-84; See also Dolgoff, 1989*e*, 13-14.

128   Carter, 1989, 185.

129   *Organise!* No. 27, 7.

130   Morris, 1992, 4.

131   ACF, 1997e, 17.

132   Morris, 1992, 4.

133   *Class War* No. 53, 3; *Class War*, No. 81, 1; *Direct Action*, No. 26, 32-3; WSM (2005).

134   Class War, 1992, 47.

135   Recent accounts that compare anarchism with the poststructuralism of Michel Foucault, Gilles Deleuze, Felix Guattari and Jean-Francois Lyotard have located areas of similarity in the belief that oppression is multi-layered and dispersed. Anarchists and radical poststructuralists consider power to be diffuse and they believe that attempts to combat heteronomous authority through the instruments of monolithic organisation merely reconstitute power and do not redistribute it (May, 1994, 12-14).

136   Lenin, 1976, 57; Lenin, 1975, 60 and 120.

137   Lenin, 1976, 61.

138   Marcuse, 1986, 21.

139   *Trotwatch*, Summer 1992, 7. This is a reference to Militant's leaders offering to help police identify rioters during the Poll Tax uprising in London in May 1990. Militant have subsequently become the Socialist Party. Tommy Sheridan, a Member of the Scottish Parliament was, until November 2004, the leader of the Scottish Socialist Party.

140   Jacobs, 1974, 135.

141   At least according to the class struggle anarchists. See, for instance, Pugh, 2000, 8.

142   Greenslade, 1997, 7.

143   Institute of Social Disengineering, 1994, 7.

144   *Organise!* No. 27, 7.

145   ACF, 1997e, 6.

146   Rhys, 1988e, 28.

147   May, 1994, 48.

148   Carter, 1983, 23 and 27.

149   Hart, 1997, 48.

150   Big Flame, 1981e, 6; *Green Anarchist*, No. 26, 15.

151   *London Class War* Special Issue, Shut Down Parliament, 1 and 3.

152   *Taking Liberties* No. 16, 2.

153   Apter, 1971, 9-10.

154   Marcuse's examples include 'Flower Power' and 'Black is beautiful'. The latter was an effective anti-racist slogan, which called into question the cultural expectations that had treated 'blackness' as an inferior category (Marcuse, 1969b, 36).

155   'March Against Anything' is an updated version of an early 1980s situationist-inspired publication (Marcus, 1989, 54).

156   *Attack Attack Attack*, 9.

157   *Attack Attack Attack*, 9.

158   *Organise!* Jan-March 1993, No. 29, 3.

159   Leaflet reprinted in Booth, 1996, 102.

160   Garnham, 1972, 293.

161   Garnham, 1972, 295-96.

162   Apter also considers that disrupting the symbolic order and adopting 'anti-roles' leads to the creation of new identities, rather than the abandonment of roles themselves (Apter, 1971, 8).

163   Certain subcultures involve willful transformation of meanings, and have consequently been targeted for disciplinary action by more mainstream cultures; see Hebdige, 1979.

164   Morland, 1997, 21.

165   Baldelli, 1971, 165.

166   Chan, 1995, 56. Chan has further elaborated the anarchist-pacifist position in Chan, 2004.

167   In the early 1980s, the Feminist and Nonviolence Study Group (F&NSG), a group which combined women's liberation and anti-nuclear protest with a wider socialist and libertarian analysis, described nonviolence in terms which repeat the prefigurative basis:

> It is both a principle and a technique, a set of ideas about how life should be lived and a strategy for social change. Respect for life is a fundamental feature, together with the desire for liberation. This means not deliberately killing, hurting, threatening or putting fear into others, in short not treating [the enemy] as less human than ourselves (F&NSG, 1983, 26).

168   See also Amster: 'if coercion, domination, hierarchy, and violence are eschewed as ends, we must not abide them as means, no matter how noble the aim' (Amster, 1998, 101).

169   Morland argues that the pacifists are in the majority: 'Most anarchists have little if anything to do with violence' (Morland, 1997, 21). This is unlikely to be true of the 1990s and early 2000s. Pacifist 'anarchists' are widely derided, and not considered anarchists by class-struggle libertarians, to the extent that constant efforts have been made to disassociate the one group from the other (see for instance *Do or Die*, No. 8; Meltzer, 1996, 321-22 and London Class War, 'Anti Hippy Action' leaflet 1996e).

170   See, for instance, Richards in Rooum, 1993, 50-51. It has been acknowledged that more recently *Freedom* has published more articles that are consistent with the main class struggle groups than with the pacifist liberalism of much of the post-war period.

171   The name probably came from one of the slogans used by the Freedom Network, instructing their supporters to 'Keep it Fluffy' in their demonstrations against the 1994 Criminal Justice Act. In response anarchists demanded that they 'keep it spikey' (*Organise!* No. 36, 5-6; Q. Class War in Booth, 1996, 102).

172   Harris, 1983.

173   Baldelli, 1971, 45-46.

174   See Chan, 2004, 112. If the concept of rights is extended beyond the most minimal to include structural impediments to fulfil basic human needs, then, as the philosopher Vittorio Bufacchi notes, violence becomes more pervasive, with the danger that almost everything becomes 'violence', thus rendering the term meaningless (Bufacchi, 2005, 196-97).

175   Miller, 1984, 122; see, too, Chan, 2004, 105.

176   Niebuhr, 2001, 241.

177   See, for instance, the statement of the Black Bloc Q. in Kingsworth, 2003, 55.

178   *Organise!*, No. 36, 5-6.

179   *Class War*, No. 52, 8.

180   During the Miners' Strike (1984-5) the mainstream press denigrated the strikers' communities for using violence even when those taking industrial action were the victims not the perpetrators. See, for instance, Douglass, 1986 and Douglass, 1994.

181   Niebuhr, 1941, 176.

182   Glover, 1993, 92.

183   Niebuhr, 1941, 240.

184   *Aufheben*, No.3, Summer 1994, 19.

185   If, for some bizarre reason, you want a more detailed appraisal of the pacificist sections of *Freedom* and *Green Anarchist* within the context of the Miners' Strike (1984-5), then see Franks, 2005, but I'm pretty certain you have better things to do.

186   *Black Flag Supplement* (1986e), No. 3, 5.

187   Niebuhr, 1941, 245; Christie and Meltzer, 1984, 60.

188   Jackson, 1971, 154.

189   Chan draws attention to the influence of the pacifists Ferdinand Nieuwenhuis and Bart de Ligt on European (especially Dutch) syndicalism (Chan, 2004, 107); see too Marshall, 1992, 484-85.

190   McKay, 1998, 17.

191   Wright was involved in a number of anarchist enterprises from his youth. These include the Grosvenor Square riot of 1968, street-level anti-fascist activity in the early 1970s and MA'M (Martin Wright talk at 'Enemies of the State', 1-in-12 Centre, Bradford, May 1, 1998, 19.00-21.00). Much of the information for this sub-section is derived from Wright's talk.

192   According to *The Mirror*, Martin Wright was born in the earlyto mid 1950s (*The Mirror*, June 19, 2001, 2).

193   Robins and Cohen, 1978, 108-09.

194   Class War Federation, 1999, 4.

195   Sorel, 1967, 78 and 91.

196   See, for instance, 'Mug a Yuppie' (Bone, Pullen and Scargill, 1991, 22).

197   Class War, 1992, 17-19.

198   The infamous 'Hospitalised Copper' feature was a regular section in *Class War*, (see for instance No. 30, 2; No. 48, 3; No. 78, 3 No. 82, 3; No. 83, 3, et. al.). 'Hospitalised Copper' calendars were also produced in 1991 and '92.

199   Chan, 1995, 59.

200   Chan, 1995, 60.

201   This is summed up in the slogan from 1968 that 'One non-revolutionary week-end is infinitely more bloody than a month of permanent revolution' (Gray, 1974, 83).

202   Carter, 1973, 130.

203   Carter, 1973, 21.

204   *Aufheben* No. 3, 20.

205   Wolfie and Speed et. al., 1982, 12; Sanguinetti, 1982.

206   Miller, 1984, 123.

207   *Hungry Brigade*, 1997, 2.

208   This defence of violence is not a vindication of terrorism. While Miller rightly distinguishes between violence and terrorism, in his account of anarchism and violence, all his examples of anarchist violence are drawn from terrorist incidents, thereby re-associating the two (Miller, 1984). Consequently, Miller's examples involve the use of paternalistic behaviour, or assaults on agents who are not involved in the oppression of the subjugated group, and thus Miller fails to consider types of 'violent' political acts which can be autonomous and emancipatory.

Chapter Three: Agents of Change

1   'Politically engaged poststructuralisms' is a highly ambiguous phrase, and the distinction between politically engaged and supposedly politically unengaged poststructuralisms is itself open to critical scrutiny. Nonetheless, I borrow it from Sadie Plant (amongst others), who alludes to the division in her book *The Most Radical Gesture*. In this she discusses those types of poststructuralism that playfully breaks and subverts codes as a form of contestation of power against those that 'abandon[ed...] any critical perspective.... who wander without purpose, observing recuperations with a mild and dispassionate interest..... naively offering an uncritical home to the notion of the spectacle' (Plant, 1992,150).

2   C. Ehrlich, 1996, 169.

3   Gray, 1974, 104.

4   See, for instance, Subversion:

> [T]he present day working class, whose day-to-day existence is largely passive (acquiescent towards capitalism) and the revolutionary force that can overthrow capitalism. The latter will grow out of the former, but is not identical to it. The former (which can be called the "class-

in-itself') is just a sociological category whereas the latter (the class-FOR-itself) is a revolutionary category (*Subversion*, No. 12, 14).

5   Marcuse, 1969, 326.

6   Witheford, 1994, 90-91.

7   Other anarchists, such as the authors of the 1971 American tract *Anti-Mass Methods of Organisation for Collectives* (*Anti-Mass*), have claimed to have superseded class analysis. *Anti-Mass* had its advocates within British libertarian circles; it was, for instance, reprinted in the 1980s by Christie in his *Investigative Reporters Handbook* and also re-issued by the Welsh CGH anarchist publisher. On closer examination, however, *Anti-Mass* formulation does not differ greatly from marxism. The grouping *Anti-Mass* refer to as the 'mass' is made up of 'passive' individuals who 'see themselves as objects' and are the 'products of a specific social organisation'. It is similar in most respects to the class in itself (*Anti-Mass*, 1988, 9 and 1). The 'class', which the authors of the tract distinguishes from the 'mass', as it is the first which takes the lead in revolutionary action. The class is: 'conscious of its social existence because it seeks to organise itself' and as such appears to be comparable to the class for itself (*Anti-Mass*, 1988, 1-2). The main area of difference between standard marxism and *Anti-Mass* is that the latter prescribes a particular form of organisation for 'class' formation. There are other similar examples of debates of how the oppressed subject becomes for itself without necessarily using marxist terminology, but which might be consistent with marxist categories.

8   Class struggle anarchists like Rocker are aware that brutal conditions make solidarity difficult and consequently rebellion far less likely (Rocker, 1956, 324).

9   'Revolutionaries and other impediments to revolution' (*Class War*, No. 73, 9).

10   Aufheben sees such autonomous activity or self-valorisation in some of the Squatters' and anti-roads movements of the 1990s (*Aufheben* No. 4, 24).

11   Class War, amongst others, are critical of efforts to be missionaries intervening in others' struggles to run them on behalf of the subjugated (see for instance 'This is Class War!' in *Class War* No. 77, Summer 1999, 2).

12   Albon, 'The Pieces of Silver' reprinted in Booth, 1996, 73.

13   *Lancaster Bomber*, Autumn 1994, 11 and 15. See too the criticisms of Meltzer and Christie, 1984, 61.

14   Purkis and Bowen, 1997, 196.

15   May, 1994, 53. See too the comments of Ernesto Laclau and Chantal Mouffe who see the social realm as comprising a network of intersecting and non-universal social practices (Laclau and Mouffe, 1994, 96).

16   In *A Thousand Plateaus* (Deleuze and Guattari, 1992) the main

features of the rhizome metaphor are elucidated. Rhizomes work through 'connection and heterogeneity' (difference). Their roots intersect and sometimes merge. Like viruses invading germs, the DNA transferred create new biological forms that are irreducible to either the host or the parasite; so too rhizomes create roots that are distinct from the constitutive combinations.

17   May, 1994, 96.

18   Cleaver, 1979, 52. London Autonomists, Krondstadt Kids and London Workers Group were amongst the origins of Class War when it moved from Swansea to the English capital. Red Notes, Big Flame and Workers Playtime were also influenced by the Italian *autonomia*.

19   *Green Anarchist*, No. 34e. (This edition is numbered No. 34 on the cover, but No. 33 on the inside headings. It does appear to be No. 34, as it follows a different No. 33).

20   See, for instance, Anderson and Anderson, 1998; Homocult, 1996. *Subversion* No. 12, 12-14; No. 13, 6-7; Splat Collective, P (London) and S. in *Smash Hits*, No. 2, 11-17. Homocult is close to the Andersons who are published by the Splat Collective and produce *Working Class Times*.

21   'Class War's hard image [...] meant to attract young, white males' (*Class War* No. 73, 13).

22   Rooum, 1986, 56.

23   In this chapter I examine various marxisms, rather than trying to resurrect a true 'Marxism'.

24   Flynn, 1993, 8.

25   Cleaver, 1979, 64.

26   '[W]e are not at all concerned with the odd blurry individual whose class it may not be easy to be sure about. It is quite easy to see the great majority of the middle class for what they are' (Anderson and Anderson, 1998, 20).

27   The autonomist Harry Cleaver has observed fundamental similarities between his branch of libertarian marxism and Kropotkin's writings in his paper 'Kropotkin, Self-valorization and the Crisis of Marxism'.

28   Fox, 1989, 6.

29   Cleaver, 1979, 26.

30   *Black and Green*, No. 2/3, Fall/Winter 1981-2, 24 and McKay, 1998, 17.

31   Christie and Meltzer, 1984, 59.

32   *Organise!* No. 36, 16.

33   Meltzer, 1976a, 32; Krimerman and Perry, 1966, 386.

34   Michele Barrett also notes the growth of interest in the 1970s of Gramsci and Althusser amongst the feminist and marxist intelligentsia (Barrett, 1988, 2-3). The Department of Cultural Studies has since closed (Russell, 2002). For a wider discussion on the effect of educational 'reforms' on

the research interests of universities see Harvey, 1997; Robinson and Tormey, 2003.

35   Amongst the exceptions are the Scottish sections of Militant who combined with the Socialist Workers Party in Scotland to form the Scottish Socialist Party (SSP). In 2003, they had six members elected to the Scottish Parliament. South of the border the SWP membership has fluctuated, yet it remains the undisputed largest Trotskyist grouping. For this reason the SWP is used as the counter-example by which to compare anarchism.

36   McKay, 1998, 46.

37   Se,e for instance, the recommended reading which includes a substantial selection of class-struggle anarchist magazines and contacts including: *Aufheben, Black Flag, ContraFLOW, Direct Action, Fighting Talk, Here and Now, Organise!, Smash Hits, Subversion, Wildcat* and *Y Faner Goch* (*Do or Die*, No. 7, 150-57). The Earth First! summer gathering in 1998 included sessions on class struggle anarchism by members of MA'M and former Class War activists associated with *Smash Hits*.

38   Class War, 1992, 167; Fox, 1989, 7; See too O'Brien, 1992e, 1.

39   *Anti-Mass*, 1988.

40   Rhys, 1988e, 26.

41   See, for instance, Marcuse, 1971, 82; Berkman, 1986, 58; *Virus*, No. 5, 5; *Black Flag*, No. 202, 1 and 4; *Wildcat*, No. 15, 17-22.

42   Bone, 1986, 2. Bone stressed the importance of shaking off middle class paternalism in his 'Enemies of the state' talk at the 1-in-12 Centre, Bradford, May 1, 1998, 19.00-21.00.

43   Marx, 1977, 41.

44   *Subversion* (unnumbered) No. 12e, 14.

45   Class War, 1992, 86.

46   Harman is one of the chief Marxist theoreticians for the Socialist Workers Party.

47   Harman, 1979, 38. Note that this was republished as recently as 1997.

48   Marx, 1992, 425.

49   Marx, 1992, 426.

50   Harman, 1979, 16.

51   Lenin, 1976, 30.

52   Cliff, 1996, 61-62. Cliff acknowledges that the difference between Leninists, such as himself, and anarchists and Social Revolutionaries is that the latter do not distinguish between workers and peasants (Cliff, 1996, 60).

53   Gorz claims that this is the most common reading ascribed to Marx by the radicals of 1968 (Gorz, 1997, 20).

54   Gorz and Wildcat describe a version of Marx's theory of historical materialism in order to argue against it (especially in *Wildcat* after issue 17).

55   Harman, 1979, 38.

56   Thomas, 1980, 291.

57   ACF, 1991*e*, 2.

58   Gorz, 1997, 154; Gilroy, 1991, 18.

59   Dolgoff, 1989*e*, 20.

60   Harman, 1979, 54 and *Organise!*, No. 21, 5-6.

61   See Kropotkin's *Mutual Aid* (1939), Sahlins' *Stone-Age Economics* (1972) and Perlman's *Against His-story Against Leviathan* (1983).

62   *Wildcat* No. 17, 11; *Green Anarchist* also reflects a firm commitment to the existence of a pre-history of abundance. See for instance *Green Anarchist* No. 53, Autumn 1998, 16-17.

63   *Wildcat* No. 17, 13.

64   Autonomous Plenum of Southern Germany, 1987, 30.

65   Historical materialism is the view that the productive basis of society (the forces of production) shapes the relations of production and the culture and politics of that society (the social relations). This contrasts with Idealism, which sees changes in conceptual apparatus and social relations occurring irrespective of material conditions.

66   It can often be found in primitivist writings; see Brian Morris's discussion of this in *Green Anarchist*, No. 36, 13. Bronislaw Szerszynski and Emma Tomalin also attempt to defend a 'spiritual' interpretation of environmental and anti-globalisation direct action that co-opts worldly experiences such as self-development and political resistance into a mystical realm (Szeresynski and Tomalin, 2004).

67   Lenin, 1963, 62-63.

68   Lenin, 1963, 63.

69   May, 1994, 23.

70   Thomas, 1980, 260.

71   Barr, 1991, 5-6. See also *Proletarian Gob*, No. 2, 10.

72   See, for instance, criticisms of well-meaning revolutionaries who want to manage the struggles of others (Douglass, 1999, 80; *Class War* No. 73, 2).

73   Anarchist critics point to the SWP-backed grouping Globalise Resistance who try to organise the struggle to fit into the Leninist conception of revolutionary struggle. See Tommy, 2001, 104-08 and the leaflet *Vampire Alert!: The Revolution will not be Bolshevised* reprinted in *Do or Die*, No. 9, 134-35.

74   In this subsection Marx is interpreted as conforming to the Leninist/ Gorz readings rather than autonomist and libertarian socialist versions of marxism.

75   Conway, 1987, 132. The autonomist writer Dyer-Witheford also identifies these arguments (Witheford, 1994, 87-88).

76   Gorz, 1997, 19.

77   Gorz, 1997, 24-25 and 66.

78   Gorz, 1997, 68-69.

79   Gorz, 1997, 66 and 68.

80   Gorz, 1997, 11 and 75.

81   Marx and Engels, 1977, 47.

82   F., *Subversion* No. 23, 10-11.

83   For instance, articles in *Subversion* No.s 21-3 have debated the appropriateness of the tactic of dropping out of the labour market.

84   Class War, 1992, 57-58.

85   *Counter Information* No. 47, 1; *Subversion* No. 20, 12-14; *Organise!* No. 48, 6 and 12.

86   For instance, in an article on labour struggles in America and Britain, Aufheben examine incidents in white as well as blue collar industries (*Aufheben*, No. 7, Autumn 1998, 6-25).

87   Witheford, 1994, 95: 'Word processors, remote terminals, data phones, and high speed printers are only a few of the new breakable gadgets that are coming to dominate the modern office. Designed for control and surveillance.' *Processed World* goes on to describe changes in office life that has altered the status of clerical work:

> Once considered a career that required a good deal of skill, the clerical job now closely resembles an assembly line station. Office management has consciously applied the principles of scientific management to the growing flow of paper and money, breaking the process down into components, routininizing and automizing the work, and reserving the more 'mental' tasks for managers or the new machines (Carlsson, 1990, 59).

88   Class War, 1992, 82.

89   Carlsson, 1990, 59-60 and 152.

90   Proletarian Gob, 1993, 7. See too Lamb's comments about anarchists not needing to be concerned with the internal struggles of authoritarian structures such as Militant and the scab Union of Democratic Mineworkers (Lamb, 1997, 15).

91   Later republished in 1998.

92   Anderson and Anderson, 1998, 48-50.

93   *Subversion* No. 7, 10-11; No. 11, 11. See too the letter from a Class War supporter who also describes the 'proletarianisation of the profession' but still consider its cultural status to be sufficiently high to identify teaching as a middle class profession (*Subversion* (edition unnumbered) 12e, 13).

94   Dalla Costa, 1975, 34 and 26.

95   Witheford, 1994, 95.

96   This analysis pre-dates the Autonomist movement. The Wobbly Gurley Flynn was well aware that women's reproductive role was central to the creation of an exploited work force, and consequently sites for class struggle. Sabotage, a subversion of capital imperatives, can stretch to contraception and other domestic activities (Gurley Flynn, 1995, 30-31).

97   Cleaver, 1979, 57.

98   May, 1994, 7-12.

99   Pierre Chaulieu (aka Cornelius Castoriadis, aka Paul Cardan) helped form the French *Socialisme ou Barbarie* (SouB) journal and group (Blissett, 1996, 82). SouB were significant influences on, and were influenced by, the Situationist International and the British group Solidarity. Members of the latter were active in re-forming class-struggle libertarianism throughout the 1960s and '70s. Their members were still active in the 1990s in groups such as the Splat collective, MA'M and Class War. Castoriadis's influence on libertarian thought has also been acknowledged by the ACF and *Aufheben* (Organise! No. 47, 16; *Aufheben* No. 3, 25-28 and 33).

100   Cardan, 1975e, 11 <para. 18>.

101   *Aufheben*, No. 3, 25-26.

102   Cardan, 1975e, 9 <para. 14>.

103   Class War, 1992, 58.

104   Vaneigem, 1983, 48.

105   Casey, 1989e, 18.

106   Class War, 1992, 58.

107   For instance, 'people in the bottom ten per cent (£2,700 [per annum]) now receive 14 per cent less than [they] received in 1979' (*The Guardian*, September 11, 1993, 23). Stephen Edgell claims that the decreasing ownership of wealth of the top 5% in Britain which characterised the post-war period was 'halted and even reversed, during the Thatcher era of regressive taxation' (Edgell, 1993, 107).

108   It is worth repeating that the views ascribed to 'traditional marxism' are those of the orthodox (Leninist and liberal) interpreters and not necessarily those of Marx himself. There is ample evidence, as his heterodox champions recognise, that Marx took a different view, seeing the superstructure and base as reciprical. This interpretation has been used by groups like Big flame, for instance, in their analysis of women's social position under fascism; they explain how nationalist ideology kept women out of the workplace, even when war production demanded their inclusion, indicating how the ideological superstructure influences the base (Big Flame, 1991, 7). Alternatively, autonomists prioritise the various subjectivities of labour independently from

capital (see Cleaver, 1979, Witheford, 1994). Certainly doubts have been expressed about how representative the base-superstructure analogy from the 'Preface' was of Marx's actual intent. Terrell Carver (2002) <1980>, James Farr (2002) <1986>, Scott Meikle (2002) and Paul Thomas (2002) <1976> amongst others, have suggested that the 'scientific' determinist text was given primacy was a result of Engels' confused involvement. The 'Preface' was, as Arthur Prinz notes, written primarily to reassure the Prussian censors, rather than to articulate a fully developed account of Marx's views (Prinz, 2002) <1969>.

109   Class War, 1992, 585-89; see too Fortunati, 1995.

110   May, 1994, 43-44.

111   See too later editions of *Class War*, e.g. the reply to a letter which states: 'We do not believe there is a "womanhood" that straddles classes and do not elevate "women's issues" above *class* analysis because if you do you end up with liberal politics' (*Class War*, No. 75, 11).

112   *Class War*, No. 51, 9.

113   McKay, 1998, 19 and 44; Monbiot, 1998, 181.

114   Gilroy, 1991, 15-16; Barrett, 1988, 11.

115   Fishman, 1975, 109. See too, *The Anarchist*, No. 2, 1885, 1; Thomas, 1980, 296.

116   See reports of anarcha-feminist meetings such in *Xtra* No. 2 and the reply in No.3, and the adverts for anti-authoritarian Women's Groups in *Freedom* throughout the 1970s and early 1980s.

117   *Anarchist Worker*, April 1977, No. 34, 7.

118   Big Flame, 1991, 7-8.

119   Proletarian Gob, 1993, 6.

120   Anderson and Anderson, 1998, 72.

121   Solanas, 1991.

122   See, for instance, the *Red Stocking Manifesto* quoted in Weiner, 1994, 55.

123   Ryan, D., 1989, 198-99; May, 1994, 20-21.

124   Weeks, 1998, 76.

125   Weeks, 1998, 75.

126   Turner, 1993e, 38.

127   Gilroy, 1991, 32.

128   Smith, Tucker et. al., 1982, 5.

129   See, for instance, *Wildcat* No. 16, 2-9. Similar analyses can be found in a range of anarchist sources including Smith, Tucker et.al, 1982 and Dangerous Times, 1986.

130   *Subversion* No. 10, 2-3; The cover of the 'Working Class Fight Back' edition (unnumbered) of *Class War* (fig 3.1) (also reprinted in Bone, Pullen and Scargill, 1991, 38) is described as a challenge to the identity politics of the 1980s

(Turner 1993e, 36). Identity politics often separated off the struggles by Black people and thereby closed avenues of solidarity, whilst Class War considered Black rebeliionns as a form of class struggle.

131   Tong, 1989, 183-84.

132   Tong, 1989, 185.

133   Ehrlich, 1981, 130-31.

134   ACF, 1990e, 1-2.

135   'Beyond the division of rich/poor, white/black etc is the division of power that runs through all these power relationships, and that is the oppression of women. Women are repressed (sic.) regardless of what class, colour or age they are' (Attack International, *Attack, Attack, Attack, Attack*, (henecforth *Attack*) 5). See too Class War's Sean Reilly: 'the vast bulk of working class women were untouched by feminism but have had to continue to fight in their own way against Capitalism *and a sexist society*' (original emphasis, Reilly, 1988e, 6).

136   *Green Anarchist*, No. 35, 9.

137   *Class War* No. 51, 9.

138   Class War, 1992, 65.

139   Class War, 1992, 65.

140   Ervin, 1993, 10.

141   Ervin, 1993, 3.

142   Ervin, 1993, 59.

143   Ehrlich, 1981, 116-17.

144   Ervin, 1993, 19-20 and 5.

145   Attack International, *Attack*, 15.

146   See, for instance, Black Flag's support for the American Black Autonomy group in *Black Flag* No. 212, 15. This, too, is Ervin's position. His views have been carried in: *Black Flag* No. 206, 12-15; *Do or Die* No.9, 83-98; and on a speaking tour of the UK as part of the 1994 'Anarchy in the UK' event (Bone, 1997, 10).

147   *Black Flag* No. 214, 23. Similarly, Gilroy notes how struggles on the basis of race can affect class composition (Gilroy, 1991, 32-35).

148   Reilly, 1990e.

149   Claudia, 1989e, 24; Erwin, 1993, 12.

150   See, for instance, Aufheben, 1998b, 34.

151   Laclau and Mouffe, 1996, 98-99.

152   Laclau and Mouffe, 1996, 151-53.

153   *Subversion* unnumbered, No. 12e, 11-12.

154   Law, 1983, 16.

155   Best and Kellner, 1991, 202.

156   Proletarian Gob, 1993, 7.

157   Attack International, *Attack*, 11.

158   The activists in British anarchist movements have tended to be predominantly (although not exclusively) white, male and heterosexual. This may explain their concentration on particular forms of economic oppression, as these are the ones that they experience most directly. Examples of the under-representation of other identities of the working class are legion. A Class War meeting in 1993 in Brixton in South London, an area with high proportion of people from ethnic minorities, had no Black people participating or in the audience. Similarly a Contra Flow meeting on race and class held in Brixton at the 121 Bookshop in 1997 was entirely white. Under-representation and the inadvertent but observable exclusion of women participating in class-struggle groups has been lamented in many anarchist publications (see for instance *Class War*, No. 73, 13).

159   Tong, 1989, 185.

Chapter Four: Organisation

1   Adopted by the Seventh Conference of the SI, July 1966.

2   *Organise!*, No. 42, 28.

3   Red Menace, 1986, 4.

4   'Not only the vitality of anarchism but its theoretical forms, indeed its very *raison d'être* stems from its capacity to express the aspirations of people to create their own egalitarian or at least self-administered social structures, their own forms of human consociation [friendly/co-operative association] by which they can exercise control over their lives' (Bookchin, 1998, 19).

5   Bloomfield, 1986, 159-60; see too Franks, 2005.

6   See, for instance, Jack White who, propagandising against Leninist bodies, repeats Marx's phrase 'The emancipation of the workers must be the work of the workers themselves' (White, 1998, 6). The Aims and Principles of the anarcho-syndicalist six-counties based Organise (not to be confused with the ACF/AF magazine of the same name) echo such sentiments:

> We believe that only the working class can change society from the present chaos and inequality to a society based on co-operation, mutual aid and equality. This change must be achieved by the conscious participation of the workers themselves (IWA in White, 1998, 14).

7   For instance, the French anarchist from the 1880s quoted by Miller:

> We do not believe.... in long term associations, federations, etc. In our view, a group.... should only be established at a precise point, for an

immediate action; once the action is accomplished, the same group reshapes itself along new lines, whether with the same members or with new ones... (Q. in Miller, 1984, 96).

8   *Organise!* No. 42, 20. See also Class War's assertion at the opening of the section on revolutionary organisation, 'There will be more than one organisation. This is taken for granted.' And 'we see organisations like the Class War Federation [...] playing a part, with others, in the creation and defence of a revolutionary movement within the working class. This movement will be a strong and diverse collection of the revolutionary sections of our class....' (Class War, 1992, 125-26).

9   The American anarcha-feminist Peggy Kornegger comments that in the small town in Illinois in which she grew up 'anarchy' was synonymous with 'chaos', an identification she now vehemently contests (Kornegger, 1998, 156). For examples of popular associations of 'anarchism' with 'chaos', see reports in the *Daily Mail*: Taylor, 2001, 22; Simpson, 2005, 6; Ginn, Madeley, et.al, 2005, 2. Hardman, 2005, 23.

10   Malatesta, Q. *Organise!* No. 42, 20.

11   Class War, 1992, 126.

12   Lenin, 1963, 146. Red Action, a Leninist grouping, explains that this perception of anarchism as 'chaos' is partly a media invention as anarchism does have a 'worked out political philosophy'. Nonetheless, they judge that contemporary British libertarianism is incapable of anything other than dilettante inactivity because of its beliefs in spontaneity, anti-intellectualism and lack of organisational structure (*Red Action* No. 56, 4-5).

13   Lenin does make a distinction between the necessary centralisation of revolutionary organisations, and the more flexible approach which can be taken by the non-revolutionary trade union movements (Lenin, 1963, 139-40).

14   See Miller, 1984, 96.

15   Clarke, 1983, 18.

16   Joll, 1979, 176. Miller also wonders whether the organisational inadequacies of anarchists can be attributed to the difficulty of reconciling their prefigurative, anti-hierarchical principles with the need for effective structures for co-ordinating activities (Miller, 1984, 98).

17   *Oh No Not Again*, nd, 1983e, 6.

18   Guérin, 1970, 11.

19   Guérin, 1970, 12. On the more liberal-wing, Ward appeals to similar ideas in his advocacy of spontaneous order (Ward, 1982, 30-31).

20   For instance, *Green Anarchist* publicises disparate acts of destruction, such as indiscriminate rises in youth crime, because 'community breakdown' as well as 'acts of community resistance' are 'both [....] harbingers of the coming collapse of authority' (*Green Anarchist* No. 54-55, 2).

21   The ACF argue that organisation is necessary for the achievement of aims, but that these can be 'free associations, collectives, federations, communes or "families" [which] will be fluid and flexible' (*Organise!* No. 42, 28).

22   See, for instance, Subversion's support for central planning in *Subversion* No. 14, 10.

23   S. in *Smash Hits* No. 3 (1998) advocates greater emphasis on the use of the carnivalesque in contemporary British libertarian activities. 'Carnivalesque demonstrations that challenge existing orders can also be "revolutionary", far more so than puritanical moral crusades and traditional demo[nstration]s' (S., 1998, 29).

24   See, for instance, Brinton discussing Bookchin (Brinton, 2004, 133).

25   Lenin, 1963, 70. It is not just overt Leninists who share this perception: the AWG also interpreted 'spontaneity' in this way (White, 1990, 23).

26   Plato, in *The Republic*, identifies a lack of governmental authority and complete freedom with the rise of tyrannical structures (Plato, 1986, 384-91).

27   In Britain, the proximity of secret service operatives in neo-fascist organisations during the 1960s and '70s suggests that there was an effort at promoting social instability and consequently a pretext for a stronger state apparatus. See Toczek, 1991, 15; 25; 27 and 31. Both *Lobster* and their para-political opponents *Searchlight* have suggested high level connections between the secret state and the extreme right for the purpose of being able to create political instability (Ramsay, 1992, 2-3). The *Turner Diaries,* which inspires the neo-Nazi groups in the Aryan Nations, glorifies creating social chaos in order to allow a racially pure, white minority to seize power (MacDonald, 1980).

28   See, for instance, the examples of popular journalists associating chaos with anarchism such as *Time Out*, April 2, 1998, 7.

29   Booth, 1998, 11-12.

30   *Black Flag* No. 315, 24-25.

31   *Subversion*, No. 12e, 7.

32   Malatesta, 1984, 85.

33   Freeman, 1984, 6-8 and 12.

34   Levine, 1984. Egalitarian participatory processes take various forms, such as restricting the number of occasions discussants can interject or discriminating in favour of those who have not had an opportunity to express their opinion.

35   Freeman, 1984, 6-7.

36   Marshall, 1992, 558.

37   ACF, 1990e, 14.

38   'Organisation is not contradictory to anarchism but synonymous with it – true anarchism is not disorganisation and chaos' (ACF, 1990e, 21).

39   *Proletarian Gob* gained some media attention for the stridency of its critique of mainstream journalism (see Leedham, 1994, 20), soon after it combined with *Subversion,* which folded in the autumn of 1998.

40   *Proletarian Gob* No. 1, 1

41   Pannekoek, 1978a, 59-60.

42   Gorter, 1989, 7-10 and Pannekoek, 1978c, 144.

43   Smart, 1978, 10-11.

44   Pannekoek, 1978b, 111. See too Shipway, 1987, 110-11.

45   Martin, 1997, 57-59. Despite identifying themselves primarily as anti-Leninist Communists, the councilist critique of trade unions as necessarily reformist organisations is essentially the same as Lenin's. See Lenin's condemnation of 'Economist' socialists in *What Is To Be Done* (Lenin, 1963, 84) and *"Left-Wing" Communism, An Infantile Disorder* (Lenin, 1975, 41).

46   It is distributed through BM Makhno who also distribute for Antagonism Press, the publishers of Dauvé and Martin, 1997.

47   Subversion argues that trade unions were always counterrevolutionary. 'Trade unions do not exist to change society. They were set up to fight over the division of the capitalist cake, not to take over the bakery. Indeed, without the buying and selling economy, based on wage labour, there is no role for a trade union' (Subversion, 1993e, 13).

48   *Anti-Exchange and Mart,* 1990e, 11-12.

49   Dauvé and Martin, 1997, 64.

50   Cleaver, 1979, 53.

51   Cleaver, 1979, 56.

52   Gorter, 1978, 151.

53   Gorter in 1921 tended to concentrate on 'the proletariat' (Gorter, 1978, 150-51), while Pannekoek also talked of 'the masses' (Pannekoek, 1978a, 61).

54   See for instance:

A revolution can no more be made by a big mass party or a coalition of different parties than by a small radical party. It breaks out spontaneously among the masses; action instigated by a party can sometimes trigger it off (a rare occurrence), but the determining forces lie elsewhere, in the psychological factors deep in the unconscious of the masses and in the great events of world politics (Pannekoek, 1978b, 100).

55   Pannekoek, 1978a, 66.

56   See the video *Poll Tax Riot* by ACAB, especially the footage of the BBC interview with Andy Murphy.

57   ACF, 1991e, 2.

58   Smith, Tucker, et. al., 1982, 21.

59   *Subversion* No. 10, 8.

60   Subversion, 1993, 24.

61   *Freedom* Vol. 1. No. 1, October 1886, 4.

62   See, for instance, John Rees's article in *Socialist Review* in which he criticises the anti-World Trade Organisation demonstrators in Seattle, USA for lacking the political leadership that only a political party with the correct (Leninist) strategy can offer (Rees, 2000, 10).

63   Class War, 1991, 7.

64   See, for instance, Rhys, 1988 and Nottingham Anarchist News, 1988. More recent critiques include *Class War*, No. 73, 10-12, Scott and Dawson, 1993, 10-14; Subversion, 1993e, 19-24; Trotwatch, 1992; Trotwatch, 1993 and reprints of extracts from Bob Drake's *The Communist Technique in Britain* as *Poor Lenin*, 1993.

65   Lenin, 1963, 86.

66   Lenin, 1976, 28-30.

67   Lenin, 1963, 118.

68   May, 1994, 117.

69   Lenin, 1963, 63.

70   Lenin, 1963, 164. Lenin argues that those workers who show sufficient promise as key revolutionaries should be financially supported by the revolutionary organisation so that their efforts are not wasted in earning a living. 'An agitator from among the workers who is at all talented and "promising" *must not work* in the factory eleven hours a day' but must be kept fresh for the party (Lenin, 1963, 153).

71   Lenin, 1963, 175-76.

72   Class War, 1991, 15-16.

73   For example, participating in the general election to vote a despised politician out of office (*Direct Action*, No. 6, Spring 1998, 4-5).

74   Lamb, 1997, 11.

75   Even after the Khrushchev liberalisation period, the British Communist Party was maintaining that a centralised structure was vital if the working class were to succede in overthrowing economic oppression. 'To reach victory in this struggle the working class requires leadership by a Party based on Marxism-Leninism...' (Communist Party, 1957, 3).

76   Castoriadis, 1969, 15, <para. 39>.

77   Weller in *Flux*, No. 5, 8.

78   Lenin, 1972, 39-40.

79   Lenin, 1975, 5-8.

80   Lenin, 1963, 144-45.

81   Lenin, 1963, 146.

82   Weller in *Flux*, No. 5, 10.

83   For instance, he argues that 'Left-Wing' opponents of the Bolsheviks fail because they are insufficiently disciplined to carry out their task of leading the masses (Lenin, 1975, 113).

84   Lenin, 1963, 126.

85   Lenin, 1963, 160-61.

86   Harman, 1979, 50.

87   Lenin, 1963, 167. See also Lenin's distinction between agitators and propagandists and their specific functions (Lenin, 1963, 92-93).

88   See, for instance, *Organise!*, No. 18, Feb-April 1990, 13-14.

89   Morland, 1997, 85-86.

90   Thomas, 1980, 283-84.

91   ACF, *Basic Bakunin*, 1991ea.

92   ACF, 1991e, 16.

93   *Red Action* No. 56, 4.

94   Bakunin, 1993e, 6.

95   Kropotkin, despite his advocates attempting to portray him as the anarchist saint who had 'little use for secret associations' (Avrich in Kropotkin, 1972, 10), never completely rejected freemasonry and covert associations, regarding them as effective modes of organisation (Bakunin, 1953, 192 and 277). Proudhon briefly entertained a secret conspiracy, as indeed, for a short time, did Marx (Hyams, 1979, 31).

96   See, for instance, Green Anarchist 1992, 1-3. Fears that anarchist groups are targets for surveillance and prosecution cannot be wholly dismissed as paranoid delusions as the GANDALF illustrates. For a complex and dense account of attempted state infiltration of anarchist groups see O'Hara, 1993.

97   Splat Collective, 1998, 13. The problems associated with such a strategy are unintentionally recognised by Andy Anderson because universal criteria for inclusion/exclusion are impossible to draw (Anderson and Anderson, 1998, 20-21).

98   Debord, 1983, para. 91.

99   Weller in *Flux* No. 5, 9-10. Green Anarchist introduces its organisational structure by explaining that it stands in complete opposition to 'centralised organisation like Greenpeace' (Green Anarchist, 1992, 1).

100   *The Platform*, 1989, 11.

101   *The Platform*, 1989, 14.

102   *The Platform*, 1989, 19; See too the comment:

>   The class struggle created by the enslavement of workers and their aspirations of liberty gave birth, in the oppression, to the idea of anarchism [....]

So anarchism does not derive from the abstract reflections of an intellectual or a philosopher, but from the direct struggle of workers against capitalism, from the needs and necessities of the workers, from their aspirations to liberty and equality, aspirations which become particularly alive in the best heroic period of life and struggle of the working masses (*The Platform*, 1989, 15).

103   *The Platform*, 1989, 20.
104   White, 1990, 26-27.
105   White, 1990, 24.
106   White, 1990, 26.
107   White, 1990, 27.
108   Duncan Hallas (1925-2002) was a leading theoretician for the SWP. He defined the vanguard party in terms of 'observable differences in abilities, consciousness and experience' which allow them to lead the subjugated class (Hallas, 1996, 45).
109   White, 1990, 28.
110   *The Platform*, 1989, 12.
111   *The Platform*, 1989, 21.
112   Paul, Liverpool DAM, 1991, 14. It is one of the quirks of fate to which anarchist history is particularly prone that one of the authors of *The Platform*, Archinov, four years later rejected anarchism and joined the Communist Party, publicly supporting Stalin's regime. In 1937 he was a victim of the purges. He was executed for 'trying to reintroduce anarchism into Russia' (Paul, Liverpool DAM, 1991, 15).
113   *The Platform*, 1989, 32.
114   White, 1990, 27.
115   *The Platform*, 1989, 34 and White, 1990, 25.
116   *Organise!* No. 27, 16. Malatesta's comments in 1927 seem to be aimed directly at the proposals within *The Platform* and their criticisms of then existing less centralised bodies. '[A]narchist organisations [....], in spite of all the disadvantages from which they suffer as representative bodies... are free from authoritarianism in any shape or form because they do not legislate and do not impose their deliberations on others' (Malatesta, 1984, 87).
117   *Organise!*, No. 29, 11.
118   *Organise!*, No. 29, 11.
119   *Organise!* No. 27, 16.
120   Fontenis, 1991, 13.
121   Fontenis, 1991, 8.
122   *Organise!* No. 27, 16.
123   *The Platform*, 1989, 33.

124   *Organise!* No. 27, 16.

125   Brown, 1990, 83-84.

126   See, for instance, Malatesta, 1984, 87.

127   Nechaev and his plans have been described as 'fanatic[al]', 'maniacal', 'despotic' and 'unscrupulous' (Woodcock, 1975, 162; Marshall, 1992, 283).

128   Avrich, 1987, 11 and Morland, 1997, 95.

129   Nechaev, 1989, 4. The sexism apparent in this quotation is ameliorated when Nechaev explains that women revolutionaries are as valuable as any man (Nechaev, 1989, 9).

130   'There is no such thing as a full-time "professional" revolutionary, although there are people who think they are! We are 'amateurs' and combine revolutionary work with everyday life. In the process we change and so do our lives' (Class War, 1992, 12-13).

131   Nechaev, 1989, 2-3.

132   Fishman, 1970, 13.

133   Prawdin, 1961, 67.

134   Clarke, 1983, 33.

135   Nechaev, 1989, 7.

136   Nechaev, 1989, 7.

137   Nechaev, 1989, 10.

138   Cleaver, 1984, 25.

139   'FARC that for a Game of Soldiers' in *Do Or Die, No. 10,* 146.

140   Nechaev, 1989, 10.

141   *Organise!* No. 31, 16, *Subversion* No. 12, 16 and *Do or Die*, No. 10, 146, 147-49. Likewise the WSM looks at Sinn Fein's policy of rejection of workers' self-organisation, in favour of actions co-ordinated by their bureaucrats, as evidence of their insularity and authoritarianism (WSM, 1992, 20). The terrorist group and its political body are the primary motor for change, not autonomous action by the oppressed.

142   The infiltration of existing cells and the creation of rogue cells has been the basis for one of the libertarian criticisms of cell structures, as well as a warning of how far sections of the state will go in order to protect their interests. The authors of *Like A Summer With A Thousand July's* cite the case of the Littlejohn brothers who were hired by trusted elements of Heath's Conservative Government to infiltrate the IRA and to commit bank raids in the Irish Republic in the name of Nationalist cause. The aim was to provoke anti-IRA feeling in the twenty-six counties (Wolfie, Speed, et. al., 1982, 12).

143   Sanguinetti, 1982, 58.

144   *Class War* 'Victory to the Hit Squads' edition, 1 and 3.

145   Marshall, 1992, 558.

146   Plant, 1992, 126.

147   Borum and Tilby, 2005, 220. Randy Borum is an academic at the University of South Florida; Chuck Tilby works for Eugene (Oregon) Police Department and is a speaker at FBI events.

148   Opponents have subsequently attempted to damn anarchism by association with these oppressive ideological movements by highlighting apparent similarities in organisational structure, whilst overlooking overarching differences in tactics, agency and ends. See, for instance, Tariq Ali's oxymoronic neologism 'Islamo-anarchists', Ali, 2005 and Q. Ali in Cockburn, 2005.

149   Bunyan, 1983, 48.

150   *Class War*, 'Victory to the Hit Squads' edition, 3.

151   The AB was part of the First of May Group which stretched over Europe (Meltzer, 1976b, 19-20). It 'was not a specific organisation, but a manifestation of revolutionary activism through a wide circle of the libertarian movement' (Meltzer, 1976b, 19-20).

152   Daniels, 1989, 120.

153   Daniels, 1989, 80.

154   'Frank: Yeh, but it ain't a substitute for Workers taking action....
'Jim: Well who said it was?
'Carole: Look, Frank, as far as I can see, it's a bloody good laugh, it hits Longs [the employers] in the pocket *and* it's given me something to smile about' (Daniels, 1989, 123).

155   Angry Brigade, Communiqué 9, 1984, 32.

156   Baumann, 1975, 98.

157   Bradley, 1991, 7.

158   Miller, 1984, 124.

159   Woodcock, 1975, 18.

160   Bookchin, 1993, 52.

161   ACF, 1997, 25.

162   In 1912, revolutionary syndicalism was estimated as having a worldwide following of just under 600,000 which grew in 1922 to around 1.7 million. Even in 1987 it was estimated at 100,000 (Gambone, 1997, 2-3 and 11). Other membership figures have been estimated for national revolutionary groups in the first three decades of the twentieth century for France by Mitchell, 1990, 43; The Netherlands by van der Linden, 1990, 54; Germany by Bock, 1990, 61, 68 and 70; Sweden by Persson, 1990, 85; Britain by White, 1990a, 103; Spain by Bar, 1990, 126; Italy by Betrand, 1990, 144; Portugal by Bayerlein and van der Linden, 1990, 156 and 161; Argentina by Thompson, 1990, 173-4; Mexico by Hart, 1990, 187, 189-90, 197; USA by Dubofsky, 1990, 214; Canada by Bercuson, 1990, 232; and globally in the pre-Second World War period by Thorpe, 1990, 250-51. Christie complained that the British anarchist

movement bythe early 1960s had no industrial base and was composed mainly of middle class liberals, while the Continental movements, especially in France and Spain, were, because of their syndicalist origins, still rooted in the working class (Christie, 1980, 31).

163   Kropotkin in *Black Flag*, No. 210, 26-27.

164   As the Charter of Amiens (1906) expounds:

> In the daily work of claiming better conditions the syndicate is seeking a co-ordination of work forces, a growth in the workers' well-being through the acquisition of immediate improvements such as the diminution of working hours, increase in salary etc.

> But thus necessity is only one side of the work of syndicalism: it is a preparation for complete emancipation which can only come about through the expropriation of capital. This requires the general strike as a mode of action, and considers that the syndicate, today the form of resistance groups, will tomorrow be groups of production and distribution, the foundation of social organisation....

> Consequently, as far as individuals are concerned, the Congress affirms complete freedom for any member of the syndicate to participate outside it in whatever kind of struggle corresponds to his philosophical or political ideas, asking him in exchange not to introduce into the syndical organism the opinions expressed outside (Bonanno, 1978*e*, 27).

165   Holton, 1980, 8-11.

166   The IWW are, strictly speaking, revolutionary syndicalists rather than anarcho-syndicalists. The difference is that while both reject political parties in favour of for direct workers' action as a means of bringing about fundamental changes in social and economic relations, revolutionary syndicalists are not wedded to the vision of a future society based on libertarian communist principles (see Longmore, 1985, 6-7) However, the IWW and IWA in practice barely diverge; as a result, there has been discussion towards the possibility of a merger (*Direct Action* No.74, 8). In Britain, there are convivial relations between the two with SolFed favourably reporting IWW activities (see for instance *Direct Action* No. 76, 9; *Direct Action* No. 4, 21-22 and *Direct Action* No. 6, 28).

167   White, 1998, 7. As Laurens Otter wrote in the anarcho-syndicalist SWF paper, 'Industry is the principal field on which the class war is fought' (*Direct Action* Volume 2, No. 4, 1962, 6).

168   Monatte, 1980, 217.

169   Holton, 1980, 13-5 and Price, 1998, 264.

170   Rocker, 1990e, 53; See too *Direct Action* No. 74, 10.

171   SolFed are a member of the anarcho-syndicalist Internal Worker's Association, of which the CNT is the leading member.

172   Rocker, 1990e, 53 and *Direct Action* No. 74, 10.

173   Roger Lyons, General Secretary of the Amicus union for manufacturing and science related workers, received a basic pay of £79,000, plus an additional package of nearly £10,000 per annum in 2002-3.

174   Rocker, 1990e, 80. DAM (the forerunners of SolFed) in their 'Aims and Principles' explain that 'We are fighting to abolish the state, capitalism and wage slavery in all forms and replace them by self-managed production for need, not profit' (DAM-IWA, 1991, 30).

175   This non-participation with governments, despite the CNT-FAI's role in the Republican state against the fascists in the Spanish Civil War, is taken seriously within the IWA. The CNT-AIT opposes participation in the 'Workers' Councils', a corporatist structure incorporated into the Social Chapter of the Maastricht Treaty (*Black Flag*, No. 211, 17).

176   *Direct Action*, No. 76, 12.

177   *Direct Action* No. 1, 34; See too letter from Paul F. PSWN/DAM in *Organise!* No. 29, 10.

178   Douglass, 1991, 11.

179   Martin, 1998e, 58. Unions show 'that their interests lie hand in glove with those of the employer' (*Subversion* No. 10, 5-6).

180   *Anti-Exchange and Mart*, 8.

181   Some examples of these from the postal sector are described in *Anti-Exchange and Mart*.

182   Douglass, 1999, 81 and Douglass, 1991, 11.

183   Q. *Bread and Roses*, Issue 2, Winter 97/98, 3.

184   Miller, 1984, 131.

185   Debord, writing of post-revolutionary structures (Councils) argued similarly: 'The revolutionary organisation existing before the power of the Councils (it will find its own form through struggle), for all these historical reasons, already knows that it *does not represent* the working class. It must recognise itself as no more than a radical separation from *the world of separation*.' (Debord, 1983, para 119).

186   *Direct Action* No. 76, 12.

187   Even the short-lived Syndicalist Alliance journal reported on non-workplace activities such as anti-fascist activity and environmental protests (see, for instance, *The Syndicalist*, No. 1, 16).

188   *Bread and Roses* No. 2, Winter 97/98, 4.

189   Meltzer, 1996, 16.

190   Simon, 1998, 8-9.

191   *Dockers Charter*, No. 28, September 1996, 1.

192   Mainstream newspapers found it difficult to explain the relationship between the groups and attempted to distinguish the Liverpool dockers and their supporters from the environmental protestors. (See *The Observer*, 13.4.97, 1 and 5; *The Mail on Sunday*, 13.4.97, 1 and 13; *Evening Standard* (London regional newspaper) 14.4.97, 3). See too *Do or Die,* No. 10, 23.

193   Pelaez and Holloway, 1996, 62.

194   Bookchin, 1993, 49.

195   *Red and Black*, No. 1, 30.

196   SolFed, 1994*e*, 3.

197   *Education Worker*, No. 3, Summer 1995, 3; *Education Worker* is the bulletin of SolFed's Education Workers' Network.

198   *Direct Action* No. 1, 34.

199   Woodcock, 1975, 294.

200   Miller, 1984, 129.

201   Marshall, 1992, 351-52.

202   Parry, 1987.

203   Miller, 1984, 129.

204   Mitchell, 1990, 26.

205   There were notable exceptions such as the Greenwich Park blast of 1894 and the thwarted Walsall bombings (see Nicoll, 1992, 7-12).

206   Harper, 1987, 68; See too Mitchell, 1990, 27.

207   *Black Flag* No. 211, 16.

208   Mitchell, 1987, 29.

209   Bone, 1997, 8.

210   Ryan, 1987, 12. Bone cites Ryan's article in support (Bone, 1997, 8).

211   Knoche, 1996, 350-53.

212   For instance, see Class War's celebration of the 1981 riots, in which 'whole communities rose up', and their support for working class 'community resistance' in general (Bone, Pullen and Scargill, 1991, 5 and 60). Similarly, the ACF divide 'struggles before the Revolution' into four categories, the first two being those directly in the community and industrial setting, where activities of the first type are all those forms of resistance not classified in the latter. The latter two categories, the revolutionary movement and international groupings, seek to communicate, assist and co-ordinate action across and between the first two spheres (ACF, 1997, 23-28).

213   Bone, 1997, 8. See too Class War's *Heavy Stuff*: 'we feel that the emphasis has shifted from the workplace to the community' (Ryan, 1987, 12).

214   Brown, 1990, 57.

215   Aufheben, 1998, 7-8.

216   Cleaver, who describes how the economic is still the central strategic arena of resistance, argues that work has extended beyond the traditional workplace:

> [M]ilitary violence, starvation and the violence of incarceration as well as spectacle (TV, movies, sports) and brainwashing (politics, school) [...] all of these are geared to either getting people into work or getting rid of those who won't. These methods all appear to be operations carried on at the periphery of formal waged work with the aim of reinforcing its power to organise people's time and energy. But when we examine these activities more closely we also realise that they perform the work of producing or reproducing labour power and in the process create a situation in which either the work of producing the commodity labour power or the work of producing other commodities take up as much of society's time as capital can impose (Cleaver, 1999, 8-9).

217   Aufheben, 1998, 8.

218   Aufheben, 1998, 8.

219   Class War, too, propose the 'growth of independent community groups in different areas with different emphasis [...] women's groups, black groups, prisoners and their support groups etc' [Class War, 1992, 95).

220   Casey, 1987, 17.

221   ACF, 1997, 23-24.

222   Ryan, 1987, 15-18.

223   Trotwatch, 1993, 29-30.

224   Burns, 1992, 74-75.

225   *Subversion* No. 11, 12.226 Hounslow APT Campaign in *Class War* No. 45, 4.

227   Burns, 1992, 107-09.

228   *Do or Die*, No. 8, 157.

229   'The greens and the roads protesters are the peace movement of the nineties. The peace movement achieved nothing. We've still got nuclear weapons. There's too many diversions promoted by middle class idiots wanting to get upset about roads, calfs [sic], the trees, c.f.c.s, food additives etc' (Homocult, 1996, 23).

230   *Class War* No. 41, 8-9; No. 46, 10 and No. 47, 10.

231   *Counter Information* No. 42, 4.

232   Wall, 2000, 69-71 and *Do or Die*, No. 8, 155.

233   *Do or Die*, No. 8, 157.

234   The article was reprinted in *Aufheben* No. 1, pagination refers to the

article available from the website: <http://lists.village.virginia.edu/~spoons/aut_html/Aufheben/auf1ef.htm>.

235   Aufheben, No. 1, 2-4.

236   Douglass, 1992, 19-20.

237   This section draws on a number of web published articles, predominantly by Harry Cleaver (1998), Hugh J. Martin (2000) and Stefan Wray (1998). There are discussion groups dedicated to hacktivism: these include <http://hacktivism.tao.ca/> as well as guides assisting a myriad of computer based activities on <http://www.mc2.nu/>.

238   For the sake of simplicity the Internet and World Wide Web are taken as the same thing.

239   *Direct Action*, No. 3, 21 and *Do or Die*, No. 8, 5. The mainstream press warns that J18 was planned and directed by electronic media, and that modern technology provides new opportunities for creating disruption (*Daily Telegraph*, July 19, 1999, 1; *Financial Times*, July 17, 1999, 13). The same claims were made concerning N30: '[A]narchists are urging supporters to "reclaim" the railways and underground. Militants are using the internet and e-mail to organise their campaign' (*Daily Mirror*, November 29, 1999, 27).

240   *Black Flag*, No. 218, 5-6

241   *Time*, April 2000, 3.

242   Cleaver, 1998.

243   Wray, 1998.

244   Moglen, 1999.

245   Cleaver, 1998.

246   Martin, 2000.

247   Cleaver, 1998.

248   Cleaver, 1998.

249   Cleaver, 1998.

250   *Time*, April 24, 2000, 40-1; *Do or Die*, No. 8. 5-6.

251   Rosen, 1997, 114-15.

252   Whitehead, 1996, 17-8.

253   The same is true of the N30 anti-WTO protests: 'Marches and rallies were held throughout the day by an estimated 25,000 people representing groups from environmentalists to labour' (*Financial Times*, December 1, 1999, 12), and in Britain the '[p]olice are investigating a link between the demonstrations in London and the underground "rave" dance culture' (*The Times*, December 1, 1999, 11).

254   Q. Grave in Miller, 1984, 131.

Chapter Five: Anarchist Tactics

1   Since the 1880s British anarchism has positioned itself as a revolutionary movement. Kropotkin distinguished *Freedom* from the mutualist wing of anarchism by promoting 'Revolutionary Communism' (*Freedom: A Journal of Anarchist Socialism*, April 1888, Vol. 2 No. 19, 75). See too *Class War*, No. 77, 2; *Organise!* No. 51, 23; *Workers Solidarity*, No. 49, 9; *Direct Action*, No. 7, Summer 1998, 35 and AWG, 1988, 4.

2   Class War, by no means the worst offender, in their two substantial works *A Decade of Disorder* and *Unfinished Business* include just two pages (out of nearly 300) on what makes, creates and distinguishes a revolution (Class War, 1992, 109-10).

3   Ancient Greek theorists posited that the cycle, or full revolution, meant that tumultuous events resulted in the eventual return to an original position (Calvert, 1970, 38-39). Tendencies within green anarchism, in particular primitivism, regard the revolution as containing elements of a return back to a pre-civilised society (See *Green Anarchist* No. 38, Summer 1995, 7-8).

4   Marx and Engels, 1977, 58.

5   Cunningham, 1995, 13.

6   Arendt, 1979, 21. See Plato's description of the transformation of society from timarchy into oligarchy, which in turn is superseded by democracy which is overthrown by tyranny (Plato, 1986, 356-420).

7   Arendt, 1979, 47-48.

8   Casey, 1990, 30.

9   See, for instance, Berkman's comment that the Russian Revolution is the:

> most important historic event since the Great French Revolution [...] the most significant fact in the whole known history of mankind. It is the only Revolution which aimed *de facto*, at social world-revolution; it is the only one which actually abolished the capitalist system of a country' (Berkman, 1986, 14).

He later appraised that the Bolsheviks imposed a bureaucratic counterrevolution that would require a third revolution to overthrow it (Berkman, 1986, 26 and 91).

10   Meltzer, 1976a, 40. See too Cunningham's comment that 'The first thing to consider is the kind of revolution that we are fighting for, because the ends we have in mind, will, to a large extent determine the means we use' (Cunningham, 1995, 13).

11   Although economic determinism is associated with Leninism, Lenin

himself believed that the proletariat did have relative autonomy in influencing events but only through the Party (Lenin, 1975, 42 and Cohan, 1975, 55).

12   Cohan, 1975, 56-67.

13   Cleaver, 1979, 34

14   Trotsky, 1983, 94. Trotsky held that the bureaucratisation of the transitional period could be attributed to the military threat to the Revolution and the dire economic circumstances caused by the civil war (Trotsky, 1983, 108-14). Berkman, in his criticism of the Bolshevik regime, suggests that the response to invasion and famine need not have taken a bureaucratic turn and that the choice of this strategy was partly due to the ideology of Leninism (Berkman, 1989, 67; Berkman, 1986, 39-40).

15   In *The Free* the ruling elite overcome this crisis by massive repression, while in *Breaking Free* the ending is more optimistic and open-ended.

16   Class War, 1992, 109.

17   Situationist International, 1989, 224.

18   Bey's TAZ is self-consciously Deleuzian. He advocates creating new realities through acts of autonomous creative interplay rather than through negative resistance, as the latter, in Bey's opinion, invites recuperation as well as repression (Bey, 1991, 128). He cites Deleuze and Guattari's works such as *Nomadology and the War Machine* as examples of nomadic subjects searching out possibilities for creativity (Bey, 1991, 106-07; see too May, 1993, 5).

19   Bey, 1991, 99.

20   See Green Anarchist No. 49-50, 16.

21   *Do or Die*, No.10, 167.

22   Bone, 1999, 6.

23   Bey, 1991, 105-06.

24   Bey, 1991, 132.

25   Police and local dignitaries have sought out confrontation with local movements, such as the convoy at the Battle of the Beanfield in 1985 (see Hemment, 1998, 208-9, 217-18). Judicial action did meet with active resistance, but more often a party venue closed down by the authorities just re-opened in a different site under a new name.

26   Bey, 1991, 100-01.

27   Bey, 1991, 101.

28   Braidotti, 1993, 49.

29   Braidotti, 1993, 52.

30   Bey, 1991, 104.

31   Camus, 1965, 127.

32   Burns, 1992.

33   Woodcock, 1975, 96-97. For a discussion of Stirner's individualist 'rebellion' contrasted with social revolution, see Thomas, 1980, 140-44).

34   Camus, 1965, 22.

35   Camus, 1965, 20.

36   Camus, 1965, 21.

37   Camus, 1965, 27, 213 and 215.

38   Bookchin, 1995, 9-10.

39   Fox, 1989, 6.

40   Fox, 1989, 7.

41   Thomas, 1980, 141.

42   Burns, 1992.

43   Sparks, 1996, 8-9.

44   See, for instance, Marshall, 1992, 286 and Thomas, 1980, 287.

45   The Sardinian anarchist paper *Anarkiviu* proposed an 'Antiauthoritarian Insurrectionist International' for the Mediterranean area. An English language version of the proposal is available from Elephant Editions.

46   Kedward, 1971, 56.

47   Thomas, 1980, 292.

48   Sparks, 1996, 9.

49   A proponent of the liberatory possibilities of insurrections also points to the appalling incidents at the Notting Hill carnival riots of August 26, 1985 when some Black insurgents attacked proletarian Whites, and in Brixton on September 28, 1985 when a couple of rioters raped two women. These are condemned by the author of *Rebel Violence Versus Hierarchical Violence* as examples of the latter (Dangerous Times, 1986, 2-3, 6-7). These incidents are highlighted as aberrations to the general atmosphere of recent urban uprisings where 'as usual during riots, the streets, normally alien places serving the speedy circulation of merchandise [...] become the terrain of history and community in struggle' (Dangerous Times, 1986, 8).

50   Kedward, 1971, 56.

51   See Stewart Home's letter reprinted in *Vague* 21, 94.

52   Home, 1988, 98-100.

53   KH, 1986, 6.

54   *Class War* 'another fucking royal parasite' edition, 4 and 3.

55   Smith, Speed et. al., 1982, 4, 21-22.

56   A list of 50 contacts was published in *Evading Standards* (June 18, 1999, 21), an occasionally produced, superbly executed spoof of London's regional paper the *Evening Standard*.

57   *Socialist Worker*, June 26, 1999, 15.

58   By the time of the World Trade Organisation talks held on November 30, 1999 (N30) in Seattle USA, and similar global protests planned to those of J18, the SWP had changed their minds and attempted to play a dominant role in the British response to neo-liberalism, setting up a front group called Globalise Resistance.

59   Socialist Worker, 26 June, 15. Militant (now the Socialist Party) were so against the tactic of rioting that they offered to assist in the police in naming rioters (Trotwatch, 1993, 34, see too 29-30 and 33).

60   Stereotypically uninformed tabloid columnist Carole Malone ascribed motives to the protestors of wanting state socialism, asking rhetorically if they really wanted to live in a socialist society 'like China' (Malone, 1999, 31). The historian, Dr Brian Brivati, contacted to help out *The Independent* journalist Paul Lashmar was equally confused: he too could not identify their aims (Q. Brivati, Lashmar, 1999, 3).

61   *Organise!* No. 27, 4 and Raf, 1986, 2.

62   Attack International sees riots as having the potential to build co-operative networks. '[R]iots can be frightening. The only way to overcome these barriers is by encouraging participation, and by being welcoming to others. Riots can be a time for sharing, distributing the spoils' (Attack International, *Attack,* 8).

63   Plant, 1992, 31.

64   Dangerous Times, 1986, 6.

65   Bone, Pullen and Scargill, 1991, 60.

66   Dangerous Times, 1986, 6 and 8. Riots, rather than being race riots – as the mainstream media have often portrayed them – are often meeting places of communal activity by ethnic minority and majority members of the working class (Situationist International, 1989, 154. See too Gilroy, 1991, 32 and Smith, Speed, et. al, 1982, 9-10).

67   See, for instance, the descriptions of co-operation in resisting the police and the realisation of collective power (ACAB Press, 1990, 40 and 51).

68   Plant, 1992, 31 and Wall, 2000, 115.

69   Trotwatch, 1992, 29-30.

70   Gilroy, 1991, 33.

71   Meltzer, 1986, 18.

72   Carter, 1973, 38. Woodcock gives the date as 1833 (Woodcock, 1975, 299).

73   Whitehead, 2001, 11.

74   Dubofsky, 1990, 208.

75   Malatesta, 1984, 115. See too Guérin, 1970, 81.

76   '[The mass strike] gives the most comprehensive expression to their strength as a social factor' (Rocker, 1990e, 68).

77   DAM, 1984, 8.

78   Woodcock, 1975, 19.

79   Trautmann, 1980, 193-94.

80   Rocker, 1990e, 69.

81   Luxemburg acknowledges that 'anarchism' is 'indissolubly linked' to the 'idea of the mass strike' (Luxemburg, 1986, 17).

82   Luxemburg derides anarchism for it 'simply do[es] not exist as a serious political tendency'. It is a movement whose 'historical career [...] is well-nigh ended' (Luxemburg, 1986, 16). If her account is right then it raises the question, why dedicate the opening chapter to castigating it?

83   Luxemburg, 1986, 68.

84   Harding, 1996, 68.

85   Luxemburg, 1986, 48 and 53-54.

86   Luxemburg, 1986, 47.

87   Luxemburg, 1986, 72.

88   *Direct Action*, No. 3, Summer 1997, 4.

89   Rocker, 1990e, 69.

90   Carter, 1973, 6.

91   Engels, 1958, 243.

92   Trade union historian Ray Challinor follows the Leninist line that 'Sabotage was a protest taken by workers as individuals not as a class' (Challinor, 1977, 96). Sociologists such as Laurie Taylor and Paul Walton also consider sabotage ('unplanned smashing') as a 'sign of a powerless individual or group' (Q. Taylor and Walton in Lamb, 1995, 4).

93   See, for instance, DAM who, in a pamphlet on *Direct Action in Industry*, give examples of sabotage which are restricted to machine-breaking or product destruction (DAM, 1980e, 19-20).

94   E.P. Thompson's study of Luddism in *The Making of the English Working Class* is particularly relevant here. He illustrated that Luddite machine-breaking was often carefully co-ordinated which resulted in its, albeit short-lived, success (Thompson, 1968, 605, 630).

95   Their selective use of machine-breaking rather than indiscriminate destruction is also indicative of an attempt to assert values of dignity and craft over commodity production (Thomson, 1968, 606-07).

96   Dubois, 1979, 97. Dubois' classification of Maoist writers is a little unclear as it includes Ratgeb, which was a pseudonym of a member of the Situationist International. The SI were extremely critical of Mao and the Chinese Communist Party: see, for instance, the hostile telegram sent to the Chinese Embassy by the SI reprinted in the *Situationist International Anthology* (Knabb, 1989, 345-46).

97   Negri, 1979, 126.

98   Weller, 1973e.

99   Lamb, 1995, 3.

100   Flynn, 1995, 25.

101   Dubois, 1979, 21.

102   Dubois, 1979, 14.

103   Flynn, 1995, 18.

104   Flynn, 1995, 16-17.

105   McFarlane, 1986/7, 5.

106   Thompson, 1968, 616; 641-42. Accusations of assassination might be exaggerated (Thompson, 1968, 633), but there were certainly celebrations in Luddite strongholds over the murder of Prime Minister Spencer Perceval (Thompson, 1968, 623).

107   For instance, in the difference between Bakunin's demands for the immediate abolition of the state and Lenin's desire to see it wither away.

108   DAM, 1984, 3.

109   Douglass, 1992, 23.

110   Dubois, 1979, 21.

111   Black Flame, 1981e, 24-25.

112   DAM, 1984, 4.

113   See, for instance, DAM, 1984, 4-5; DAM, 1991, 18-19; Wildcat, 1992, 12; *Merseyside Anarchist*, No. 14, February 1990, 3.

114   Luxemburg, 1986, 46.

115   Brown, 1990, 12.

116   *Dockers Charter*, 28 September, 1996, 2-3.

117   See *Merseyside Anarchist*, No. 15, March 1990, 2. Striking drivers distributed a phone number which people could still call to gain assistance.

118   *Class War* No. 38, 3.

119   DAM, 1980e, 16.

120   Dubois, 1976, 90-91.

121   Rocker, 1990e, 71.

122   *Class War*, No. 38, 3.

123   Gorz, 1997, 41 and 48.

124   Gorz, 1997, 50.

125   Negation, 1975, 41.

126   Negation, 1975, 52-53.

127   Negation, 1975, 54-55 and 90.

128   Negation, 1975, 73 and 75.

129   Lamb, 1995, 5; See Weller, 1973e and Dubois, 1979, 67.

130   The exception being the CGT prior to the First World War when it was anarchist-dominated. In this period it did support sabotage, and did so again under more orthodox leadership during the Nazi-occupation of France. Following 'liberation', however, it rejected the tactic (Dubois, 1979, 68).

131   *Class War*, No. 38, 3.

132   *Class War*, No. 38, 3.

133   Solidarity, 1986, 33.

134   Brown, 1990, 15.

135   Lamb, 1995, 4.

136 'Percentage of fast-food restaurant workers who admit to doing "slow, sloppy work" on purpose: 22' (Harper's Index, *Harper's*, May 1991, 7 Q. Sprouse, 1992, 122). Kolinko-agents and friends, the authors of an automonist marxist analysis into call centres, identify everyday sabotage such as making the computer workstation crash, deliberately cutting off phone calls, and physically manipulating office wiring to prevent efficient use (Kolinko-agents and friends, 2002, 99-100).

137 Flynn, 1995, 11-12.

138 Linebaugh, 1993, 122-23.

139 Linebaugh, 1993, 134.

140 Dubois, 1979, 46.

141 Flynn, 1995, 21 and Brown, 1990, 13.

142 Dubois, 1976, 35-37.

143 Gorz, 1997, 39.

144 Gorz, 1997, 39-40.

145 Gorz, 1997, 39 and Flynn, 1995, 18.

146 Emphasis in original - Negri, 1979, 124.

147 Flynn, 1995, 30.

148 Tronti, 1979, 7-21. Negri, 1979, 93-117; Tronti is regarded as the 'father of European workerism' as he has collaborated with Negri and other autonomists on their journal *Quaderni Rossi*. Tronti was a member of the mainstream Leninist Italian Communist Party although he was critical of many aspects of orthodox marxism and the Communist movement (Red Notes, 1979, 21 and Wright, 2000, 82).

149 Dubois, 1979, 56.

150 Aufheben, 1998, 12.

151 Dubois, 1979, 109. See too Franco Platania discussing the situation of the Italian Communist Party: 'I couldn't understand the Communist Party blokes in the [FIAT] factory. They made it a point of honour never to be faulted in their work by the foreman' (Platania, 1979, 176). Current groups such as Reclaim the Streets had some of their origins in the dole autonomous environmental protests of the early 1990s (McKay, 1996, 202).

152 Negri, 1979, 127.

153 *Class War* 'We Have Our Own Idea of Time and Motion' edition, 3.

154 Douglass, 1992, 19.

155 This is the basis of some of Bookchin's criticisms of the egoism of 'lifestyle anarchism' (Bookchin, 1995, 50).

156 Fox, 1989, 6.

157 Attack International, *Attack*, 24. See too the letter by F (Liverpool) in *Subversion* which posits the greater revolutionary potential of unemployment: 'Jobs/wages invariably leads us to shackling ourselves to the baubles that

capitalism dangles before us incessantly - drop out and do something that hurts capitalism instead of meandering along inside its poxy system' (*Subversion*, No. 23, 10). Subversion did not agree.

158   Aufheben, 1998, 13-14.

159   Platania, 1979, 172; 'I wonder if I can sneak home early? I'm half asleep anyway – they'll never miss me' (*Class War*, 'We Have Our Own Idea of Time and Motion' edition, 3).

160   Dubois, 1979, 54.

161   Decadent Action 'helped organise campaigns such as National Phone In Sick Day' (Murray, 1997, 9). The idea was later recuperated (recuperation being the process by which a radical idea is embraced by dominant groupings, torn from its original proponents and used against them) in an advertising campaign for Karrimor outdoor equipment (Cassidy, 1999, 5).

162   A flier advertising the day suggests 'Take a day off work or go sick on 18/6/99'. Leaflet produced by the J18 network (contact given as: J18discussion@ gn.apc.org).

163   Miller, 1984, 99. Following the suicide bomb attacks on 7 July 2005 on London transport, many commentators have asserted a tactical and even ideological connection between theocratic radical Islam (the ideological faction widely accepted as the progenitors of the outrages) and anarchists, because of the supposed similarity between propaganda by deed and the indiscriminate attacks against civilians, see for instance Ali, 2005; Ghannoushi, 2005 and Stewart, 2005.

164   Woodcock, 1975, 308.

165   Miller, 1984, 98.

166   Parry, 1987, 11.

167   Parry, 1987, 13.

168   Targets included The French Chamber of Deputies, President Sadi Carnot, the house of President Benoit, the state prosecutor Bulot and the Lobau barracks in Paris as well as illegitimate assaults such as Ravachol's murder of two old women who ran an iron-mongers shop (Woodcock, 1975, 283-94 and Joll, 1964, 128-38).

169   Woodcock, 1975, 292-93.

170   *Black Flag Supplement* No. 3, 5.

171   Parry, 1987, 28.

172   Attack International, *Attack*, 13.

173   Parry, 1987, 15.

174   Parry, 1987, 24-25 and 28.

175   Parry, 1987, 59.

176   Kerr, 1998-99, 34.

177   Hoffman, 1971, vi.

178   ACF, 1997, 22.

179   A grouping close to the Green Anarchist movement.

180   Herman and Chomsky, 1988; Chomsky, 1993; Institute of Social Disengineering, 1994; Class War's Neil Warne, 1991, 16.

181   Institute of Social Disengineering, 1994, 7.

182   Editorial, *Direct Action*, No. 1, Autumn 1996, 1.

183   When Militant (now the separate Socialist Party) were infiltrating the Labour Party they claimed that they were 'a paper not a party' (Rhys, 1988, 27).

184   Atton, 1999, 35-36.

185   Otter, 1971, 8.

186   Atton, 1999, 26.

187   Atton, 1999, 45.

188   See, for instance, the account of Swansea's *Alarm* by I. (Bristol), 1998, 8-9.

189   Lenin, 1963, 165 and 168-69.

190   Atton, 1999, 33.

191   Atton, 1999, 41-42.

192   The ACF write: 'Please feel welcome to contribute articles to *Organise!* as long as they don't conflict with our Aims and Principles we will publish them. (Letters, of course, need not agree with our A&Ps [Aims and Principles] at all)' (*Organise!* No. 51, 2). See too *ContraFLOW*, August/September 1995, 2; *Smash Hits* No. 1, 1 and its marginal modification in *Smash Hits* No. 3, 1 and *Direct Action* No. 11, 2.

193   See, for instance, *ContraFLOW* which positively invites critical appraisal of its contents anf production (*Contraflow* No. 24, Jan-Mar 1998, 2).

194   Drake, 1993, 7.

195   The democratisation of production that aims to 'break down the barrier between producers and consumers' is identified, by Paul Rosen, as the 'punk "access aesthetic"', which he considers to be closely connected to anarchism (Rosen, 1997, 99-100).

196   *Animal*, No. 3, 1; See too the review in *Black Flag* No. 214, 28. The content being more important than production values is also discussed by I. (Bristol), 1998.

197   *Solidarity* No. 13, 5-6.

198   Godwin, 1971, 250.

199   Godwin, 1986, 121; See too Marshall, 1984, 77.

200   See, for instance, William Dixon's 'Obituary: Class War' in *Radical Chains* No. 5 and Analysis, 'The Passing of An Old Warrior', *Weekly Worker* (CPGB), July 17, 1997. Criticism also comes from within the libertarian milieu: see, for instance, *Aufheben* No. 6, 41.

201   *Aufheben* No.6, 41.

202   Thayer, 1965, 153.

203   Trautmann, 1980, 138.

204   See, for instance, *Xtra!*, *Police News: For Nonviolent Authoritarianism*, Gravesend's *The Gravedigger* and *Swansea's Angry Side*. Purkis finds it too in Donald Rooum's Wildcat cartoon, a mainstay of *Freedom* (Purkis, 1997, 78), which is often reprinted in *Workers Solidarity*.

205   Class War, 1991e, 13.

206   Bone, 1987, 6-7.

207   Class War, 1991e, 12.

208   *Class War* No. 73, 4.

209   Bone, 1987, 9.

210   Although, as John O'Farrell has pointed out, comedy is never sufficient, oppressive leaders from Hitler to (a lesser extent) Thatcher were objects of satire:

> Because 'satire' is what I did, I had always tried to pretend to myself it was a worthy and important pursuit [...]. I had read a book entitled *Wit as Weapon* which described the importance of the Berlin cabaret as a form of opposition to the Nazis in the 1930s. At the back of my mind was a niggling worry. If my historical knowledge served me right, weren't the Nazis in a fairly strong position by the end of the 1930s? (O'Farrell, 1998, 260)

211   Class War, 1991e, 10-12.

212   *Aufheben*, No. 6, 40-41.

213   *Aufheben*, No. 6, 41.

214   *Aufheben*, No. 6, 41-42. See too Red Menace, *Anarchism Exposed* 1986e, 2-3.

215   *Class War* No. 73, 2.

216   Dixon, 1997, 33.

217   'Enemies of the State' talk, 1 in 12 Centre Bradford, May 1, 1998.

218   Yates, 1997, 1.

219   See *Class War* No. 59, 13.

220   Yates, 1997, 4.

221   Red Menace claim that from the start there were diverse political traditions in Class War (Red Menace, 1986e, 2).

222   Even if it means denying people help who require and deserve it (Class War, 1992, 134).

223   Dixon, 1997, 33.

224   Class War sold T-shirts, golf umbrellas, mugs, cigarette lighters, car window stickers, car tax disc holders and badges (*Class War* No. 41, 14).

225   Other publications such as Attack International's *Attack Attack Attack Attack* were intended to be sold at the price customers were choosing to pay, leaving open the possibility that they could be taken for free (*Attack Attack Attack Attack*, 1).

226   *Organise!*, No. 46, 8.

227   American primitivists, such as the collective behind *Fifth Estate*, also use computers for making their magazine. The collective proudly announce that they 'hate it', but seem content that their politics should involve something they despise (for a sympathetic account of *Fifth Estate* see Millett, 2004, 73-97).

228   Shlong, 1994, 11.

229   Davies, 1997, 64.

230   See *Organise!* No. 35, 13-14 and 15-16; *Organise!* No. 36, 17; *Organise!* No. 40, 16-17; *Organise!* No. 41; 16-17; *Organise!* No. 43, 12-13 and 13-15; *Organise!* No. 44, 9-11.

231   Jappe, 1999, 49.

232   Plant, 1992, 86-87.

233   For some examples from the SI see Gray, 1974, 70-71, 89, 108-09 and 152. The SI also included some unaltered excerpts from cartoon strips to highlight their conservative banality through juxtaposition with their own text and illustrations, see Gray, 1974, 27 and 104.

234   Dickinson, 1997, 47.

235   *Attack Attack Attack Attack*, 11, Daniels, 1989; *Class War*, No. 41, 1 and *Class War* No. 64, 1.

236   Kenny, 1988*e*, 17.

237   See, for instance, the car billboard advertisement for the Fiat 127, which used the slogan 'If it were a lady, it would get its bottom pinched'. The chauvinist presumptions (that viewers are male, assault is harmless flattery and that women are passive objects to be fawned upon) are uncovered and ridiculed by the illicit addition: 'If this lady was a car she'd run you down' (see *Crowbar*, No. 48, 3).

238   Plant, 1992, 145 and Rosen, 1997, 103-06.

239   *Class War* No. 73, 5.

240   Situationist International, 1989c, 45.

241   Plant, 1992, 32.

242   Plant, 1992, 20-21.

243   Debord, 1989, 22.

244   Situationist International, 1989b, 43.

245   Situationist International, 1989b, 44.

246   Situationist International, 1989b, 44 and Debord, 1989, 23.

247   Wall, 2000, 63.

248 Plant, 1992, 31.

249 Debord, 1983, para 4.

250 Law, 1993a, 30-31.

251 Orlowski, 1994, 17.

252 Bone, 1997, 9.

253 Home, 1988, 95.

254 Home, 1988, 100.

255 N. and Others, 1997, 15.

256 See N. and Others, 1997, 14.

257 Institute for Social Disengineering, 1994, 70.

258 'Journalists [....] are always trying to make you say something that will support whatever angle they have decided to take' (*Do or Die*, No. 7, 36).

259 Institute of Social Disengineering, 1994, 73.

260 N. and Others, 1997, 15.

261 Class War produced a leaflet arguing against pacifism. The diatribe interested journalists and their editors and was printed in 1994 by Britain's most popular tabloid: 'in effect, the *Sun* just reprinted and distributed four million copies of our leaflet' (*Class War* No. 73, 9).

262 Institute for Social Disengineering, 1994, 76.

263 Institute for Social Disengineering, 1994, 73.

264 Institute of Social Disengineering, 1994, 76.

265 Debord, 1983, para 11.

266 Chomsky, 1993; Herman and Chomsky, 1988.

267 Orlowski, 1994, 18.

268 Porton, 1999, 232. Anarcho-syndicalists such as Dolgoff derided individualist anarchists who glorified the artist above all others: 'half-assessed artists and poets who object to organisation and want to play only with their belly buttons' (Porton, 1999, 235).

269 From No. 50 (1991) to No. 73 (1997) there were 129 letters published in *Class War*. The gender of some correspondents cannot be determined as they were signed with initials (DD), under collective group names (Tyneside Anarchist Group) or had gender neutral given names (Maz). Of those in which a reasonable presumption of gender can be assumed, 68 (89%) were by men and 8 (11%) by women (54 were unclassified, with one letter being signed by two people).

270 Bone, 1997, 9.

271 As Alexandra Skirda describes in his thorough history of anarchist organisation, whilst the early anarcho-syndicalists advocated a diversity of tactics, the creation of revolutionary syndicates was 'the central objective' (Skirda, 2002, 77).

272 Linebaugh, 1993 and Thompson, 1977.

273   Marx, 1967, 167-68.

274   Engels, 1958, 242-43.

275   Linebaugh, 1993, 162 and 168-73.

276   '[We] shall ally ourselves with the intrepid world of brigands, who are the only true revolutionaries in Russia' (Nechaev, 1989, 10, para. 25).

277   See, for instance, Class War's 'No muggers' sticker (reprinted in *Class War* No. 77, 14) and the statement of principles of the ABC.

We will not support:

- Anyone involved in anti-social and oppressive crime, i.e. rape, child abuse, racist attacks, *on that basis alone*:

- Crime which is anti-working class, eg mugging/burgling other working class people, in short robbing your own (*Taking Liberties*, No. 19, 1).

278   New roads bring health risks of 'childhood asthma, glue ear, and skin complaints' all for the sake of the quicker mobilisation of commodities (Welsh and McLeish, 1996, 28 and 36).

279   Aufheben, 1998, 108.

280   Incidents of GM cross-contamination resulting in such problematic features as greater herbicide resistance amongst wild plants has been reported by Sean Poulter in *The Daily Mail* (2005) and by Paul Brown in *The Guardian* (2005); see too *The Guardian* July 26, 2005, 7.

281   Welsh and McLeish, 1996, 36-37.

282   Welsh and McLeish, 1996, 33.

283   Aufheben, 1998, 108.

284   ttack International, *Attack*, 10.

285   *Anarchist Theft* No. 1, 1997e, 9.

286   *Anarchist Theft*, No. 1, 10.

287   Attack International, *Attack*,10.

288   *Class War*, Unnumbered '*The Best Cut of All* edition', 6; See too the graffiti 'Don't mug me, MUG A YUPPIE!!!, MUG A YUPPIE!!!, pictured in Kenny, 1988e, 17.

289   Attack International, *Attack*, 15.

290   Berkman, 1987, 68-69.

291   During the revolution in Spain, liberated areas distributed land under different property arrangements: some opted for collectivisation, others chose more individualist arrangements (Souchy Bauer, 1982, 39). Some adaptations which recreated a wages system were not consistent with anarchist anti-hierarchical precepts (see *Subversion*, unnumbered <No. 12e>, 9-10).

292   Class War, 1992, 109-10.

293   Miller, 1984, 126.

294   Nozick, 1988, 251-52.

295   Kennedy, 1995, 175-76.

296   Attack International, *Attack*, 10.

297   Attack International, *Attack,* 10.

298   Crawfurd, 1991, 4-5.

299   Colin Ward, a supporter of the Freedom Press Group, was involved in the 1946 squatting movement. He points out that the squatters who create the shanty towns in Africa and the Americas are acting in accordance with anarchist principles, but they are not popularly associated with anarchism, unlike the 1960s squatting movement in the United Kingdom (Ward, 1982, 29 and 69-71).

300   Bailey, 1973, 105.

301   See Sam, 1996, 8.

302   Wates and Wolmar, 1980, 36 and 45.

303   Bailey, 1973, 102 and Broad, 1978.

304   Goodman, 1972, 22.

305   See Sam, 1996, 5.

306   Advisory Service for Squatters, 1996, 6.

307   Wates and Wolmar, 1980, 42-43 and Reilly, 1990e, 8.

308   Wates and Wolmar, 1980, 33.

309   *Crowbar* No. 45, 4-7.

310   Begbie, 1996, 71.

311   Angela, 1996, 76, McKay, 1996, 175 and Jackson, 1987, 25.

312   Wates and Wolmar, 1980, 175.

313   *Merseyside Anarchist*, No. 28, 18.

314   Fourier, Saint-Simon and Owen also considered the possibility of building new societies in the body of the existing order. This tactic is also used by some fascist groups. The Aryan Nations and anti-federal state militia in the USA have set up compounds based on the precepts of their own ideologies.

315   *Green Anarchist*, No. 39, Autumn 1995, 24. The editors of *Green Anarchist* advised caution on the grounds of security (the respondents' names were to be published) not because they judged the project to be inappropriate.

316   *Merseyside Anarchist* describes the Crabapple community as being 'firmly middle class in terms of membership' No. 26, April 1991, 12.

317   Vidal, 1996, 3.

318   Monbiot, 1996, 2-3.

319   Monbiot, 1996, 3.

320   *Green Anarchist* No. 38, Summer 1995, 20.

321   Marx, 1967, 110.

322   *Merseyside Anarchist* No. 26, April 1991, 12.

323   Italian autonomists and Israeli anarchists have also stood candidates in elections. These nominees were prisoners who would be released under parliamentary rules if elected. In the case of Toni Negri, who was successfully elected, his immunity was revoked (see Wilson, 1999).

324   *Solidarity* No. 13, Winter 1986-87, 11-12. Other examples of anarchist influenced groupings partaking in electoral activity would include the Bristolian Party in the 2003 and 2004 council elections. Some anarchists were involved with and supported the Independent Working Class Association, which in 2004 had three members elected onto Oxford City Council, and also stood in London's mayoral elections in 2004, winning over 50,000 votes.

325   Coleman, 1987, 93 and SPGB, 1993, 22.

326   Palmer, 1988e, 2.

327   Palmer, 1988e, 2.

328   Bone, 1997, 9.

329   Palmer, 1988e, 2.

330   Bone reports that the *Alarm* candidates fared well, gaining 'an average of 28 per cent of the vote in the wards where we stood' (*Solidarity* No. 13, Winter 86-87, 12). Howard Moss, however, suggests that Bone has embroidered the level of support, although even under Moss's figures they gathered far greater support than most 'lefty groups' (*Solidarity* No. 20, Spring 1989, 16).

331   Challinor, 1977, 44 and Coleman, 1987, 92-94.

332   *Aufheben*, No. 4, Summer 1995, 3.

333   See Best, 1994, 47-50; Best and Kellner, 1991, 117 and Plant, 1992, 153.

334   Baudrillard's article 'The Year 2000 Will Not Take Place', which anticipates his infamous article 'The Gulf War Did Not Take Place', develops this theme of acceleration leading to a diminution, and ultimately evaporation, of consequences (Baudrillard, 1986, 19).

335   Best and Kellner, 1991, 131.

336   Baudrillard, 1983, 46.

337   Q. Decadent Action, *Scotland on Sunday*, August 31, 1997, 9.

338   Best and Kellner, 1991, 131.

339   See the interview with Decadent Action in *Class War* No. 76, 7.

340   Baudrillard, 1987, 19-20.

341   Best and Kellner, 1991, 121.

342   Baudrillard, 1983, 10.

343   Baudrillard, 1983, 12-13.

344   Plant, 1992, vi-vii.

345   Home, 1990, v; Home's description of Art Strike in *Here and Now* is consistent with traditional class struggle anarchism, placing it alongside other

forms of proletarian struggle which create social structures to contest capitalist domination (Home, 1990, v). In the *Art Strike Handbook* and *Art Strike Papers*, the Baudrillardian elements are more explicit (*Art Strike Handbook*, 38).

346   See, for instance, Newman, 2001. Sasha K. (Villon) persuasively argues that Newman overstates the degree to which the classical anarchists were dependent upon a humanist essentialism (Villon, 2005).

347   For instance, Brendt's comment that the 'Art strike has a Zen quality tearing down logic but leaving nothing in its place' (Ball, 1991, 19).

348   Plant, 1992, vii.

349   Baudrillard, 1983, 37-38.

350   *The Independent*, Saturday, June 27, 1998, 2; Morris, 1998, 4; Bird, 2002 and Gray, 2002, 4.

351   *Sunday Mirror*, May 23, 1999, 14 and *The Mirror*, Monday May 24, 1999, 7.

Conclusion

1   Slogan of Mayday 2000.

2   June 18, 1999, November 30, 1999 and Mayday 2000.

3   *The Sun*, May 2, 2000, 1; *The Mirror*, May 2, 2000, 1; *The Daily Express*, May 2, 2000, 1

4   See, for instance, the invitation to 'Name and nail the yobs' with the telephone number of the newspaper and the police's Crimestoppers number printed below the photographs of demonstrators (*The Mirror*, 2.5.00, 4-5), and 'Find these animals', Sullivan, Whitaker and Parker, 2000.

5   For a full list of events see the conference programme *Mayday 2000: anti-capitalist ideas and action*.

6   *Daily Mail*, May 2, 2000, 1.

7   *The Guardian*, April 20, 2000, 13.

8   See, for instance, *The Guardian*, April 20, 2000, 13; *The Sunday Times*, News Review Section, April 31, 2000, 1. Such hysteria has become a feature of all major anarchist demonstrations. The anti-capitalist congregation against the G8 in Edinburgh in July 2005 was met with headlines promising their readers authoritarian suppression of the anarchist threat, see for instance: 'Police prepare to make thousands of arrests at G8 Army barracks to be used as holding camps for violent anarchists who are already finding their way into Britain', *The Sunday Telegraph*, June 12, 2005, 4 and 'Army placed on standby for G8', Chamberlain, 2005.

9   For instance the Nicky Campbell phone-in on BBC Radio Five Live, May 2, 2000, 9.00am-10.00am

10   *Today in Parliament*, BBC Radio 4, 2.5.2000, 11.30pm.

11   Fishman, 1975, 117-18 and 215.

12   BBC News, 'Blair defends anti-terror plans', Friday, 16 September 2005, 08:01 GMT, <http://news.bbc.co.uk/1/hi/uk_politics/4251516.stm>, last accessed September 16, 2005.

Abbreviations and Acronyms

AB – Angry Brigade.
ABC – Anarchist Black Cross.
ACAs – Anarchist Communist Association.
ACDG – Anarchist Communist Discussion Group.
ACF – Anarchist Communist Federation.
AF – Anarchist Federation.
AFB – Anarchist Federation of Britain.
APCF – Anti-Parliamentary Communist Federation.
APTU – Anti-Poll Tax Union.
ATUN – Anarchist Trade Union Network (see too TUNA).
AWA – Anarchist Workers Association.
AWG – Anarchist Workers Group.
AYN – Anarchist Youth Network.
BAIU – British Association of Industrial Unions.
BSP – British Socialist Party.
CAG – Clydeside Anarchist Group.
CND – Campaign for Nuclear Disarmament.
CP – Communist Party.
CWF – Class War Federation.
CWO – Class War Organisation.
DAM – Direct Action Movement.
EF! – Earth First!
F&NSG – Feminist and Nonviolence Study Group
GACF – Glasgow Anarchist Communist Federation.
GAG – Glasgow Anarchist Group.
GA – Green Anarchist.
GAN – Green Anarchist Network.
IDL – Industrial Democracy League.
IN – Industrial Network.
ISEL – Industrial Syndicalist Education League.
IUDA – Industrial Union of Direct Actionists.
IWGB – Industrial Workers of Great Britain.
IWW – Industrial Workers of the World.
KSL – Kate Sharpley Library.

LCG - Libertarian Communist Group.
LCDG – Libertarian Communist Discussion Group.
LDG – Leeds Discussion Group.
LEL – Labour Emancipation League.
NMP –Newham Monitoring Project
NVDA – Non-Violent Direct Action.
ORA – Organisation of Revolutionary Anarchists.
RCP – Revolutionary Communist Party.
RTS – Reclaim the Streets.
SDF – Social Democratic Federation.
SI - Situationist International.
SL – Socialist League.
SLP – Socialist Labour Party.
SolFed – Solidarity Federation.
SPGB – Socialist Party of Great Britain.
SPL – Syndicalist Propaganda League.
SSP – Scottish Socialist Party.
SyF – Syndicalist Fight.
SWF – Syndicalist Workers Federation.
SWP – Socialist Workers Party.
TUNA – Trade Union Network for Anarchists (see ATUN).
WOMBLES – White Overall Movement Building Liberation through Effective Struggles.
WSF – Workers Solidarty Federation.
WRP – Workers Revolutionary Party.
WSM – Workers Solidarity Movement.

Groups by Organisational Structure 1985 - 2002

Group	Organisational Structure	Organisation Theory	Location in the Workplace
A(C)F	Federalist	The Manifesto of Libertarian Communism	None
AWG*	Centralist	The Organisational Platform of the Libertarian Communists (The Platform)	Mixed
AYN+*	Federalist/Network	None	None
CWF	Alternated from Network to Federal to Centralised and back to Federal	Favourable to The Platform	Little
CWO*	Centralist	None	None
Organise (Six Counties)*	Federal	Aims and Principles of the IWA	Main
Freedom	Centralist	None	None
GA	Network	None	None
SolFed/DAM	Federal	Aims and Principles of the IWA	Main but no longer exclusive
Subversion*	Centralist/Federal	None	None
Syndicalist Alliance*	Federal	None	Exclusive
Trade Union Network for Anarchists*	Federal/Network	None	Primary
Workers Solidarity Movement	Federal/Centralised	The Platform	Mixed

Key   * No longer existent   + Post 2000

Bibliography

Guide To Footnotes and Bibliography

In many source materials there is no issue date. In these cases, an estimated date of publication has been given followed by '*e*'. Also, many pieces do not contain pagination. In these cases, to help enable efficient checking of sources, page numbers have been given with the front cover counting as page one. Pseudonyms have only been matched with the authors, either with permission, or when the matter has already been published or otherwise publicly known, such as in an open meeting.

In primary source material, where an author has been given, then the bibliography records the article under that author. Where the article is unsigned, it is credited to the group producing the journal. If the article is anonymous, it is classified under the group publishing it, and where no publisher is recorded, the article is classified under its title. Books are *italicised*, as are pamphlets and magazines.

The National Library of Scotland and the British Library contain many of the texts mentioned in this book; however, a large number of materials are not included in these collections. Highly recommended sources include the Kate Sharpley Library (contact at BM Hurricane, London, WC1 3XX). Copies of many of the cited materials may be found through AK Distribution, A Distribution, Freedom Press, Housmans and Porcupine Bookshops in London. In many cases, but regrettably not all, copies of sources cited in the bibliography are available from the compiler of this bibliography. I am grateful to Mike Craven, Adenike Johnson, David Lamb, Bill Whitehead, Millie Wild and Rowan Wilson for allowing me access to their archives.

Texts have been split into two broad categories. The first 'primary texts' are those written from an avowedly 'anarchist' or anti-state communist perspective. 'Secondary texts', conversely, are commentaries (which may still be compatible with anarchism but were not authorially positioned or generally viewed as promoting anarchism) or texts explicitly espousing a competing viewpoint. In order to assist in finding the anarchist texts which are referred to in this book, I have marked those still in print and available from the AK Press British or American catalogue with an asterix (*), those still in print but only available through other distributors have been indicated by (+), and those which are accessible online are prefixed by (~). Please note that the texts that are currently available may be different editions to those cited in the bibliography. Whilst every effort was made to make this as accurate as possible, texts do go in and out of print, similarly items appear and disappear from the web, plus I mess up from time to time.

Primary Sources

121 Bookshop (1991), *The Glasgow Rent Strikes 1915*, London: 121 Bookshop.

* Ablett, N., Hay, W., Mainwaring, W. and Rees N. (1991e), *The Miners' Next Step*, London: Germinal and Phoenix Press.

* ACAB Press (1990), *Poll Tax Riot*, London: ACAB Press.

Advisory Service for Squatters (1996e), *Squatters Handbook* 10th Edition, London: Advisory Service for Squatters.

Aldred, G. (1943), *Communism: Story of the Communist Party*, Glasgow: The Strickland Press.

_____ (1957), *No Traitors Gait: The autobiography of Guy Aldred*, Glasgow: The Strickland Press.

* Anarchist Communist Federation (1990e), *Anarchism - As We See It*, ACF.

* _____ (1991ea), *Basic Bakunin*, Coventry: Anarchist Communist Editions.

* _____ (1991eb), *The Role of the Revolutionary Organisation*, London: Anarchist Communist Editions.

_____ (1996), 'Anarchist Communism in Britain' in *Organise!* No. 42, Spring 1996.

_____ (1997), *Beyond Resistance: A revolutionary manifesto for the millennium*, Second Edition, London: Anarchist Communist Editions.

_____ (1997ea), *Against Parliament For Anarchy*, London: Anarchist Communist Editions.

_____ (1997eb), *Where There's Brass There's Muck: Ecology and anarchism*, London: Anarchist Communist Editions.

Anarchist Workers Group (1988a), *Founding Statement*, Huddersfield: AWG.

_____ (1988b), *In Place of Compromise*, Huddersfield: AWG.

(1991e), *Anarchist 1992 Yearbook*, London: Phoenix Press.

(1992e), *Anarchist 1993 Yearbook*, London: Phoenix Press.

(1993e), *Anarchist 1994 Yearbook*, London: Phoenix Press.

(1994e), *Anarchist Year Book 1995*, London: Phoenix Press.

(1995e), *Anarchist Year Book 1996*, London: Phoenix Press.

(1996e), *Anarchist Year Book 1997*, London: Phoenix Press.

(1998), *Anarchist Year Book 1998*, London: Phoenix Press.

Anderson, A. and Anderson, M. (1991e), *Why the 'Revolutionaries Have Failed*, Moseley: Splat Collective.

_____ (1998), *The Enemy is Middle Class*, Manchester: Openly Classist.

Andrew (1998), 'Another View From Ireland' in *Conference Report and Personal Accounts of Mayday 1998: Bradford May 1st to 4th 1998*, London: London Mayday Group.

Antiauthoritarian Insurrectionalist International (Promoting Group) (1993), *For an Anti-Authoritarian Insurrectionist International: Proposal for a debate*, London: Elephant Editions/Bratach Dubh.

* (1988), *Anti-Mass Methods of Organisation for Collectives*, Pencader, Wales: CGH Services.

+ Angela (1996), 'Autonomous Centre of Edinburgh' in S. Wakefield, and Grrrt <fish> , eds., *Not For Rent: Conversations with creative activists in the UK*, Amsterdam, The Netherlands: Evil Twin Publications.

Apter, D. and Joll, J. (1971), eds., *Anarchism Today*, London: Macmillan.

Apter, D. (1971), 'The Old Anarchism and the New' in D. Apter and J. Joll, eds., *Anarchism Today*, London: Macmillan.

* Aufheben (1998), 'The politics of anti-road struggle and the struggles of anti-road politics: The case of the No M11 Link Road campaign' in G. McKay, ed., *DiY Culture: Party and Protest in Nineties Britain*, London: Verso.

_____ (1998b), *Dole Autonomy Versus the Re-Imposition of Work: Analysis of the Current Tendency to Workfare in the UK*, Brighton: Aufheben.

Autonomous Plenum of Southern Germany (1987), translated Luke, R. 'Down with Capitalism' in *Class War: The heavy stuff*, No. 1.

Autonomy (1989e), *Socialist Opportunist*, Oxford: Autonomy.

~ Baird, C., Baird, M., Caldwell J., Raeside, B. & Raeside, J. (1994a), 'Anarchism in Scotland: Part 1' in *Scottish Anarchist*, No. 1, 20-22, also available on-line at <http://www.spunk.org/library/groups/gl/sp000136.txt>.

~ _____ (1994b), 'Anarchism in Glasgow Part 2', *Scottish Anarchism*, Number 2, also available on-line at <http://www.spunk.org/library/groups/gl/sp000136.txt>.

Bakunin, M. (1956), translated by Maximoff, G. *The Political Philosophy of Bakunin*, London: Collier Macmillan.

+ _____ (1984), translated by Kenafick, *Marxism, Freedom and the State*, London: Freedom Press.

* _____ (1993e), *Bakunin on Violence: Letter to S. Nechayev*, New York, USA: Anarchist Switchboard.

Baldelli, G. (1971), *Social Anarchism*, Harmondsworth: Penguin.

Ball, E. (1991), 'Just Say No' in Home, S., *Art Strike Papers*, Stirling, Scotland: AK Press.

Barker, J. (1998), Review Article of '*Anarchy in the UK: The Angry Brigade*' in *Transgressions*, No. 4.

Barr, J. (1991e), 'Question Marx', *Heavy Stuff*, No. 4.

* Barrot, J. (1992), {aka Dauve, G.} *Fascism Antifascism*, Sheffield: Pirate Press.

* _____ (2003), 'Critique of the Situationist International' in S. Home, ed., *What is Situationism?: A reader*, Edinburgh, Scotland: AK Press.

* Baumann, B. (1979), *Terror or Love*, London: John Calder.

Bear, P. (1988), *Once Upon A Time There Was A Place Called Notting Hill Gate....,* London: B. M. Blob.

Beckman, M. (1993), *The 43 Group,* London: Centreprise Publications.

* Becky (2001), 'An Italian Job', in One Off Press, ed, *On Fire: The battle of Genoa and the anti-capitalist movement',* npl: One Off Press.

+ Begbie, A. (1996), 'Pollok Free State' in S. Wakefield and Grrrt <fish>, eds., *Not For Rent: Conversations with creative activists in the UK,* Amsterdam, The Netherlands: Evil Twin Publications.

* Berkman, A. (1986), *The Russian Tragedy,* London: Phoenix Press.

* _____ (1987), *ABC of Anarchism,* London: Freedom Press.

* _____ (1989), *The Bolshevik Myth,* London: Pluto Press.

Big Flame (1981e), *Organising to Win,* Liverpool: Big Flame.

_____ (1991), *Sexuality and Fascism,* London: 121 Bookshop.

Black, B. (1997), 'Why Not Take a Holiday?', *Green Anarchist* No. 49/50, Autumn 1997.

+ _____ (1997b), *Anarchy After Leftism,* Columbia, USA: Columbia Alternative Library.

Blob, B. (1982), *Like a Summer With a Thousand July's* (sic), London: B. M. Blob.

BM Makhno (1989e), *Anti Exchange and Mart,* London: BM Makhno.

* Bonanno, A. (1978e), *Critique of Syndicalist Methods: Trade-unionism to anarcho-syndicalism,* Port Glasgow, Scotland: Bratach Dubh.

Bone, I. (1987), 'Intro', *Class War: The Heavy Stuff,* No. 1.

_____ (1988e), 'Why We Hate Yuppies', *Class War the Heavy Stuff,* No. 2.

_____ (1997), 'I Started... So I'll Finish It!', *Animal,* Issue 1 [see too *Smash Hits* No. 1].

* _____ (1999), *Anarchist!,* London: Movement Against the Monarchy.

+ Bone, I., Pullen A. and Scargill, T,. (1991), *Class War: A decade of disorder,* London: Verso.

* Bookchin, M. (1970), *Listen Marxist!,* York: York Anarchist Group.

* _____ (1993), 'Deep Ecology, Anarchosyndicalism and the Future of

Anarchist Thought' in M. Bookchin, et. al., eds., *Deep Ecology and Anarchism: A polemic*, London: Freedom Press.

* _____ (1995), *Social Anarchism or Lifestyle Anarchism: An unbridgeable chasm*, Edinburgh, Scotland: AK Press.

+ _____ (1998), 'Anarchism: Past and present' in H. Ehrlich, ed., *Reinventing Anarchy, Again,* Edinburgh, Scotland: AK Press.

Booth, S. (1993), *City Death*, Camberley: Green Anarchist Books.

_____ (1994), 'The Dogma of Class Denied', *Green Anarchist* No. 34, Spring 1994 (inside says issue No. 33).

_____ (1996), *Into the 1990's* [sic.] *with Green Anarchist*, Camberley: Green Anarchist Books.

Booth, S. (1998), 'The Irrationalists' in *Green Anarchist* No. 51, Spring 1998.

Bradley, Q. (1991), 'Join the Angry Side', *Northern Star* 17 Oct - 24 Oct 1991.

* Brinton, M. (2004*), For Workers' Power*, Edinburgh: AK Press.

Broad, C. (1978), 'Anarchy and the Art of Motor-Cycle Maintenance', *Anarchy* No. 26,

+ Brown, L. S. (1998), 'Beyond Feminism: Anarchism and human freedom' in H. Ehrlich, ed., *Reinventing Anarchy, Again,* Edinburgh, Scotland: AK Press.

Brown, T. (1990), *Syndicalism*, London: Phoenix Press.

* Burns, D. (1992), *Poll Tax Rebellion*, London and Stirling, Scotland: Attack International and AK Press.

* Cardan, P. {Castoriadis} (1975*e*), *Redefining Revolution*, London: Solidarity.

* Carlsson, C. (1990), *Bad Attitude: The 'Processed World' anthology*, London: Verso.

Casey, J. (1990*e*), 'The Seventies' in *The Heavy Stuff* No. 3.

Castoriadis, C. (1969), *Socialism or Barbarism*, London: Solidarity.

+ _____ (1988), translated by David Ames Curtis, *Political and Social Writings, Volume 1: From the critique of bureaucracy to the positive content of socialism*, Minneapolis, USA: University of Minnesota Press.

Causet, C. (1988*e*), 'The End of Anarchism', *Class War: The Heavy Stuff* No. 2.

+ Chomsky, N. (1986), 'The Manufacture of Consent' in D. Roussopoulos, ed., *The Anarchist Papers*, London: Pluto Press

Christie, S. (1980), *The Christie File*, Sanday, Orkney Isles: Cienfuegos Press.

_____ (1983e), *The Investigative Researcher's Handbook*, London: BCM Refract.

* _____ (2004), *Granny Made Me an Anarchist*, London: Scribner.

Christie, S. and Meltzer, A. (1984), *The Floodgates of Anarchy*, London: Kahn and Averill.

* Class War Federation (1991), *This is Class War: An introduction to the Class War Federation* Stirling, Scotland: AK Distribution.

+ _____ (1992), *Unfinished Business...* Stirling, Scotland: AK Press and Class War Federation.

_____ (1999), *21st Century Class War*, London: Class War Federation.

Claudia (1989e), *I, Claudia*, London: Class Whore.

* Cleaver, H. (1979), *Reading Capital Politically*, Brighton: The Harvester Press.

~ _____ (1998), 'The Zapatistas and the International Circulation of Struggle: Lessons suggested and problems raised' at <http://www.eco.utexas.edu/faculty/Cleaver/lessons.html>, last accessed 7, December 2005.

~ _____ (1999), 'Work is STILL the Central Issue!' paper at 'The Labour Debate' conference, Labour Studies Seminar Series, Warwick University, Wednesday 24 February 1999, see too <http://www.eco.utexas.edu/Homepages/Faculty/Cleaver/workiscentralissue.htm>, last accessed 7, December 2005.

* Cohn-Bendit, D. and Cohn-Bendit, G. (1968a), *Obsolete Communism the Left-Wing Alternative*, London: Penguin.

Cohn-Bendit, D. and Sartre, J. (1968b), 'Daniel Cohn-Bendit interviewed by Jean-Paul Sartre' in Savagot, Geismar et. al. (1968), translated by B. Brewster, *The Student Revolt: The activists speak*, London: Panther.

Collectableanorak (1998e), *Collectable anorak: Some thoughts*, Sheffield: Colleactableanorak.

* Cores, G. (1992), *Personal Recollections of the Anarchist Past*, London: Kate Sharpley Library.

Crass (1982), *A Series of Shock Slogans and Mindless Token Tantrums*, London: Existencil Press (issued with *Christ - The Album*).

Crawfurd, H. (1991), 'Helen Crawfurd's Account' in 121 Bookshop (1991), *The Glasgow Rent Strike*, London: 121 Bookshop.

Cunningham, R. (1995), *Red and Black Revolution*, No. 2, 1995-6.

* Dalla Costa, M. and James, S. (1975), *The Power of Women and the Subversion of the Community*, Bristol: Falling Wall.

* Daniels, J. (1989), *Breaking Free*, London: Attack International.

* Dauve, G. (1997a), {aka Barrot, J.}, 'Capitalism and Communism' in Dauve, G. and Martin, F. (1997), *The Eclipse and Re-Emergence of the Communist Movement*, London: Antagonism Press.

* _____ (1997b), 'Leninism and the Ultra-Left' in Dauve, G. and Martin, F. (1997), *The Eclipse and Re-Emergence of the Communist Movement*, London: Antagonism Press.

Dauve, G. (1999e), *When Insurrectionists Die*, London: Antagonism Press.

* Dauve, G. and Martin, F. (1997), *The Eclipse and Re-Emergence of the Communist Movement*, London: Antagonism Press.

* de Angelis, M. (2001), 'From Movement to Society' in One Off Press, ed, *On Fire: The battle of Genoa and the anti-capitalist movement'*, npl: One Off Press.

* Debord, G. (1983), *Society of the Spectacle*, Detroit, USA: Red and Black.

* _____ (1989), 'Report on the Construction of Situations and on the International Situationist Tendency's Conditions of Organisation and Creation' in K. Knabb, ed., *Situationist International Anthology*, Berkeley, USA: Bureau of Public Secrets.

* Debord, G. and Wolman, G. (1989), 'Methods of Detournement' in K. Knabb, ed., *Situationist International Anthology*, Berkeley, USA: Bureau of Public Secrets.

Direct Action Movement (1980e), *Direct Action in Industry*, Manchester: DAM-IWA.

_____ (1984), *Strike Action*, London: DAM-IWA and Dark Star.

* _____ (1991), *Winning the Class War: An anarcho-syndicalist strategy*, Manchester: DAM-IWA .

Dixon, W. (1997), 'Obituary: Class War', *Radical Chains*, No. 5.

* Do or Die! (2003), 'Down with Empire! Up with Spring!' in *Do or Die* No. 10.

Dolgoff, S. (1989e), *A Critique of Marxism*, Minneapolis, USA: Soil of Liberty.

Douglass, D. (1991), *Refracted Perspective: The left, working class trade unionism and the miners*, London: 121 Bookshop/Anarchist Centre.

_____ (1992e), *Coal Communities in Conflict: 'Heavy Stuff' special Edition*, npl: Class War.

* _____ (1999), *All Power to the Imagination- Revolutionary class struggle in the trade unions and the petty bourgeois fetish of organisational purity*, London: Class War.

Drake, B. (1993), *Poor Lenin: Extracts from 'The Communist Technique in Britain'*, Leeds: Irate Press.

+ Ehrlich, C. (1981), 'The Unhappy Marriage of Marxism and Feminism: Can it be saved' in l. Sargent, ed., *Women And Revolution: A discussion of the unhappy marriage of marxism and feminism*, Quebec, Canada: Black Rose.

+ _____ (1998), 'Socialism, Anarchism, and Feminism' in H. Ehrlich, ed., *Reinventing Anarchy, Again*, Edinburgh, Scotland: AK Press.

+ Ehrlich, H. (1998), 'Anarchism and Formal Organisation' in H. Ehrlich, ed., *Reinventing Anarchy, Again,* Edinburgh, Scotland: AK Press.

Eigol, R. (1994), 'Smash the Shitbags!' in *Green Anarchist*, No. 36, Winter 1994.

Evans, K. (2000), *Some Simple Questions Mr Straw*, Sheffield: Kate Evans.

Everett (1992e), *A Short History of Political Violence*, npl <Londone>, npb <ACFe> (see *Organise!* No. 29, 14).

Fabbri, L. (1987), translated by C. Bufe, *Bourgeois Influences on Anarchism*, San Francisco, USA: Arcata Press.

Flood, A. (1994), 'The Left (part 1): Ashes to Phoenix?', *Red and Black Revolution*, No. 1.

* Flynn, E. (1993), *Sabotage: The conscious withdrawal of the workers efficiency* London: Pentagon b.

Fontenis, G. (1991), *Manifesto of Libertarian Communism*, London: Anarchist Communist Editions.

Fortunati, L., (1995), translated by H. Creek, *The Arcane of Reproduction: Housework, prostitution, labor and capital*, Brooklyn, USA: Autonomedia

~ Fox, N. (1989), 'Anarchism in the Thatcher Years', *Socialism From Below*, Volume 1, No. 1, available online at: <http://flag.blackened. net/revolt/awg/awg_thatcher1.html>.

* Freeman, J. (1984), 'The Tyranny of Structurelessness' in *Untying the Knot: Feminism, anarchism and organisation*, London: Dark Star and Rebel Press.

* Gambone, L. (1995), *Syndicalism in Myth and Reality*, npl: Red Lion Press.

Goldman, E. (1969), *Anarchism and Other Essays*, New York, USA: Dover.

Gombin, R. (1971), 'The Ideology and Practice of Contestation Seen Through Recent Events in France' in D. Apter and J. Joll, eds., *Anarchism Today*, London: Macmillan.

Gorter, H. (1978), 'The Organisation of the Proletariat's Class Struggle' in D. Smart, ed., *Pannekoek's and Gorter's Marxism*, London: Pluto Press.

~ Gorter, H. (1989), *Open Letter to Comrade Lenin*, London: Wildcat: <http://www.left-dis.nl/uk/open0.htm>.

+ Graham, R. (1996), 'The Anarchist Contract' in H. Ehrlich, ed., *Reinventing Anarchy, Again*, Edinburgh, Scotland: AK Press.

+ Gray, C. (1974), ed., *Leaving the 20th Century: The incomplete work of the Situationist International*, Brussels, Belgium: Free Fall.

+ Goaman, K. (2004), 'The Anarchist Travelling Circus: Reflections on contemporary anarchism, anti-capitalism and the international scene' in J. Purkis, and J. Bowen, eds., *Changing Anarchism: Anarchist theory and practice in a global age*, Manchester: Manchester University Press, 163-180.

Green Anarchist (1992), *Contacts Briefing*, npl: npb <available through Oxford Green Anarchist>.

Guerin, D. (1970), translated by Mary Klopper, *Anarchism*, New York, USA: Monthly Review Press.

+ Hardt, M. and Negri, T. (2001), *Empire*, London: Harvard University Press.

Hart, L. (1997), 'In Defence of Radical Direct Action: Reflections on civil disobedience, sabotage and nonviolence' in J. Purkis and J. Bowen, eds., *Twenty-First Century Anarchism: Unorthodox ideas for a new millennium*, London: Cassell.

~ Harvey, D. (1997), 'Alienation, Class And Enclosure in UK Universities', <http://lists.village.virginia.edu/listservs/spoons/ aut-op-sy.archive/papers/harvie.alienation> also in (2000) *Capital and Class*, No. 71.

+ Herman, E. and Chomsky, N. (1988), *Manufacturing Consent: The political economy of the mass media*, New York, USA: Pantheon Books.

* Hoffman, A. (1971), *Steal This Book*, London: Four Walls Eight Windows.

Holman, C. (1989), 'Party or Class?', *Socialism from Below* Vol. 1, No. 1 .

Home, S. (1990), 'On the Art Strike' in *Art/Anti-Art Supplement, Here and Now*, No. 10.

Homocult (1996), see Splat Collective (1996).

Hungry Brigade (1997), *What Do We Want?*, npl: Hungry Brigade.

Hutchings, J. (1998), 'How do we organise?', *Black Flag* issue 213.

I. [Bristol] (1998), 'Alarm Calling!', *Smash Hits* No. 3.

Imrie, D. (1995), 'The "Illegalists"', *Anarchy: A Journal of Desire Armed*, No. 41, Vol. 14, No. 3, Winter 1995.

* Institute of Social Disengineering at Oxfin (1994), *Test Card F: Television, mythinformation and social control*, Edinburgh: AK Press.

Jackson, F. (1987), *Squatting in West Berlin*, London: Hooligan Press.

Jacobs, M. (1995), translated by Doug Imrie, '"Why I Became A Burgular": Marius Jacobs' last words to the court', *Anarchy: A journal of desire armed*, No. 41, Vol. 14, No. 3, Winter 1995.

Jennings (1994), 'Corrupting Left Intellectual Culture', *Here and Now*, No. 15.

* Jones, B. (1991), *Left-Wing Communism in Britain 1917-21: An infantile disorder?*, Sheffield: Pirate Press and Black Star.

Kate Sharpley Library (1983e), *Kate Sharpley Library*, London: Kate Sharpley Library.

Kendall, W. (1969), *The Revolutionary Movement in Britain*, London: Wiedenfield and Nicolson.

Kenny, S. (1988e), 'Culture Class and Politics' in *Class War: The Heavy Stuff*, No. 2.

Kerr, G. (1998-9), 'Hobson's Choice: The "Good Friday Agreement" and the left' in *Red and Black Revolution: A magazine of libertarian communism*, No. 4, 1998-9.

K. H. (1986), 'Riots and their Respondents' in *Here and Now* No.3, Spring 1986.

* Khayati, M. (1989), 'Captive Words: Preface to a situationist dictionary' in K. Knabb, ed., *Situationist International Anthology*, California, USA: Bureau of Public Secrets.

Kimmerman, L. and Perry, L. (1966), *Patterns of Anarchy: A collection of writings on the anarchist tradition,* New York, USA: Doubleday and Company.

* Knabb, K. (1989), ed. and trans, *Situationist International Anthology*, California, USA: Bureau of Public Secrets.

Kolinko-Agents and Friends (2002), *Hotlines: Call centre inquiry, communism*, Oberhausen, Germany: Kolinko.

Komboa Ervin, L. (1993), *Anarchism and the Black Revolution*, Second Edition, npl: npb (the first edition was produced by the North American Anarchist Black Cross).

Komboa Ervin, L., Abron, J., et. al. (2002), 'Black Autonomy: Civil rights, the Black Panthers and today' in *Do or Die*, No. 9.

+ Kornegger, P. (1998), 'Anarchism: the feminist connection' in H. Ehrlich, ed., *Reinventing Anarchy, Again,* Edinburgh, Scotland: AK Press.

Krimerman, L. and Perry, L. (1966), eds., *Patterns of Anarchy*, Doubleday-Anchor.

* Kropotkin, P. (1939), *Mutual Aid*, Penguin Books.

Kropotkin, P. (1970), *Kropotkin's Revolutionary Pamphlets*, New York, USA: Dover Publications.

* _____ (1972), *The Conquest of Bread*, London: Penguin Books.

+ _____ (1992), translated by L. Friedland and J. Piroshnikoff, *Ethics: Origin and Development*, Montreal, Canada: Black Rose Books.

_____ (1997e), 'Syndicalism and Anarchism', *Black Flag* Issue 210.

~ Lamb, D. (1977e), *Mutinies: 1917 - 1920*, London and Oxford: Solidarity (London) and Solidarity (Oxford), available online at <http://www.geocities.com/cordobakaf/mutinies.html>.

_____ (1995), 'Introduction' to Gurley Flynn, E. *Sabotage: The conscious withdrawal of the workers' efficiency*, London: Pentagon.

~ _____ (1997), 'Libertarian Socialism: Means and Ends', *Animal* Issue 1, available online at: <http://www.geocities.com/CapitolHill/Lobby/2379/lamb.htm>.

* Law, L. (1983), *More of the Shame*, London: Spectacular Times.

* _____ (1983), *The Bad Days Will End*, London: Spectacular Times.

* _____ (1989e), *Cities of Illusion*, London: Sepectacular Times.

* _____ (1993a), *Images and Everyday Life*, London: Spectacular Times.

* _____ (1993b), *The Media*, London: Spectacular Times.

* Levine, C. (1984), 'The Tyranny of Tyranny' in J. Freeman and C. Levine, *Untying the Knot: Feminism, anarchism and organisation*, London: Dark Star and Rebel Press.

Lipman, M. (1980), *Memoirs of a Socialist Businessman*, London: Lipman Trust.

London Mayday Group (1998), *Conference Report and Personal Accounts of Mayday 1998 Bradford May 1st to 4th 1998*, London: London Mayday Group.

Longmore, C. (1985), *The IWA Today*, London: DAM-IWA .

Luton, D. (1987), 'World Economics', *Class War: The heavy stuff*, No. 1.

* McKay, G. (1996a), Senseless Acts of Beauty: Cultures of resistance since the Sixties, London: Verso.

_____ (1996b), 'Is that anarchy I see going on in the seminar room', *New Statesman*, 30 August, 1996.

* _____ (1998), 'DiY Culture: Notes towards an intro' in G. McKay, ed., *DiY Culture: Party and protest in nineties Britain*, London: Verso.

~ Makhno, N., Mett, I., Archinov, P. et. al. (1989), *Organisational Platform of the Libertarian Communists*, Dublin, Ireland: Workers Solidarity Movement, available online at <http://flag.blackened.net/revolt/platform/plat_preface.html>.

* Martin, F. (1997), 'The Class Struggle and its Most Characteristic Aspects in Recent Years' in G. Dauve and F. Martin, eds., *The Eclipse and Re-Emergence of the Communist Movement*, London: Antagonism Press.

(2000), *Mayday 2000: Anti-capitalist ideas and action: Conference programme*, London: npb.

* McCartney, W. (1992e), *Dare to be a Daniel! A history of one of Britain's earliest syndicalist unions 38 Strikes Fought - 38 Won! The life and struggles of an agitator and the fight to free the catering slaves of the West End of London (1910-1914)*, London: Kate Sharpley Library.

McFarlane, J. (1986/7), 'The Demise of the Class Object' in *Here and Now*, No. 4, 1986/7.

McNaughton, E. (1988e), *Wapping: The story of a year of struggle*, npl: npb.

Meltzer, A. (1976a), *The Anarchists in London: 1935 - 1955*, Sanday, Orkney Islands: Cienfuegos Press, 1976.

_____ (1976b), *The International Revolutionary Solidarity Movement: A study of the origins and development of the revolutionary anarchist movement in Europe 1945 - 1973 with particular reference to the First of May Group*, Sanday, Orkney Islands: Cienfuegos Press.

* _____ (1986), *Anarchism: Arguments for and against*, London: Black Flag.

* _____ (1992e), *First Flight: The Origins of Anarcho-Syndicalism in Britain*, London: Kate Sharpley Library.

_____ (1996a), 'Red, Black and Green' in *Direct Action*, No. 1, Autumn 1996.

* _____ (1996b), *I Couldn't Paint Golden Angels: Sixty years of commonplace life and anarchist agitation*, Edinburgh, Scotland: AK Press.

+ Merrick (1997), *Battle for the Trees*, London: Godhaven Ink.

Monatte, P. (1980), 'Syndicalism an Advocacy' in G. Woodcock, ed., *The Anarchist Reader*, Glasgow, Scotland: Fontana/Collins.

Morris, R. (1992), 'More than a 24 hour virus' in *Socialism from Below Election Special*, London: AWG.

N and others (1997), 'A Short Rant in Response!', *Smash Hits: A discussion bulletin for revolutionary ideas*, October 1997.

N, B.M. Combustion (1997), 'What's it Forum', *Smash Hits: A discussion bulletin for revolutionary ideas*, October 1997.

Narodnik (1918), 'The Social Significance of the Russian Revolution' *The Spur*, Vol. III, No. 2, January-February, 1918.

* Nechayev, S. (1989), *Catechism of the Revolutionist*, Violette Nozieres Press and Active Distribution.

~ Negation (1975), translated P. Rachleff and A. Wallach, *Lip and the Self-Managed Counter-Revolution*, Detroit, USA: Black and Red, available online at: <http://www.geocities.com/~johngray/lip.htm>.

~ Negri, T. (1979), translated by Red Notes, 'Capitalist Domination and Working Class Sabotage' in Red Notes, ed., *Working Class Autonomy and the Crisis: Italian Marxist texts of the theory and practice of a class movement*, London: Red Notes and Conference of Socialist Economists Book Club, available at: <http://www. geocities.com/cordobakaf/negri_sabotage.html>, last accessed 8 December, 2005.

* Nicoll, D. (1992), *Life in English Prisons (100 years ago)*, London: Kate Sharpley Library.

Nottingham Anarchist News (1988), *One Step Beyond: Or smash the Revolutionary Communist Party*, npl <Londone>, Pirate Press and Phoenix Press.

(1983e), *Oh Dear, Not Again*, npl: Serendipity.

O'Hara, L. (1993), *A Lie Too Far: 'Searchlight', Hepple and the left*, London: Mina Enterprises.

* One Off Press (2001), *On Fire: The battle of Genoa and the anti-capitalist movement*, npl: One Off.

Otter, L. (1971), *Theory and Praxis in Anarchist Organisation*, Heslington: Organisation of Revolutionary Anarchists.

Palmer, T. (1988e), 'Introduction: The Kensington By-Election', *Class War: The heavy stuff*, No. 2.

Pannekoek, A. (1978a), 'Marxist Theory and Revolutionary Tactics' in D. Smart, ed., *Pannekoek's and Gorter's Marxism*, London: Pluto Press.

_____ (1978b), 'World Revolution and Communist Tactics' in D. Smart, ed., *Pannekoek's and Gorter's Marxism*, London: Pluto Press.

_____ (1978c), 'Afterword to World Revolution and Communist Tactics' in D. Smart, ed., *Pannekoek's and Gorter's Marxism*, London: Pluto Press.

Parker, S. (1980), 'Anarchism and the Proletarian Myth', *Freedom: anarchist review*, 26 April 1980, Vol. 41, No. 8.

Paul, Liverpool DAM (1991), 'Rewriting History: The politics of the AWG', *Merseyside Anarchist Newsletter* No. 28, June 1991.

+ Peacock , A.(1999), *Two Hundred Pharaohs Five Billion Slaves*, London: Reknaw / Repetitive Fame Injury Press.

Pelaez, E. and Holloway, J. (1996), 'The Dialogue of San Cristobal', *Common Sense* No. 20.

Pengham, A. (1987), 'Anarcho-Communism' in M. Rubel and J. Crump, eds., *Non-Market Socialism in the Nineteenth and Twentieth Centuries*, Basingstoke: MacMillan.

Peters, M. (1995/6), '"A Posthumous Fame"?', *Here and Now: Guy Debord Supplement* in *Here and Now* No. 16/17.

Plant, S. (1990), 'When Blowing the Strike is Striking the Blow' in *Art/Anti-Art Supplement, Here and Now*, No. 10.

Platania, F. (1979), '23 Years at FIAT' translated by Red Notes, in Red Notes, ed., *Working Class Autonomy and the Crisis: Italian Marxist texts of the theory and practice of a class movement*, London: Red Notes and Conference of Socialist Economists Book Club.

PNR (1992), *Green Anarchism: Its origins and influences*, Camberley: Alder Valley @'s

Proletarian Gob (1993), *Anarchist Communism or Death! What is Class Struggle Anarchist Communism,* London: BM Makhno.

+ Proudhon, P. (1994), *What is Property?*, Cambridge: Cambridge University Press.

* Pugh, J. (2000), *Working Class First!,* Anti-Capitalist Debate Press.

+ Purkis, J. and Bowen, J. (1997), *Twenty-First Century Anarchism: Unorthodox ideas for a new millennium*, London: Cassell.

* _____ (2004), *Changing Anarchism: Anarchist theory and practice in a global age*, Manchester: Manchester University Press.

Raf (1986/7), 'Letters: Riots crossfire' in *Here and Now* No. 4, Winter 1986/7.

(1986), *Rebel Violence V. Hierarchical Violence: A chronology of anti-hierarchical violence in mainland UK, July 1985 - May 1986*, npl, npb (*AK Distribution 1993 Catalogue* accredit it to Combustion).

Red Menace (1986e), *Anarchism Exposed!*, London: Red Menace.

Red Notes (1979), ed., *Working Class Autonomy and the Crisis: Italian Marxist texts of the theory and practice of a class movement*, London: Red Notes and Conference of Socialist Economists Book Club.

Reknaw / Repetitive Fame Injury Press, see Peacock, A.

Reid, J. and Savage, J. (1987), *The Incomplete Works of Jamie Reid*, London: Faber and Faber.

Reilley, S. (1990e), 'The Middle Class', *Class War: The heavy stuff* No. 3.

Rhys, G. (1988e), 'Class War's Rough Guide to the Left', *Class War: The heavy stuff* No. 2.

* Richards, V. (1989), *The Left and World War II: Selections from the anarchist journal 'War Commentary' 1939-1943*, London: Freedom Press.

* Rimbaud, P. (1998), (aka Ratter, J.), *Shibboleth My Revolting Life*, Edinburgh, Scotland: AK Press.

~ Robinson, A. and Tormey, S. (2003), 'New Labour's neoliberal *Gleichschaltung*: The case of higher education', *The Commoner*. No.7. Spring/Summer, 2003, <http://homepage.ntlworld.com/simon.tormey/articles/New%20Labour%20HE%20White%20Paper.pdf>, last accessed, 15 July, 2005.

* Rocker, R. (1990e), *Anarcho-Syndicalism*, London: Phoenix Press.

_____ (1956), translated by Joseph Leftwick, *London Years*, London: Robert Anscombe and Co. Ltd/Rudolf Rocker Book Committee.

Rooum, D. (1986), 'Anarchism is About Individuals' in Freedom Press (1986), *Freedom A Hundred Years: October 1886 to October 1986*, London: Freedom Press.

* _____ (1992), *What is Anarchism? An introduction*, London: Freedom Press.

Rosen, P. (1997), '"It was easy, it was cheap, go do it!" Technology and Anarchy in the UK Music Industry' in J. Pukis and J. Bowen, eds., *Twenty-First Century Anarchism: Unorthodox ideas for a new millennium*, London: Cassell.

+ Roussopoulos , D. ed. (1986), *The Anarchist Papers*, Montreal, Canada: Black Rose Books.

Ryan, S. (1987), 'Politics and Its Relation to the Masses' in *Class War: The heavy stuff* No. 1.

S. (1998), 'The Problem is You', *Smash Hits* No. 3.

+ Sam (1996), '*Squall* Magazine, London' in S. Wakefield and Grrrt <fish>, eds., *Not For Rent: Conversations with creative activists in the UK*, Amsterdam, The Netherlands: Evil Twin Publications.

* Sanguinetti, F. (1982), translated by l. Forsyth and M. Prigent, *On Terrorism and the State*, London: Chronos.

Scott, S. and Dawson, T. (1993), *Which Way Forward for the Working Class?*, Bradford: Workers' Council Publications.

~ SDEF! (1999), 'Give Up Activism' in *Reflections on June 18*, npl: npb, see too <http://www.geocities.com/kk_abacus/ioaa/guactivism.html>.

Shlong, H (1994), 'Fuck the Media? Fuck the Mediators!' in *Green Anarchist* No. 36, Winter 1994.

Simon, H. (1998), 'Liverpool Dockers' Dispute' in *Collective Action Notes*, No. 14/15

Situationist International, (1974), edited and translated by C. Gray, *Leaving the 20th Century: The incomplete work of the Situationist International*, Brussels, Belgium: Free Fall.

* _____ (1989a), 'Six Postscripts to the Previous Issue' in K. Knabb, ed., *Situationist International Anthology*, Berkeley, USA: Bureau of Public Secrets.

* _____ (1989b), 'Preliminary Problems in Constructing a Situation' in K. Knabb, ed., *Situationist International Anthology*, Berkeley, USA: Bureau of Public Secrets

* _____ (1989c), 'Definitions' in K. Knabb, ed., *Situationist International Anthology*, Berkeley, USA: Bureau of Public Secrets.

Smart, D. (1978), ed., *Pannekoek's and Gorter's Marxism*, London: Pluto Press.

~ Solidarity (1986), *Paris: May 1968*, London: Dark Star Press and Rebel Press, available online at: <http://flag.blackened.net/revolt/disband/solidarity/may68.html>.

Solidarity Federation (1995e), *Solidarity Federation: Powerless? Frustrated? Angry? - An outline of our ideas about organisation and what we are fighting for today*, Manchester: Solidarity Federation - International Workers' Association.

_____ (1998), *SolFed: An introduction to Solidarity Federation*, Manchester: Solidarity Federation.

+ Sorel, G. (1967), translated by T. Hume and J. Roth, *Reflections on Violence*, London: Collier-Macmillan.

Splat Collective (1996), *Educating Who About What: The circled 'A' and its parasites*, Manchester: Black Economy Books.

_____ (1998), 'Critique of the Final Issue of Class War', *Smash Hits* No. 2.

* Sprouse, M. (1992), ed., *Sabotage in the American Workplace: Anecdotes of dissatisfaction, mischief and revenge*, San Francisco, USA and Edinburgh, Scotland: Pressure Drop Press and AK Press.

Stafford, D. (1971), 'Anarchists in Britain Today' in D. Apter and J. Joll, eds., *Anarchism Today*, London: Macmillan.

Stirner, M. (1993), *The Ego and Its Own: The case of the individual against authority*, London: Rebel Press.

Subversion (1993e), *Labouring in Vain*, Manchester: Subversion.

* Tommy (2001), 'Trots and Liberals' in One Off Press, *On Fire: The battle of Genoa and the anti-capitalist movement*, npl: One Off Press.

+ Szerszynski, B. & Tomalin, E. (2004), 'Enchantment and its Uses: Religion and spirituality in environmental direct action', in J. Purkis and J. Bowen, eds., *Changing Anarchism: Anarchist theory and practice in a global age*, Manchester: Manchester University Press.

+ Trautmann, F. (1980), *The Voice of Terror: A biography of Johann Most*, London: Greenwood Press.

Tronti, M. (1979), translated by Red Notes, 'The Strategy of Refusal' in Red Notes, ed., *Working Class Autonomy and the Crisis: Italian Marxist texts of the theory and practice of a class movement*, London: Red Notes and Conference of Socialist Economists Book Club.

Trotwatch (1992), *Trotwatch: An anarchist commentary on the left*, Nottingham: Trotwatch.

_____ (1993), *Carry on Recruiting!: Why the Socialist Workers Party dumped the 'downturn' in a 'dash for growth' and other party pieces*, Nottingham and Edinburgh, Scotland: Trotwatch and AK Press.

Turner, E. (1993e), 'Revolution as Merchandise' in *Here and Now*, No. 13.

(1992), *Urban Attack: A primer for direct action*, npl: Really Fucking Angry Books.

* Vaneigem, R. (1983), *The Revolution of Everyday Life*, London: Rebel Press.

* Ward, C. (1982), *Anarchy in Action*, London: Freedom.

* _ _ (1987), *A Decade of Anarchy 1961-1970*, London: Freedom Press.

Warne, N. (1991), 'Language and Power', *Heavy Stuff*, No. 4.

Wedling, J. (1997), 'History of the Black Flag', *Fifth Estate*, Vol. 32, No. 1 (349), Summer 1997.

~ Weller, K. (1973e), *The Lordstown Struggle and the Real Crisis in Production*, London: Solidarity. See too <http://www.af-north.org/lordstown.html>, last accessed August 25, 2005.

Weller, K. (1992), 'The Ken Weller Interview' in *Flux,* No. 5, Autumn, 7-11.

Welsh, I. and McLeish (1996), 'The European Road to Nowhere: Anarchism and direct action against the UK roads programme' in *Anarchist Studies* Vol. 4, No. 1, March 1996.

Welsh Socialists (1996), *Extreme Democracy: We are the Welsh Socialists*, Wrecsam (Wrexham), Wales: The Welsh Socialists.

Weir, J. (1985), *The Angry Brigade 1967-1984: Documents and chronology*, London: Elephant Editions.

~ White, J. (1990), 'Anarchist Organisation: The next step' in *Socialism from Below* Vol. 1, No.2, available online at: <http://flag.blackened.net/revolt/awg/anar_org_2.html>, last accessed 8 December, 2005.

White, J. (1991), 'No Justice - No Peace! Why the Peace Movement Failed' in *Socialism from Below* Vol. 1, No. 4.

_____ (1992), 'Breaking the New Consensus' in *Socialism from Below Election Special*, London: AWG.

White, J. and Gordon, M. (1991), 'After the Peace Dividend, It's War as Usual' in *Socialism from Below* Vol. 1, No. 3.

White, J. R. (1998), *The Meaning of Anarchism*, Belfast, Northern Ireland: Organise! The Voice of Anarcho-Syndicalism.

Wildcat (1986e), *How Socialist is the Socialist Workers Party?*, Manchester: Wildcat.

_____ (1992), *Outside and Against the Unions: A communist response to Dave Douglass' text "Refracted Perspectives"*, London: Wildcat.

* Wise, D. and Wise, S. (1996), 'The End of Music' in S. Home, ed., *What is Situationism?: A reader*, Edinburgh, Scotland: AK Press.

* Woodcock, G. (1980), ed., *The Anarchist Reader*, Glasgow: Fontana/Collins.

Workers Playtime (nd), *The Playtime Omnibus: A miscellany for young people compiled by The Workers Playtime Group*, London: Phoenix Press.

Workers Solidarity Movement (1992), *Ireland and British Imperialism*, Dublin, Ireland: Workers Solidarity Movement.

_____ (2005), 'Call this choice?', <http://flag.blackened.net/revolt/wsm/election/ callthischoice.html>, last accessed October 4, 2005.

+ Zerzen, J. (1994), *Future Primitive: And other essays*, Columbia, USA: Autonomedia.

Anarchist Magazines and Newspapers Consulted

(issues included where known)

Alternative Green (No. 3).

The Anarchist: A Revolutionary Review (1885).

Anarchist Black Cross Bulletin (Nos. 2-6, 9).

Anarchist Lancaster Bomber (Nos. 8-10).

Anarchist Theft (No. 1).

Animal (Nos. 1-4).

Attack, Attack, Attack, Attack: The Voice of Respectable Moderation (1988e).

Aufheben (Nos. 1-13).

Bad Attitude (Nos. 5-6).

Big Flame (No. 92).

Black and Green (2/3, 1981/2).

Black Flag (newspaper) (Nos. 164, 167, 171, 178, 190-02, 194).

Black Flag (magazine) (Vol. III Nos. 9-10, 1974, Volume VII 5D, No. 10, 202-22).

Black Flag Quarterly (Volume VII, Nos. 4-5).

Bread and Roses (No. 2).

Catalyst (No. 1, Winter 1987/88).

Class War (some early editions undated and unnumbered, 17, 19, 28-73)

Class War (Nos. 74-88) (editions of the provisional faction).

Class War: The Heavy Stuff (Nos. 1-5).

Class Whore (unnumbered, undated <1987e>).

Contra Flow (various between September 1993-August/September 1995 and Nos. 20-24).

Counter Information (Nos. 33, 35-36, 42, 44, 47-49).

Crowbar: Squatting news (Nos. 45, 48).

Der Arbeiter Fraint (various 1885-1921).

Direct Action (Nos. 19, 22, 36, 32-33, 39, 43, 50-51, 57, 74-80) (newspaper).

Direct Action (Nos. 1-29) (magazine).

Dissent (No. 1).

Do or Die: Voices from Earth First! (Nos. 1-10).

Earth First! Action Update Issue 52, October 1998.

East Midlands Anarchist Bulletin (various).

Education Worker (Nos. 2-3) (magazine).

Education Worker (No. 5) (newspaper).

East Midlands Anarchist Bulletin (No. 43).

Evading Standards (various 1997-9).

Fighting Talk: Bulletin of Anarchists in the Unions (No. 1).

Freedom (various 1886-1918).

Freedom (various 1979-96).

Flux (Nos. 1-6).

Green Anarchist (Nos. 26, 29-31) (magazine).

Green Anarchist (Nos. 32-51) (newspaper).

The Guillotine (Nos. 1-2).

Hate Mail

Here and Now (Nos. 1, 3-4, 9-18).

Insurrection (No. 3) (newspaper).

Insurrection (Nos. 4 May 1988, 5 Autumn 1988) (magazine).

Liberation: Paper of the Anarchist Communist Federation (No. 2).

London Calling.

London Resistance.

Merseyside Anarchist (Nos. 17-26).

Nottingham Anarchist News (No. 20, 1989).

Organise!: For Class Struggle Anarchism (Nos. 15-60) (see *Virus*).

Pink Pauper.

Public Service Workers' Network (Nos. 6-7, Spring - Autumn 1995).

Proletarian Gob (Nos. 1-6).

Radical Chains (Nos. 2-5).

The Red Menace (Nos. 1-3).

Resistance (various from 1-49).

Scottish Anarchist (No.s 1-3).

SchNEWS (Vol 1. No. 3 and Nos. 10, 11, 13, 14, 17, 19, 20, plus email editions 1998-2006).

The Spur (1917-19).

Socialism from Below (Nos. 1-4).

Solidarity (various).

Swansea Angry Side (nd, un 1987e).

Smash Hits: A discussion bulletin for revolutionary ideas (1-3).

Stateless: Quarterly review of the North East Anarchist Federation (Vol. 1, No. 1).

Subversion (Nos. 1, 6-20).

Taking Liberties (Nos. 4-5, 9-13) (magazine).

Taking Liberties (Nos. 15-20) (newspaper).

Trotwatch (1).

Variant (various)

Vague (Nos. 20-23).

Virus (Nos. 1, 3, 5, 7, 11-13).

Where's My giro? Newsletter of Brighton Against Benefit Cuts (No. 2).

Wildcat (4-5, 8, 10-3, 15-18).

Workers Solidarity (Nos. 29-30, 34-41) (magazine).

Workers Solidarity (Nos. 42-51) (newspaper).

Xtra!: The paper of the armchair terrorist (Nos. 3-6).

Other Socialist Papers Consulted

Black Dwarf.
Militant.
Morning Star.
Now That's What I Call Marxism.
Red Action.
Red Mole.
Revolution.
Socialist Review.
Socialist Standard.
Socialist Worker.
Weekly Worker (CPGB).
Workers' Hammer.

Workers' Revolution.

Workers' Vanguard.

World Revolution.

Others

Dockers Charter (Nos. 12, 14-15).

The Miner (1983-85).

Theses

Whitehead, B. (1997), *The Goldfish and the Revolutionary Anti-Poll Tax Campaign: The student nurses' campaign against the Poll Tax in Derby and elsewhere*, Ruskin College, Oxford.

TV Programmes

Counterblasts, Get Rid of the Royals, MA'M, BBC2, 14.3.99, 19.30-20.00.

Heart of the Matter, BBC1, 23.3.97.

Videos

"... And I Know Why I Stand Here." (Hamburg, Germany: Millerntor Roar!).

Poll Tax Riot (London: ACAB).

Riot Against the Royals (London: Movement Against the Monarchy).

Websites

AK Press and Distribution: <http://www.akuk.com/>.

Anarchist Communist Federation: See Anarchist Federation.

AnarchaFeminism: <http://www.geocities.com/Paris/2159/anrfem.html>.

Anarchist Federation: <http://flag.blackened.net/af/>.

Anarchist Trade Union Network (see too Anarchist Workers Network): <http://www.geocities.com/CapitolHill/Parliament/2522/>.

Anarchist Youth Network: <http://www.enrager.net/ayn/index.php>.

Anarchist Workers Network: <http://www.awn.org.uk>.

Antagonism: <http://www.geocities.com/CapitolHill/Lobby/3909/index. html>.

Aufheben: <http://www.geocities.com/aufheben2/>.

Autonomous Centre Edinburgh: <http://autonomous.org.uk/ace/>.

Black Flag: <http://flag.blackened.net/blackflag/>.

Campaign Against Prison Slavery: <http://www.enrager.net/caps/ index.php>.

Class Against Class: <http://www.geocities.com/cordobakaf/index. html>.

Class War: <http://classwaruk.org/>.

Commoner, The: <http://www.commoner.org.uk/>.

Corporate Watch: <http://www.corpwatch.org/>.

Earth First!: <http://www.eco-action.org/efau/aulast.html>.

Green Anarchy Archive: <Green Anarchy Archive>.

Herefordshire Anarchist Group: <http://www.eco-action.org/efau/ aulast.html>.

Industrial Workers of the World: <http://www.iww.org/>.

Indymedia:<www.uk.indymedia.org>.

Libcom.org (libertarian community and organising resource for Britain): <www.libcom.org>.

International Workers Association: <http://www.iwa-ait.org/>.

Midnight Notes: <http://www.tao.ca/~midnightnotes/>.

Movement Against the Monarchy: <http://www.geocities.com/ CapitolHill/Lobby/1793/>.

Postanarchism: <http://www.geocities.com/ringfingers/postanarchism. html>.

Raise the Fist: <http://www.raisethefist.com/index1.html>.

Reclaim the Streets: <http://rts.gn.apc.org/>.

Revolutionary Anti-authoritarians of Color (US): <http://passionbomb. com/race/>.

SchNEWS: <http://www.schnews.org.uk/>.

Solidarity Federation: <http://www.solfed.org.uk/>.

Spunk Library: <http://www.spunk.org/>.

Subversion: <http://www.geocities.com/knightrose.geo/>.

Urban 75: <http://www.urban75.com/>.

WOMBLES : <http://www.wombles.org.uk/>.

Secondary Texts

Ali, T. (2005), 'Why They Happened: The London bombings', *Counterpunch*, July 8, 2005, <www.counterpunch.org/ tariq07082005.html>, last accessed, July 28, 2005.

Ali, T. and Watkins S. (1998), *1968: Marching in the streets*, London: Simon and Schuster.

Amster, R. (1998), 'Anarchism as Moral Theory: Praxis, Property, and the Postmodern' in *Anarchist Studies* Vol. 6, No. 2, October 1998.

Analysis (1992), 'The Passing of An Old Warrior' in *Analysis*, London: Analysis <available from Analysis, 27 Old Gloucester Street, London WC1N 3XX>.

Arendt, H. (1979), *On Revolution*, Harmondsworth: Penguin.

Aristotle (1963), *Ethics*, London: Dent.

_____ (1980), *Ethics*, Harmondsworth: Penguin.

Atton, C. (1999), '*Green Anarchist*: A case study of collective action in the radical media' in *Anarchist Studies* No. 7, Vol. 3, March 1999.

Bailey, R. (1973), *The Squatters*, Harmondsworth: Penguin.

_____ (1994), *Homelessness What Can Be Done: An immediate programme of self-help and mutual-aid*, Oxford: Jon Carpenter.

Banham, R., Barker, P., Hall, P. and Price, C. (1969), 'Plan/Non-Plan: An experiment in freedom', *New Society*, March 20, 1969.

Bar, A. (1990), 'The CNT: The glory and tragedy of Spanish anarchosyndicalism' in M. van der Linden and W. Thorpe, eds., *Revolutionary Syndicalism: An international perspective*, Aldershot: Scolar.

Barker, C. and Kennedy, P. (1995), eds., *To Make Another World: Studies in protest and collective action*, Aldershot: Avebury.

Barrett, M. (1988), *Women's Oppression Today: The marxist feminist encounter*, London: Verso.

Barry, N., (1986), *On Classical Liberalism and Libertarianism*, Basingstoke: MacMillan.

Baudrillard, J. (1983), translated by P. Foss, J. Johnston and P. Patton, *In the Shadow of the Silent Minorities or, The End of the Social and Other Essays*, New York, USA: Semiotext(e) Foreign Agents.

_____ (1986), 'The Year 2000 Will Not Take Place', in E. Grosz, T. Threadgold, D. Kelly, A. Choldenko and E. Colless, eds., *Futur*Fall: Excursions into post-modernity*, Sydney, Australia: Power Institute Publications, 18-28.

_____ (1987), translated by B. Schutze, and C. Schutze, *The Ecstacy of Communication*, New York, USA: Semiotext(e) Foreign Agents.

Bayerlein, B. and van der Linden, M. (1990), 'Revolutionary Syndicalism in Portugal' in M. van der Linden and W. Thorpe, eds., *Revolutionary Syndicalism: An international perspective*, Aldershot: Scolar.

Beauchamp, T. and Childress, J. (1989), *Principles of Biomedical Ethics*, Third Edition, Oxford: Oxford University Press.

Beckett, F. (1995), *Enemy Within: The rise and fall of the British Communuist Party*, London: Merlin Press.

Bercuson, D. (1990), 'Syndicalism Sidetracked: Canada's one big union' in M. van der Linden and W. Thorpe, eds., *Revolutionary Syndicalism: An international perspective*, Aldershot: Scolar.

Bernstein, R. (1976), *The Restructuring of Social and Political Theory*, Oxford: Basil Blackwell.

Bertrand, C. (1990), 'Revolutionary Syndicalism in Italy' in M. van der Linden and W. Thorpe, eds., *Revolutionary Syndicalism: An international perspective*, Aldershot: Scolar.

Best, S. (1994), 'The Commodification of Reality and the Reality of Commodification: Baudrillard, Debord, and postmodern theory' in D. Kellner, ed., *Baudrillard: A critical reader*, Oxford: Blackwell.

Best, S. and Kellner, D. (1991), *Postmodern Theory: Critical Investigations*, Basingstoke: Macmillan.

Beynon, J. and Dunkerley, D. (2000), eds., *Globalization: The reader*, London: Athlone.

Bird, S. (2002), 'Violence after victory', *The Times*, June 17, 2002.

Blissett, L. (1996), 'From *Socialisme ou Barbarie* to Communism or Civilisation', *Transgressions* No. 2/3, August 1996.

Bloomfield, B. (1986), 'Women's Support Groups at Maerdy' in R. Samuel, B. Bloomfield and G. Boanas, eds., *The Enemy Within: Pit villages and the miners' strike of 1984-5*, London: Routledge and Kegan Paul, 154-65.

Bock, H. (1990), 'Anarchosyndicalism in the German Labour Movement: A rediscovered minority tradition' in M. van der Linden and W. Thorpe, eds., *Revolutionary Syndicalism: An international perspective*, Aldershot: Scolar.

Borum, R. and Tilby, C. (2005), 'Anarchist Direct Actions: A challenge for law enforcement' in *Studies in Conflict and Terrorism*, No. 28, 201-23, available at <chuck.mahost.org/weblog/anarchist_direct_actions.pdf>, last accessed, July 27, 2005.

Braidotti, R. (1993), 'Discontinuous Becomings. Deleuze on the Becoming-Woman of Philosophy' in *The Journal of the British Society of Phenomenology*, Vol. 24, No. 1, January 1993.

Breines, W. (1982), *Community and Organisation in the New Left, 1962-1968: The great refusal*, New York, USA: Praeger.

Bright, M. (2002), 'The Observer Profile: Angela Mason' in *Observer* News Pages, November 24, 2002, 27.

Brockes, E. (2000), 'Working Lives: Who dares swindles', *The Guardian*, June 21, 2000, 6.

Brown, P. (2005), 'Weed discovery brings calls for GM ban', *The Guardian*, July 26, 2005, 7.

Bryson, B. (1996), *Notes From A Small Island*, London: Black Swan.

Bufacchi, V. (2005), 'Two Concepts of Violence' in *Political Studies Review*, Volume 3, No. 2, April, 193-204.

Bunyan, T. (1983), *The History and Practice of the Political Police in Britain*, London: Quarter Books.

Burchill, J. and Parsons, T. (1978), *"The Boy Looked at Johnny": The obituary of rock and roll*, London: Pluto Press.

Burns, A. (1973), *The Angry Brigade*, London: Quartet Books.

Byrne, P. (1997), *Social Movements in Britain*, London: Routledge.

Byrnes, D. (2002), 'How to avoid a smack on the bun', *The Independent*, Wednesday, April 24, 2002, 14.

Cadogan, P. (1972), 'From Civil Disobedience to Confrontation', in R. Benewick and T. Smith, eds., *Direct Action and Democratic Politics*, London: George Allen and Unwin Ltd.

Call, L. (1999), 'Anarchy in the Matrix: Postmodern anarchisms in the novels of William Gibson and Bruce Sterling' in *Anarchist Studies*, October 1999.

Calvert, P. (1970), *Revolution*, London: Macmillan.

Camus, A. (1965), translated by Bower, A. *The Rebel*, Harmondsworth: Penguin Books.

Carling, A. (1992), 'Bread First then Ethics', in P. Wetherby, ed., *Marx's Theory of History: The contemporary debate*, Aldershot: Avebury.

Carter, Alan. (1989), 'Outline of an Anarchist Theory of History', D. Goodway, ed., *For Anarchism: History, theory, and practice*, London: Routledge.

Carter, April. (1973), *Direct Action and Liberal Democracy*, London: Routledge and Kegan Paul.

_____ (1983), *Direct Action*, npl: CND.

Carver, T. (2002), 'Marx, Engels and Dialectics' in S. Meikle, ed., *Marx*, Dartmouth: Ashgate, also available in *Political Studies* (1980), No. 28, 353-63.

Cassidy, J. (1999), 'It's Anarchy in the Advertising Media' in *The Big Issue*, January 18-24 1999 .

Challinor, R. (1977), *The Origins of British Bolshevism*, London: Croom Helm.

Chamberlain, G. (2005), 'Army placed on standby for G8', *The Scotsman*, Tuesday, June 28, 2005, 12.

Chan, A. (1995), 'Anarchists, Violence and Social change: Perspectives from today's grassroots', *Anarchist Studies*, Volume 3, No. 1, 45-68.

_____ (2004), 'Violence, Nonviolence, and the Concept of Revolution in Anarchism', *Anarchist Studies*, Volume 12, No. 2, 103-23.

Clandestine Revolutionary Indigenous Committee - General Command of the Zapatista Army of National Liberation (2005), 'Zapatista Army Of National Liberation, Mexico: Sixth declaration of the Selva Lacandona', <http://www.ezln.org/documentos/2005/sexta1.en.htm>, last accessed August 7, 2005.

Clarke, F. (1983), *Will-o'-the-Wisp: Peter the Painter and the Anti-Tsarist terrorists in Britain and Australia*, Melbourne, Australia: Oxford University Press.

Cleaver, E. (1984), *Soul on Ice*, New York, USA: Dell/Ramparts.

Cliff, T. (1986), 'Introduction' to Luxemburg, R., *The Mass Strike*, London: Bookmarks.

_____ (1996), 'Trotsky on Substitutionism' in Cliff and Hallas et. al. (1996) *Party and Class*, London: Bookmarks.

Cockburn, A. (2005), '*Counterpunch Diary*: Islamo-Anarcs or Islamo-Fascists', *Counterpunch*, Weekend Edition, July 23/24, 2005, <www.counterpunch.org/cocburn07252005.html>, last accessed 28 July, 2005.

Cohan, A. (1975), *Theories of Revolution: An introduction*, London: Nelson.

Cohen, G. (2002), 'The Structure of Proletarian Unfreedom' in R. Goodin and P. Pettit, eds., *Contemporary Political Philosophy: An anthology*, Oxford: Blackwell.

Coleman, S. (1987), 'Impossiblism' in M. Rubel, and J. Crump, eds., *Non-Market Socialism in the Nineteenth and Twentieth Centuries*, Basingstoke: Macmillan.

Communist Party (1957), *Inner Party Democracy*, London: Communist Party.

Conrad, J. (1986), *The Secret Agent*, Harmondsworth: Penguin.

Cooper, C. (1989e), *Mere Anarchy*, London: Libertarian Alliance.

Crump, J. (1987), 'Non-Market Socialism in the Twentieth Century' in M. Rubel and J. Crump, eds., *Non-Market Socialism in the Nineteenth and Twentieth Centuries*, Basingstoke: MacMillan Press.

Cunningham, J. (1990), 'Poll Tax (The Riot Aftermath): Shadowy source of violent revolt', *The Guardian*, April, 2, 1990.

Dangerfield, G. (1997), *The Strange Death of Liberal England*, London: Serif.

Deuleuze, G. and Guattari, F. (1992), trans. B. Massumi, *A Thousand Plateaus: Capitalism and schizophrenia*, London: Athlone Press.

Diamond, M. (1994), 'Anarchy's Heyday', *BBC Worldwide*, January 1994.

Dickinson, R. (1997), *Imprinting the Sticks: The alternative press beyond London*, Aldershot: Gower.

Dubofsky, M. (1990), 'The Rise and Fall of Revolutionary Syndicalism in the United States' in M. van der Linden and W. Thorpe, eds., *Revolutionary Syndicalism: An international perspective*, Aldershot: Scolar.

Economic League, The (1986), *Companies Under Attack*, London: The Economic League Ltd.

_____ (1991ea), 'The State of Anarchy: I' reprinted in *Anarchist 1992 Yearbook*, London: Phoenix Press

_____ (1991eb), 'The State of Anarchy: II' reprinted in *Anarchist 1992 Yearbook*, London: Phoenix Press.

Edgell, S. (1993), *Class*, London: Routledge.

Engels, F. (1958), translated by W. Henderson and W. Chaloner, *The Condition of the Working Class in England*, Oxford: Basil Blackwell.

Farr, J. (2002), 'Marx's Laws' in S. Meikle, ed., *Marx*, Dartmouth: Ashgate, also in *Political Studies*, No, 34, 1986, 202-22.

Fishman, W. (1975), *East-End Jewish Radicals 1874-1914*, London: Duckworth.

_____ (1970), *The Insurrectionists*, London: Methuen and Co.

Fountain, N. (1988), *The Underground: The London alternative press 1966-74*, London: Comedia/Routledge.

Franks, B. (2005), 'British Anarchisms and the Miners' Strike',*Capital and Class*, No. 87, 227-54.

Garnham, N. (1972), 'Direct Action, Democratic Participation and the Media' in R. Benewick and T. Smith, eds., *Direct Action and Democratic Politics*, London: George Allen and Unwin.

German, L. (1996), 'The role of the Revolutionary Party' in The Socialist Workers Party, eds., *What do we mean by revolution?*, London: Socialist Workers Party.

Ghannoushi, S. (2005), 'Al-Qaida: The wrong questions', Aljazeera. Net, July 29, 2005, <http://english.aljazeera.net/NR/exeres/ 25D45C98-471B-4A36-8253-F2120BEA180F.htm>, last accessed August 25, 2005.

Gilroy, P. (1992), *There Ain't No Black in the Union Jack: The cultural politics of race and nation*, London: Routledge.

Ginn, K., Madeley, G., Thompson, D. and Macaskill, G. (2005), 'The battle of Bannockburn II', *Daily Mail*, Section ED_SC1_04; 2.

Goodman, R. (1972), *After the Planners*, Harmondsworth: Penguin.

Godwin, W. (1986), *Selected Writings*, London: Freedom Press.

Gorz, A. (1983), *Farewell to the Working Class: An essay on post-industrial socialism*, London: Pluto Press.

Gray, R. (2002), 'World Cup 2002: Prisoners riot over world cup blackout', *The Mirror*, Thursday, June 13, 2002, 4.

Grayeff (1994), *Aristotle and His School*, London: Duckworth.

Greenslade, R. (1997), 'Nice One Sun, Says Tony', *The Guardian* Media Page; Pg. T2.

Hall, P. (1992), *Cities of Tomorrow*, Oxford: Blackwells.

Hallas, D. (1996), 'Towards a Revolutionary Socialist Party' in T. Cliff and D. Hallas et. al. eds., *Party and Class*, London: Bookmarks.

Hardie, W. (1968), *Aristotle's Ethical Theory*, Oxford: Clarendon Press.

Harding, N. (1996), *Leninism*, Basingstoke: MacMillan.

Hardman, R. (2005), 'March to justice that descended into another riot', *Daily Mail*, 23.

Harman, C. (1979), *How Marxism Works*, London: Socialist Workers Party.

_____ (1996), 'Party and Class' in T. Cliff and D. Hallas, et. al. eds., *Party and Class*, Bookmarks, London.

_____ (1996b), 'The General Strike' in Socialist Workers Party (1996), *What Do We Mean By Revolution?*, London: Socialist Workers Party.

Harper, C. (1987), *Anarchy: A graphic guide*, London: Camden Press.

Harris, J. (1983), 'The Morality of Terrorism', *Radical Philosophy*, No. 33, Spring 1983.

Hart, J. (1990), 'Revolutionary Syndicalism in Mexico' in M. van der Linden and W. Thorpe, eds., *Revolutionary Syndicalism: An international perspective*, Aldershot: Scolar.

Harvey, D. (1996), *The Condition of Postmodernity: Enquiry into the origins of cultural change*, Oxford: Blackwell.

Hayek, F. (1973), *Law, Legislation and Liberty: Volume 1 Rules and order*, London: Routledge and Kegan Paul.

Hebdige, D. (1979), *Subculture: The meaning of style*, London: Methuen.

Hegel, G. (1977), *Phenomenology of Spirit*, Oxford: Oxford University Press.

Hemment, D. (1998), 'Dangerous Dancing and Disco Riots: The northern warehouse parties' in McKay, *DiY Cultures: Party and protest in nineties Britain*, London: Verso.

Hencke, D. (2000), 'Left blacklist man joins euro fight', *The Guardian*, September 9, 2000, 7.

_____ (2003), 'Blair loyalist to stand down from leadership of Amicus union', *The Guardian*, July 12, 2002, 14.

Henshaw, D., (1989), *Animal Welfare: The story of the Animal Liberation Front*, Glasgow: Fontana/Collins.

Hewison, R. (1986), *Too Much: Art and society in the sixties 1960-75*, London: Methuen.

Holton, R. (1980), 'Syndicalist Theories of the State' in *Sociological Review*, Vol. 28, No.1.

Home, S. (1988), *The Assault on Culture: Utopian currents from Lettrisme to Class War*, London: Aporia Press and Unpopular Books.

_____ (1993), *No Pity*, Edinburgh, Scotland: AK Press.

_____ (1995), *Cranked Up Really High*, Hove: Codex.

Honderich, T. (1980), *Violence for Equality*, Harmondsworth: Penguin Books

Humphrey, R. (1951), *Georges Sorel, Prophet Without Honour: A study in anti-intellectualism*, Cambridge, Massachusetts, USA: Harvard University Press (facsimile).

Hursthouse, R. (1987), *Beginning Lives*, Oxford: Blackwell.

Hutchings, V. (1992), 'Election Watch: Passive wanking' in *New Statesman*, April 10, 1992.

Hyams, E. (1979), *Pierre-Joseph Proudhon*, London: Murray.

Jacobs, J. (1974), *The Death and Life of Great American Cities: The failure of town planning*, Harmondsworth: Penguin Books.

Jappe, A. (1999), translated by Nicholson-Smith, D., *Guy Debord*, London: University of California Press.

Joll, J. (1964), *The Anarchists*, London: Eyre and Spottiswoode.

Jones, G. (1999), 'Stop the anarchy', *The Mirror*, Monday, 29 November, 1999, 17.

Jones, V. (2001), 'French Protestors destroy GM crops', BBC News Online, Sunday, 26 August, 2001, <http://news.bbc.co.uk/1/hi/world/europe/1510463.stm>, last accessed, 27 May, 2005.

Jordan, T. (2002), *Activism!: Direct action, hacktivism and the future of society*, London: Reaktion.

Kant, I. (1959), *Foundations of the Metaphysicas of Morals and What is Enlightenment?*, Indianapolis USA: Liberal Arts Press.

_____ (1991), *The Metaphysics of Morals*, Cambridge: Cambridge University Press.

Kellner, D. (1984), *Herbert Marcuse and the Crisis of Marxism*, Basingstoke: MacMillan.

_____ (1994), ed., *Baudrillard: A Critical Reader*, Oxford: Blackwell.

Kingsnorth, N. (2003), *One No, Many Yeses: A journey to the heart of the global resistance movement*, London: Free Press.

Klein, N. (2000), *No Logo*, London: Flamingo.

Laclau and Mouffe, *Hegemony and Socialist Strategy: Towards a radical democratic politics*, London: Verso.

Lashmar, P. (1999), Now is Another Season of Our Heated Discontent', *The Independent*, Tuesday, June 22, 1999, 3.

Leedham, R. (1994), 'Short Cuts: In Gob we trust', *The Guardian*, Weekend Section, 40.

Lefebvre, H. (1988), ' Toward a Leftist Cultural Politics: Remarks occasioned by the centenary of Marx's death' in Nelson and Grossberg, eds., *Marxism and the Interpretation of Culture*, London: Macmillan.

Lenin, V. (1963), translated by S. V. and Patricia Utechin, *What is to be Done*, Oxford: Clarendon.

_____ (1965), translated by A. Koptseva, *On Utopian and Scientific Socialism*, Moscow, Russia: Progress Publishers.

_____ (1972), edited by E. Fischer and translated by A. Bostock, *Lenin in His Own Words*, London: Allen Lane the Penguin Press.

_____ (1975), *"Left-Wing" Communism, An Infantile Disorder*, Peking, China: Foreign Languages Press.

_____ (1976), *The State and Revolution*, Peking, China: Foreign Languages Press.

Linebaugh, P. (1993), *The London Hanged: Crime and civil society in the eighteenth century*, Harmondsworth: Penguin.

Locke, J. (1993), *Two Treatises on Government*, Cambridge: Cambridge University Press.

Lull, J. (2000), 'Globalization' in J. Beynon, and D. Dunkerley eds., *Globalization: The reader*, London: Athlone.

Luxemburg, R. (1986), *The Mass Strike*, London: Bookmarks.

Lynch, M. (1995), *Trotsky: The permanent revolutionary*, London: Hodder and Stoughton.

Macdonald, A. (William L. Pierce) (1980), *The Turner Diaries*, Arlington, USA: National Vanguard Books.

MacGregor, I. (1986), with Taylor, R., *The Enemies Within: The story of the Miners' Strike, 1984-5*, London: Collins.

Malone, C. (1999), 'The howling mob just bite the hands that feed them', *Sunday Mirror*, 20 June 1999, 31.

Malyon, T. (1998), 'Tossed in the Fire and They Never Got Burnt: The Exodus Collective' in G. McKay, ed., *DiY Culture: Party and protest in nineties Britain*, London: Verso.

Marcus, G. (1989), *Lipstick Traces: A secret history of the twentieth century*, London: Secker and Warburg.

Marcuse, H. (1969a), 'Revolutionary Subject and Self-Government', *Praxis* No. 5.

_____ (1969b), *An Essay on Liberation*, London: Allen Lane the Penguin Press.

_____ (1971), *Soviet Marxism: A critical analysis*, Harmondsworth: Penguin.

_____ (1988), *From Luther to Popper*, London: Verso.

Marshall, P. (1984), *William Godwin*, London: Yale University Press.

_____ (1992), *Demanding the Impossible: A history of anarchism*, London: HarperCollins.

Martin, H. (2000), 'Hacktivism: The new protest movement' at <www.spark-online.com/april00/printhappy7.0/martin.htm>, last accessed 11 August, 2005.

Marx, K. (1967), T. Bottomore and M. Rubel, eds., *Selected Writings in Sociology and Social Philosophy*, Harmondsworth: Penguin.

_____ (1977), D. McLellan, ed., *Selected Writings*, Oxford: Oxford University Press.

_____ (1992), *Early Writings*, Harmondsworth: Penguin.

Marx, K. and Engels, F. (1977), *Manifesto of the Communist Party*, Moscow, Russia: Progress Publishers.

May, T. (1993), 'The System and Its Fractures: Gilles Deleuze on Otherness' in *Journal of the British Society for Phenomenology*, Vol. 24, No. 1, January 1993.

_____ (1994), *The Political Philosophy of Poststructuralist Anarchism*, Pennsylvania, USA: The Pennsylvania State University Press.

McKay, G. (1998), ed., *DiY Culture: Party and protest in nineties Britain*, London: Verso

McLellan, D. (1973), *Karl Marx His Life and Thought*, London: The MacMillan Press.

_____ (1988), *Marx*, London: Fontana.

Meikle, S. (2002), 'Introduction', *Marx*, Dartmouth: Ashgate.

Melucci, A. (1996), *Challenging Codes: Collective action in the information age*, Cambridge: Cambridge University Press.

Miller, D. (1984), *Anarchism*, London: J. M. Dent and Sons.

Miller, J. (1987), *"Democracy in the Streets"*, New York, USA: Simon and Schuster.

Millett, S. (2004), 'Technology is Capital: *Fifth Estate*'s critique of the megamachine' in J. Purkis and J. Bowen, eds., *Changing Anarchism: Anarchist theory and practice in a global age*, Manchester: Manchester University Press.

Mises, L. von (1949), *Human Action*, London: W. Hodge.

Mitchell, B. (1990), 'French Syndicalism: An experiment in practical anarchism' in M. van der Linden and W. Thorpe, eds., *Revolutionary Syndicalism: An international perspective*,

Miyoshi, M. (2000), 'Perspectives on Globalisation' in J. Beynon and D. Dunkerley, eds., *Globalization: The reader*, London: Continuum.

Moglen, E. (1999), 'Anarchism Triumphant: Free software and the death of copyright', *First Monday*, <http://emoglen.law.columbia.edu/publications/anarchism.html>.

Mommsen, W. (1989), *The Political and Social Theory of Max Weber*, London: Polity.

Monbiot, G. (1996), 'Second Front: Common cause and effect', *The Guardian*, Section 2, 16 October, 1996, 2-3.

_____ (1998), 'Reclaim the fields and country lanes! The Land is Ours campaign', in G. McKay, *DiY Culture: Party and Protest in nineties Britain*, London: Verso.

Morland, D. (1997), *Demanding the Impossible?: Human nature and politics in nineteenth-century social anarchism*, London: Cassell.

_____ (2004), ' Anti-Capitalism and poststructuralist anarchism' in J. Purkis, and J. Bowen, eds., *Changing Anarchism: Anarchist theory and practice in a global age*, Manchester: Manchester University Press, 23-38.

Morris, L. (1998), 'Violence mars end of match - English and Argentine supporters in separate trouble', *Evening Chronicle* (Newcastle).

Mosbacher, M. (1996), *The British Communist Movement and Moscow: How the demise of the Soviet Union affected the Communist Party and its successor organisations*, London: Libertarian Alliance.

Mueller, T. (2003), 'Empowering Anarchy: Power, hegemony, and anarchist strategy' in *Anarchist Studies*, Vol. 11, No. 2.

Murray, G. (1997), 'Anarchists armed with credit cards plan to bring down the system', *Scotland on Sunday*, August 31, 1997, 9.

Neibuhr, R. (1942), *Moral Man and Immoral Society*, London: Charles Scribener's Sons.

_____ (2001), *Moral Man and Immoral Society*, London: Westminster John Knox Press.

Nelson, C. and Grossberg, L. (1988), *Marxism and the Interpretation of Culture*, Urbana, USA: University of Illinois Press.

Newman, S. (2001), *From Bakunin to Lacan: Anti-authoritarianism and the dislocation of power*, Oxford: Lexington Press.

Nozick, R. (1988), *Anarchy, State, and Utopia*, Oxford: Blackwell.

O'Brien, (1992e), 'A Haunting Spectre', *Analysis* (photocopy from Trevor Bark's archive).

O'Farrell, J. (1998), *Things Can Only Get Better: Eighteen miserable years in the life of a Labour supporter 1979-1997*, London: Black Swan.

Orlowski, A. (1994), 'Yippie for the Pranksters', *New Statesman and Society*, 9 September, 1994.

Paine, T. (1953), *Common Sense and Other Political Writings*, New York, USA: Liberal Arts Press.

_____ (1983), *Rights of Man*, Harmondsworth: Penguin.

Parkin, F. (1968), *Middle Class Radicalism: The social bases of the British Campaign for Nuclear Disarmament*, Manchester: Manchester University Press.

Parry, G. (1978), *John Locke*, London: George Allen and Unwin.

Parry, R. (1987), *The Bonnot Gang*, London: Rebel Press.

Persson, L. (1990), 'Revolutionary Syndicalism in Sweden before the Second World War' in M. van der Linden and W. Thorpe, eds., *Revolutionary Syndicalism: An international perspective*, Aldershot: Scolar .

Plant, S. (1990), 'The Situationist International: A case of spectacular neglect' in *Radical Philosophy* No. 55.

_____ (1992), *The Most Radical Gesture: The Situationist International in a post-modern age*, London: Routledge.

_____ (1993), 'Nomads and Revolutionaries', *Journal of the British Society for Phenomenology*, Vol. 24, No. 1, January 1993.

Police Monitoring and Research Group (1987), *Policing Wapping: An account of the dispute 1986/7*, London: London Strategic Policy Unit.

Porton, R. (1999), *Film and the Anarchist Imagination*, London: Verso.

Poulter, S. (2005), 'GM trials spawn', *The Daily Mail*, July 26, 2005, 12

Prawdin, M. (1961), *The Unmentionable Nechayev: A Key to Bolshevism*, George Allen and Urwin.

Price, C. (1984), *Cedric Price: Architectural Association Works II*, London: Architectural Association.

Price, R. (1998), 'Contextualizing British Syndicalism, c.1970-c.1920', *Labour History Review* Vol 63, No. 3.

Prinz, A. (2002), 'Background and Ulterior Motive of Marx's "Preface" of 1859', in S. Meikle, ed., *Marx*, Dartmouth: Ashgate, also *Journal of the History of Ideas*, 1969, No. 30, 437-50.

Purkis, J. (1995), 'Daring to Dream: Idealism in the philosophy, organization and campaigning strategies of Earth First!' in C. Barker and P. Kennedy, eds, *To Make Another World: Studies in protest and collective action*, Aldershot: Avebury.

Routledge, P. and Simons, J. (1995), 'Embodying Spirits of Resistance', *Environment and Planning D: Society and space*, 1995, Volume 13.

Quail, J. (1978), *The Slow Burning Fuse*, London: Paladin.

Ramsay, R. (1992), 'Our *Searchlight* Problem' in *Lobster* No. 24.

Rees, J. (2000), 'The Battle After Seattle', *Socialist Review*, No. 237, Jan. 2000.

Ritter, A. (1980), *Anarchism: A theoretical analysis*, Cambridge: Cambridge University Press.

Robins, D. and Cohen, P. (1978), *Knuckle Sandwich: Growing up in the working class city*, Harmondsworth: Penguin.

Rose. D. (1985), 'Woman's 'death' sparked off night of violence / Riots in Brixton, London' in *The Guardian*, 30 September.

Rousseau, J. (1983), *The Social Contract and Discourses*, London: Dent.

Runkle, G. (1972), *Anarchism: Old and new*, New York, USA: Delta.

Russell, B. (2002), 'Pioneering university department to close', *The Independent Online edition*, 29 August 2002,<http://education.independent.co.uk/news/article131253.ece>, last accessed 7 December, 2005.

Ryan, M. (1989), *Marxism and Deconstruction*, Baltimore, USA: John Hopkins University Press.

Sadler, S. (1998), *The Situationist City*, London: MIT Press.

Sargisson, L. (1996), *Contemporary Feminist Utopianism*, London: Routledge.

Scase, R. (1992), *Class*, Buckingham: Open University Press.

Scruton, R. (1985), *The New Left*, London: Longmans.

Sheehan, S. (2003), *Anarchism*, London: Reaktion.

Shipway, M. (1987), 'Council Communism' in M. Rubel and J. Crump, eds, *Non-Market Socialism in the Nineteenth and Twentieth Centuries*, Basingstoke: MacMillan Press.

Simons, J. (1995), *Foucault and the Political*, London: Routledge.

Skirda, A. (2002), *Facing the Enemy: A history of anarchist organisation from Proudhon to May 1968*, Edinburgh: AK Press.

Smith, J. W. (1991), *AIDS, Philosophy and Beyond: Philosophical dilemmas of a modern pandemic*, Aldershot: Avebury.

Smith, T. (1972), 'Protest and Democracy' in R. Benewick and T. Smith, eds., *Direct Action and Democratic Politics*, London: George Allen and Unwin.

Socialist Party of Great Britain (1993), *Socialist Principles Explained: The object and declaration of principles of the Socialist Party of Great Britain*, London: Socialist Party of Great Britain.

Socialist Workers Party (1996), *What Do We Mean By Revolution?*, London: Socialist Workers Party.

Solanas, V. (1991), *SCUM Manifesto*, London: Phoenix Press.

Souchy Bauer, A. (1982), translated by A. Bluestein, *With the Peasants of Aragon*, Sanday, Orkney and Minneapolis, USA: Cienfuegos and Soil of Liberty.

Sparks, C. (1996), 'Insurrection' in Socialist Workers Party, *What Do We Mean By Revolution*, London: The Socialist Workers Party.

Stewart, G. (2005), 'Al Qaeda, Victorian style', *Times On-Line*, August 5, 2005, <http://www.timesonline.co.uk/article/0,,1072-1721466,00.html>, last accessed August 5, 2005.

Stiglitz, J. (2002), *Globalization and its discontents*, Harmondsworth: Penguin.

Sullivan, M., Whitaker, T. and Parker, N. (2000), 'Find these animals', *The Sun*, May 2, 2000.

Taylor, B. (2001), 'Guide to anarchy that promises a monopoly on Mayday mayhem', *Daily Mail*, April 23, 2001, 22.

Taylor, C. (1993), *Philosophy and the Human Sciences*, Cambridge University Press.

Thayer, (1965), *The British Political Fringe*, London: Blond.

Thomas, P. (1980), *Karl Marx and the Anarchists*, London: Routledge and Kegan Paul.

_____ Thomas, P. (2002), 'Marx and Science' in S. Meikle, ed., *Marx*, Dartmouth: Ashgate, also available in *Political Studies*, No. 24, 1976, 1-23.

Thompson, E. (1977), *The Making of the English Working Class*, Harmondsworth: Penguin.

Thompson, R. (1990), 'Argentine Syndicalism: Reformism before revolution' in M. van der Linden and W. Thorpe, eds., *Revolutionary Syndicalism: An international perspective*, Aldershot: Scolar.

Thorpe, W. (1990), 'Syndicalist Internationalism before World War II' in M. van der Linden and W. Thorpe, eds., *Revolutionary Syndicalism: An international perspective*, Aldershot: Scolar.

Toczeck, N. (1991), *The Bigger Tory Vote: The covert sequestration of the bigotry vote*, Edinburgh, Scotland: AK Press.

Tong, R. (1989), *Feminist Thought: A comprehensive introduction*, Boulder, USA: Westview Press.

Trotsky, L. (1996), 'The Class, the Party and the Leadership' in T. Cliff and D. Hallas et. al. eds., (1996) *Party and Class*, London Bookmarks.

TUC (2004), 'No room for complacency on union membership', July 30 2004, <http://www.tuc.org.uk/the_tuc/tuc-8365-f0.cfm>, last accessed 7, August 2005.

Vague, T. (1997), *Anarchy in the UK: The Angry Brigade*, Edinburgh: AK Press.

van der Linden, M. (1990), 'The Many Faces of Dutch Revolutionary Trade Unionism' in M. van der Linden and W. Thorpe, eds., *Revolutionary Syndicalism: An international perspective*, Aldershot: Scolar.

van der Linden M. and Thorpe, W. (1990), 'The Rise and Fall of Revolutionary Syndicalism' in M. van der Linden and W. Thorpe, eds., *Revolutionary Syndicalism: An international perspective*, Aldershot: Scolar.

Vidal, J. (1996), 'Second Front: The seeds on stony ground', *The Guardian*, Section 2, October 16, 1996, 3-4.

Villon, S. (2005), 'Post Anarchism or Simply Post-Revolution', Killing King Abacus Site, <http://www.geocities.com/kk_abacus/other/postanarchism.html>, last accessed September 16, 2005.

Wall, D. (2000), *Earth First! and the Anti-Roads Movement: Radical environmentalist and comparative social movements*, London: Routledge.

Waterhouse, R. and Connett, D. (1990), 'Black flag casts long shadow of violent history; Were the poll tax rioters anarchists or just yobbos?', *The Independent*, April 8, 1990, 4.

Waterman, P. (2001), *Globalization, Social Movements and the New Internationalisms*, London: Continuum.

Wates, N. and Wolmar, C. (1980), eds., *Squatting: The real story*, London: Blackrose Press.

Weber, M. (1995), *Max Weber Selections in Translation*, Cambridge: Cambridge University Press.

Weiner, G. (1994), *Feminisms in Education: An introduction*, Buckingham: Open University Press.

Welsh, I. (2000), *Mobilising Modernity: The nuclear movement*, London: Taylor and Francis.

White, J. (1990a), 'Syndicalism in a Mature Industrial Setting: the Case of Britain' in M. van der Linden and W. Thorpe, eds., *Revolutionary Syndicalism: An international perspective*, Aldershot: Scolar.

Widgery, D. (1989), *Preserving Disorder*, London: Pluto Press.

Willener, A. (1970), *The Action-Image Society: On cultural politicization*, London: Tavistock.

Wilson, R. (1999), 'Inside the Radiant City' in *Philosophers Magazine*, No. 8.

Witheford, N. (1994), 'Autonomist Marxism and the Information Society', *Capital and Class* No. 52 .

Wray, S. (1998), 'Electronic Civil Disobedience and the World Wide Web of Hactivism' found at <http://www.nyu.edu/projects/wray/wwwhack.html>.

Wolff, R. (1976), *In Defence of Anarchism*, London: Harper Torchbooks.

Woodcock, G. (1975), *Anarchism*, Harmondsworth: Penguin.

_____ (1992), 'Introduction' to Kropotkin, *Ethics: Origins and Development*, Montréal, Canada: Black Rose Books.

Yates, R. (1997), 'Want to smash the state? Call a plumber', *The Observer*, Review Section, March 16, 1997.

A

The Libertarian Socialist Movement in Britain & Ireland

Anarchist Federation (British Section of the International of Anarchist Federations), BM ANARFED, London, WC1N 3XX
info@afed.org.uk
www.afed.org.uk

Aufheben (magazine), Brighton & Hove Unemployed Workers Centre, PO Box 2536, Rottingdean, brighton, BN2 6LX
aufheben99@yahoo.co.uk
www.geocities.com/aufheben2

Black Flag (magazine), BM Hurricane, London, WC1N 3XX
BlackFlag@lycos.co.uk
http://flag.blackened.net/blackflag/

Class War Federation, PO Box 467, London, E8 3QX
londoncwf@yahoo.co.uk
www.classwaruk.org

Freedom (newspaper),
84b Whitechapel High Street, London, E1 7QX
info@freedompress.org.uk
www.freedompress.org.uk

Organise!, PO Box 505, Belfast, BT12 6BQ
organiseireland@yahoo.ie
www.organiseireland.org

Solidarity Federation (British Section of the International Workers Association), PO Box 29, SW PDO, Manchester, M15 5HW
solfed@solfed.org.uk
www.solfed.org.uk

Workers Solidarity Movement, PO Box 1528, Dublin 8,Ireland
wsm_ireland@yahoo.com
http://struggle.ws/wsm

BRINTON, Maurice
For Workers' Power - Selected Writings
paperback   £12.00
AK Press
1904859070

At long last, the collected works of the principal writer, translator and thinker of the Solidarity Group, one of the most active and influential libertarian socialist organisations of the 1960s and early 1970s. Includes writing on topics ranging from the Paris Commune to Paris 1968, via Wilhelm Reich, the Portuguese Revolution, The Irrational in Politics, The Belgian General Strike of 1960, The Bolsheviks and Workers' Control and of couse, the work of Paul Cardan/Cornelius Castoriadis. From the workplace, to the streets, to the bedroom, Brinton writes critically and honestly on the nuts and bolts of a free humanity, laying to rest the arguments against a genuinely libertarian socialism. Edited by David Goodway.

CHOMSKY, Noam
Chomsky On Anarchism
paperback   £11.00
AK Press
1904859208

"Chomsky is familiar with the key that opens forbidden doors."
[Eduardo Galeano] One of the world's leading radical intellectuals
moves beyond criticism. Chomsky's vision of an anarchist future. We
all know what Noam Chomsky is against. His scathing analysis of
everything that's wrong with our society reaches more and more people
every day. His brilliant critiques of - among other things - capitalism,
imperialism, domestic repression and government propaganda,
have become mini-publishing industries unto themselves. But, in
this flood of publishing and republishing, very little ever gets said
about what exactly Chomsky stands for, his own personal politics,
his vision of the future. Not, that is, until Chomsky on Anarchism,
a groundbreaking new book that shows a different side of this best-
selling author: the anarchist principles that have guided him since he
was a teenager. This collection of Chomsky's essays and interviews
includes numerous pieces that have never been published before, as
well as rare material that first saw the light of day in hard-to-find
pamphlets and anarchist periodicals. Taken together, they paint a
fresh picture of Chomsky, showing his life-long involvement with the
anarchist community, his constant commitment to nonhierarchical

Noam Chomsky

models of political organization, and his
hopes for a future world without rulers. For
anyone who's been touched by Chomsky's
trenchant analysis of our current situation,
as well as anyone looking for an intelligent
and coherent discussion of anarchism itself,
Chomsky on Anarchism will be one of this
season's most exciting, and surprising,
reads. Noam Chomsky is one of the world's
leading intellectuals, the father of modern
linguistics, an outspoken media and foreign
policy critic, and tireless activist. He lives
in Boston, Massachusetts.

SKIRDA, Alexandre.
Translator - SHARKEY, Paul
Facing the Enemy - a History of Anarchist Organization from Proudhon to May 1968
paperback   £12.00
AK Press
1902593197

The finest single volume history of European Anarchism is finally available in English in Paul Sharkey's elegant translation. Drawing on decades of research, Alexandre Skirda traces anarchism as a major political movement and ideology across the 19th and 20th centuries. Critical and engaged, he offers biting and incisive portraits of the major thinkers, and more crucially, the organizations they inspired, influenced, came out of and were spurned by. Opinionated and witty, he is equally at home skewering the actions of the early anarchist Victor Serge as he is the Paris chief of police who organized undercover "anarchist bombers" in an attempt to infiltrate and discredit the movement. Skirda argues that the core problem for anarchists has been to create a revolutionary movement and envision a future society in which the autonomy of the individual is not compromised by the need to take collective action. How anarchists have grappled with that question in theory and practice make up the core of the

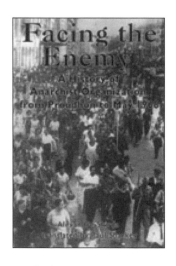

book. Bakuninist secret societies; the Internationals and the clash with Marx; the Illegalists, bombers and assassins; the mass trade unions and insurrections; and, of course, the Russian and Spanish Revolutions are all discussed through the prism of working people battling fiercely for a new world free of the shackles of Capital and the State.

Friends of AK Press + Distribution

In the last 12 months AK Press has published a number of new titles. We aim to continue this output of radical material along with reprints of existing work. However, not only are we financially constrained as to what (and how much) we can publish, we already have a huge backlog of excellent material we would like to publish sooner rather than later. If we had the money, we could easily publish thirty titles in the next 12 months...

Friends of AK Press is a way in which you can directly help us to try to realise many more such projects, much faster. Using the standing order form provided. Friends pay a minimum of £15 per month (of course we have no objection to larger sums!).

In return as a Friend you will receive one copy FREE of EVERY new AK Press title, usually in 3 or 4 parcels per year. You are also entitled to 10% discount off EVERYTHING featured in the current AK Distribution catalogue on any and every order. (When ordering please indicate that you are a Friend.) If you so wish, you can be acknowledged as a Friend in all new AK Press titles.

We also run a scheme where groups or individuals can sponsor a whole book. (Please contact us for more details) **ak@akedin.demon.co.uk**.

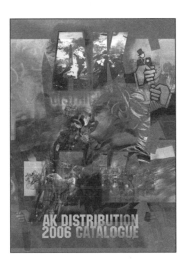

To browse and order from the complete list of all available titles go to

www.akuk.com   www.akpress.org